The Complete Works of John Owen

The Complete Works of John Owen

The Trinity

Vol. 1 *Communion with God*

Vol. 2 *The Trinity Defended: Part 1*

Vol. 3 *The Trinity Defended: Part 2*

Vol. 4 *The Person of Christ*

Vol. 5 *The Holy Spirit—His Person and Work: Part 1*

Vol. 6 *The Holy Spirit—His Person and Work: Part 2*

Vol. 7 *The Holy Spirit—The Helper*

Vol. 8 *The Holy Spirit—The Comforter*

The Gospel

Vol. 9 *The Death of Christ*

Vol. 10 *Sovereign Grace and Justice*

Vol. 11 *Justification by Faith Alone*

Vol. 12 *The Saints' Perseverance: Part 1*

Vol. 13 *The Saints' Perseverance: Part 2*

Vol. 14 *Apostasy from the Gospel*

The Christian Life

Vol. 15 *Sin and Temptation*

Vol. 16 *An Exposition of Psalm 130*

Vol. 17 *Heavenly-Mindedness*

Vol. 18 *Sermons and Tracts from the Civil Wars (1646–1649)*

Vol. 19 *Sermons from the Commonwealth and Protectorate (1650–1659)*

Vol. 20 *Sermons from the Early Restoration Years (1669–1675)*

Vol. 21 *Sermons from the Later Restoration Years (1676–1682)*

Vol. 22 *Miscellaneous Sermons and Lectures*

The Church

Vol. 23 *The Nature of the Church: Part 1*

Vol. 24 *The Nature of the Church: Part 2*

Vol. 25 *The Church Defended: Part 1*

Vol. 26 *The Church Defended: Part 2*

Vol. 27 *The Church's Worship*

Vol. 28 *The Church, the Scriptures, and the Sacraments*

Hebrews

Vol. 29 *An Exposition of Hebrews: Part 1, Introduction to Hebrews*

Vol. 30 *An Exposition of Hebrews: Part 2, Christ's Priesthood and the Sabbath*

Vol. 31 *An Exposition of Hebrews: Part 3, Jesus the Messiah*

Vol. 32 *An Exposition of Hebrews: Part 4, Hebrews 1–2*

Vol. 33 *An Exposition of Hebrews: Part 5, Hebrews 3–4*

Vol. 34 *An Exposition of Hebrews: Part 6, Hebrews 5–6*

Vol. 35 *An Exposition of Hebrews: Part 7, Hebrews 7–8*

Vol. 36 *An Exposition of Hebrews: Part 8, Hebrews 9–10*

Vol. 37 *An Exposition of Hebrews: Part 9, Hebrews 11–13*

Latin Works

Vol. 38 *The Study of True Theology*

Shorter Works

Vol. 39 *The Shorter Works of John Owen*

Indexes

Vol. 40 *Indexes*

The Complete Works
of John Owen

THE TRINITY

VOLUME 7

The Holy Spirit—
The Helper

John Owen

INTRODUCED AND EDITED BY
Andrew S. Ballitch

GENERAL EDITORS
Lee Gatiss and Shawn D. Wright

WHEATON, ILLINOIS

The Holy Spirit—The Helper

Copyright © 2023 by Crossway

Published by Crossway
          1300 Crescent Street
          Wheaton, Illinois 60187

Cover design: Jordan Singer

Marble Paper Artist: Vanessa Reynoso, Marbled Paper Studio

First printing 2023

Printed in China

Scripture quotations marked KJV are from the King James Version of the Bible. Public domain.

Hardcover ISBN: 978-1-4335-6020-0
ePub ISBN: 978-1-4335-8576-0
PDF ISBN: 978-1-4335-8574-6
Mobipocket ISBN: 978-1-4335-8575-3

Library of Congress Cataloging-in-Publication Data

Names: Owen, John, 1616–1683, author. | Ballitch, Andrew S., editor.
Title: The Holy Spirit — the Helper / John Owen ; edited and introduced by
Andrew S. Ballitch ; Lee Gatiss and Shawn D. Wright, general editors.
Other titles: Pneumatologia. Selections
Description: Wheaton, Illinois : Crossway, 2023. | Series: The complete works of John Owen ; volume 7 | Includes
    bibliographical references and index.
Identifiers: LCCN 2022004734 (print) | LCCN 2022004735 (ebook) | ISBN 9781433560200 (hardcover) | ISBN
    9781433585746 (pdf) | ISBN 9781433585753 (mobipocket) | ISBN 9781433585760 (epub)
Subjects: LCSH: Holy Spirit—Early works to 1800.
Classification: LCC BT121.3 .O94 2022 (print) | LCC BT121.3 (ebook) | DDC 231/.3—dc23/eng/20220615
LC record available at https://lccn.loc.gov/2022004734
LC ebook record available at https://lccn.loc.gov/2022004735

Crossway is a publishing ministry of Good News Publishers.

RRDS		32	31	30	29	28	27	26	25	24	23
15	14	13	12	11	10	9	8	7	6	5	4	3	2	1

Volume 7

Contents

Works Preface   *vii*

Editor's Introduction   *1*

The Reason of Faith   *71*

The Causes, Ways, and Means of Understanding the Mind of God   *209*

General Index   *351*

Scripture Index   *363*

Works Preface

JOHN OWEN (1616–1683) is one of the most significant, influential, and prolific theologians that England has ever produced. His work is of such a high caliber that it is no surprise to find it still in demand more than four centuries after his birth. As a son of the Church of England, a Puritan preacher, a statesman, a Reformed theologian and Bible commentator, and later a prominent Nonconformist and advocate of toleration, he is widely read and appreciated by Christians of different types all over the globe, not only for the profundity of his thinking but also for the depth of his spiritual insight.

Owen was born in the year that William Shakespeare died, and in terms of his public influence, he was a rising star in the 1640s and at the height of his power in the 1650s. As chaplain to Oliver Cromwell, dean of Christ Church, and vice-chancellor of Oxford University, he wielded a substantial degree of power and influence within the short-lived English republic. Yet he eventually found himself on the losing side of the epic struggles of the seventeenth century and was ousted from his position of national preeminence. The Act of Uniformity in 1662 effectively barred him from any role in the established church, yet it was in the wilderness of those turbulent post-Restoration years that he wrote many of his most momentous contributions to the world of theological literature, despite being burdened by opposition, persecution, family tragedies, and illness.

There was an abortive endeavor to publish a uniform edition of Owen's works in the early eighteenth century, but this progressed no further than a single folio volume in 1721. A century later (1826), Thomas Russell met with much more success when he produced a collection in twenty-one volumes. The appetite for Owen only grew; more than three hundred people had subscribed to the 1721 and 1826 editions of his works, but almost three thousand subscribed to the twenty-four-volume set produced by William H. Goold from 1850 onward. That collection, with Goold's learned introductions and notes, became the standard edition. It was given a new lease on life when the Banner of Truth Trust reprinted it several times beginning in 1965, though without some of Owen's Latin works, which had appeared in Goold's edition, or his massive Hebrews commentary, which Banner did eventually reprint in 1991. Goold corrected various errors in the original seventeenth- and eighteenth-century publications, some of which Owen himself had complained of, as well as certain grammatical errors. He thoroughly revised the punctuation, numeration of points, and Scripture references in Owen and presented him in a way acceptable to nineteenth-century readers without taking liberties with the text.

Since the mid-nineteenth century, and especially since the reprinting of Goold's edition in the mid-twentieth century, there has been a great flowering of interest in seventeenth-century Puritanism and Reformed theology. The recent profusion of scholarship in this area has resulted in a huge increase of attention given to Owen and his contribution to these movements. The time has therefore come to attempt another presentation of Owen's body of work for a new century. This new edition is more than a reprint of earlier collections of Owen's writings. As useful as those have been to us and many others, they fail to meet the needs of modern readers who are often familiar with neither the theological context nor the syntax and rhetorical style of seventeenth-century English divinity.

For that reason, we have returned again to the original editions of Owen's texts to ensure the accuracy of their presentation here but have conformed the spelling to modern American standards, modernized older verb endings, reduced the use of italics where they do not clarify meaning, updated some hyphenation forms, modernized capitalization both for select terms in the text and for titles of Owen's works, refreshed the typesetting, set lengthy quotations in block format, and both checked and added Scripture references in a consistent format where necessary. Owen's quotations of others, however, including the various editions of the Bible he used or translated, are kept as they appear in his original. His marginal notes and footnotes have been clearly marked in footnotes as his (with "—Owen" appearing at the end of his content) to distinguish them from editorial comments. Foreign languages such as Greek, Hebrew, and Latin (which Owen knew and used extensively) have been translated into modern English, with the original languages retained in footnotes for scholarly reference (also followed by "—Owen"). If Goold omitted parts of the original text in his edition, we have restored them to their rightful place. Additionally, we have attempted to regularize the numbering system Owen employed, which was often imprecise and inconsistent; our order is 1, (1), [1], {1}, and 1st. We have also included various features to aid readers' comprehension of Owen's writings, including extensive introductions and outlines by established scholars in the field today, new paragraph breaks marked by a pilcrow (¶), chapter titles and appropriate headings (either entirely new or adapted from Goold), and explanatory footnotes that define archaic or obscure words and point out scriptural and other allusions in the text. On the rare occasions when we have added words to the text for readability, we have clearly marked them using square brackets. Having a team of experts involved, along with the benefit of modern online database technology, has also enabled us to make the prodigious effort to identify sources and citations in Owen that Russell and Goold deliberately avoided or were unable to locate for their editions.

Owen did not use only one English translation of the Bible. At various times, he employed the Great Bible, the Geneva Bible, the Authorized Version (KJV), and his own paraphrases and translations from the original languages. We have not sought to harmonize his biblical quotations to any single version. Similarly, we have left his Hebrew and Greek quotations exactly as he recorded them, including the unpointed Hebrew text. When it appears that he has misspelled the Hebrew or Greek, we have acknowledged that in a footnote with reference to either *Biblia Hebraica Stuttgartensia* or *Novum Testamentum Graece*.

This new edition presents fresh translations of Owen's works that were originally published in Latin, such as his Θεολογούμενα Παντοδαπά (1661) and *A Dissertation on Divine Justice* (which Goold published in an amended eighteenth-century translation). It also includes certain shorter works that have never before been collected in one place, such as Owen's prefaces to other people's works and many of his letters, with an extensive index to the whole set.

Our hope and prayer in presenting this new edition of John Owen's complete works is that it will equip and enable new generations of readers to appreciate the spiritual insights he accumulated over the course of his remarkable life. Those with a merely historical interest will find here a testimony to the exceptional labors of one extraordinary figure from a tumultuous age, in a modern and usable critical edition. Those who seek to learn from Owen about the God he worshiped and served will, we trust, find even greater riches in his doctrine of salvation, his passion for evangelism and missions, his Christ-centered vision of all reality, his realistic pursuit of holiness, his belief that theology matters, his concern for right worship and religious freedom, and his careful exegetical engagement with the text of

God's word. We echo the words of the apostle Paul that Owen inscribed on the title page of his book Χριστολογία (1679), "I count all things but loss for the excellency of the knowledge of Christ Jesus my Lord, for whom I have suffered the loss of all things, and do count them but dung that I may win Christ" (Phil. 3:8).

Lee Gatiss
CAMBRIDGE, ENGLAND

Shawn D. Wright
LOUISVILLE, KENTUCKY, UNITED STATES

Editor's Introduction

Andrew S. Ballitch

JOHN OWEN AND THE HOLY SPIRIT

Born into a humble, moderately Puritan clergy family during the reign of James I (1566–1625) and ordained as a priest in the Church of England under Charles I (1600–1649), John Owen (1616–1683) became a preacher to the Long Parliament in 1646, preacher of the regicide in 1649, and chaplain to Oliver Cromwell (1599–1658) during the invasions of Ireland and Scotland in 1649 and 1650. His academic career boasted the positions of dean of Christ Church, Oxford, from 1651 to 1660 and vice-chancellor of the university from 1652 to 1657. Owen's was a principal voice in Cromwell's religious settlement, and he became involved in the downfall of Richard Cromwell (1626–1712) in 1659, which precipitated the Restoration of the Stuart monarchy in 1660. Owen's recent biographer, Crawford Gribben, sums up the latter decades of his life this way: "The changing legal and cultural circumstances of the reign of Charles II (1630–1685) forced Owen to withdraw from public life and facilitated the re-energizing of his already prolific publishing career in defense of high Calvinist theology and the toleration of Protestant dissenters."[1] One of the most significant fruits of this reenergized publishing career was his work on the Holy Spirit.

Owen's contribution to pneumatology was purposefully and self-consciously new. Few have dared such a detailed exposition of the doctrine of the Holy Spirit, and fewer still accomplished a masterpiece on the topic. If Owen's commentary on Hebrews is the epitome of his exegesis, his treatises on the Holy Spirit represent his mature theological reflection, occupying

---

[1] Crawford Gribben, *John Owen and English Puritanism: Experiences of Defeat*, Oxford Studies in Historical Theology (New York: Oxford University Press, 2016), 1.

1

the last decade of his life. His Πνευματολογια, or, *A Discourse concerning the Holy Spirit* (1674) is a stand-alone treatment of the Holy Spirit's nature and mission, operation in the Old Testament, work of regeneration, and role in sanctification. But his pen continued, and he completed five smaller treatises on various aspects of the Spirit's work: *The Reason of Faith* (1677); *The Causes, Ways, and Means of Understanding the Mind of God* (1678); *The Holy Spirit in Prayer* (1683); and *The Holy Spirit as a Comforter* published posthumously with *A Discourse of Spiritual Gifts* (1693). These five shorter treatises constitute volumes 7–8 of the present *Works* and address the topics of illumination, biblical interpretation, extemporaneous prayer, Christian comfort, and ordinary and extraordinary spiritual gifts, all centering on and unified by the role of the Spirit.

This introduction will proceed with two primary goals, which also determine its organization. The first is to provide an adequate, but by no means comprehensive, historical context. Owen did not write his treatises in a vacuum. He had concerns, experiences, and interlocutors that motivated and informed his writing. These must be identified and accounted for if true comprehension of Owen's ideas and theology is to be achieved. In this vein, a brief narrative of the events leading to the Restoration of the English monarchy, the rise of the episcopal Church of England, and the formation of English Dissent will be provided, followed by a treatment of Roman Catholicism in this milieu and the sectarians, with particular focus on the Quakers and Socinians. The importance of these topics and groups will become apparent in due course. The second goal is to offer a thematic discussion of each treatise, including an outline of the arguments and the noting of major themes. Addressing these two topics will aid the reader in understanding Owen and serve as a guide in the eminently worthy endeavor of reading his writings themselves.

The Restoration Church of England and English Dissent

The tumultuous middle decades of seventeenth-century England could rightly be categorized as wars of religion, wars largely precipitated by Charles I. He threw his royal support behind a revolution in the Church of England, he provoked rebellions in both Ireland and Scotland, he compromised the relationship between crown and Parliament, with civil war in all three British kingdoms ensuing. The period beginning with the dissolution of Parliament in 1629 until the Long Parliament commenced in 1640 is conventionally referred to as the personal rule of Charles Stuart. He raised money in creative and unpopular ways and saw the emergence of a strong Roman Catholic presence at his court.[2] But most significantly, Charles backed William Laud (1573–1645), whose meteoric rise through ecclesiastical ranks took him from bishop of Bath and Wells to archbishop of Canterbury (1633) via a stint as bishop of London.

Moderate Calvinism had remained the accepted orthodoxy under James I, but changing beliefs under his son Charles were accompanied by changing attitudes toward worship. For English Arminians of the late 1620s and 1630s, and, most importantly, for Laud, God's grace was conveyed primarily through the sacraments. Sermons told people about God, whereas God could be experienced directly through the sacraments, especially through the Lord's Supper. This had major implications for places of worship. Not only did Laud launch an effort of beautification; he demanded that Communion tables be replaced with permanent altars and that they be railed off in the east end of churches. This appalled the Puritans because the changes smacked of transubstantiation and the Mass. Laudians did not just repudiate the predestinarian doctrines of mainstream Reformed Christianity; they insisted on ceremonies in a style consciously opposed to Puritan sensitivities. The episcopacy became nonnegotiable. Moreover, Laudians assumed a posture toward the Church of Rome that saw it as a true church in error, rather than no church at all and opposed to legitimate Christianity. All of this top-down policy had the full support of the king and at times was brutally enforced.[3]

When Charles decided to force a version of the Book of Common Prayer on his Scottish Presbyterian realm, war ensued and quickly spread. The Scots drew up a national covenant and took up arms against the king. This rebellion, known as the Bishops' War (1639–1640), bankrupted Charles and was a royal failure. Because only Parliament could levy taxes, Charles reluctantly summoned it in 1640. The Short Parliament was decidedly anti-Laud and opposed to arbitrary government, and Charles dismissed it after only three weeks. The convocation of the clergy that met parallel to the Short Parliament and continued after its dismissal produced a set of canons that doubled down on Laudianism and seemed to be aimed deliberately at enflaming the situation. The infamous "etcetera oath" that gave bishops a blank check regarding what they could demand of clergy and churches received the Scots' ire. At this point, the Scottish Covenanters invaded the North, and Charles was forced

2 John Spurr, *The Post-Reformation: Religion, Politics and Society in Britain, 1603–1714*, Religion, Politics, and Society in Britain (Harlow, UK: Pearson, 2006), 60–68.

3 Doreen M. Rosman, *The Evolution of the English Churches, 1500–2000* (Cambridge: Cambridge University Press, 2003), 74–79; Spurr, *Post-Reformation*, 72–80.

to call what came to be known as the Long Parliament, which began in 1640 and continued in one form or another until 1653.[4]

Divisions broke into violent civil war in 1642. Royalists cited obligations to conscience and honor in justification for their support of the king, as well as a general detestation of rebellion. Parliamentarians were persuaded that true religion was in mortal danger. Charles believed in a divine right of kings and absolute monarchy. He would not compromise or even negotiate about the heavy handedness of his reign to that point. To oppose the king, in his estimation, was to oppose God. Add this to suspicions of Roman Catholicism—which found evidence in Charles's Catholic wife, Laud's imposing of Catholic externals in worship, and the rebellion of Irish Catholics in the name of the king in 1641—and the result was the raising of armies. Parliament was determined to complete what the Reformation had started more than one hundred years earlier and ensure the establishment of true Protestantism. The year 1643 saw Royalist victories, but things began to shift with the Scottish alliance expressed as the Solemn League and Covenant. The pendulum swing gained unstoppable momentum in 1644 with Parliament's establishment of the New Model Army, culminating in Charles's surrender in 1646. The next three years included failed negotiations with Charles and the New Model Army's quelling of uprisings in both Ireland and Scotland with Oliver Cromwell at the helm, as well as its purging from Parliament all those opposed to putting the king on trial for treason. The Rump Parliament (1648–1653), consisting of what was left of the members of Parliament, found Charles guilty of treason, which was followed in January 1649 by the previously unthinkable and internationally shocking regicide.[5]

The machinery of government and the Church of England infrastructure collapsed in the chaos of the early 1640s. Bishops lay low or went into hiding, but the end result was still the execution of Laud in 1645 and the dissolution of the office of bishop entirely in 1646. This opened space for a variety of voluntary congregations and sects, and the unfettered promotion of ideas through an uncensored press. The Westminster Assembly, an advisory body to Parliament, began work in 1643 to create a new constitution, directory of worship, and confession for the English Church. The ninety English divines making up the Assembly well represented Puritanism, which divided mostly

---

4 Rosman, *Evolution of the English Churches*, 85; Spurr, *Post-Reformation*, 86–87.

5 Rosman, *Evolution of the English Churches*, 86–94; Spurr, *Post-Reformation*, 94–99, 112–14. Spurr notes that the English Civil Wars caused 180,000 casualties, 3.6 percent of the total population, and brought greater government intrusion and heavier taxation than anything threatened by Charles (100).

into Presbyterian and Independent factions. Parliament committed itself to the former through the Solemn League and Covenant, but the latter coincided with Cromwell's sympathies; eventually, the Independents would have their day. But for some time, the Church of England existed without leadership or institutions. Parliament eventually banned the Book of Common Prayer and ordered the Westminster Assembly's Directory for Public Worship to be used in its place, though this was largely unenforceable. With the rise of the Independents to greater prominence, the mood in general changed to one of toleration and religious liberty for sectarians.[6]

The 1650s were a decade of political crisis in which responsibility for bringing order to an unstable and turbulent society fell to Cromwell, who never successfully handed over power to a civilian government. Officially, the Rump Parliament governed in the absence of a king and the House of Lords. Propaganda touted the government as a representative republic, but the situation was tenuous. The execution of the king stoked Royalist sympathies in Ireland and Scotland, and the threat of Charles II's gaining continental support loomed large. The Rump sold off royal lands and made essential military improvements. Cromwell not only defended England from Ireland and Scotland but also conquered these countries. In the aftermath of Charles's beheading, the only two groups retaining some authority were the army and the Rump. As a leader in both, Cromwell attempted to bridge the gap. He eventually dismissed the Rump in 1653, as it had become, in his estimation, woefully inefficient at accomplishing its purpose of reform, and set up a provisional assembly, the Barebones Parliament (1553), in its place. Lasting only six months, Barebones gave way to Cromwell's becoming Lord Protector of the Commonwealth.[7]

As attempts at a religious and political settlement were continually disappointed, Cromwell gave his attention to security and reform of sin in society. His five-year tenure as Protector (1653–1658) was a period of peace, broad toleration for orthodox Protestants, unofficial toleration of unorthodox sects who did not disturb the peace, and the legislation of holiness in the Puritan mold. He appointed his son Richard his successor at his death in 1658, which turned out to be a mistake, as the younger Cromwell was able to control neither the army nor Parliament. The Puritan project failed, disillusion reigned, and Charles II was invited by Parliament to take the throne.[8]

---

6 Spurr, *Post-Reformation*, 101–7.
7 Rosman, *Evolution of the English Churches*, 98; Spurr, *Post-Reformation*, 120–22. Spurr argues that Cromwell's subduing of Ireland was also a campaign to exact revenge for the 1641 rebellion. The massacre of five thousand civilians took place under Cromwell's direction (120).
8 Spurr, *Post-Reformation*, 124–39.

Charles II was no absolutist. Rather, he was determined to keep his throne and indulge his appetites. Regarding religion, he was apathetic unless involvement in religious disputes became politically advantageous.[9] His interests in the years immediately after the Restoration lay in moderation, a conciliar tone, and promises of compromise. From 1660 to 1662, significant lobbying and negotiation happened. The Presbyterians wanted inclusion in the church settlement. Congregational and radical groups desired toleration of their independent worship. Acceptance of a range of Protestant opinions initially looked hopeful; the spirit seemed to be one of reconciliation. Charles even offered bishoprics to some high-profile Presbyterians—proposing presbytery within episcopacy—confirmed the majority of Cromwellian clergy without episcopal ordination or a religious test, and made Puritans his chaplains. But compromise divided the purist and pragmatic Presbyterians, Independents did not want inclusion at all, the number of Puritan members of Parliament fell, Thomas Venner (1608–1661) and his Fifth Monarchist uprising (1657) changed the societal mood, and attempts at a comprehensive, big-tent Anglican Church ultimately failed.[10]

The 1662 Act of Uniformity, with its Book of Common Prayer, was an intentional purge. The prayer book was imposed exclusively, it alone could be used in worship, and all other forms of worship were outlawed. It mandated episcopal ordination. It demanded that clergy stand before their congregations and affirm the prayer book without reservation or qualification, denounce taking up arms against the king, and condemn the Solemn League and Covenant. The act was designed to be intolerable to Puritans, and it surely was. Roughly one thousand beneficed ministers, schoolteachers, and university fellows gave up their positions, bringing the ejected number to two thousand since the Restoration.[11] Uniformity of worship was in contest with comprehensive and tolerant religion, a battle the former would finally win within the Church of England.[12]

A series of laws known as the Clarendon Code tried to stamp out the very existence of nonconformity, with the rise of dissenting denominations as the net result. The 1661 Corporation Act required all officials to receive Communion in the Church of England. In 1664, the Conventicle Act outlawed

---

9 Spurr, *Post-Reformation*, 154.

10 N. H. Keeble, "Introduction: Attempting Uniformity," in *"Settling the Peace of the Church": 1662 Revisited*, ed. N. H. Keeble (New York: Oxford University Press, 2014), 2–10.

11 The number of those ejected is disputed, and lowered, in Lee Gatiss, *The Tragedy of 1662: The Ejection and Persecution of the Puritans*, Latimer Studies 66 (London: Latimer Trust, 2007).

12 Keeble, "Introduction: Attempting Uniformity," 17–22.

religious gatherings of more than four people, not including one's family or servants, that did not use the prayer book. The Five Mile Act of 1665 forbade ejected clergy from coming within five miles of their previous parishes. The 1670 Conventicle Act was particularly malicious. It authorized the seizure of property to cover the cost of fines, penalized officials who failed to prosecute, and ordered one-third of the fines be issued to informants. These measures were carried out with varying degrees of zeal and found opponents at every level of society.[13]

Politics took a sudden turn in 1672 with Charles's pro-French foreign policy amid war with the Dutch, when he attempted the Declaration of Indulgence to gain the favor of the dissenting movement in his realm as well as to please the French with whom he was secretly negotiating. This indulgence gave relative freedom to dissenting churches that registered with the government, but Charles was forced to revoke the declaration in 1673 because of anti-Catholic backlash. The final decade or so of Charles's reign was marked by the Popish Plot (1678) and Exclusion Crisis (1679–1681). The latter arose from Parliament's attempts to bar James II (1633–1701), Charles's brother, from the royal line of succession because of his conversion to Roman Catholicism. The situation was tumultuous to a degree similar to the one that had led to civil war. While revolution was this time avoided, English society became deeply politicized, with the partisan labels of Whig and Tory coming into play at this juncture. Most Dissenters were Whig exclusionists, and Anglican Tory royalists feared another Puritan revolt. Tory reaction brought the worst persecution of Dissent in the Restoration period.[14]

The short reign of James II, beginning in 1685, was one marked by reforms supportive of toleration and liberty of conscience that led to the Glorious Revolution of 1688–1689. James supported the Repealers, who wanted to reverse the laws penalizing religious nonconformity, and settled on a strategy that privileged reform rather than repression. He often did not exact penalties for nonconformity in an effort to co-opt, rather than coerce, opponents. As a Roman Catholic granting toleration of Roman Catholics, along with other religious minorities, James evoked increasing opposition from the Whigs and alienated the Tories, who feared freedom for Catholics might result in a Catholic takeover of the country. The Glorious Revolution resulted when Parliament invited William of Orange (1650–1702), married to James's daughter

---

13 Dewey D. Wallace Jr., *Shapers of English Calvinism, 1660–1714: Variety, Persistence, and Transformation*, Oxford Studies in Historical Theology (New York: Oxford University Press, 2011), 21.

14 Spurr, *Post-Reformation*, 58–68.

Mary (1662–1694), to invade England and stymie a Catholic dynasty. His forces met little to no armed resistance, and William and Mary were installed as dual monarchs. The 1689 Act of Toleration that ensued gave freedom of worship to orthodox Protestant Dissenters.[15]

The rise and fall of John Owen's public life coincided with the rise and fall of the Puritan project that began with the Civil War and ended with the demise of the Commonwealth in 1660. The Laudian reforms at Oxford forced Owen to abandon his academic prospects as a student at Oxford University in 1637. After five years of living in obscurity, at the outbreak of civil war, Owen moved to London, sided with Parliament, and made a name for himself by taking advantage of the lax publishing restrictions.[16] Beginning in 1646, he was regularly invited to preach before Parliament, even as he was siding with the Independent New Model Army and its vision of general toleration against the Presbyterian Parliament and its desire for national religious uniformity. His transfer of allegiance occasioned his becoming the "unofficial preacher-in-chief of the revolutionary regime."[17] He preached to the Rump Parliament the day after Charles I was beheaded, and he participated in military tours to Ireland and Scotland as Cromwell's personal chaplain and confidant. Cromwell then gave Owen his academic positions in the senior leadership of Oxford University.[18] Frustrated with failed attempts at a religious settlement and the perceived declension of Cromwell's court, Owen fell out of favor with the Cromwell family and became associated with those opposed to Richard. By the time of the Restoration, Owen had returned to clerical life as the pastor of a gathered congregation.[19] He lived the rest of his days in the context of social exclusion, political retaliation, and, at times, severe persecution, though Owen himself was sheltered from extreme forms of the latter. But he learned to navigate the treacherous times and made some of his most enduring theological contributions during this period.[20] In a pamphlet from 1681 entitled *A Dialogue between the Pope and the Devil, about Owen and Baxter*, an anonymous author adeptly and satirically described the press, calling it "as large as Hell; and, like a Horse-Leach, it sucks, and is never satisfied." And in reference to Owen's vast output, the pamphlet said he had

---

15 Scott Sowerby, *Making Toleration: The Repealers and the Glorious Revolution*, Harvard Historical Studies 181 (Cambridge, MA: Harvard University Press, 2013), 3–17.
16 Gribben, *John Owen and English Puritanism*, 36–44.
17 Gribben, *John Owen and English Puritanism*, 69–90. For the quote, see p. 90.
18 Gribben, *John Owen and English Puritanism*, 108–17.
19 Gribben, *John Owen and English Puritanism*, 180.
20 Gribben, *John Owen and English Puritanism*, 211.

"a kind of ambitious itch to scribble."[21] Owen published tirelessly in his final decades, some of the fruits of his labor being these treatises on the Holy Spirit.

Church of Rome

Catholicism was doubly stigmatized in the English imagination, as it was both foreign and familiar. Catholics were foreign, different, and therefore necessarily inferior. At the same time, they were close and threatening.[22] At times posing a real threat, but most often only a perceived one, an English Catholic community existed throughout the sixteenth and seventeenth centuries while its country forged a Protestant identity. This community was marked by a struggle resulting from conflicting allegiances. Remaining true to pope, king, and conscience; maintaining religious integrity; and at the same time displaying basic English loyalty proved at times impossible, which regularly played into the politics of persecution and plots.[23]

Many English Catholics maintained the Roman faith throughout the tumultuous reigns of the Tudors Henry (r. 1509–1547), Edward (r. 1547–1553), and Mary (r. 1553–1558), and under Elizabeth's (r. 1558–1603) church settlement. This community underwent something of a revival beginning in the 1570s as Jesuit missionaries and seminary priests brought to it leadership and a voice. Forced to worship in secret, always marginalized and sometimes persecuted, this underground Catholic community of recusants solidified in the later years of Elizabeth's long tenure on the throne. As the movement became linked in the official and public mind with treasonable conspiracy in alliance with Spain, the attitude of English Catholics changed to missionary status as a minority under a seemingly permanent Protestant settlement.[24]

Catholics in England seemed to have a friend, though not a sympathizer, in James I. If never explicitly with words, implicitly with his actions, James made life easier for nonconformists of all stripes. At the succession of his son Charles I, prospects for the Catholic community looked the brightest they had in generations. England as a missionary province with a small, slightly expanding Catholic population is evidenced by the increased

21 *A Dialogue between the Pope and the Devil, about Owen and Baxter* (London, 1681), 1.

22 Raymond D. Tumbleson, *Catholicism in the English Protestant Imagination: Nationalism, Religion, and Literature, 1660–1745* (Cambridge: Cambridge University Press, 1998), 1.

23 For a treatment of the struggle of English Catholics through the lens of conflicting allegiances, see Kenneth L. Campbell, *The Intellectual Struggle of the English Papists in the Seventeenth Century: The Catholic Dilemma*, Texts and Studies in Religion 30 (Lewiston, NY: E. Mellen, 1986).

24 Michael A. Mullett, *Catholics in Britain and Ireland, 1558–1829*, Social History in Perspective (New York: St. Martin's, 1998), 22.

number of Jesuits in the early Stuart years. Eighteen Jesuits in 1598 grew to 193 in 1639. The relative relief and lack of harassment came at a cost, however. The Crown acquired a stake in Catholic survival through recusancy fines. A fiscalized penal system was regularized into compositions, or periodic payments to the king in lieu of recusancy fines. This system served as a framework for Catholic survival leading up to the Civil War, albeit an increasingly expensive one. As Charles looked for alternative sources of income in the 1630s, compositions rose from six thousand to thirty-two thousand pounds per year.[25]

English Catholics met a crisis in the Civil War. They suddenly declined from the status of relative favor to being persecuted. Renewed suffering beset the community, and above all its priests, that had built a comparatively stable existence in England over the previous decades. Antipopery raged, and security turned to extreme danger, including brutal executions. While Puritans threatened the Crown, they blamed the Catholics. Pro-Catholic advisors had led Charles to invade Scotland. Catholics stirred up rebellion in Ireland. All the while Archbishop Laud, to some a crypto-Catholic, attempted to make the Church of England look like the Church of Rome. Or so the reasoning went, and the Puritans had to oppose Charles to keep Roman influences out of England's national church.[26] Anti-Catholic rhetoric rose as it had under Elizabeth, when suspicions were high regarding English-Catholic cooperation with Spain. Or as it had in the wake of the Gunpowder Plot (1605). Now the Irish Rebellion (1641) especially intensified anti-Catholicism so as to portray both Stuart absolutism and Laudianism as popish in their essence and to mobilize Protestant parliamentarians to declare war against their king. Catholics were painted as a treasonous, ruthless, and murderous liability.[27]

Protestant fears of the Catholics as a solid military support for Charles were exaggerated, but propagandists painted the royalist forces in the north as a "Catholic army." This, added to conspiracy, meant that Catholics did not fare well in Parliament-controlled lands during the Civil War or anywhere in the country in its aftermath. At the same time, real possibilities materialized for accommodation between English Catholics and the government in the late 1640s and 1650s.[28] Yes, there were two executions during Oliver Cromwell's time in power, though he was not in favor of them; eight priests were

25 Mullett, *Catholics in Britain and Ireland*, 24–26.
26 Campbell, *Intellectual Struggle of English Papists in the Seventeenth Century*, 224.
27 Arthur F. Marotti, *Religious Ideology and Cultural Fantasy: Catholic and Anti-Catholic Discourses in Early Modern England* (Notre Dame, IN: University of Notre Dame Press, 2005), 147.
28 Mullett, *Catholics in Britain and Ireland*, 72–74.

arrested in 1657, though they were subjected only to the Lord Protector's mocking. This stood in marked contrast to the brutality of antipopery in the early 1640s.[29] The 1650s were overall a mild decade for Catholics in England. Congregations largely functioned quietly and unnoticed. Cromwell's secretary, John Rushworth (1612–1690) assisted Catholic gentry in preserving their estates. Cromwell himself entertained leading Catholics such as Lord Arundell (ca. 1607–1694), Lord Brudenell (ca. 1583–1663), and Sir Kenelm Digby (1603–1665).[30]

Charles II showed promise of toleration, especially in the months leading up to the Restoration and its early years, but he had to retract promises and commitments. While true toleration did not materialize, Catholic numbers increased, and hopes seemed to be high. By the 1670s, "popery" was a well-worn umbrella term of abuse for almost anything politically objectionable to mainstream thought. The Jesuits, properly viewed as the political arm of the Roman Catholic Church on the continent, were particularly repulsive to the English mind. The "Popish Plot" of 1678 was a last attempt to drum up fears of popery as sedition. The middle of the 1680s saw recusancy fines drop to a negligible sum and very few arrests. The last clerical execution was 1681. Systematic persecution of nonconformity fizzled out across the board.[31]

The hysteria around the Popish Plot from 1678 to 1681 began with a rumor excited by Titus Oates (1649–1705), which gained traction because of a pattern of suspicion aimed at Catholics.[32] Fears of Catholics had been on the rise as a result of Charles's pro-French foreign policy, French expansion under Louis XIV (1638–1715), and the conversion of James Stuart to Catholicism.[33] Oates, the son of a Baptist preacher, was received into the Catholic Church and went to Jesuit colleges in France and Spain. He returned to England touting evidence of a Catholic conspiracy to bring England back under Roman ecclesiastical rule. The paranoia stirred up by Oates, though with an elaborate fiction, was exploited by the Crown's opposition. They were unhappy with the favor the king showed to France and Catholics associated with monarchial absolutism.[34] These years made it obvious that persecution of Catholics had little to do with religion; political popery was not the same

29 John Coffey, *Persecution and Toleration in Protestant England, 1558–1689*, Studies in Modern History (Harlow, UK: Pearson, 2000), 157–58.
30 J. C. H. Aveling, *The Handle and the Axe: The Catholic Recusants in England from Reformation to Emancipation* (London: Blond and Briggs, 1976), 175–76.
31 Mullett, *Catholics in Britain and Ireland*, 76–79.
32 Sowerby, *Making Toleration*, 80.
33 Tumbleson, *Catholicism in the English Protestant Imagination*, 2.
34 Marotti, *Religious Ideology and Cultural Fantasy*, 158.

thing as religious Catholicism. As the former was resolved, persecution of the latter dissipated.[35]

The efforts of Charles II and then especially James II to offer indulgence to Catholics in the 1670s and 1680s were interpreted by many as attempts to reimpose the monopoly of the Church of Rome. James's protoleration strategy, which of course did not exclusively benefit Catholics, was his undoing.[36] Indeed, for those living in the seventeenth century, the date that Catholicism's fate was sealed as a minority sect was different from how it is reckoned by historians looking back.[37] Whatever the favor enjoyed by Catholics under James II, a dramatic downturn took place at the Glorious Revolution. Catholics were severely handicapped in society along with the rest of noncommunicant Anglicans, and at the same time anti-Catholicism served as nationalistic fuel for the emerging Protestant British Empire.

The fact of the matter is this: a Catholic community existed in England throughout Owen's lifetime and at times even flourished to a degree. International Catholicism was Tridentine, which by definition gave it an anti-Protestant posture. Owen, as part of the international Reformed movement—reading and sometimes writing in Latin, the language of international scholarship and politics—was very much aware of the Catholic Counter-Reformation. Whether real or imagined, the specter of Roman Catholicism was ever present in the minds of seventeenth-century Englishmen, Owen included. The fear extended both to homegrown Catholic sedition and to external threats such as Spain and France.

Owen was reared within the Puritan movement, which self-identified as true Protestantism in juxtaposition to both the medieval Catholicism of England's past and all of its accretions in the Church of England. This religious outlook and fervor was fueled partially by the remembrance of bloody persecution under Mary Tudor in the middle of the sixteenth century and events like the failed invasion of the Spanish Armada at the end of the century or the Gunpowder Plot at the beginning of the seventeenth century. Such events would have been instilled in Owen's mind, and the warnings they messaged against the Church of Rome could not have been missed. The Irish Rebellion happened during Owen's early adulthood, just before his rise to prominence. The Popish Plot dominated the last years of his life. Owen listened and con-

---

35 Campbell, *Intellectual Struggle of English Papists in the Seventeenth Century*, 225; Mullett, *Catholics in Britain and Ireland*, 78.
36 This is Sowerby's primary argument in *Making Toleration*.
37 Alexandra Walsham, *Charitable Hatred: Tolerance and Intolerance in England, 1500–1700*, Politics, Culture and Society in Early Modern Britain (Manchester: Manchester University Press, 2008), 16.

tributed to the anti-popery rhetoric of the middle decades of the seventeenth century. While the treatises in this volume are not focused on anti-Roman polemics, Owen often does self-identify in contradistinction to Catholicism, which makes perfect sense given his context.

In Owen's discussions of the Holy Spirit as illuminator, comforter, and spiritual gift giver, Roman Catholicism serves as an explicit foil for his arguments. In *The Reason of Faith* (1677) and *Causes, Ways, and Means* (1678), Owen navigates between an overemphasis on reason, on the one hand, and the Spirit, on the other, when interpreting the Bible. In so doing, he carefully avoids an appeal to anything like the Roman curia; the Catholic appeal to tradition illustrates what must be rejected. In *The Holy Spirit as a Comforter* (1693), Owen weighs in on the Protestant and especially Puritan emphasis of an individual's assurance of his or her salvation. The Spirit is given to and indwells the believer, resulting in assurance of final salvation by guaranteeing its completion. The Catholic Church supplants the Spirit's work in this regard with the sacramental system, a system that professedly cannot provide ultimate assurance. Further, in *A Discourse of Spiritual Gifts* (1693), Owen wants to distance himself from the enthusiasm of radical dissent with all of its spiritual excesses. Even more, however, Owen views the rise of the Church of Rome, with its authoritarian pope and superstition, as a by-product of the neglect of true spiritual gifts. Ministry is supernatural and at the same time ordinary.

Owen's *The Work of the Holy Spirit in Prayer* (1682) contrasts the Spirit's work in prayer with liturgical impositions (or set forms of prayer) and mental prayer, both of which are negatively illustrated by the Church of Rome. If it were a treatise on prayer in general, it would be a measly offering, but with its focus on the Spirit's work, and with Owen's sights set on liturgical prayers, explicitly in the context of the Church of Rome, this treatise brings clarity and provides insight to an important communal and private Christian experience. In his preface, Owen lays out his design to combat the worship of Roman Catholicism, summarized by the blanket designation "prayers of human composure." It should be noted that much of Owen's criticism parallels the Puritan tradition's criticism of the Church of England and its prayer book. The decades following the Restoration were not the first time that Puritans shrouded their condemnation of prayer book worship with explicit reference to Roman Catholicism. The 1620s and 1630s had witnessed the same tactic.[38] Owen's readers knew exactly what he was doing.

38 See Tom Webster, *Godly Clergy in Early Stuart England: The Caroline Puritan Movement, c.1620–1643*, Cambridge Studies in Early Modern British History (Cambridge: Cambridge University Press, 1997).

Owen's censure of prayer book worship caused significant controversy among Dissenters in the several years following his death. Richard Baxter (1615–1691), in *Catholic Communion Defended against Both Extremes* (1684), interacts with a supposedly widely circulated manuscript of Owen's that enumerated twelve arguments for separation from the Church of England. Baxter quotes the manuscript verbatim as he takes issue with the conclusion, and the content is consistent with Owen's *The Work of the Holy Spirit in Prayer*. The author of the manuscript is arguing for separation from the Church of England's worship based on the regulative principle of worship.[39] Baxter makes clear that he remains unconvinced, as his defense of his own participation in communion with the established church makes clear.[40] This precipitated a fury of publication. For example, an anonymous defender of Owen, in *A Vindication of the Late Reverend and Learned John Owen* (1684), challenged Baxter by concluding that the twelve arguments manuscript was not even Owen's work. It was simply not as accurate and tightly argued as the sources confirmed to be Owen's.[41] Owen's anonymous vindicator and Baxter continued to go back and forth.[42] Isaac Chauncy (1632–1712), Owen's successor as pastor of the church in London, also weighed in on the debate in his *A Theological Dialogue*, in which he set the words of Baxter's initial discourse in dialogue with Owen, for whom Chauncy himself spoke.[43] Baxter's *Whether Parish Congregations Be True Christian Churches* was his capstone to the whole debate.[44] Baxter's penchant

---

39 The regulative principle is the belief that public worship services are to be conducted using only the distinct elements affirmed in Scripture. This view is opposed to the normative principle, which teaches that those things not expressly forbidden in Scripture are indifferent and can indeed be used in worship. See Terry L. Johnson, *Worshipping with Calvin: Recovering the Historic Ministry and Worship of Reformed Protestantism* (Darlington, UK: Evangelical, 2014).

40 Richard Baxter, *Catholic Communion Defended against Both Extremes* (London, 1684), preface. Baxter's issue with separation goes back to his differences with Owen in the 1650s regarding the comprehension of the Cromwellian church settlement. See Paul Chang-Ha Lim, *In Pursuit of Purity, Unity, and Liberty: Richard Baxter's Puritan Ecclesiology in Its Seventeenth-Century Context*, Studies in the History of Christian Thought 112 (Leiden: Brill, 2004); Sungho Lee, "All Subjects of the Kingdom of Christ: John Owen's Conceptions of Christian Unity and Schism" (PhD diss., Calvin Theological Seminary, 2007); Tim Cooper, "Why Did Richard Baxter and John Owen Diverge? The Impact of the First Civil War," *The Journal of Ecclesiastical History* 61, no. 3 (2010): 496–516.

41 A Hearty Friend of All Good Men, *A Vindication of the Late Reverend and Learned John Owen* (London, 1684), 1.

42 Richard Baxter, *Catholic Communion Doubly Defended* (London, 1684); A Lover of Truth and Peace, *Vindiciae revindicate* (London, 1684).

43 Isaac Chauncy, *A Theological Dialogue* (London, 1684).

44 Richard Baxter, *Whether Parish Congregations Be True Christian Churches* (London, 1684).

for criticizing Owen and others has been well documented, by both his contemporaries and his twenty-first-century biographers.[45]

However, Baxter was not alone in his interaction with Owen's views on liturgical prayers. In a kind of anthology of leading Independents, published under the title *The Lawfulness of Hearing the Public Ministers of the Church of England*, Owen is cited to demonstrate that not only is hearing the word preached in the Church of England acceptable; there is nothing wrong with hearing the Book of Common Prayer liturgy either. It is argued that Owen condemns composing forms of prayer for private use, but not the use of forms per se or that churches may collectively agree on prescribed forms by common consent. Further, liturgical forms are not intrinsically evil, according to Owen; God will accept them when they are sincere, even though they do not conform precisely to the word of God. Rather, Owen—as represented in this compendium—is setting up a better-and-best continuum.[46] But a review of the references to Owen's *The Work of the Holy Spirit in Prayer* reveals that this is not what Owen is communicating at all. Rather, Owen is responding to a very specific argument—namely, that believers who can pray on their own would benefit from occasionally using prescribed forms. He is not speaking to the lawfulness of prescription in corporate worship. Owen does leave room for real communion with God through liturgical forms in cases where the heart is prepared and motives are appropriate and where they are performed in ignorance. But he is not setting up a better-and-best dichotomy. He strongly denounces set forms as essentially obstructive to true prayer and worship and therefore unlawful.[47] Despite this fact, Thomas Pittis includes a quotation from Owen's *The Work of the Holy Spirit in Prayer* on the title page of his *A Discourse of Prayer: Wherein This Great Duty Is Stated, so as to Oppose Some Principles and Practices of Papists and Fanatics*. Even though Pittis argues that those who separate "under the pretense of greater Reformation, and a more pure, and Evangelical, Worship, do not pay homage, in their prayers, to the great God, in such a manner as is suitable to his Attributes, man's dependence, and that infinite distance betwixt their Creator, and themselves";[48] even

---

45 *A Winding Sheet for Mr. Baxter's Dead* [. . .] *Wherein the Reverend and Learned Dr. Owen Is Further Vindicated* (London, 1685); Tim Cooper, *John Owen, Richard Baxter and the Formation of Nonconformity* (Burlington, VT: Ashgate, 2011).

46 *The Lawfulness of Hearing the Public Ministers of the Church of England* (London, 1683), 38.

47 See chap. 11 of *A Discourse of the Work of the Holy Spirit in Prayer*, in vol. 8.

48 Thomas Pittis, *A Discourse of Prayer: Wherein This Great Duty Is Stated, so as to Oppose Some Principles and Practices of Papists and Fanatics* (London, 1683), 242.

though he sees the end of extemporary prayer as rash and irreverent and at times nonsensical or worse;[49] nonetheless, he still wants to take advantage of Owen's influence for his own ends.[50] On the subject of liturgical forms, Owen was leveraged by friends and enemies, and by both those inside and outside the established church.

Also in his preface to *The Work of the Holy Spirit in Prayer*, Owen takes aim at mental prayer, contemplation that does not engage the mind but rather empties it. He recalls that it was Hugh Cressy's (1605–1674) *The Church-History of Brittany* and its disparagement of what Owen considered the biblical position on the subject of prayer that served as the impetus for Owen's treatise to begin with. Cressy received his initial education at Oxford before serving as chaplain to Viscount Falkland. This post put him at the center of the Great Tew Circle for a number of years. He later boasted that he had been the one who initially introduced Socinian works to England.[51] Cressy converted to the Church of Rome when he became convinced that if the Bible alone was authoritatively to be judged by reason, then the Socinians were right. He did not want to concede orthodoxy, so he converted in 1646 and continued his education in Paris at the Sorbonne. When he took Benedictine orders, he spent seven years at a monastery in Douai, later becoming chaplain to Charles II's wife. Cressy demonstrated his great learning in his ecclesiastical history of England, in which he leveraged manuscript evidence to demonstrate that the history of the English Church was thoroughly and consistently Roman.[52] One element of this was the practice of contemplative prayer, the discussion of which certainly includes some harsh words aimed at the Protestant alternative. Cressy says,

> The most perfect manner of prayer in esteem with them is such a tedious, loud, impetuous, and uncivil conversation with God, as they see practiced by their preachers, which is no better than a mere artificial sleight and facility easily obtained by custom and a quick imagination, and may be in perfection practiced by persons full of inordinate, sensual, revengeful, and immortified passions.[53]

49 Pittis, *Discourse of Prayer*, 313.
50 For an example, see Pittis, *Discourse of Prayer*, 353.
51 Oliver Lawson Dick, ed. *Aubrey's Brief Lives: Edited from the Original Manuscripts and with a Life of John Aubrey* (Ann Arbor, MI: University of Michigan Press, 1957), 56.
52 Joseph Gillow, *A Literary and Biographical History, or Bibliographical Dictionary of the English Catholics*, vol. 1 (New York: Burt Franklin, n.d.), 592–93.
53 Serenus Cressy, *The Church-History of Brittany, or England, from the Beginning of Christianity to the Norman Conquest* (Rouen, 1668), "Preface," 43.

This public dismissal from a prominent and learned Roman Catholic instigated Owen's public reply.

Revolutionary Sectarians

The middle decades of the seventeenth century were indeed decades of religious war in England. King and bishop tried to make the Church of England less Reformed and more ritualistic. Thus, when monarchy and episcopacy called for taxes to be raised and the prayer book to be imposed on Scotland, Parliament united against them. In this context, censorship broke down, the army became a political actor, and the ever-changing government became more tolerant than ever before; and so the sectarians abounded. However, the temptation to see these sects or movements as discrete, easily identifiable bodies must be avoided. They were groups of people clustered around certain sets of ideas, but without a centralized structure or formal membership. Moreover, fluidity and overlap abounded; it was not unusual for people to move from identification with one sect to another. The sectarians tended to share a common yet broad concern: the rejection of the established church maintained by compulsory tithes and a desire for toleration and freedom of conscience. They pushed things beyond what even the Interregnum government allowed and challenged accepted wisdom and practice. While most appeared and vanished within these few decades, together they comprised an important element of Owen's historical landscape. For that reason, the most important sects will be briefly described in turn.

Baptists

The seventeenth-century English Baptists were characterized by nonliturgical worship, with an emphasis on preaching and believer's baptism. They were attacked with the label of Anabaptist, a stereotype that conjured particular fear and loathing in their context, but it was an illegitimate designation. The Baptists were the inheritors of the Puritan-become-Separatist movement associated with Robert Browne (ca. 1550–1633), taking the implications of the regulative principle of worship to their logical conclusions—namely, application to ecclesiology and the ordinances. By midcentury, two distinct groups were apparent: the Particular Baptists, stemming from independent London congregations associated with Henry Jacob (1563–1624), on the one hand, and the General Baptists, with roots in the Amsterdam church led by John Smyth (ca. 1570–1612) and Thomas Helwys (ca. 1550–ca. 1616), on the other. The former got their name from their traditional Protestant soteriology, the latter from their Arminian sympathies. However, they agreed that believer's baptism was the entry into church membership. And while immersion was

attacked with satire by their religious opponents, the real threat posed by
Baptists was the breaking up of social cohesion caused by their independence.
Rejection of the church equaled rejection of the state. The Particular Baptists
especially worked hard to affirm submission in matters not of conscience and
separate themselves from political radicals, while General Baptists showed
some overt support for the Levellers. Both welcomed Cromwell's government
but were disillusioned like so many others when it failed to fully deliver the
desired reforms. This disenchantment led some to join the Fifth Monarchy
Men. With Restoration imminent, Baptists committed to live peaceably with
whatever government would be established but remained stalwart against
compulsory religion. The Baptists had served as a breeding ground for radical
sects during the century's middle decades and later consolidated to become
an established and at times respected dissenting denomination.[54]

Levellers

The core of the Leveller platform was individual liberty and rights, but leaders did not necessarily share the same starting point; nor did they agree how
their theoretical positions should be applied. For instance, Richard Overton
(fl. 1640–1663) wrote *An Arrow against All Tyrants and Tyrany* (1646) developing an argument for political rights based on natural law, while John
Lilburne (ca. 1614–1657) came to similar conclusions based on the Bible in
London's Liberty in Chains (1646). The movement lasted only six years, beginning with the publication *A Remonstrance of Many Thousand Citizens* in July
1646. The philosophy was basically this: God created people equal, and no
one therefore had a God-given right to rule or govern over another. Government exists by consent of the governed. Ultimate sovereignty resided in the
people, and thus government could act only by the will of the people. The
aim was to purge undemocratic elements from the government—especially
the House of Lords—and make the House of Commons truly democratic in
practice. Even with a representative government, though, Levellers advocated
for freedom of conscience, equitable justice, and the right of property. The
Leveller movement's primary concern was practical, not theological, meaning
the short-lived coalition included various religious persuasions.[55]

54 Michael A. G. Haykin, *Kiffin, Knollys and Keach: Rediscovering English Baptist Heritage* (Leeds: Reformation Today, 1996); B. R. White, *The English Baptists of the Seventeenth Century* (London: Baptist Historical Society, 1983); Stephen I. Wright, *The Early English Baptists, 1603–1649* (Woodbridge, UK: Boydell, 2006).
55 Andrew Bradstock, *Radical Religion in Cromwell's England: A Concise History from the English Civil War to the End of the Commonwealth*, International Library of Historical Studies 58

Diggers

On the fringe of the Leveller movement were the "True Levellers" or Diggers. No tension between democracy and the maintenance of property rights existed in the Digger mind. The poor needed economic, not just political, freedom and this would be accomplished by the communal ownership of land. And this was not merely an appeal or theory. The group cultivated and planted land not their own, hoping to incite the process of making the earth a "common treasury." The first reports of the Diggers appear in 1649 after Gerrard Winstanley (1609–1676) received direction in a trance to help usher in the kingdom of God, a kingdom which included no buying or selling, nor categories of ownership such as "mine" and "yours." He set up a community, which quickly drew attention and was officially harassed, with the hope that the vision would spread. Other communities were also established. Digger ideology was radical and its theology unorthodox. The earth, in Winstanley's teaching, was originally created for all to share equally. He does not use the category of the fall to explain the problem of humanity, but rather the biblical narrative of the strong, rich, and powerful struggling against the weak, poor, and powerless. Adam rises up in every man to take what is not his, and the second Adam, Christ, overcomes this impulse. Redemption is corporate, a communal event that includes the spurning of buying and selling. Because self-interest is not innate but rather caused by the system of buying and selling, if the latter is eradicated, a prelapsarian state is possible. Christ is not distinct from the saints, in Winstanley's mind, and the second coming is his welling up in his followers, not a personal return. The resurrection can be similarly explained. Christ is still buried, waiting to rise up in believers. The Diggers clearly rejected the theological system of the established church and anything that could be described as orthodox Christian religion wholesale. The main community was violently broken up, and the movement sputtered out, its adherents being absorbed into the ranks of various other sects. Winstanley himself became a Quaker.[56]

(London: I. B. Tauris, 2011), 27–36. See also G. E. Aylmer, *The Levellers in the English Revolution*, Documents of Revolution (Ithaca, NY: Cornell University Press, 1975); Henry Noel Brailsford, *The Levellers and the English Revolution* (Stanford, CA: Stanford University Press, 1961); Andrew Sharp, ed., *The English Levellers*, Cambridge Texts in the History of Political Thought (Cambridge: Cambridge University Press, 1998).

56 Bradstock, *Radical Religion in Cromwell's England*, 51–70. See also Andrew Bradstock, *Faith in the Revolution: The Political Theologies of Müntzer and Winstanley* (London: SPCK, 1997); John Gurney, *Brave Community: The Digger Movement in the English Revolution*, Politics, Culture and Society in Early Modern Britain (Manchester: Manchester University Press, 2007).

Ranters

Even more extreme in the eyes of the establishment were the Ranters. They primarily rose out of Baptist and Seeker ranks, and while there were no real leaders, no formal membership, and hardly an identifiable movement at all, there were Ranters.[57] Men like Abiezer Coppe (1619–1672), Joseph Salmon (fl. 1647–1656), and Jacob Bauthumley (1613–1692) drew attention with their crass antinomianism. The Ranter creed was that there is no sin, because if God indwelt a person it was impossible to sin and ergo the law was irrelevant. This article of faith flowed from strong mystical and pantheistic convictions. God in all things made everything and anything good. What made the Ranters radical was not so much this theology as their obvious readiness to act on it and take it to the extreme. Sexual immorality, drunkenness, sacrilege, and blasphemy abounded. Ranterism was short-lived, with an active period from 1649 to 1651, at the end of which an act was passed to put an end to the socially threatening behavior and ideas. Such people were not going to endure persecution or have any qualms about the path of least resistance. They strove to shock with their license. And shock they did.[58]

Fifth Monarchists

The Fifth Monarchy Men combined organization with a political agenda. They were millenarians, and they were committed to actively bringing the millennial reign about at any cost. They looked eagerly for the second coming of Christ, which would usher in his thousand-year reign of peace on Earth. Indeed, his return was their raison d'être. The execution of Charles and its aftermath were unmistakable signs and the fulfillment of prophecy. Fifth Monarchists placed Daniel 2, God's establishing a fifth and eternal kingdom, alongside Revelation 20, the picture of the millennium. The resulting progression went like this: Assyria, Babylon, Greece, Rome—which was extinguished with the Roman Catholic sympathizer Charles—then king Jesus, the fifth monarch. The movement was solidified when hopes of ushering in the kingdom were dashed in 1651 by the Rump Parliament and then in

57 The Seekers were a movement beginning in the 1620s that dismissed all organized churches as corrupt and awaited God's further revelation. See Nicholas McDowell, *The English Radical Imagination: Culture, Religion, and Revolution, 1630–1660*, Oxford English Monographs (Oxford: Oxford University Press, 2003).

58 Bradstock, *Radical Religion in Cromwell's England*, 76–86. See also Jerome Friedman, *Blasphemy, Immorality, and Anarchy: The Ranters and the English Revolution* (Athens, OH: Ohio University Press, 1987); A. L. Morton, *The World of the Ranters: Religious Radicalism in the English Revolution* (London: Lawrence and Wishart, 1970).

1653 by Cromwell himself and his Barebones Parliament. Christopher Feake (1612–1683) and Henry Jessey (1603–1663) were leaders who emerged during these early days. The group denounced Cromwell, but they largely agreed that they would need a clear sign before using force against him. Some claimed to receive messages from God in dreams and visions. The year 1657 saw the infamous attempt at uprising by Thomas Venner. This and other efforts were thwarted as Cromwell took great interest in the development of the movement and went to great lengths to keep it suppressed, especially in the ranks of his army. The Restoration was, of course, functionally the end of the Fifth Monarchists, and by century's end they were no more.[59]

Muggletonians

Lastly, the Muggletonians emerged in 1652 with the cousins Lodowicke Muggleton (1609–1698) and John Reeve (1608–1658). Reeve received a special communication from God that the pair were the two last witnesses from the book of Revelation, comparing himself to Moses and Muggleton to Aaron. Reeve wrote the apology for the movement the same year, *A Transcendent Spiritual Treatise*, arguing that his revelation was superior from that claimed by other sects, because his came from outside himself. God spoke to him audibly. Reeve may have been the genius behind the movement, but it assumed Muggleton's name as he singlehandedly led the group for forty years. The Muggletonians thought they were living in the last days, but they were no millenarians. They expected the second coming of Christ to usher the last judgement in immediately. They were dispensationalists with a Trinitarian view of history; the age of the Spirit had begun with the divine revelation to Reeve. They were predestinarians, which separated them from most other sects with whom they shared an emphasis on the Spirit over the words of Scripture. What gave them appeal was the power of the two witnesses to know whether an individual was numbered among the elect or not. With the witnesses, it became possible to have not only salvation but also assurance. Blessing and cursing based on this special insight became a distinctive of Muggletonian ministry. However, the group remained small, as adherents did not initiate conversations about their message. In their view, someone they encountered might be saved, but if they heard the message of the two witnesses and rejected it, they would certainly be damned. They were unitarians, understanding God to have a spiritual, and yet circumscribed body.

---

59 Bradstock, *Radical Religion in Cromwell's England*, 117–24. See also B. S. Capp, *The Fifth Monarchy Men: A Study in Seventeenth-Century English Millenarianism*, (London: Faber, 1972).

So the Father became a physical, mortal human—Jesus—for a time, before taking on immortality again. After this, with the exception of the revelation to Reeve, God was disinterested in his people. He took no notice of prayers and was unmoved by suffering, to such an extent that nothing was gained from martyrdom or self-denial. The result of these beliefs was an informal piety. No prayer, no proselytizing, no ministers, no regular services. Just gatherings, often in taverns or alehouses, where leaders surfaced, and discussions were had. The Muggletonians were political quietists small in number and, as such, existed as a kind of unnoticed society after the Restoration into the twentieth century.[60]

Owen witnessed firsthand the rise of these religious sects in the 1640s and 1650s, and in some cases was very much aware of their continuance later into the seventeenth century. This sectarian milieu resulted, he thought, from failures on two fronts: the doctrine of Scripture and the doctrine of the church. Owen's *Causes, Ways, and Means* (1678) establishes a legitimate method of biblical interpretation, one that does not leave the meaning of Scripture open-ended. Further, the Spirit never contradicts the word, so whether it is Digger redefinition of sin or Ranter antinomianism, any teaching contrary to Scripture is categorically false, regardless of where it is claimed to have originated. Even more pointedly, the Spirit does not work apart from the word, so claims to special revelations, whether Fifth Monarchist or Muggletonian, are simply not true. Like all extraordinary spiritual gifts, prophecy and all the other extrabiblical revelation—"enthusiasm," as it was called in the seventeenth century—ended with the extraordinary offices of New Testament prophets and apostles. Enthusiasm was a threat that was given life by many of these sects, and it not only undermined Owen's conception of the authority and function of Scripture but also devalued the ordinary spiritual gifts and offices through which Christ provides for his church, as Owen outlines in *A Discourse of Spiritual Gifts* (1693). Owen shared many of the sectarian concerns; however, he believed that Scripture and the ordinary means of grace given by God to his church provided the answers and resources necessary for response to the legitimate apprehensions. The Muggletonian emphasis on assurance, for example, Owen shared. But rather than revising orthodox Christianity, he penned a biblical treatise on the certainty of salvation in *The Holy Spirit as a Comforter* (1693). The 1640s and 1650s turned the world upside down and violently shook it up, with the Restoration attempting to put things back

---

60 Bradstock, *Radical Religion in Cromwell's England*, 139–55. See also William M. Lamont, *Last Witnesses: The Muggletonian History, 1652–1979* (Aldershot, UK: Ashgate, 2006).

in their place.[61] What Owen experienced during those decades, and what was allowed promulgation, required a doubling down on emphases traditionally present in Christian theology, emphases such as the authority of Scripture, the coupling of word and Spirit, the Spirit's provision of ministerial gifts, and the Spirit's role in consolation. Owen's delay until his final decade may be explained by his overall constructive writing project, which throughout his life seems to have been systematic rather than reactionary, while at the same time sensitive to his historical context.

Quakers

The Quakers, like so many other English sectarians in the seventeenth century, emerged out of the upheaval of the Civil War, when church hierarchy and censorship were abolished. However, unlike most other sects, they transformed into one of the main dissenting denominations after the Restoration. And while this evolution must be briefly outlined for historical context, it is important at the outset to observe that the movement's theology changed very little, which is why Owen positioned himself so strongly against the Quakers, even at the end of his life when the Friends were all but established as a respectable dissenting denomination.

Most histories of the Quakers begin in the 1650s, but the first definite event in Quaker history was the interaction between George Fox (1624–1691) and Elizabeth Hooton (1600–1672) in late 1646. Fox, the father of Quakerism and its foremost leader during his lifetime, had spent the previous few years wandering England, disenchanted with the hypocrisy of established religion. He became convinced of an "inner light," something every individual possessed, which constituted ultimate authority and required obedience. The recognition of and submission to this inner light was the way of salvation, and it had major ramifications for traditional Christianity, implications that we will explore shortly. When Fox met Hooton, who was part of a Baptist meeting, she sympathized with him and took him in as a kind patron. She was convinced of his message by the first recorded instance of quaking and devoted herself to what was originally known pejoratively as Quakerism, dying in Jamaica as a missionary.[62]

---

61 Such phraseology, descriptive of the period, was made famous by Christopher Hill, *The World Turned Upside Down: Radical Ideas During the English Reformation* (London: Maurice Temple Smith, 1972).

62 Rosemary Anne Moore, *The Light in Their Consciences: Early Quakers in Britain, 1646–1666* (University Park, PA: Pennsylvania State University Press, 2000), 6; Hilary Hinds, *George Fox and Early Quaker Culture* (Manchester: Manchester University Press, 2011), 65–73.

From 1647 to 1649, the Friends grew among those with sectarian tendencies, those with little time for the ordained ministry and prescribed ritual, as Fox and his followers continued to travel. In 1649, Fox landed himself in prison, the first of many times, for shouting down a priest and attacking the idea that Scripture was the final authority for the Christian. Such incidents were sporadic and took place initially in the countryside of England. Given that the Friends were unorganized and lacked a presence in London, they did not attract official government notice as a societal threat during their early expansion. As Fox traveled, he recruited sympathizers, and by the close of 1652, he had amassed the leaders who would carry the movement through the seventeenth century. Richard Farnworth (d. 1666), William Dewsbury (ca. 1621–1688), Margaret Fell (1614–1702), and James Naylor (ca. 1618–1660) were first. Fell's estate, Swarthmoor Hall, served as the base of operations as the early movement organized, and Fell served as its chief administrator. Naylor, who would become infamous in the movement's history, was the only person to be considered an equal colleague with Fox during the founder's lifetime. These were followed by George Whitehead (1636–1723), a London businessman and conservative theological force later in the century; Edward Burrough (1633–1663), political pamphleteer and theologian; William Caton (1636–1665), missionary to Holland and Germany; and Richard Hubberthorne (1628–1662), eloquent preacher and writer. The Friends were well positioned to rapidly expand in the mid-1650s.[63]

Adherents began delivering the message, the movement built momentum, and by 1655 one could find Quaker meetings throughout the country, with international efforts as well. Fox was organizing and writing pamphlets and letters of advice. Evangelistic pairs were strategically sent into cities and towns, sometimes finding a warm welcome, often among Baptists, sometimes not, which simply meant open-air preaching to whomever would hear. Teams of women were especially open to hostility. By the time the government noticed the Quakers in mid-century, there were thousands of them, and it was too late to just stamp them out by force, a policy implemented with great effect in other sectarian cases. In December 1654, leaders of the Friends gathered to discuss theology, a procedure for discipline, a policy for official publication, and other such matters that amounted to the movement's regionalization and standardization. By the end of the decade, their numbers had increased to the range of thirty thousand to sixty thousand, and their ranks included a majority of small businessmen and artisans.[64]

63   Moore, *Light in Their Consciences*, 7–19.
64   Moore, *Light in Their Consciences*, 22–34.

The first major breach in the movement came in 1656 with the notorious James Naylor affair. Naylor, Fox's unquestioned number two within the Quaker movement and probably his equal from an external vantage, sided with Martha Simmons (1624–1665), a London meeting leader who had been chaffing under the leadership. While at her house, Naylor had a mental breakdown of sorts. An already tense relationship with Fox was irreparably damaged when, at the direction of Simmons, who was convinced that Naylor was Christ returned, Naylor reenacted the triumphal entry on his way into Bristol. He was arrested, charged with blasphemy, whipped, pilloried, and branded. Naylor gave the Quaker's opponents an easy target and showed contradiction in what was supposed to be the leading of an infallible inner light. In his wake, Fox consolidated his leadership, writing pamphlets on essentially every matter that concerned Quakers. After Naylor, the excesses of early Quakerism were subdued.[65]

Politically, things became quite unstable after Protector Cromwell's death in 1658. What had to that point been a modest Quaker political program, one that really included only toleration and exemption from the mandated tithe, increased in its demands and pressure.[66] During the process of Restoration, Fox and his leadership tried to ensure calm. Avoidance of Quaker involvement, especially violent involvement, on either side of the political and religious turmoil was the goal. But hopes for a favorable religious settlement for sectarians were dashed in 1661 when the Fifth Monarchists revolted. Persecution came, and, in response, Fox and the Friends committed themselves unequivocally and publicly to nonresistance and passivism. Their meetings were banned, censorship was reinstated, and the refusal to take oaths penalized. Oppression relaxed in 1664. The Quakers had survived, largely unbowed, and despite sporadic persecution for a few more decades, the dissenting denominations were never in serious danger of extinction again.[67]

Within only a few years, the Quakers went from a radical sect to an introverted denomination that used the language of traditional Christianity more and more. Quaking in meetings all but disappeared, and the movement was drawn to respectability. In response to internal division and in order to weather systematic persecution, the Quakers ratcheted down discipline, and expressions of the Spirit were formally regulated by leaders. The early charismatic Quaker movement was replaced by a denomination, the Religious Society of Friends, a transformation that was complete by the end of the

65 Moore, *Light in Their Consciences*, 35–40.
66 Bradstock, *Radical Religion in Cromwell's England*, 113.
67 Moore, *Light in Their Consciences*, 179–82.

seventeenth century. The denomination's shift toward theological orthodoxy and political respectability was ultimately demonstrated in the inclusion of the Quakers in the Toleration Act of 1689.[68]

Owen's career spanned much of this transformation. He had lived through Quaker radicalism, and in his opinion a change in respectability did not equal a change in substance. Owen held the post of vice-chancellor at Oxford University, making him responsible for discipline, when the Quakers first appeared in the university town. Elizabeth Fletcher (ca. 1638–1658) and Elizabeth Leavens (d. 1665) came preaching the message of the inner light in 1654, and to get the students' attention, Fletcher walked seminaked through the streets.[69] Owen accused the women of blaspheming the Holy Spirit and profaning the Scriptures, and had them whipped and expelled from the town. Two years later, Owen was present at Whitehall Palace when Fox had an audience with Cromwell, in which the Quaker leader passionately proselytized the lord protector.[70] Despite such encounters, Owen's concern was theology, not tone. This explains his sustained theological polemic throughout his prolific writing career.

Owen's antagonism toward the Quakers stemmed primarily from their overemphasis on the Holy Spirit, or in their own jargon, "inner light." They came from a tradition of emphasis on the Spirit, but unlike the Reformers and Puritans, they saw no need for the safeguards of tradition or even biblical authority. By championing the inner light, Friends did away with doctrines and practices considered foundational to Christianity. As a result, the charge of heresy was quickly applied to the movement. It was the Quaker belief that all people had the inner light from God, which included potential saving power. This contradicted Owen's doctrines of predestination and the atonement, because to Quakers all people are in essence partially saved. The only thing necessary to effect salvation was obedience to the inner light, with or without explicit knowledge of Jesus Christ and his sacrificial death on the cross. Because the inner light linked men and women directly to God, the Quakers disposed of the ordinances of baptism and the Lord's Supper and the idea of set prayer or liturgical worship forms. Further, there

---

68 Moore, *Light in Their Consciences*, 214–28; David L. Wykes, "Friends, Parliament and the Toleration Act," *The Journal of Ecclesiastical History* 45 (1994): 42–63.

69 This method was not unique. See Kenneth L. Carroll, "Early Quakers and Going Naked as a Sign," *Quaker History* 67 (1978), 80. Neither was it unusual for women to be in public leadership roles within Quakerism. See Teresa Feroli and Margaret Olofson Thickstun, eds., *Witness, Warning, and Prophecy: Quaker Women's Writing, 1655–1700* (Toronto: Iter, 2018).

70 Michael A. G. Haykin, "John Owen and the Challenge of the Quakers," in *John Owen: The Man and His Theology*, ed. Robert W. Oliver (Phillipsburg, NJ: P&R, 2002), 133–34.

was no need for a clerical hierarchy, whether formally in the institutional church or informally through education and training.[71]

John 1:9, "that was the true Light, which lighteth every man that cometh into the world" (KJV), served as the biblical warrant for the Quakers' distinct message. It bore witness to or described the Friends' experience. "Every individual was born with the light of Christ, which, though darkened by sin, was never fully extinguished."[72] The one convinced by the Quaker message allowed this inner light to overcome sin and unite the soul with Christ. It was from this that the rest of Quaker theology flowed. And it was this passage that Owen set his sights on in his concentrated attack of 1658, *Pro Sacris Scripturis Excercitationes adversus Fanaticos.*[73] Owen argues that Scripture is the word of God, that it is authoritative, and that it is perfect. He then contrasts this with the Quaker doctrine of the inner light, and he goes to the exegetical heart of the matter. Owen explains that the referent of the participle "coming" is the Light, not every man: "It is not said that Christ illuminates every man coming into the world, but rather that he, coming into the world, illuminates every man," every man meaning all of God's people, not all people without exception.[74] So Johannine illumination is not natural, or something that all people experience. It is spiritual. And this illumination by the Spirit is inseparable from the word. This emphasis on the Scripture in answer to the Quaker undermining of biblical authority would remain a concern for Owen almost two decades later.

In the late 1670s, when Owen wrote his twin treatises on illumination, *The Reason of Faith* and *Causes, Ways, and Means*, the Quakers, despite their developing coolness, formality, and respectability, were one of his primary interlocutors.[75] Their doctrine of the inner light seemed to destroy the need for Scripture as revelation. It was not so much that they dismissed the Bible as a source of authority but that they held it to have no supreme authority, which could limit the inspiration of the indwelling Spirit. It was the inner light that tested the word, not the reverse. By relegating the authority of Scripture,

---

71 Adrian Davies, *The Quakers in English Society, 1655–1725*, Oxford Historical Monographs (Oxford: Clarendon, 2000), 15–19. See also Hinds, *George Fox and Early Quaker Culture*, 13–32.

72 Matthew Barrett and Michael A. G. Haykin, *Owen on the Christian Life: Living for the Glory of God in Christ* (Wheaton, IL: Crossway, 2015), 40.

73 For English translation, see John Owen, "A Defense of Sacred Scripture against Modern Fanaticism," in *Biblical Theology: The History of Theology from Adam to Christ*, trans. Stephen P. Westcott (Grand Rapids, MI: Soli Deo Gloria, 2014).

74 Owen, "Defense of Sacred Scripture," 852.

75 Evidence of the Quakers' influence on the literary scene is illustrated in Thomas N. Corns and David Loewenstein, eds., *The Emergence of Quaker Writing: Dissenting Literature in Seventeenth-Century England* (Portland, OR: Frank Cass, 1995).

the Quakers undermined its necessity. Owen blasted both positions as intolerable. Scripture is the objective light by which the knowledge of Christ is transmitted into our minds. There is no knowledge without Scripture. And the Spirit is the light that illuminates the mind by the means of the Scriptures. Owen responded strongly to the Quaker movement's improper appeal to the Spirit, an overemphasis that has earned the Friends the description "the most extreme of the godly Puritans."[76] But if the Quakers took the Puritan appeal to the Spirit too far, there was another group, the Socinians, who overextended the Puritan application of reason.

Socinians

During Owen's lifetime, Socinianism went from being a nonissue in England to the primary polemical opponent of Reformed Protestants. The Socinians are most often understood as rationalists who applied their reason to the biblical text, concluding that the Trinity and the atonement are absurd. While this is true, central also were claims about religion, freedom, and human nature, which help to explain the singularly extreme reaction to the Socinian caricature.[77]

Faustus Socinus (1539–1604) offered a reinterpretation of Christianity that sought to place morality at the heart of the religion by reconceiving virtue and justice.[78] He taught that Christ saves through his teaching and example, not by atoning for sins. The challenge, then, became to explain how and why a person might choose to follow Christ's commands, a choice that must be voluntary in order to be virtuous. The doctrine of human depravity had to be revisited. Nothing in nature inevitably put people into relationship with God, positively or negatively. In Socinus's conception of freedom, no room existed for original sin or innate knowledge of God. Human beings are presented with revelation, and therefore a choice must be made with their reason. Scripture, for Socinus, is trustworthy upon historical analysis and

---

76 Davies, *Quakers in English Society*, 15.

77 This insight is Sarah Mortimer's primary contribution in *Reason and Religion in the English Revolution: The Challenge of Socinianism*, Cambridge Studies in Early Modern British History (Cambridge: Cambridge University Press, 2010). Hers was the first full treatment of Socinianism in more than fifty years and one of the only modern contributions that does not view the movement through a Unitarian confessional lens. For these reasons, this description will rely heavily on her work. See also Paul C. H. Lim, *Mystery Unveiled: The Crisis of the Trinity in Early Modern England*, Oxford Studies in Historical Theology (Oxford: Oxford University Press, 2012).

78 For studies on Socinus's life and thought, see Lech Szczucki, ed., *Faustus Socinus and His Heritage* (Kraków: Polska Akademia Umiejętności, 2005).

textual criticism, and it reveals Christ as a man who demonstrated virtuous living, with the afterlife as its motivating reward. God is not required to punish sin or exact satisfaction as a prerequisite to forgiveness, and because sin is fundamentally a debt, God has the right, but not a duty, to punish. This protected God's freedom in Socinus's estimation. Additionally, Socinus dismantled the doctrine of the Trinity. This he did primarily by conceiving of God in legal terms, drawing from his legal background, which dismissed the classical metaphysical category of substance or essence. Divinity is power and authority, which can be transmitted or transferred, but not divided. So the relationship between God and Christ was one of subordinate "divinity" based on received authority.[79]

Socinus's division of nature and true religion, revealed only in Christ, necessitated a contrast between Christ's law and both natural law and the related Old Testament law. For traditional Protestants, natural law, which was articulated in Old Testament commandments, contained all duties required of people, thus justifying state established religion. Socinus taught pacifism and critiqued resistance theory—including self-defense—ideas that were explosive in Europe in the sixteenth and seventeenth centuries. While Socinus's radical ideas were tempered by his second-generation followers, they continued to develop his theology.[80] This Socinian evolution took place under the direction of leaders such as Johann Crell (1590–1633) as they operated on the international theological stage, interacting most significantly with the Remonstrant heirs like Hugo Grotius (1583–1645) and Simon Episcopius (1583–1643).[81]

In the early decades of the seventeenth century, Protestants on the continent viewed the Socinians as a disunifying force during a time of Roman Catholic resurgence. The same could be said of the Arminians, and they were indeed lumped together with Socinians during the Dutch Remonstrant crisis. With the conclusion of the Synod of Dort (1618–1619), the Reformed world had learned just how destructive of a weapon the charge of Socinianism could be. But Socinianism was peculiarly absent from discussions in England until the 1630s. This is understandable, given the fact that the anti-Calvinists in England were High Churchmen. They were not interested in emphasizing individual faith and morality the way both Arminians and Socinians did. As for the Puritans, they were consumed with the Church of England's apparent

---

79 Mortimer, *Reason and Religion in the English Revolution*, 15–21, 35.
80 Mortimer, *Reason and Religion in the English Revolution*, 23–31.
81 For detailed studies of such interchange, see Martin Mulsow and Jan Rohls, eds., *Socinianism and Arminianism: Antitrinitarians, Calvinists, and Cultural Exchange in Seventeenth-Century Europe*, Brill's Studies in Intellectual History 134 (Leiden: Brill, 2005).

movement even more toward the Church of Rome's liturgical practices. However, when religious controversy was officially forbidden in the 1620s, asserting justification by faith polemically against the Socinians was a safe way to try to protect the national church from Arminianism and Roman leanings as well.[82]

The two decades of upheaval between the start of the British Civil War and the Restoration of the monarchy (1640–1660) saw sustained efforts to both bring together natural law and Christianity and tear them asunder. The Great Tew Circle, representing the only positive interaction with Socinian ideas before the Civil War, supported the king and attacked the whole concept of a right of self-preservation and the resistance theory used by supporters of Parliament as justification for taking up arms. Socinianism and royalism were polemically conflated. During the Interregnum, when attention shifted to establishing a church settlement, Socinian concepts were used by some, such as Henry Hammond (1605–1660), to divide nature and Christianity on yet another front. Hammond defended episcopacy and argued that the church's doctrine and polity must be based on the law of Christ. The fact that the church was a voluntary community, separate from any civil government, meant Parliament could not legitimately establish religion. This Socinian method of argumentation that placed a wedge between natural law and Christianity did not always result in anti-Trinitarianism, but it often did.[83]

Including Trinitarianism in the church settlement did not turn out to be as simple as it would have seemed. It was accomplished largely by recasting the problem of heterodoxy in general as the problem of Socinianism in the early 1650s. Support for liberty of conscience was strong in this context, but the line was more often than not drawn at blasphemy and subversion. The Socinians provided both. The Independents gave the most concerted effort to defining heresy as they sought the toleration of Protestants who differed on disputable matters of doctrine and practice. When Parliament was under pressure to defend the inclusion of the Trinity in the church settlement on intellectual grounds, Owen led the charge in attacking those who explicitly denied the Trinity, showing that anti-Trinitarianism was intolerable without being forced in reality to defend the doctrine. This was significant because the whole project of a state-sanctioned church settlement relied on wedding natural law and Christianity, but the desire to include the Trinity coupled with the challenge of grounding the concept in natural theology or the explicit

82 Mortimer, *Reason and Religion in the English Revolution*, 40–45.
83 Mortimer, *Reason and Religion in the English Revolution*, 88–107, 117–32.

wording of Scripture had all but paralyzed the process. It was John Biddle (1615–1662), especially his English translation of the Racovian Catechism in 1652, who provided a suitably unpopular backdrop, a Socinian one, against which Owen proposed his own ecclesiastical vision.[84]

By 1655, Owen and his cobelligerents were genuinely concerned about the infiltration of Socinianism in England, an anxiety that was not misplaced. Socinianism must not be associated with Biddle and his circle alone, for alarming tenets existed in the popular writings of Grotius and Episcopius as well. For Owen, most concerning was the separation of Christianity and natural law, which undermined the principles upon which religious unity in England was being sought in the Commonwealth, at least officially. His two most significant works against Socinianism were *Dissertation of Divine Justice* (1653) and *Defense of the Gospel* (1655). Oliver Cromwell commissioned the latter in answer to Biddle's *A Twofold Catechism* (1654), but Owen was clearly also determined to address the historical-theological development of Grotius's and others' ideas, which undermined the universal principles appealed to in much of Reformed theology. Owen took aim at Grotius's *Annotationes*, published in the 1640s, which modeled a historical method of biblical interpretation that undermined Trinitarian readings of key Scripture passages. Orthodox theological concepts like the atonement and the Trinity had not only to be proven true, but justification for the magistrate's defense and promotion of them had to be made. For this constructive project, Owen turned to Thomism to back up what he found in Scripture.[85]

Socinianism in the second half of the seventeenth century became increasingly diverse, as Socinians and Socinian ideas mixed with other people and ideas throughout Western Europe. The new Socinians appealed to ignorance on matters of theological speculation and biblical interpretation. They were skeptics. Some adopted Cartesian thought, or Lockean epistemology, or other early Enlightenment thinking. But there was a unity around anti-Trinitarianism and appealing to reason alone in biblical interpretation.[86] This appeal to reason and the heterodox conclusions derived from it were what Owen relentlessly attacked. Even if he did not see explicit Socinianism everywhere, he observed in Restoration England the twin appeals to reason

84 Mortimer, *Reason and Religion in the English Revolution*, 177–81, 194–97. For an extensive treatment of John Biddle, see H. John McLachlan, *Socinianism in Seventeenth-Century England* (London: Oxford University Press, 1951).
85 Mortimer, *Reason and Religion in the English Revolution*, 205–10, 222–28.
86 Muslow, "The 'New Socinians,'" in Mulsow and Rohls, *Socinianism and Arminianism*, 49–79. See also Lee Gatiss, "Socinianism and John Owen," *Southern Baptist Journal of Theology* 20, no. 4 (2016): 43–62.

in approaching Scripture and to ignorance when forced to handle theological claims, so he continued to polemically engage Socinianism until the end of his life.[87] In Owen's dual treatises on the Spirit's work of illumination, *The Reason of Faith* and *Causes, Ways, and Means*, both written in his last decade, Socinianism is one of his primary interlocutors. He desired to temper the Socinian appeal to reason with the necessity of the Spirit in both believing and understanding the Bible, and he explicitly referenced Socinianism throughout the project. Like many of Owen's formulations, this did not become mainstream.

In the England of Owen's final decades, reason was usually portrayed in a positive light and given a role in religion. Owen and much of English Dissent granted it a place. But Anglicans especially presented the Church of England as reasonable religion. For Socinians, Arminians, and Anglicans, especially those of the Latitudinarian kind, the emphasis was placed on understanding the literal meaning of Scripture and applying it. Christ's teaching was easy to understand when evaluated with human reason, but tough to practice. No technical, specialized theological language seemed necessary. There was no need for scholastic distinctions or dogmatics. Moreover, after the radicalism of the sectarians, with their spiritual excesses during the Civil War and Interregnum, reason appeared to be the safest way to move forward.[88]

OWEN'S TREATISES

The Reason of Faith (1677)[89]

As Owen observed the divine origin of the Scriptures coming under attack and their authority being undermined, he purposed to defend the traditional concept of Scripture's self-authentication made efficient by the Holy Spirit. But he had to avoid several theological pitfalls while doing so. He carefully distinguished himself from the Quakers and their spiritualism, which resulted in practical fideism in the terms of apologetic discourse. Adherents of the Church of Rome accused Protestants of holding a Quaker position, of faith based on private testimony or immediate revelation. Owen also went about his defense of Scripture in distinction from the rationalistic arguments found

---

87 For illustrations of these appeals, see Douglas Hedley, "Persons of Substance and the Cambridge Connection," in Mulsow and Rohls, *Socinianism and Arminianism*, 225–40.

88 Mortimer, *Reason and Religion in the English Revolution*, 236–39.

89 This was published by Nathaniel Ponder, who published several of Owen's works and John Bunyan's *The Pilgrim's Progress*. Owen, in fact, may have introduced Ponder to Bunyan. See N. H. Keeble, "Bunyan's Literary Life," in *The Cambridge Companion to Bunyan*, ed. Anne Dunan-Page (Cambridge: Cambridge University Press, 2010), 18.

in the Church of England. Further, so-called proof of the inspiration and authority of Scripture based on objective evidence was being established effectively by other authors. What Owen attempts is a biblical synthesis in *The Reason of Faith*, which grounds belief in Scripture itself, witnessed to by the Spirit, a witness evidenced experientially in the life of the individual believer.

As Owen's title page reveals, he primarily concerns himself with the cause and nature of faith in this treatise. And it is important to note at the outset that when Owen uses the term *faith* in the context of this treatise, he usually is referencing not saving faith but divine and supernatural belief that Scripture is the word of God. Indeed, the foremost question on his mind in writing this treatise was, Why do Christians believe the Scripture to be God's word? In short, his answer is this: The reason of faith is God's authority and veracity revealing themselves in the Scriptures and by them. The ground of this faith is experimental—the renewing and sanctifying effect of divine truth, as proposed in Scripture—upon the mind. The work of the Holy Spirit is the efficient cause of such belief, but not the objective ground or evidence upon which faith rests.

Responding to three short questions with three short answers gets to the heart of Owen's project. What do Christians believe? Revelation—namely, the Bible. How do Christians believe revelation? Illumination. Why do Christians believe the Bible? The Scripture's self-authentication. So illumination, in *The Reason of Faith*, is assent to Scripture's self-authentication, which is enabled by the work of the Holy Spirit alone. I define *illumination* at this juncture because, in his preface, Owen identifies his treatise as the first installment of a two-part work on the Spirit of illumination, the second part being his treatise *The Causes, Ways, and Means of Understanding the Mind of God*. This latter work extends his initial definition of illumination by adding the Spirit's work in understanding the mind of God in Scripture to the Spirit's work in establishing belief that Scripture is the word of God.

Chapter 1: The Subject Stated

Owen opens his *The Reason of Faith* in chapter 1 by enumerating six premises regarding revelation. He asserts: (1) Revelation is the only objective cause of illumination. (2) Revelation was originally given immediately. (3) Scripture is sufficient. (4) Scripture is now the only external means of supernatural illumination, because it is the sole repository of all divine revelation. (5) However, subordinate means of making Scripture effectual, such as personal study and the ministry of the word, are not negated; in fact, they are assumed and required. (6) For Scripture to be a sufficient external cause of illumination, two things are required. First, we must believe it to be revelation, for learning cannot equate to illumination if the Bible is studied as any other book. Second, we must understand the mind of God as it is revealed and expressed in the Scriptures, which, again, is the subject of Owen's second treatise on the Spirit of illumination.

Chapter 2: What It Is Infallibly to Believe the
Scripture to Be the Word of God, Affirmed

In chapter 2, Owen, staying on the topic of revelation, moves to a discussion of grounding faith in the certainty of that revelation. He first draws the distinction between the material object of faith, which is the content proposed in Scripture, and the formal object, or cause, of faith. The latter is where Owen's interest lies. Further, the faith he is concerned about is nothing less than divine and supernatural faith. The infallibility of this faith is not an inherent quality in the human subject; rather, it is the authority and veracity of God revealing the material object of faith that is the formal object, the ground or reason of faith. And as God's full and exclusive revelation, it is Scripture, even more precisely, that provides the ground of faith. So faith is supernatural because the Holy Spirit produces it in the mind. It is infallible because of its formal reason—namely, Scripture, which is God's revelation. And it is divine or opposed to what is merely a human belief. Owen concludes that the ground for accepting Scripture as divine revelation is "solely . . . the evidence that the Spirit of God, in and by the Scripture itself, gives unto us that it was given by immediate inspiration from God." In the rest of this treatise, Owen attempts to expound this conclusion and its implications.

Chapter 3: Sundry Convincing External Arguments for Divine Revelation

Owen argues for the impossibility of believing with certainty upon fallible evidence, including all external arguments for the inspiration of Scripture. External arguments serve as no ground of faith, but they do confirm faith against temptations, oppositions, and objections, and so Owen provides a treatment of them in chapter 3. He gives weight to the antiquity of Scripture, its preservation, the divine content found in it, the church's testimony to it, and its effects. After highlighting these five external arguments, Owen reinforces his initial point that while these adequately answer the objections of rational and unbiased persons, alone such arguments, at best, invoke a moral assurance of the truth of Scripture. In Owen's words,

> Although those external arguments, whereby learned and rational men have proved, or may yet further prove, the Scripture to be a divine revelation

given of God, and the doctrine contained in it to be a heavenly truth, are of singular use for the strengthening of the faith of them that do believe, by relieving the mind against temptations and objections that will arise to the contrary, as also for the conviction of gainsayers; yet to say that they contain the formal reason of that assent which is required of us unto the Scripture as the word of God, that our faith is the effect and product of them, which it rests upon and is resolved into, is both contrary to the Scripture, destructive of the nature of divine faith, and exclusive of the work of the Holy Ghost in this whole matter.

External arguments persuade but do not result in divine and supernatural faith, for they are still in the realm of the natural, human, and fallible. They present probability, not infallible certainty.[90]

Chapter 4: Moral Certainty, the Result of
External Arguments, Insufficient
Chapter 4 is Owen's dismantling of the idea that what he has labeled moral certainty, the by-product of external arguments for the divine origin of Scripture, is sufficient reason of faith. He accomplishes this by arguing directly for moral certainty's insufficiency and then by comparing it to the certainty wrought by the Spirit. The arguments against moral certainty's sufficiency are four:

1. The proper object of divine faith is divine revelation. When revelation was given, it was to be accepted as such purely on the basis that it was God, in relationship with his people, who gave it. Consider the Decalogue, where the preamble is merely "I am the Lord your God." No external arguments seem necessitated. Christ and the apostles follow the same pattern in the New Testament, where the expectation existed that revelation was to be accepted on its own account.
2. Moral certainty is the effect of reason, and therefore negates the need for a work of the Holy Spirit.
3. Assent can be of no other nature than the evidence upon which it is built. Ergo, if the evidence is fallible, the assent is necessarily fallible.
4. Believing Scripture with human faith overthrows believing the content of Scripture with divine faith, for there is no consistent or, more

90 Note a similar attitude toward external arguments in John Calvin, *Institutes of the Christian Religion*, ed. John T. McNeill, trans. Ford Lewis Battles (Philadelphia: Westminster John Knox, 1960), 1.7.4.

importantly, biblical warrant for a distinction in belief applied to revelation and the things revealed.

While moral certainty may compel some level of obedience, it falls short of the infallible certainty produced by the Holy Spirit alone. At this point, Owen is inquiring after the power whereby an individual is enabled to believe the Scriptures, not the reason why one believes. The former pertains to the subject, or the human mind, while the latter to the object, or Scripture. Owen states that the work of the Spirit in this regard is "saving illumination of the mind, and the effect of it is a supernatural light, whereby the mind is renewed." And "hereby we are enabled to discern the evidences of the divine origin and authority of the Scripture that are in itself, as well as assent unto the truth contained in it; and without it we cannot do so." The two hindrances to faith, when revelation is proposed, are natural blindness after the fall and the prejudices produced by Satan. External arguments can aid faith only in the latter realm. The spiritual blindness resulting from fallen human nature can be overcome only by a miraculous work of God the Spirit. However, the content of this spiritual illumination is not immediate revelations of things not before revealed, but rather an internal revelation of that which is outward and antecedent unto it—namely, Scripture. There exists a difference in kind here. Illumination in this sense is the freeing of the mind from darkness, ignorance, and prejudice, while positively enabling the discernment of spiritual things. It is not the divine impartation of knowledge. So back to an earlier question, How do we believe that Scripture is the word of God? Owen answers, "It is because the Holy Ghost has enlightened our minds, wrought faith in us, and enabled us to believe." Yet again, this is how, not why, we believe.

Owen gives significant space to clarifying that the internal testimony of the Spirit is not the reason of faith. He asserts, "It is the common opinion of Protestant divines that the testimony of the Holy Ghost is the ground whereon we believe the Scripture to be the word of God," though he wants to qualify this. The witness of the Spirit is not why we believe, but it is significant, even indispensable, nonetheless. The point is crucial for Owen, one reason being that the Church of Rome accused Protestants of settling the ground and assurance of faith in the soul of the individual. The point is also important for Owen's intention in identifying the role of the Spirit in the execution of our obligation to believe the Scriptures. Though not the formal object of faith, the testimony of the Spirit does effectually persuade, and this effectual work of the Spirit is indispensable. In his conclusion to chapter 4, Owen summarizes, "Although no internal work of the Spirit can be the formal reason of our faith, or that which it is resolved into, yet is it such as without it we can never sincerely believe as we ought, nor be established in believing against temptations and objections."

Chapter 5: Divine Revelation Itself the Only Foundation and Reason of Faith

To this point, Owen has laid a foundation of descriptions, definitions, and distinctions, a prolegomenon establishing what the reason of faith is not. In chapter 5, he wades into what he calls the principal part of his treatise, raising one more question about the work of the Spirit in the believer's assent to Scripture. The question: What is the work of the Spirit regarding the objective evidence available concerning Scripture? He answers quite pointedly,

> We believe the Scripture to be the word of God with divine faith for its own sake only; or, our faith is resolved into the authority and truth of God only as revealing himself unto us therein and thereby. And this authority and veracity of God do infallibly manifest or evince themselves unto our faith, or our minds in the exercise of it, by the revelation itself in the Scripture, and no otherwise. Or, "Thus saith the Lord," is the reason why we ought to believe, and why we do so; why we believe at all in general, and why we believe anything in particular. And this we call the formal object or reason of faith.

This is the Spirit's work because he immediately authored the whole of Scripture, and both in it and through it gives testimony to the divine truth and origin of it. How the Spirit does this Owen will explore in chapter 6. But before he does so, he firmly plants the concept of Scripture itself being the only reason of faith in an exegetical argument and the express example of the prophets and apostles, making a critical distinction at the outset. The question is where faith rests, not what arguments are available to prove that Scripture is revelation. Because faith rests in Scripture alone, the ministerial proposal of Scripture is a means of believing itself. When the word is proclaimed extraordinarily, by the prophets and apostles under inspiration, or ordinarily, through the ministry of the church, hearers are obliged to believe without any further evidence. This leads to the doctrine of Scripture's self-authentication.

Chapter 6: The Nature of Divine Revelations

Owen approaches the fact that Scripture is self-authenticating by way of response to an objection, which is the content of chapter 6. The objection is that everyone who experiences a proposition of the Scripture would believe if Scripture evidences itself to be the word of God, at least if it is self-evident in the same way that the sun manifests itself by light or fire by heat. Owen answers this objection first with some epistemological considerations and second by surveying how Scripture evidences its divine origin and authority.

Owen splits up knowledge into three categories: instinct, rational consideration, and faith. Faith by definition is assent upon testimony. God appeals to all three; his appeals to the first two are known as general revelation. The existence of God, for instance, is utterly apparent simply because of the existence of the world. And as to rational capacities, God's works of creation and providence provide the material needed to make further insights into the nature, being, and properties of God. But the appeal to faith comes through special revelation, through Scripture, accepted upon testimony. This mode of knowledge rises above reason, but it is not irrational, for the same God who reveals himself to faith reveals himself also to reason and instinct, ensuring absolute consonance of general and special revelation. However, though dissonance is an impossibility, Owen argues that the appeal to faith through Scripture takes precedence. Human beings can infallibly know God through all three, but God's word is implanted with vastly more details about himself and his properties, such that it is uniquely self-evident. Further, the capability of assenting to truth upon testimony is the most noble faculty and power of human nature, part of what constitutes the soul and separates God's image bearers from the rest of his creatures. Failure to assent to Scripture when it is proposed is a problem with the subject, not the object, an insurmountable problem from a human perspective; the problem is the spiritual blindness associated with the fall and sinful suppression of the truth. Faith becomes capable of giving assent "because God works it in us and bestows it upon us for this very end." Owen goes on:

> Yea, our faith is capable of giving an assent, though of another kind, more firm, and accompanied with more assurance, than any given by reason in the best of its conclusions. And the reason is, because the power of the mind to give assent upon testimony, which is its most noble faculty, is elevated and strengthened by the divine supernatural work of the Holy Ghost.

God imbued such a power unto the revelation of himself by his word.

Moving to how Scripture evidences its divine origin and authority, Owen teases out "the way and means whereby they evidence themselves unto us, and the Scripture thereby to be the Word of God, so as that we may undoubtedly and infallibly believe it so to be." He posits, "There must be some testimony or witness in this case whereon faith does rest. And this we say is the testimony of the Holy Ghost, the author of the Scriptures, given unto them, in them, and by them." This testimony consists of Scripture's excellency and efficiency. With regard to the former, Owen understands Scripture to have details and impressions subjectively left in it and upon it by the Holy Spirit, of all the excellencies and properties of the divine nature. And as to the efficiency of Scripture, the Spirit wields power and authority in it and by it over the minds and consciences of men. Without the experience of divine efficacy, no one does or can believe; nonetheless, the divine effects are conversion, conviction, illumination, awe, and consolation. The Bible evidences itself as revelation by the stamp of the divine nature upon it and the miracles God works in the souls of individuals through it.

Chapter 7: Inferences from the Whole

In chapter 7, Owen concludes his work by drawing three inferences from what he has argued and by answering objections to his project. First, the three considerations:

1. Evidence of the divinity of Scripture or the reason of faith is equally obvious to all believers.
2. The assent of faith brings more assurance than any assent that is the effect of science upon demonstrable principles. Here, Owen explicitly employs the scholastic distinction between assurance of evidence and assurance of adherence. The certainty of faith exceeds science in the latter, while less so in the former. In any case, as applied to the concern at hand—namely, the certainty that Scripture is the word of God—the assurance of adherence exceeds the assurance of evidence because scientific evidence appeals only to the mind, while evidence by faith operates also on the will.
3. Denial of the first two inferences or the separation of the internal work of the Holy Spirit (enabling belief) from his external work (evidencing Scripture's divinity in and by it) undermines divine truth and substitutes persuasion through probability.

Finally, Owen answers a few objections to these three inferences. To those who say that it disadvantages Christian religion to take away its rational grounds, especially in the task of convincing unbelievers, Owen responds that proving the doctrine of Christ and the doctrine of Scripture are two different things, though they are connected. The bottom line is that the apostles convinced unbelievers through their preaching, not rational argumentation. To those who propose that if Scripture is self-evident, then either all would accept it or the evidence lies in the efficacy of the Spirit in the mind, Owen counters that he does not deny the necessary work of the Spirit but that this work is the objective evidence upon which faith is built; and again, faith is assent upon testimony. Related to this objection is the resulting idea that none are obligated to believe outside of those who have faith wrought in them by the Spirit. Owen answers that the Spirit is the efficient cause of belief, but not the reason why we believe. Further, obligation has nothing to do with power or ability; we are responsible to receive Scripture as the word of God upon the evidence it gives in itself. Through Owen's responses, he clarifies even further the reason of faith and its implications. Illumination accounts for the untold majority of Christians who have unshakable, yet perhaps uneducated or inarticulate, confidence in the Scriptures.

The Causes, Ways, and Means of Understanding the Mind of God (1678)[91]

Owen takes a mediating position in *The Causes, Ways, and Means of Understanding the Mind of God*, his treatise on biblical interpretation, between the irrationalism of the Quakers and the rationalism of the Socinians, without appealing to tradition or something like the curia as the Church of Rome does. All three of these groups subordinate the authority of Scripture: the Quakers to the inward light; the Socinians to human reason; the Church of Rome to tradition, practically determined by the pope. Owen wants to protect the right of private interpretation by the ordinary believer, while providing a method of interpretation that genuinely safeguards biblical authority. He agrees with Protestants in general on the sufficiency of Scripture itself as the rule of faith and practice, when it is understood according to the Spirit's illumination.

The Causes, Ways, and Means of Understanding the Mind of God comes as Owen's second installment on the topic of the Holy Spirit's illumination. The first, *The Reason of Faith*, articulated the evidence or grounds on which we receive Scripture as divine. In *Causes*, Owen offers the method by which we understand the divine mind revealed in Scripture. This second work's nine chapters may be divided thus: chapters 1–6 expound the Holy Spirit as the principal efficient cause of right interpretation, and chapters 7–9 explain the means of proper understanding.

91 Published by Nathaniel Ponder.

In the preface, Owen defends the perspicuity of Scripture. This first step in the argument forms a foundation for the entirety of the treatise, the design of which is to compel the employment of obvious means in the interpretation of Scripture. Perspicuity is fundamental because the ordinary course of subordinating the authority of Scripture is leveling questions at its clarity or sufficiency and then proposing an alternative authority. For this reason, it is worth quoting Owen's definition of perspicuity:

> The substance of what we plead for is, that such is the wisdom, goodness, and love of God toward mankind, in the grant that he has made unto them of the revelation of himself, his mind and will, in the Scripture, as that no one person does or can fail of attaining all that understanding in it and of it which is any way needful for his guidance to live unto God in his circumstances and relations, so as to come unto the blessed enjoyment of him, but by the sinful neglect of the means and duties prescribed by him for the attainment of that understanding, and want of a due dependence on those spiritual aids and assistances which he has prepared for that end.

Chapter 1: Introduction

Chapter 1 serves as Owen's introduction and quickly builds on this foundation of perspicuity. The Spirit's role in illumination is again tied to Scripture itself. Just as belief in the Bible does not depend on the church or any person, neither does the understanding of those things contained in it; rather, they are both part of the Spirit's one work of illumination, which he accomplishes in tandem with the word. So Owen's "principal design" is this:

> To manifest that *every believer may, in the due use of the means appointed of God for that end, attain unto such a full assurance of understanding in the truth, or all that knowledge of the mind and will of God revealed in the Scripture, which is sufficient to direct him in the life of God, to deliver him from the dangers of ignorance, darkness, and error, and to conduct him unto blessedness.*[92]

Owen's category of full assurance of understanding is of utmost importance, for in order to suffer for the truth or perform any act of obedience to God properly, one must be utterly persuaded that he or she has grasped divine revelation. This brings Owen to his primary question: How may anyone attain

---

92 All italics in quotations from Owen appear in the original.

right understanding of the meaning and sense of the Scriptures? Or, to ask the same question another way, How can anyone perceive the mind of God in Scripture or what he intends to reveal?

Owen provides a summary of his whole argument in seven points, which he will expand in the course of the treatise, to answer this chief question. The Spirit is the principal efficient cause of understanding Scripture correctly, such that without his work of illumination, Scripture cannot be properly understood. Here are the heads undergirding this conclusion:

1. We do not need any new, immediate revelations to understand Scripture.
2. This understanding does not depend on the instruction or interpretation of tradition, valuable as the history of the church's interpretation is.
3. However, mere natural reason does not bring proper understanding.
4. So a special work of the Spirit in the supernatural illumination of our minds is necessary.
5. Illumination alone results in full assurance of understanding.
6. Such certainty does not result from "our reason and understanding merely in their natural actings, but as they are elevated, enlightened, guided, conducted, by an internal efficacious work of the Spirit of God upon them."
7. There are two means of right biblical interpretation. First, there are Christian duties such as prayer and Scripture meditation; second, there are disciplinary means such as those that come through formal education in the arts and sciences.

For Owen, Scripture is the final arbiter of all things, so it is the authority even in how it is to be interpreted. Therefore, he moves in chapter 2 to the biblical evidence for the Spirit's role in illumination.

Chapter 2: The Holy Spirit as the Principal Efficient Cause of Understanding Scripture: Part 1

Owen appeals first to Psalm 119 for biblical evidence for the necessity of divine illumination of Scripture; specifically, he explicates 119:18: "Open thou mine eyes, that I may behold wondrous things out of thy law." The "law" in this verse is a reference to the Pentateuch, the prophets, and the other writings constituting the Old Testament—in short and by implication, the whole of the Christian canon. The "wondrous things" the psalmist prays to behold are those wonderful things pertaining to Christ. And three things are assumed here in the request for beholding wonderful things: the necessity of Scripture, our duty and privilege to understand it, and our need of the Spirit's help. Likewise, we are to pray for the enabling of God. Owen anticipates the objection that while those in the Old Testament needed their eyes opened in this way, Christians have the wonderful things revealed to them clearly in Christ and the New Testament. He answers the objection with an appeal to 2 Corinthians 3:13–18, particularly Paul's concept of a double veiling. One veil was put on Moses's face, but another covered the Israelites' hearts. The first veil consisted in obscurity in instruction, which types, shadows, and parables darkened. It is this veil that the revelation of Jesus Christ and the doctrine of the gospel removed. The second veil involves the ignorance, darkness, and blindness that cover the understanding of human beings by nature. This covering is removed only by the effectual work of the Spirit.

Similarly, in Ephesians 1:17–19,[93] Paul prays for revelation, though not for new information. He requests enablement to discern things already revealed. Owen illustrates this request with the concept of a telescope. The telescope causes perception, and reveals only in the sense that it brings into view a reality that already exists. Owen understands Paul to ask for explicitly what the psalmist pleaded for implicitly under the category of wonderful things. He prays that the Ephesians would know these things in a way they could not naturally, in no way implying that they were foolish or uneducated. Rather, their minds, like all human minds, were darkened by sin. The apostle prayed for eyes to be opened, for an internal work of illumination, a work of the Spirit, since he is the immediate author of all supernatural effects and operations in his people.

Chapter 3: The Holy Spirit as the Principal Efficient Cause of Understanding Scripture: Part 2

In chapter 3, Owen presents more biblical evidence for the Spirit as the principal efficient cause of Scriptural understanding and then contrasts this with false knowledge. Referencing John 16:13 and the Spirit's leading into all truth, Owen states that this work of the Spirit is "his work to give us a useful, saving understanding of all sacred truth, or the mind of God as revealed in

---

93 Owen's quotation: "That the God of our Lord Jesus Christ, the Father of glory, may give unto you the Spirit of wisdom and revelation in the knowledge of him: the eyes of your understanding being enlightened, that you may know what is the hope of his calling, and what the riches of the glory of his inheritance in the saints, and what is the exceeding greatness of his power to us-ward who believe."

the Scripture." Jesus here promised the Spirit to help those who believe fulfill their duty to acquire right understanding of Scripture, the only deposit of all spiritual, divine, supernatural revelation. First John 2:20 and 2:27, then, speak of the Spirit as unction or anointing. According to Owen, the entire design of the apostle in these verses is this:

> *All divine truths necessary to be known and to be believed, that we may live unto God in faith and obedience, or come unto and abide in Christ, as also be preserved from seducers, are contained in the Scripture, or proposed unto us in divine revelations. These of ourselves we cannot understand unto the ends mentioned; for if we could, there would be no need that we should be taught them by the Holy Spirit. But this is so, he teaches us all these things, enabling us to discern, comprehend, and acknowledge them.*

And the full assurance of understanding comes from the teacher, God the Holy Spirit, who is infallible. Because of this infallibility, this confidence rises above what any other evidence or demonstration could possibly provide, whether appeals to tradition by Roman Catholicism, on the one hand, or to rationalism by Socinianism, on the other.

Before showing the contrast of false knowledge, Owen summarizes the biblical teaching this way: "*that it is the Holy Spirit who teaches us to understand aright the mind and will of God in the Scripture, without whose aid and assistance we can never do so usefully nor profitably unto our own souls.*" With this in the background, Owen raises the question of knowledge in the case of the unbeliever, making five points in answer:

1. He distinguishes between knowledge and acknowledgment. The former by itself affects only the speculative part of the mind. The latter "gives the mind an experience of the power and efficacy of the truth known or discovered, so as to transform the soul and all its affections into it, and thereby to give a 'full assurance of understanding' unto the mind itself."

2. "To know a thing as the mind of God, and not to assent unto its truth, implies a contradiction." Owen asserts, "I shall never grant that a man understands the Scripture aright who understands the words of it only, and not the things which are the mind of God in them." An example of knowledge in the absence of acknowledgement is the Jews. The rabbis understand the words of the Bible impeccably in the original Hebrew, yet they miss the mind of God.

3. False knowledge informs but fails to illuminate.
4. Therefore, it fails to bring full confidence in understanding.
5. Finally, false knowledge falls woefully short of enabling trust and adherence motivated by love; thus, prayers ought to be in earnest for the Spirit's help.

Chapter 4: The Nature and Effects of Illumination

Chapter 4 shifts from the necessity of the Spirit's illumination to the nature and effects of that work. Owen offers five effects, each of which he finds in Scripture. One effect of illumination is the opening of our eyes, as already discussed. He states, "This is the sum of what we plead: there is an efficacious work of the Spirit of God opening our eyes, enlightening our understandings or minds, to understand the things contained in the Scripture, distinct from the objective proposition of them in the Scripture itself." Illumination, then, is more than the propositions of Scripture. It is a distinct work of the Spirit. Scripture is the content. Illumination is the grasping of that content. Other biblical descriptions of the effects of illumination include transfer from darkness into light, giving of understanding, teaching, leading, guiding into the truth, and shining into the heart. The nature of illumination is portrayed as light, understanding, and wisdom. Light is the "spiritual ability to discern and know spiritual things." The "introduction of light into the mind is the proper effect of illumination."

Chapter 5: Ignorance

Chapter 5 serves as a fitting parenthesis, an aside on the causes of ignorance and its remedy, before setting back on the main course of articulating the means of illumination. Owen prefaces his treatment of the general and particular causes of ignorance with a reminder that ignorance results from human deficiency. Human ignorance of divine truth is not a problem with Scripture. Rather, universally, natural vanity and darkness deprave the human mind. Left to itself, the human mind will seize the Scripture to its own destruction when presented with it. The particular causes of ignorance flow from the heart, which incline individuals to prejudice and perversion of the truth. At the forefront of these affections is pride, which in this case results in a carnal confidence in one's own wisdom and ability. Other affections resulting in ignorance are love of honor and praise, resolute adherence to corrupt traditions and errors, love of sin, and spiritual sloth. Owen concludes, "While the minds of men are thus affected, as they cannot understand and receive divine, spiritual truths in a due manner, so are they ready and prone to embrace whatever is contrary thereunto." Thus, there is a special work of the Spirit of God in the renovation of our minds, enabling us to learn the truth as we ought.

The Holy Spirit removes hindrances by communicating spiritual light. He frees, delivers, and purges the mind of corrupt affections. Owen explicitly states that what people can understand without giving glory to God or bringing spiritual advantage to themselves is not his concern. But, positively, the Spirit implants spiritual habits and principles contrary to corrupt affections, such as humility, meekness, godly fear, reverence, and submission of the soul. Owen summarizes,

> Now all these graces whereby men are made teachable, capable of divine mysteries, so as to learn the truth as it is in Jesus, to understand the mind of God in the Scriptures, are wrought in them by the Holy Spirit, and belong unto his work upon our minds in our illumination. Without this the hearts of all men are fat, their ears heavy, and their eyes sealed, that they can neither hear, nor perceive, nor understand the mysteries of the kingdom of God.

So illumination is a matter of the will and affections. But it will become clear that in Owen's reasoning, even if this is the initial, indispensable step, there is more to the Spirit's work of illumination.

Chapter 6: Inspiration and Perspicuity

In chapter 6, Owen transitions to the means of illumination, which is none other than Scripture itself. The composing and disposal of Scripture is another part of the Spirit's work. Owen states it this way:

> The Holy Spirit of God has prepared and disposed of the Scripture so as it might be a most sufficient and absolutely perfect way and means of communicating unto our minds that saving knowledge of God and his will which is needful that we may live unto him, and come unto the enjoyment of him in his glory.

Owen navigates this topic by considering the genre and clarity of Scripture. As to its genre, Scripture is not a systematic theology. God used a kind of literary conglomerate to reveal himself, which forces one to conclude that this must be the best way. And it does make sense upon reflection. Owen observes that this approach allows for flexibility in the context of reception. He finds it instructive that the purpose of Scripture is not primarily, or exclusively, knowledge, but rather transformation. Scripture's genre makes the preaching ministry necessary, as well as diligence and perseverance in continually reckoning with biblical teaching.

Regarding the clarity of Scripture, Owen presents a thoroughly Protestant doctrine of perspicuity. He claims, *"The mind of God in all things concerning our faith and obedience, in the knowledge whereof our illumination does consist, is clearly revealed therein."* Yet because Scripture is divine revelation, it must be read and received, not like any other book, but as the word of the living God. And it follows that the mind must be freed by the Spirit, as previously noted, and that the truth cannot be mined in humanity's natural strength and ability. Still, Owen is forceful in his assertion that the necessity of supernatural illumination in no way infringes on Scripture's perspicuity. So, what about difficult passages? For this Owen distinguishes between hard to understand and hard to interpret. The former category includes things of a mysterious nature, such as the Trinity, the incarnation, eternal decrees, and the new birth. Truths such as these are above the ability of natural human reason to comprehend, but they are clearly expressed in Scripture. Difficult-to-interpret passages challenge us in the manner of their presentation. Owen has in mind allegories, parables, mystical stories, allusions, unfulfilled prophecies, ancient references, and rarely used words. Any truths necessary for faith and obedience revealed in such obscure places will be taught clearly elsewhere in Scripture. This conclusion springs from the doctrine of perspicuity and results in the concept of collation, the interpretive principle that within the canon clearer passages inform our reading of less clear passages. Another important interpretive principle introduced by Owen at this point is the analogy of faith, which he defines as the sum total of what Scripture clearly teaches regarding faith and obedience. The analogy of faith limits the possible meanings of any passage of Scripture to what is orthodox. With these two principles—collation and the analogy of faith—it can legitimately be maintained that Scripture is clear and that it provides for its own interpretation.[94]

Chapter 7: Biblical Interpretation

Thus far, Owen has presented illumination as it pertains to the mind and Scripture. What is as yet unexplored is the Spirit's role in the actual application

---

94 For more on Puritan biblical interpretation, specifically the concepts of perspicuity, collation, and the analogy of faith, see Andrew S. Ballitch, *The Gloss and the Text: William Perkins on Interpreting Scripture with Scripture*, Studies in Historical and Systematic Theology (Bellingham, WA: Lexham, 2020), 63–72.

of our minds to understanding and interpreting Scripture. The helps or means afforded by the Spirit for this purpose are three: spiritual, disciplinary, and ecclesiastical. And the purpose, most basically, is understanding the mind of God as revealed in Scripture through the human authors. The aim is the divine author's intended meaning, which is subtly yet significantly different from the end goal of interpretation being human authorial intent. These two are never in opposition, given Owen's doctrine of inspiration; and at the same time, the fact that there is a divine author is what makes Scripture revelation. There are at minimum two senses of Scripture, or at least two ways of reading or understanding it: one illuminated by the Spirit, and the other not. While Owen does not develop the point, he seems to indicate that unilluminated understanding is the grammatical and historical intent of the human author and that illuminated interpretation goes further. The latter concerns the theological significance, that meaning intended by the Spirit, which at times may be above and beyond the meaning intended by the human author. Owen illustrates this by referencing Jewish interpretation of the Old Testament. The rabbis understand it in its original Hebrew as well as anyone, grasping the grammatical sense, construction, and propositions contained in it perfectly. Yet they understand "the words of it only, and not the things which are the mind of God in them." Therefore, they do not truly understand Scripture. It is no coincidence that the title of Owen's treatise refers to understanding the mind of God particularly and that his most consistent referent throughout the treatise when discussing the sense, meaning, or intention of the text is that intended by the Spirit.

At the top of the list of spiritual means of interpretation, Owen places prayer, which in this context is a fervent, earnest plea for the Spirit's help. The following promise is attached:

> Whoever, in the diligent and immediate study of the Scripture to know the mind of God therein so as to do it, does abide in fervent supplications, in and by Jesus Christ, for supplies of the Spirit of grace, to lead him into all truth, to reveal and make known unto him the truth as it is in Jesus, to give him an understanding of the Scriptures and the will of God therein, he shall be preserved from pernicious errors, and attain that degree in knowledge as shall be sufficient unto the guidance and preservation of the life of God in the whole of his faith and obedience.

The one who will sincerely pray for help in understanding the Scriptures will not fall into soul-destroying error and will indeed comprehend the truths necessary for faith and obedience. Other spiritual means included by Owen are: readiness to conform the mind and heart to the doctrines found in Scripture; practical application of those doctrines; an ongoing intention for growth and progress in knowledge motivated by love for the truth and the experience of its excellence; and, finally, the ordinary ordinances of worship. Owen reinforces time and again that the spiritual means in no way supplant learning, study, and the use of reason in the interpretation of Scripture. However, Scripture is not an ordinary book, and thus the spiritual means must precede the disciplinarian means if true understanding is to be achieved.

Chapter 8: Rules for Biblical Interpretation

Having treated the spiritual means of interpretation, Owen turns in chapter 8 to what he terms disciplinarian means. These include study of the original languages, history, geography, and chronology, and the use of methodical reason. Owen begins by warning that such means are morally indifferent. He proposes that when applied to the interpretation of Scripture, disciplinarian means may be used properly, bringing blessing from the Holy Spirit, or abused, seducing people to trust in their own understanding. Concerning the biblical languages, Owen offers balance in proposing the advantages of learning Hebrew and Greek while instilling confidence in the exposition of good translations. History, geography, and chronology allow for consideration of historical context in the interpretive process. At the same time, Owen cautions against applying chronology strictly and minutely to history.[95] Reason applied to Scripture in interpretation enables judgement of the sense and logical deductions. However, Owen quickly dispels the notion of authoritative systems of logic. He asserts that it would be a presumptuous mistake to reduce all reasoning in Scripture to any single system or to assume that anyone can "fathom the depths of Scripture senses" by imperfect human reason.[96] Moreover, every interpretation must be tested by the analogy of faith, no matter how reasonable or logical it may seem. Again, the disciplinary means

95 This contrasts with the efforts of other Puritans who elaborated significantly and confidently on the dating of biblical chronology and even prophecy. E.g., William Perkins, *A Digest or Harmony of the Books of the Old and New Testament*, in *The Whole Works of That Famous and Worthy Minister of Christ in the University of Cambridge, M. William Perkins*, vol. 2 (London: John Legatt, 1631); and James Ussher, *Annales Veteris Testamenti, a prima mundi origine deducti, una cum rerum Asiaticarum et Aegyptiacarum chronico, a temporis historici principio usque ad Maccabaicorum initia producto* (1650).

96 Owen's view here is counterevidence to the Ramist thesis regarding Puritan theology and exegesis. E.g., Donald K. McKim, *Ramism in William Perkins' Theology*, American University Studies VII, Theology and Religion 15 (New York: Peter Lang, 1987).

may be abused, but added to the foundational spiritual means, they are used by the Spirit in the work of illumination.

Chapter 9: Biblical Interpretation and the Church

In his concluding chapter, Owen addresses the ecclesiastical means of biblical interpretation. He begins by challenging the concepts of universal tradition and consent of the church fathers, claiming that these simply are nonexistent outside the analogy of faith, which, of course, is derived from Scripture itself. For Owen,

> the sole use of ecclesiastical means in the interpretation of Scripture is in the due consideration and improvement of that light, knowledge, and understanding in, and those gifts for the declaration of, the mind of God in the Scripture, which he has granted unto and furnished them with who have gone before us in the ministry and work of the gospel.

In short, God's promise to lead his people into all truth and maintain a gospel witness through his church enables us to consider the interpretations of saints throughout the ages with great benefit as we interpret the Scriptures ourselves.

The Work of the Holy Spirit in Prayer (1682)[97]

Owen's treatise on prayer is an attack on set forms of prayer and an argument for free (unwritten and unmemorized) prayer. As previously noted, Owen felt compelled to write on the subject in response to Hugh Cressy's rather abrasive dismissal of the Reformed Protestant position in his *Church-History of Brittany*. But Owen's project is larger than merely an apologetic against the Church of Rome and its false worship flowing from its composed prayers. Two ideas dominate. Prayers of human composure in the national Restoration Church of England's Book of Common Prayer and the neglect of prayer among other churches are Owen's twin concerns.

Owen begins by asserting the necessity, benefit, and use of prayer in general. This goes without saying, in fact. No true religion exists without prayer. All religion consists principally in prayer. And so the design of his discourse, in Owen's own words, is that when it comes to prayer, "nothing more requisite in our religion than that true apprehensions of its nature and use be preserved in the minds of men, the declaration and defense of them, when they

---

97 Published by Nathaniel Ponder.

are opposed and unduly traduced, is not only justifiable but necessary also." Owen understands prayer according to the Spirit to be under attack by the imposition of liturgical forms.

The questions Owen seeks to answer include the nature of the work of the Spirit in aiding and assisting believers in their praying according to the mind of God and the effects and fruit of that work. The sum of what he pleads, from Scripture and experience, is this:

> Whereas *God has graciously promised his Holy Spirit, as a Spirit of grace and supplications, unto them that do believe, enabling them to pray according to his mind and will, in all the circumstances and capacities wherein they are, or which they may be called unto, it is the duty of them who are enlightened with the truth hereof to expect those promised aids and assistances in and unto their prayers, and to pray according to the ability which they receive thereby.*

After summarizing his claim, he lays out eight general principles, which warrant enumerating, since they serve as a foundation for the treatise as a whole:

1. It is the duty of every person to pray for himself or herself. The existence of God simply demands it.
2. It is the duty of some to pray for others. Here, Owen is thinking of fathers, husbands, pastors, and the like.
3. Whoever prays is obligated to pray as well as possible.
4. And the best prayer includes intense, sincere actings of our minds through the greatest assistance we can attain.
5. The duty of prayer is achievable with the aid of God himself.
6. God expressly commands his people to pray, but not to compose written prayers for themselves, much less others.
7. Assistance is promised to believers to enable them to pray according to the will of God. However, at the same time, no help is promised for composing prayers for others.
8. Prayers given in Scripture have everlasting use but give no warrant for compositions unto the same end. This final principle leads Owen to the dominant topic in his preface, an earnest plea against set forms of prayer.

Owen stops short of determining set forms of prayer as inherently sinful, absolutely unlawful, or entirely vitiating of acceptable worship, but neither does he have anything positive to say about them. Taking the Missal (or

Roman Catholic Mass book) as a case study, he highlights the abuses and corruptions engendered by liturgical forms. While the Missal's development was slow, it eventually imposed worship of human composure as divine and brought with it several unfortunate results. One was the doctrines of the Mass and transubstantiation. The Church of Rome came to believe what it first admitted in prayer. This theology of the Lord's Supper could not have conceivably developed without enforceable set forms of prayer. Another disastrous result was the rise of arbitrary ceremonies that came to adorn the devised prayer forms, leading to superstition and idolatrous practices. A third calamitous outcome was the imposition of the Missal, enforced at times even to the point of death. These consequences further served as catalysts for the cessation of true spiritual and ministerial gifts.

Owen proceeds to build upon the foundation laid in his preface in three movements. In chapters 1–3, he details the biblical evidence for true prayer. Chapters 4–7 exposit the nature of the Spirit's work. And then chapters 8–9 draw out the duties associated with the Spirit's gift of prayer. Owen concludes the treatise with two separate discussions, one on what he calls "mental prayer" and one on prescribed forms, in chapters 10–11, which are significant for historical context and will be handled briefly in turn.

Chapter 1: The Use of Prayer, and the Work of the Holy Spirit Therein

In chapter 1, Owen reasserts the duty of prayer, narrows his subject to the gracious operation of the Holy Spirit in prayer, and argues for the significant relevance of the topic. He observes that the great animosity between different groups on the issue of prayer arises from the fact that prayer is the hinge on which all other differences concerning worship depend. By looking in detail at two passages of Scripture, Owen evinces "that there is promised and actually granted a special work of the Spirit of God in the prayers or praises of believers under the New Testament."

Chapter 2: Zechariah 12:10 Opened and Vindicated

Zechariah 12:10 is the passage upon which Owen's treatise is built. The manner of the fulfillment of what is promised—namely, "the Spirit of grace and supplications"—is expressed by "I will pour out." The pouring out of God's Spirit will be plentiful in the days of the gospel. The promise is addressed to the whole church. The Spirit is efficiently the Spirit of supplication in two ways. One, "by working gracious inclinations and dispositions in us unto this duty." Two, "by giving a gracious ability for the discharge of it in a due manner." For Owen, Zechariah 12:10, properly understood, proves "*that God has promised under the New Testament to give unto believers, in a plentiful manner or measure, the Spirit of grace and of supplications, or his own Holy Spirit, enabling them to pray according to his mind and will."* Next, Owen turns his attention to the witness of the New Testament.

Chapter 3: Galatians 4:6 Opened and Vindicated

Galatians 4:6 reports the fulfillment of the Old Testament promise and expresses the nature of the Spirit's work in prayer. Believers are the subjects of the bestowal of the Spirit's gift, which is the enabling of adopted sons and daughters to act like just that, children of God. What Owen claims from this passage is this: The Spirit "does actually incline, dispose, and enable them to cry 'Abba, Father,' or to call upon God in prayer as their Father by Jesus Christ." Having exegetically underpinned the reality of the Spirit's role in legitimate prayer, Owen turns to a detailed exposition of the nature of the Spirit's work.

Chapter 4: The Nature of Prayer

In chapter 4, Owen outlines human deficiency with regard to the practice of prayer, explaining Romans 8:26. He begins with a definition of prayer, which he articulates as "a gift, ability, or spiritual faculty of exercising faith, love, reverence, fear, delight, and other graces, in a way of vocal requests, supplications, and praises unto God." The fact is, the Spirit supplies and furnishes the mind with what ought to be prayed for in general and in particular. Moreover, without the special aid of the Holy Spirit, none of us knows what to properly pray for. We do not have any accurate estimation of what we need, no conception of the promises of God, which are the measure of prayer, no grasp of the end, goal, or purpose of prayer. The Spirit must supply both the matter and the manner of prayer.

Chapter 5: The Work of the Holy Spirit as to the Matter of Prayer

Owen describes the Spirit's resource of the matter of prayer in chapter 5. In short, "he alone does, and he alone is able to give us such an understanding of our own wants as that we may be able to make our thoughts about them known unto God in prayer and supplication." According to Owen, the principal matter concerns faith and unbelief. Human beings have no conception of either the deprivation of their nature or the grace of God apart from the work of the Spirit. Regarding humanity's perception of this deprivation of nature and the grace of God, Owen memorably states, "Nature is blind, and cannot see them; it is proud, and will not own them; stupid, and is senseless of them." The Spirit acquaints us not only with an impression of our needs but also with the grace and mercy prepared in the promises of God for our relief. These are the measure of prayer, the boundaries within which we pray. Owen argues, "We must pray with our understanding, that is, understand what we pray for. And these things are no other but what God has promised, which if we are not regulated by in our supplications, we ask amiss." Finally, the Spirit supplies the end of prayer. In other words, he guides and directs believers to petition from the right motivations and for proper purposes—namely, the glory of God and the improvement of holiness. In sum, the Spirit teaches believers what to pray for as they ought by furnishing and filling their minds with the matter of prayer.

Chapter 6: The Due Manner of Prayer, Wherein It Does Consist

After supplying the matter of prayer, the Spirit works the manner of prayer in the believer. This consists in the realm of the will and affections. The two are inseparable, for prayer by definition is the obedient acting of the whole soul toward God. The Spirit again does what individuals are unable to do themselves. He conforms the will and works affection in believers suitable for what they are praying about; therefore, he is the fountain of inexpressible fervency and delight. Delight in God as the object of prayer consists in three main things. First, the sight or prospect of God on his throne of grace, ready through Jesus Christ to dispense mercy to supplicant sinners. Second, a sense of God's relation unto us as Father. Third, the boldness and confidence that we have in our access to God in the act of prayer. Delight also flows from a focus on Christ, our access to the Father, the only way and means of our acceptance with God. The Spirit is as much behind how the Christian prays as he is the source of the content of those prayers.

Chapter 7: The Nature of Prayer in General, with
Respect unto Forms of Prayer and Vocal Prayer

Chapter 7 concludes Owen's section on the nature of prayer with a discussion of Ephesians 6:18. Here, Paul does not reference praying by an extraordinary or miraculous gift; rather, praying in the Spirit is the constant duty of all believers, which also illegitimates set forms of prayer. Answering the question "how they are enabled to pray in whose minds the Holy Ghost does thus work as a Spirit of grace and supplication" speaks to both of these faulty notions of prayer. Owen answers the question in brief this way: "Those who are thus affected by him do never want a gracious ability of making their addresses unto God in vocal prayer, so far as is needful unto them in their circumstances, callings, states, and conditions." As a result, set forms are absolutely unnecessary for the believer. And as for the argument that set forms benefit the unregenerate, Owen has another answer: Those unregenerate persons who are given over to sin cry out only when they are in distress. For these people, set forms serve like a charm. Others who attend to prayer out of duty, if their desire becomes sincere, would be hindered by set forms. In all cases, "it cannot be denied but that the constant and unvaried use of set forms of prayer may become a great occasion of quenching the Spirit, and hindering all progress or growth in gifts or graces," just as "those who will never enter the water but with flags or bladders under them will scarce ever learn to swim." Owen will return to prescribed prayer forms in the final chapter of his treatise, but his flow of argument at this point moves from the reality and nature of true prayer to the resulting duties.

Chapter 8: The Duty of External Prayer by Virtue of a Spiritual Gift Explained and Vindicated

Having expressed the internal, spiritual nature of the duty already, and the exercise of the Spirit's grace therein, Owen transitions to prayer's external performance in chapter 8. His point is this:

> There is a *spiritual ability given unto men by the Holy Ghost, whereby they are enabled to express the matter of prayer, as taught and revealed in the manner before described, in words fitted and suited to lead on their own minds and the minds of others unto a holy communion in the duty, to the honor of God and their own edification.*

So even the words prayed are from the Spirit and therefore are unprescribed. The argument proceeds this way: All people are obligated to pray as they are able, according to their condition, relations, occasion, and duty. All examples of prayer in Scripture are unprescribed. Every command in Scripture to pray is according to one's abilities. And ability includes the conscientious, diligent use of all means—involving the searching of both the heart and the Scriptures—which God has ordained to improve prayer. Abilities also include natural talents of invention, memory, and elocution. Yet external prayer is a gift. Words and expression are an adjunct of the internal gift discussed thus far in Owen's treatise.

Chapter 9: Duties Inferred from the Preceding Discourse

The expression of prayer is a gift inseparable from the internal work of the Spirit. Owen, however, combats the claim that everyone with the grace therefore has the gift, and vice versa. It is true that "all those in whom the Spirit of God does graciously act faith, love, delight, desire, in a way of prayer unto God, have an ability from him to express themselves in vocal prayer." Though it does not follow that everyone who appears to have the gift also has the grace. For instance, the unregenerate can publicly pray unto the edification of others. Interestingly, Owen does explicitly allow for unvocal prayer, but insists that even this must still be expressed in words in the mind. The significance of this point becomes apparent in chapter 10. Like all other spiritual duties, we need the Spirit in prayer's faithful completion, otherwise nothing would exist to separate the regenerate and unregenerate exercise of it. Further, the effects of prayer are so great that it would be impious not to attribute it to God. Prayer is a gift from God from beginning to end.

The duties that follow from Owen's conception of prayer add up to glorifying God for the great privilege the Spirit of grace and supplication brings and its diligent use. Owen describes the appropriate exercise of prayer and divides the topic into three parts. First, it is our duty to use the gift to the inestimable advantage for our own souls. Second, the duty includes our natural faculties. Owen states that prayer "is freely bestowed, but it is carefully to be preserved. It is a gospel talent given to be traded with, and thereby to be increased." This includes constant consideration and observation of ourselves and Scripture, which serves as a mirror, presenting both what we are and what we ought to be. It entails meditation on God's glorious excellencies and the mediation and intercession of Christ. It requires frequency in exercise and constant fervency and intention of mind and spirit. Third, it is our duty to use prayer unto the ends for which it is bestowed by God. Prayer is a means to stir up faith, love, delight, joy, and the like, as well as to benefit others, specifically our families, churches, and societies. With this exhortation to faithfulness in the duties of prayer, Owen concludes his unified argument regarding the Spirit's role in prayer to focus on two parentheses, mental and prescribed forms of prayer.

Chapter 10: Of Mental Prayer as Pretended Unto by Some in the Church of Rome

Owen sets his sights in chapter 10 pointedly on mental prayer as it exists in the Church of Rome. Cressy's definition of mental prayer, in *Church-History of Brittany*, the work that inspired Owen's treatise, is "pure spiritual prayer, or a quiet repose of contemplation; that which excludes all images of the fancy, and in time all perceptible actuations of the understanding, and is exercised in signal elevations of the will, without any force at all, yet with admirable efficacy." It requires "an entire calmness and even death of the passions, a perfect purity in the spiritual affections of the will, and an entire abstraction from all creatures."[98] In opposition to this concept, Owen insists on the use of the intellect. The experience of true prayer is through the faculties of the soul; it does not circumvent them. It is not as if we can pray in our "will and its affections without any actings of the mind or understanding." Further, so-called mental prayer is impossible to verify, given that it brings no benefit or edification to the church or any member of it. Owen warns, "The use of words is necessary in this duty, from the nature of the duty itself, the command of God, and the edification of the church." Whatever mental prayer is, in Owen's estimation, it is not true prayer.

Chapter 11: Prescribed Forms of Prayer Examined

In his final chapter, Owen handles prescribed forms of prayer, attending to their origin, supposed advantages, and lawfulness. The origin of prescribed forms is clearly human, for the Spirit is not promised to assist in their composition. As to the claimed advantages, for those who have the gift of free prayer by the Spirit, there is none. For those with a comparably low ability to pray for themselves, there is also no benefit, for set forms will only keep them from maturing. For those who do not yet have a desire to pray, other means are at their disposal, including the sincere consideration of themselves and Scripture and the ordinary means of grace. For those that claim personal experience of spiritual advantage, Owen refrains from disputing this, but points rather to God's gracious blessing of his children, even when they fail to order everything according to his word. As to the lawfulness of prescribed forms, Owen comes short of condemning them as unlawful in themselves, at which point he only alludes to the regulative principle of worship but does not pursue it. Owen leaves room for the lawful private use of prescribed forms, though he is suspicious of the benefit even in this setting, while he would prefer their exclusion from public worship.

The Holy Spirit as a Comforter (1693)

In his treatise *The Holy Spirit as a Comforter*, Owen handles the signally Puritan topic of assurance. Owen is concerned to offer the believer the comfort in life and in death that can come only from the Spirit himself.

98 Cressy, *Church-History of Brittany*, preface, paras. 42–43; quoted in Owen.

At the same time, he elevates ordinary believers through his discussion of the anointing of the Spirit, a conspicuously Protestant motif. This treatise perhaps also best illustrates, in this volume, Owen as expositor of Scripture, as he carefully exegetes what Scripture means in reference to the Spirit as unction, seal, and earnest.

Chapter 1: The Holy Ghost the Comforter of the Church by Way of Office

Owen's work on the Holy Spirit as comforter proceeds in three stages. He first defines the office, then discusses its discharge, and then follows with a description of its effects.

Chapter 1 handles the office, working through the four things that constitute any office. First, there is the trust. The Spirit has the comfort, consolation, and support of believers entrusted to him. Christ's ascension did not mean that he stopped loving and caring for his disciples. He had to go to make intercession for them, which was part of his work that remained toward God. The other part of his remaining work respects the church and individual believers, which he gave to the Spirit. While the Spirit did not commence being comforter when Jesus left, he was at that time promised to be the comforter. Regenerate people were unaware of his ministry or dispensation beforehand. So Christ is still comforter, but by his Spirit.

A mission, name, and work are the three other elements constituting an office. The Spirit's special mission consists of his commissioning to be comforter by the Father and Son. His special name is Paraclete, found first in John 14:16. It is not distinctive with respect to his person, but denominative with respect to his work, used by Jesus as a proper name with respect to his office. The concept of comforter is principally ascribed to the Spirit in this name. The whole context of the promise in John 14–16 verifies this. As our "advocate," as the word is often rendered, he offers consolation—not, of course, as an advocate with God, but for the church in, with, and against the world. The Spirit serves as our advocate by undertaking our protection and defense. And he does so in three primary ways. First, by suggesting and supplying pleas and arguments to witnesses resulting in the conviction of their opponents. Second, in and by his communication of spiritual gifts, both extraordinary and ordinary, with their effects visible to the world. Third, by the internal efficacy of the preached word—namely, conviction, which effects either belief or rejection. The final aspect of an office is a special work. For the Spirit as comforter, this is "to support, cherish, relieve, and comfort the church, in all trials and distresses." This will be more fully expressed in Owen's discussion of particular effects of the office.

Chapter 2: General Adjuncts or Properties of the Office of a Comforter, as Exercised by the Holy Spirit

In chapter 2, Owen treats the discharge of this office, which includes four primary features. One of the properties of the office is infinite condescension. The Spirit's work as comforter is on behalf of men and women, individual human beings, sinful individuals at that. Another property is unspeakable love, as he works by tenderness and compassion. This is fitting given Trinitarian relations:

> In all the actings of the Holy Ghost toward us, and especially in this of his susception of an office on the behalf of the church, which is the foundation of them all, his love is principally to be considered, and that he chooses this way of acting and working toward us to express his peculiar, personal character, as he is the eternal love of the Father and the Son.

Benefits, gifts, or kindnesses bring comfort or consolation only if they proceed from love. And there was indeed infinite love in the acceptation of this office by the Spirit.[99] A third property is power, infinite power as the foundation for unshakable consolation. Only divine power can alleviate consciences and bring full assurance, driving away the disconsolations believers face. Only omnipotence can overcome the opposition from Satan. Finally, an unchangeable dispensation is a feature of the office of comforter. To whom the Spirit is given, he abides with forever, which is true both for individuals and the church unto the consummation of all things.

Chapter 3: Unto Whom the Holy Spirit Is Promised and Given as a Comforter; or the Object of His Acting in This Office

Chapters 3 and 4 transition to the effects of the Spirit's role as comforter with an assertion about whom the Spirit is given to and an explanation of his inhabitation of recipients. Chapter 3 argues that only believers are given the Spirit. Owen says it this way: "All his actings and effects as a comforter are confined unto them that believe, and do all suppose saving faith as antecedent unto them." This is not the first saving work, however. Regeneration precedes it, for "he comforts none but those whom he has before sanctified."

99 For a discussion and critique of this Augustinian conception of the Spirit, see Colin Gunton, *Theology through the Theologians: Selected Essays, 1972–1995* (London: T&T Clark, 2003), chap. 7.

Chapter 4: Inhabitation of the Spirit the First Thing Promised

Inhabitation, or indwelling, is the great foundational privilege upon which all others depend. Owen carefully distinguishes what the indwelling of the Spirit is from what it is not. This inhabitation is not the Spirit's essential omnipresence, or an expression of the cause for the effect, or a hypostatic union. Neither is it a union or relation immediately between the Spirit and believers, who are related in such a way to Christ. Rather, it is the actual person of the Holy Spirit who is promised to believers. The fact that he inhabits so many at one time illustriously demonstrates his eternal glory. This indwelling is the spring of his gracious operations in us; it is "the hidden spring and cause of that inexpressible distance and difference that is between believers and the rest of the world." The person of the Spirit inhabits believers as the promised comforter.

Chapter 5: Particular Actings of the Holy Spirit as a Comforter

The final three chapters of Owen's treatise describe three particular ways the Spirit comforts—as an unction, a seal, and an earnest. The Spirit as unction, or the Spirit's anointing, is the first in natural order. Owen constructs a biblical argument for what this anointing consists in, contrasting this with arguments that the anointing is the doctrine of the gospel, the testimony of the Spirit to the truth of the gospel, or the chrism (anointing in the rites of baptism, confirmation, and holy orders) and extreme unction (anointing the sick and dying) of the Church of Rome. Owen provides a biblical theology of anointing, beginning with the claim that all things dedicated or consecrated in the Old Testament were anointed with oil. All such types were fulfilled in Jesus Christ, the anointed one, whose anointing was with the Spirit. The unction of Christ consisted in the full communication of the Spirit in all his graces and gifts needed in Christ's human nature and for his work. Though this was essentially a single work, it was carried out, of course, in degrees. Believers have their unction immediately from Christ, consisting in the communication of the Spirit. It is like Christ's, but to an inferior degree. The Spirit's "first, peculiar, special effect as an unction"—and here Owen references his previous treatises *The Reason of Faith* and *Causes, Ways, and Means*—"is his teaching of us the truths and mysteries of the gospel by saving illumination." This anointing also dedicates believers as kings and priests, a dedication unto God, resulting in special privilege. From 1 John 2:20, 27, Owen concludes that the principal benefit of the Spirit as unction is the stability of belief. This anointing is "an effectual means of their preservation, when a trial of their stability in the truth shall befall them." Further, "nothing will give stability in all seasons but the wisdom and knowledge which are the effects of this teaching," teaching which includes "all things," or the whole life of faith, including joy and consolation.

Chapter 6: The Spirit a Seal, and How

Owen is not entirely satisfied with comparisons to human sealing in attempting to understand the Spirit as a seal. For example, discussions of the Spirit putting forth his power in the preservation of believers, as in something highly valuable being sealed up for safety and inviolability, fall short of the rich meaning of sealing. Rather, Owen compares the sealing of believers with the sealing of Christ, which demonstrated God's owning of him, his approbation of him, and manifested that God the Father would take care of Christ and preserve him. He summarizes,

> This sealing of the Son is the communication of the Holy Spirit in all fullness unto him, authorizing him unto, and acting his divine power in, all the acts and duties of his office, so as to evidence the presence of God with him, and his approbation of him, as the only person that was to distribute the spiritual food of their souls unto men.

Owen then defines the Spirit's sealing of believers as God's "gracious communication of the Holy Ghost unto them, so to act his divine power in them as to enable them unto all the duties of their holy calling, evidencing them to be accepted with him both unto themselves and others, and asserting their preservation unto eternal salvation." In both the case of Christ and believers, the sealing is the communication of the Spirit unto them, and the effects are the gracious operations of the Spirit, enabling them to live according to their radical callings. For believers specifically, God, by the sealing of the Spirit, gives testimony that they are his, assurance of that relationship, and evidence to the world, while also protecting them unto final consummation.

Chapter 7: The Spirit an Earnest, and How

When discussing the Spirit as an earnest, Owen is again unsatisfied with human illustrations, this time with transactional language. The Spirit is really neither a pledge or collateral, nor an earnest or down payment, as if God is somehow in anyone's debt or as if a business deal has been struck. Giving security to something future is as far as the metaphor goes. In God's case, he is unilaterally bestowing grace. Believers are given a foretaste of the future now by the Holy Spirit, who also guarantees that future. The Spirit is an "earnest," Owen's preferred term, of our inheritance, which, under forfeiture, needed to be purchased for us by Christ. "The way whereby we come to have an interest in Christ, and thereby a right unto the inheritance, is by the participation of the Spirit of Christ," argues Owen. By communication of the Spirit, we are made joint heirs with Christ; therefore, he is the earnest of our inheritance. He is the firstfruits of the full harvest to come, a spiritual and eternal redemption. In Owen's estimation, nothing could be more comforting.

A Discourse of Spiritual Gifts (1693)

In Owen's analysis of spiritual gifts, he has two primary aims. First, to explain what spiritual gifts are, distinguishing the ordinary from the extraordinary gifts, the latter being no longer operative. And second, to elevate the ordinary gifts as the God-given, sufficient means for building the church. These purposes arose out of the enthusiasm found in the seventeenth-century religious sects, as well as the prevalent charismatic manifestations. They also explain the rise of the Roman Catholic Church, for it was the neglect of the ordinary gifts that resulted in that sacramental institution. And it was the misguided grasping at the extraordinary gifts that occasioned superstition and endless miracle accounts there. As Owen completes his objectives, he protects the balance between the inward and outward call to ministry and insists that the ministry of the gospel cannot be done in human power.

Chapter 1: Spiritual Gifts, Their Names and Significations

Owen's examination of spiritual gifts consists of brief discussions of their name and nature, followed by a treatment of their distribution as both extraordinary and ordinary, which forms the body of the treatise. The definition Owen provides is this: spiritual gifts "are free and undeserved effects of divine bounty." From the human perspective, they are spiritual powers aimed at a certain end. But most basically, they are undeserved gifts. To get at the nature of spiritual gifts, Owen enumerates the similarities and differences with saving graces. The commonalities are three. First, both spiritual gifts and saving graces are purchased by Christ for his church. Christ distributes gifts as the only legitimate weapons of the warfare that consists in the establishing and edifying of the church. Second, they share the same immediate efficient cause. They both are wrought by the power of the Holy Spirit. Third, they both are designed unto the good, benefit, ornament, and glory of the church. Grace gives the church an invisible life; gifts give it a visible profession. In Owen's words, "That profession which renders a church visible according to the mind of Christ, is the orderly exercise of the spiritual gifts bestowed on it, in a conversation evidencing the invisible principle of saving grace."

Chapter 2: Differences between Spiritual Gifts and Saving Grace

The differences between spiritual gifts and saving graces are seven. Graces are the fruit of the Spirit; gifts are the effects of his operation. Graces proceed from electing love, gifts from temporary election. Graces are the essential effects of the covenant; gifts are part of the outward administration. Graces proceed from the priestly office of Christ, gifts from his kingly office. Graces cannot be lost, though they can decay, while gifts can be taken away. Graces are bestowed primarily for the individual's good, gifts for the benefit of others. Principally, graces possess the whole soul, whereas gifts are present in the mind or theoretical intellect, meaning that while grace necessarily transforms the soul and its presence guarantees that one belongs to Christ, the same cannot be said of gifts. Here Owen protects the distinction between the invisible and visible church and makes sense of false professors of Christianity who appear to be saved.

Chapter 3: Of Gifts and Offices Extraordinary; and First of Offices

Transitioning to extraordinary spiritual gifts, Owen explains first extraordinary offices, then the gifts themselves and their origin, duration, use, and end. Offices in general exist whenever there is power and a duty to be performed by it. Extraordinary offices include also an extraordinary call and the bestowal of extraordinary power. The three extraordinary offices are apostle, evangelist, and prophet. Owen explains the special calling and exceptional power attached to each office.

Chapter 4: Extraordinary Spiritual Gifts

The extraordinary gifts themselves are listed in 1 Corinthians 12:4–11. At the outset of the discussion of this list, Owen distinguishes between gifts that exceed the whole power and faculties of humanity, including miracles and healings, and endowments and improvements of the faculties of the minds of men, such as wisdom, knowledge, and utterance. This distinction is significant because the latter gifts differ only in degree from the ordinary gifts continually dispensed throughout the history of the church. The first gift in Paul's list is word of wisdom. Owen understands this as wisdom itself, specifically the wisdom promised to the apostles in the face of adversaries. It also includes special wisdom for the management of gospel truths for the edification of the church. Word of knowledge is "such a peculiar and special insight into the mysteries of the gospel, as whereby those in whom it was were enabled to teach and instruct others." This was initially needed in the church by immediate revelation. Faith, often understood in the context of troubles and trials or suffering, is "a peculiar confidence, boldness, and assurance of mind in the profession of the gospel and the administration of its ordinances." Gifts of healing are referenced in the plural because of their free communication unto many persons. They are distinct from miracles for several reasons. They are a sign unto believers, rather than unbelievers. There is a peculiar goodness and relief toward mankind in them. The kindness, love, and compassion demonstrated in them results in appreciation and obedience flowing from gratitude. Miracles are an immediate effect of divine power exceeding all created abilities. In the context of the early church, Owen claims, "this gift of miracles was exceedingly useful, and necessary unto the propagation of the gospel, the vindication of the truth, and the establishment of them that did believe." Prophecy refers to both the faculty of prediction and the ability to declare the mind of God from the word by the special and immediate revelation of the Holy Spirit. Discerning of spirits was the ability to judge between the Spirit's work and Satan's plagiarized counterfeits. Finally, in reference to tongues and their interpretation, Owen asserts that tongues were sometimes understood by the speakers and the church and at other times not. While tongues were effectual for the propagation of the gospel to unbelievers, interpretation was added that the church might be edified by the gift.

Chapter 5: The Origin, Duration, Use, and End
of Extraordinary Spiritual Gifts

The extraordinary gifts and extraordinary offices ended together, coinciding with the establishment of the early church. However, Owen does not rule out the possibility of God continuing to work miraculously. He says, "It is not unlikely but that God might on some occasions, for a longer season, put forth his power in some miraculous operations, and so he yet may do, and perhaps does sometimes." When the extraordinary gifts were operative, they were the glory, honor, and beauty of the church. They were aimed at setting up, planting, advancing, and propagating the kingdom of Christ in the establishment of the church. Those chosen and called for this purpose were enabled by these gifts. Such persons were of course insufficient in themselves, as God purposed the gospel to suffer every disadvantage humanly speaking. It was by the gifts that preaching was rendered effectual. Miracles filled the world with an apprehension of the divine power accompanying the gospel and its preachers. The extraordinary spiritual gifts left no doubt that Christ and the message of his apostles were divine revelation.

Chapter 6: Of Ordinary Gifts of the Spirit

Owen initiates his discussion of the ordinary gifts of the Spirit in the context of the continuation of the ministry of the church. The designation of ordinary must not be understood as in any way pejorative or diminishing. Ordinary simply separates these gifts from the miraculous gifts. They differ only in degree from what the extraordinary office holders possessed. The term also designates the continued supply of gifts throughout the continuation of the ordinary state of the church. Before addressing the gifts themselves, Owen dissects the ministry itself. The ministry is itself Christ's gift to the church, acquired by his humiliation and death, distributed when he ascended unto his exaltation, and consisting in spiritual gifts. The ministerial office continues as the spiritual gifts are continually dispensed and recognized by the church in its calling of ministers. The aim of the ministry is the edification of the church, through protection and the service of the word. The gifts of the Spirit enable ministers to discharge their responsibilities.

Chapter 7: Of Spiritual Gifts Enabling the Ministry to the Exercise and Discharge of Their Trust and Office

The ordinary spiritual gifts are much more than mere natural abilities, and they are antecedently necessary to legitimate a minister. In other words, they come from God, and therefore the outward call of the church alone, though essential, is insufficient. Owen's main claim is this:

> There is a special dispensation and work of the Holy Ghost in providing able ministers of the New Testament for the edification of the church, wherein the continuance of the ministry and being of the church, as to its outward order, does depend; and that herein he does exert his power and exercise his authority in the communication of spiritual gifts unto men, without a participation whereof no man has de jure, any lot or portion in this ministration.

Owen supports this claim with an argument of eight propositions:

1. Christ has promised to be present with his church, and
2. this promised presence is by his Spirit.
3. It is secured by an everlasting, unchangeable covenant.

4. The gospel is called the ministration of the Spirit and ministers of it the ministers of the Spirit.

5. The end for which the Spirit is promised is the preservation of the church in the world, and

6. the communication of gifts is the means to this end.

7. As such, they are indispensable for gospel administrations.

8. And all of this is demonstrably true in the experience of the church in any age.

But what of the actual ordinary gifts of the Spirit?

Chapter 8: Of the Gifts of the Spirit with Respect
Unto Doctrine, Worship, and Rule

Owen concludes his treatise with a taxonomy of ministerial gifts. There are three categories, gifts that pertain to the doctrine, worship, and rule of the church.

First, gifts concerning doctrine help accomplish the primary duty of the ministry—namely, the dispensation of the doctrine of the gospel to the church through preaching. The Spirit gives wisdom, knowledge, or understanding—all designations of the same concept—of the mysteries of the gospel. These can be distinguished, but all speak to acquaintance with and comprehension of doctrine necessary for preaching. In short, the Spirit provides

> such a comprehension of the scope and end of the Scripture, of the reve-
> lation of God therein, such an acquaintance with the systems of particular
> doctrinal truths, in their rise, tendency, and use, such a habit of mind in
> judging of spiritual things, and comparing them one with another, such a
> distinct insight into the springs and course of the mystery of the love, grace,
> and will of God in Christ, as enables them in whom it is to declare the
> counsel of God, to make known the way of life, of faith and obedience unto
> others, and to instruct them in their whole duty to God and man thereon.

The Spirit also gives skill in dividing the word properly, in culling doctrines from the biblical text and applying them. To do this aright, the minister must be well acquainted with his flock and aware of how God's grace operates on minds and hearts, the nature of temptation and the obstacles to faith and obedience, and spiritual diseases and remedies. The last gift concerning preaching is the gift of utterance. Far from natural speaking ability, the gift of utterance is freedom in the declaration of truth—holy confidence, authority, and gravity in expression.

The remaining ministerial gifts are those touching worship and the rule of the church. The gifts concerning worship can be summarized under the heading "prayer," which includes confession, supplication, thanks, and praise. Owen does not treat this in any length but rather points the reader to his *The Work of the Holy Spirit in Prayer*. Gifts concerning the rule of the church are spiritual, with nothing in common with the administration of the powers of the world. They consist in the "humble, holy, spiritual application of the word of God or rules of the gospel" to the church.

The ministry gifts that fall into these three categories are dispensed to church members at large as well. When gifts are attached to duties rather than offices, as in the case of ministers, they are to be exercised in the building up of the body. The gifts are not communicated by extraordinary infusion. They are not attainable in people's diligence alone. But means are ordinarily used in their realization and growth. The gifts ought to be prepared for through the inculcation of humility, meekness, and teachability. They ought to be prayed for and faithfully exercised when granted. Ministry, true ministry, the kind that does in fact build the church and further the cause of the gospel, cannot be done in human power.

Conclusion

In these treatises, Owen ought not be viewed as an innovator but rather as a brilliant synthesizer, adding extraordinary detail to conventional theological loci—in this case, pneumatology. His discussions of the Holy Spirit in these five treatises place him comfortably within the Puritan Protestant stream of the great orthodox tradition of Christianity. While one must look elsewhere in Owen's corpus—to his Πνευματολογια, or, *A Discourse concerning the Holy Spirit* (1674)—to find his explicit handling of the doctrine of the Holy Spirit as hammered out in the fourth century and faithfully developed by Augustine (354–430) and the Latin West, in these shorter treatises his orthodox Trinitarianism is on full display in his insistence upon the divinity of the Spirit and his continual attestation to his personal agency. For instance, regarding the Spirit's work of illumination, Owen insists that only because he is God can the Spirit reveal the mind of God as it is communicated in the Scriptures. Or in the context of prayer and comfort, it is the Spirit's special responsibility to comfort God's people and generate true prayer, not the Father's or the Son's. Likewise, it is the Spirit who dispenses ministerial gifts, both extraordinary and ordinary, which were purchased by the Son in obedience to the Father. The operations of the Godhead are inseparable in Owen's theology, yet the Spirit, like the Father and the Son, has a particular and distinct role. Owen confessed God the Holy Spirit as the third person of the Trinity with Christians throughout the ages.

Owen was also impeccably Protestant, particularly a Protestant of the Reformed stripe. Consider his attitude toward external arguments for the validity of Scripture. With John Calvin (1509–1564), he argues that faith, or infallible certainty of the divine origin of Scripture, can come only from the Spirit's illumination of the Scripture's own witness.[100] Or consider the essential role of the Spirit in his method of biblical interpretation. Owen agrees with a previous generation of English Protestants, notably William Whitaker (1548–1595) and William Perkins (1558–1602), that while all mental powers and educational helps at one's disposal should be utilized, the Spirit must bring true understanding as he interprets Scripture with Scripture itself.[101] Or note his abhorrence of written prayers and with them all prescribed forms of worship. Owen is in good company here with many in the Reformed tradition, as it defined itself in contradistinction to post-Reformation Lutheranism; he stood together with Protestants such as John Cotton (1585–1652), Thomas Hooker (1586–1647), and Thomas Shepard (1605–1649), who argued similarly and fled England for freedom from prayer book worship.[102] Or take the issue of assurance. Owen's friend Thomas Goodwin (1600–1680), for instance, taught that the sealing of the Spirit referenced in Ephesians 1:13 and 4:30 was a second work of grace giving immediate assurance of salvation.[103] Owen did not follow this theological innovation; rather, he interpreted the sealing of the Spirit as the communication of the Spirit himself to the believer. Assurance is an effect of this sealing, not the sealing itself. Owen was relentlessly Protestant, and historically Protestant, standing in consistent opposition to internal as well as external foes, whether Roman Catholic or Arminian, Socinian or Quaker.

---

100 Calvin, *Institutes*, 1.7.4.

101 William Whitaker, *A Disputation on Holy Scripture: Against the Papists, Especially Bellarmine and Stapleton*, trans. William Fitzgerald (Cambridge: Cambridge University Press, 1849), 415; William Perkins, *The Arte of Prophesying*, in *The Whole Works of That Famous and Worthy Minister of Christ in the University of Cambridge, M. William Perkins*, 2:651.

102 John Cotton, *The Way of the Churches of Christ in New-England* (London, 1645), 65; Thomas Hooker, *A Survey of the Summe of Church-Discipline. Wherein the Way of the Churches of New-England Is Warranted Out of the Word, and All Exceptions of Weight, Which Are Made against It, Answered* (London, 1648), 5–6; Thomas Shepard, *A Treatise of Liturgies, Power of the Keyes, and of Matter of the Visible Church. In Answer to the Reverend Servant of Christ, Mr. John Ball* (London, 1652), 36–58.

103 See Thomas Goodwin's sermon on Ephesians 1:13–14, in *The Works of Thomas Goodwin*, vol. 1, *Containing an Exposition on the First Chapter of the Epistle to the Ephesians* (1861; repr., Eugene, OR: Wipf and Stock, 2009), 227–39.

Owen was an orthodox Protestant and also a Puritan. He was born and raised a Puritan, suffered for nonconformity in the Church of England, triumphed as a Puritan, and then shaped the dissenting community during the decades of its inception. Owen contributed to Puritanism's emphasis on Scripture-saturated piety, as evidenced in these treatises. As he focused on illumination, prayer, comfort, and spiritual gifts, it was ever with an eye on the life of the believer. It is the individual whose mind is illuminated unto biblical understanding. The individual offers prayer unmediated to God. The individual receives comfort from the indwelling Holy Spirit as the guarantee of eternal life. The individual is gifted spiritually for ministry based on the offices and responsibilities to which he or she is called. This focus on individual Christians has led some to the conclusion that Owen's was a subjectivist piety that eventually blossomed in revivalist evangelicalism, a piety not rooted in ecclesiology.[104] Certainly Owen's evangelical successors picked up on legitimate emphases he made. However, the church looms large in these treatises concerning the Holy Spirit. The church plays a role in biblical interpretation. The church is the context where prayers of human composure have no place. The officers of the church are recipients of spiritual gifts. Owen was ever the churchman, with a distinctly Puritan piety.

Nathaniel Mather (1631–1697) evaluates John Owen's works in his preface to *The Holy Spirit as a Comforter* and *A Discourse of Spiritual Gifts*, and his appraisal certainly rings true and summarizes well why Owen was appreciated in the seventeenth century and is still of great interest today:

I doubt not but the discerning reader will observe such excellencies shining out in this and other of this great author's writings, as do greatly commend them to the church of God, and will do so in after ages, however this corrupt and degenerate generation entertain them. They are not the crude, and hasty, and untimely abortions of a self-full, distempered spirit, much less the boilings-over of inward corruption and rottenness put into a fermentation; but the mature, sedate, and seasonable issues of a rich magazine of learning, well digested with great exactness of judgment. There is in them a great light cast and reflected on, as well as derived from, the Holy Scriptures, those inexhaustible mines of light in sacred things. They are not filled with vain, impertinent jangling, nor with a noise of multiplied futilous distinctions, nor with novel and uncouth terms foreign to the things of God, as the manner of some writers is *ad nauseam usque*. But there is in them a happy and rare conjunction of firm solidity, enlightening clearness, and heart-searching

104 Gribben, *John Owen and English Puritanism*, 271.

spiritualness, evidencing themselves all along, and thereby approving and commending his writings to the judgment, conscience, spiritual taste, and experience of all those who have any acquaintance with and relish of the gospel.

Owen offers insight even today—if not always because of his conclusions, then because of his questions and disciplined biblical thinking. Though Roman Catholics and Quakers may no longer be perceived as the menaces to Reformed Protestantism they once were, institutionalism, celebrity pastors, and theological heroes, on the one hand, and individualism, privatism, and spiritual excess, on the other, are perennial issues when it comes to biblical interpretation. While debates over what should or should not be included in gathered worship according to Scripture have often given way to pragmatism and cultural accommodation, the church ought to continually ask how its worship might be most pleasing to God as he has indicated in his word. Christians still need comfort, and the Spirit is still able to provide the assurance of faith. The question of how Christ provides for his church after its establishment in the days of the apostles, whether through ordinary or extraordinary spiritual gifts, is one that Christians have wrestled with since the early church. The list could go on, drawn from volumes 7–8 alone, but the point is this: Mather was right. Christians have been and will be able to read Owen with immense benefit in every generation. This was the heart of one of Owen's eulogizers, when he wrote these lines of verse, commemorating his fallen hero:

His *Fame* will *Live* to lat'st Posterity,
In's *Theo—Christo—Pneumatology*:
And various *Volumes* more; where we may find
How in's *Great Soul, Rich Gifts* and *Grace* were *joyn'd*.
His *Learned Tongue* (which [living] did impart,
Its Message from his *Own*, to th' *Hearers Heart*;
And *taught* those *Truths* whose *Worth & Excellence*,
Were *Felt before*, by's *own Experience*)
Alas, is *Silenc'd* now! But 's *Pious Pen*,
Do's and will *Preach* to Multitudes of Men;
Such *Sound* and *Weighty* Doctrines do's unfold,
As are by th' *Scripture-Touchstone* prov'd *true Gold*.[105]

105 *An Elegy on the Death of That Learned, Pious, and Famous Divine, Doctor John Owen* (London, 1683); emphasis original.

THE REASON
OF FAITH

or,
An Answer unto That Inquiry,
"Wherefore We Believe the
Scripture to Be the Word of God."
With the Causes and Nature of That Faith
Wherewith We Do So.
Wherein the Grounds Whereon the Holy
Scripture Is Believed to Be the Word of
God with Faith Divine and Supernatural,
Are Declared and Vindicated.

By John Owen, D.D.

———

If they hear not Moses and the prophets, neither will
they be persuaded, though one rose from the dead.

LUKE 16:31

———

London, Printed for Nathaniel Ponder,
at the Peacock in the Poultry, near
Cornhill: 1677

The Reason of Faith
Contents

To the Reader   *75*

1   The Subject Stated: Preliminary Remarks   *81*

2   What It Is Infallibly to Believe the Scripture to Be the Word of God, Affirmed   *91*

3   Sundry Convincing External Arguments for Divine Revelation   *97*

4   Moral Certainty, the Result of External Arguments, Insufficient: Four Arguments against the Sufficiency of Moral Certainty   *127*

5   Divine Revelation Itself the Only Foundation and Reason of Faith   *153*

6   The Nature of Divine Revelations: Their Self-Evidencing Power Considered, Particularly That of the Scriptures as the Word of God   *167*

7   Inferences from the Whole: Some Objections Answered   *187*

Appendix   *197*

Owen's treatise did not originally have chapter divisions. These divisions and titles have been adapted from the William Goold edition of 1862. They are fitting both with regard to the content and flow of the treatise and are stylistically consistent with the original chapter titles found in Owen's other works.

To the Reader

HAVING ADDED a brief account of the design, order, and method of the ensuing discourse in an appendix at the close of it,[1] I shall not here detain the reader with the proposal of them; yet some few things remain which I judge it necessary to mind him of. Be he who he will, I am sure we shall not differ about the weight of the argument in hand; for whether it be the truth we contend for or otherwise, yet it will not be denied but that the determination of it, and the settling of the minds of men about it, are of the highest concern unto them. But whereas so much has been written of late by others on this subject, any further debate of it may seem either needless or unseasonable. Something, therefore, may be spoken to evidence that the reader is not imposed on by that which may absolutely fall under either of these characters. Had the end in and by these discourses been effectually accomplished, it had been altogether useless to renew an endeavor unto the same purpose. But whereas an opposition unto the Scripture, and the grounds whereon we believe it to be a divine revelation, is still openly continued among us, a continuation of the defense of the one and the other cannot reasonably be judged either needless or unseasonable.¶[2]

Besides, most of the discourses published of late on this subject have had their peculiar designs, wherein that here tendered is not expressly engaged. For some of them do principally aim to prove that we have sufficient grounds to believe the Scripture, without any recourse unto or reliance upon the authoritative proposal of the Church of Rome, which they have sufficiently evinced[3] beyond any possibility of rational contradiction from their

---

1   Owen includes an appendix at the end of this treatise enumerating his presuppositions, points of argument, and authors who agree with him.
2   The ¶ symbol indicates that a paragraph break has been added to Owen's original text.
3   I.e., provided evidence for.

adversaries. Others have pleaded and vindicated those rational considerations whereby our assent unto the divine origin of it is fortified and confirmed, against the exceptions and objections of such whose love of sin and resolutions to live therein tempt them to seek for shelter in an atheistical contempt of the authority of God, evidencing itself therein. But as neither of these are utterly neglected in the ensuing discourse, so the peculiar design of it is of another nature; for the inquiries managed therein—namely, "What is the obligation upon us to believe the Scripture to be the word of God? What are the causes, and what is the nature of that faith whereby we do so? What it rests on and is resolved into, so as to become a divine and acceptable duty?"—do respect the consciences of men immediately, and the way whereby they may come to rest and assurance in believing. Whereas, therefore, it is evident that many are often shaken in their minds with those atheistical objections against the divine origin and authority of the Scripture which they frequently meet with, and that many know not how to extricate themselves from the ensnaring questions that they are often attacked withal about them—not for want of a due assent unto them, but of a right understanding what is the true and formal reason of that assent, what is the firm basis and foundation that it rests upon, what answer they may directly and peremptorily give unto that inquiry, "Wherefore do you believe the Scripture to be the word of God?"—I have endeavored to give them those directions herein that, upon a due examination, they will find compliant with the Scripture itself, right reason, and their own experience. I am not, therefore, altogether without hopes that this small discourse may have its use, and be given out in its proper season.¶

Moreover, I think it necessary to acquaint the reader that, as I have allowed all the arguments pleaded by others to prove the divine authority of the Scripture their proper place and force, so where I differ in the explication of anything belonging unto this subject from the conceptions of other men, I have candidly examined such opinions and the arguments wherewith[4] they are confirmed, without straining the words, caviling[5] at the expressions, or reflections on the persons of any of the authors of them. And whereas I have myself been otherwise dealt with by many, and know not how soon I may be so again, I do hereby free the persons of such humors and inclinations from all fear of any reply from me, or the least notice of what they shall be pleased to write or say. Such kind of writings are of the same consideration with me as those multiplied false reports which some have raised concerning me, the

---

4 I.e., by which.
5 I.e., raising a frivolous objection.

most of them so ridiculous and foolish, so alien from my principles, practices, and course of life, as I cannot but wonder how any persons pretending to gravity and sobriety are not sensible how their credulity and inclinations are abused in the hearing and repetition of them.¶

The occasion of this discourse is that which, in the last place, I shall acquaint the reader with. About three years since I published a book about the dispensation and operations of the Spirit of God. That book was one part only of what I designed on that subject.[6] The consideration of the work of the Holy Spirit, as the Spirit of illumination, of supplication, of consolation, and as the immediate author of all spiritual offices and gifts, extraordinary and ordinary, is designed unto the second part of it. Hereof this ensuing discourse is concerning one part of his work as a Spirit of illumination, which, upon the earnest requests of some acquainted with the nature and substance of it, I have suffered to come out by itself, that it might be of the more common use and more easily obtained.

May 11, 1677

---

6 Πνευματολογια, or, A Discourse concerning the Holy Spirit: Wherein an Account Is Given of His Name, Nature, Personality, Dispensation, Operations, and Effects; His Whole Work in the Old and New Creation Is Explained; the Doctrine concerning It Vindicated from Oppositions and Reproaches. The Nature also and Necessity of Gospel Holiness; the Difference between Grace and Morality, or a Spiritual Life unto God in Evangelical Obedience and a Course of Moral Virtues, Are Stated and Declared (1674).

The Reason of Faith

or,
The Grounds Whereon the Scripture Is Believed
to Be the
Word of God with Faith Divine
and Supernatural

1

The Subject Stated

Preliminary Remarks

THE PRINCIPAL DESIGN of that discourse whereof the ensuing treatise is a part, is to declare the work of the Holy Ghost in the illumination of the minds of men. For this work is particularly and eminently ascribed unto him, or the efficacy of the grace of God by him dispensed (Eph. 1:17–18; Heb. 6:4; Luke 2:32; Acts 13:47; 16:14; 26:18; 2 Cor. 4:4; 1 Pet. 2:9). The objective cause and outward means of it are the subjects at present designed unto consideration; and it will issue in these two inquiries.

1. On what grounds, or for what reason, we do believe the Scripture to be the word of God with faith divine and supernatural, as it is required of us in a way of duty?
2. How or by what means we may come to understand aright the mind of God in the Scripture, or the revelations that are made unto us of his mind and will therein?

For by illumination in general, as it denotes an effect wrought in the minds of men, I understand that supernatural knowledge that any man has or may have of the mind and will of God, as revealed unto him by supernatural means, for the law of his faith, life, and obedience. And this, so far as it is comprised in the first of these inquiries, is that whose declaration we at present design, reserving the latter unto a distinct discourse by itself also.[1] Unto the former some things may be premised.

---

1 This is a reference to the second treatise in this volume, *The Causes, Ways, and Means of Understanding the Mind of God as Revealed in His Word, with Assurance Therein* (1678).

DIVINE REVELATION: SIX PREMISES

1. Supernatural revelation is the only objective cause and means of supernatural illumination. These things are commensurate. There is a natural knowledge of supernatural things, and that both theoretical and practical (Rom. 1:19; 2:14–15). And there may be a supernatural knowledge of natural things (1 Kings 4:31–34; Ex. 31:2–6). But unto this supernatural illumination it is required both that its object be things only supernaturally revealed, or as supernaturally revealed (1 Cor. 2:9–10), and that it be wrought in us by a supernatural efficiency, or the immediate efficacy of the Spirit of God (Eph. 1:17–19; 2 Cor. 4:6). This David prays for, גל עיני, "Reveal," or "uncover mine eyes," bring light and spiritual understanding into my mind, "that I may behold (ἀνακεκαλυμμένῳ προσώπῳ, 'with open face,' or as in the Syriac, באפא גליחא, 'with a revealed or uncovered face,' the veil being taken away [2 Cor. 3:18]) wondrous things out of thy law" (Ps. 119:18). The light he prayed for within did merely respect the doctrine of the law without. This the apostle fully declares (Heb. 1:1–2). The various supernatural revelations that God has made of himself, his mind and will, from first to last, are the sole and adequate object of supernatural illumination.

2. This divine external revelation was originally, by various ways, which we have elsewhere declared, given unto sundry persons immediately, partly for their own instruction and guidance in the knowledge of God and his will, and partly by their ministry to be communicated unto the church.[2] So was it granted unto Enoch, the seventh from Adam, who thereon prophesied, to the warning and instruction of others (Jude 14–15). And to Noah, who became thereby a preacher of righteousness (2 Pet. 2:5). And to Abraham, who thereon commanded his children and household to keep the way of the Lord (Gen. 18:19). And other instances of the like kind may be given (Gen. 4:26; 5:29). And this course did God continue a long time, even from the first promise to the giving of the law, before any revelations were committed to writing, for the space of 2,460 years; for so long a season did God enlighten the minds of men by supernatural, external, immediate, occasional revelations. Sundry things may be observed of this divine dispensation, as

---

2   Owen is likely referring to his *Of the Divine Original, Authority, Self-Evidencing Light, and Power of the Scriptures; with an Answer to That Inquiry, How We Know the Scriptures to Be the Word of God; also, a Vindication of the Purity and Integrity of the Hebrew and Greek Texts of the Old and New Testament; in Some Considerations on the Prolegomena and Appendix to the Late Biblia Polyglotta. Whereunto Are Subjoined Some Exercitations about the Nature and Perfection of the Scripture, the Right of Interpretation, Internal Light, Revelation, Etc.* (1659).

(1) That it did sufficiently evidence itself to be from God unto the minds of those unto whom it was granted, and theirs also unto whom these revelations were by them communicated. For during this season Satan used his utmost endeavors to possess the minds of men with his delusions, under the pretense of divine, supernatural inspirations; for hereunto belongs the origin of all his oracles and enthusiasms[3] among the nations of the world. There was, therefore, a divine power and efficacy attending all divine revelations, ascertaining and infallibly assuring the minds of men of their being from God; for if it had not been so, men had never been able to secure themselves that they were not imposed on by the crafty deceits of Satan, especially in such revelations as seemed to contain things contrary to their reason, as in the command given to Abraham for the sacrificing his son (Gen. 22:2). Wherefore, these immediate revelations had not been a sufficient means to secure the faith and obedience of the church if they had not carried along with them their own evidence that they were from God. Of what nature that evidence was we shall afterward inquire. For the present I shall only say, that it was an evidence unto faith, and not to sense; as is that also which we have now by the Scripture. It is not like that which the sun gives of itself by its light, which there needs no exercise of reason to assure us of, for sense is irresistibly affected with it. But it is like the evidence which the heavens and the earth give of their being made and created of God, and thereby of his being and power. This they do undeniably and infallibly (Ps. 19:1–2; Rom. 1:19–21). Yet it is required hereunto that men do use and exercise the best of their rational abilities in the consideration and contemplation of them. Where this is neglected, notwithstanding their open and visible evidence unto the contrary, men degenerate into atheism. God so gave out these revelations of himself as to require the exercise of the faith, conscience, obedience, and reason of them unto whom they were made, and therein they gave full assurance of their proceeding from him. So, he tells us that his word differs from all other pretended revelations as the "wheat does from the chaff" (Jer. 23:28). But yet it is our duty to try and sift the wheat from the chaff, or we may not evidently discern the one from the other.

(2) The things so revealed were sufficient to guide and direct all persons in the knowledge of their duty to God, in all that was required of them in a way of faith or obedience. God from the beginning gave out the knowledge of his will πολυμερῶς, "by sundry parts and degrees"; yet so that every age and season had light enough to guide them in the whole obedience required

---

3   I.e., claims of receiving extrabiblical, external, immediate revelations after the close of the canon.

of them, and unto their edification therein. They had knowledge enough to enable them to offer sacrifices in faith, as did Abel; to walk with God, as did Enoch; and to teach their families the fear of the Lord, as did Abraham. The world perished not for want of sufficient revelation of the mind of God at any time. Indeed, when we go to consider those divine instructions which are upon record that God granted unto them, we are scarce able to discern how they were sufficiently enlightened in all that was necessary for them to believe and do; but they were unto them "as a light shining in a dark place." Set up but a candle in a dark room, and it will sufficiently enlighten it for men to attend their necessary occasions therein; but when the sun is risen, and shines in at all the windows, the light of the candle grows so dim and useless that it seems strange that any could have advantage thereby. The Sun of Righteousness is now risen upon us, and immortality is brought to light by the gospel. If we look now on the revelations granted unto them of old, we may yet see there was light in them, which yields us little more advantage than the light of a candle in the sun. But unto them who lived before this Sun arose, they were a sufficient guide unto all duties of faith and obedience. For

(3) There was during this season a sufficient ministry for the declaration of the revelations which God made of himself and his will. There was the natural ministry of parents, who were obliged to instruct their children and families in the knowledge of the truth which they had received. And whereas this began in Adam, who first received the promise, and therewith whatsoever was necessary unto faith and obedience, the knowledge of it could not be lost without the willful neglect of parents in teaching, or of children and families in learning. And they had the extraordinary ministry of such as God entrusted new revelations with, for the confirmation and enlargement of those before received, who were all of them preachers of righteousness unto the rest of mankind. And it may be manifested that from the giving of the first promise, when divine external revelations began to be the rule of faith and life unto the church, to the writing of the law, there was always alive one or other, who, receiving divine revelations immediately, were a kind of infallible guide unto others. If it was otherwise at any time, it was after the death of the patriarchs, before the call of Moses, during which time all things went into darkness and confusion. For oral tradition alone would not preserve the truth of former revelations. But by whom these instructions were received, they had a sufficient outward means for their illumination, before any divine revelations were recorded by writing. Yet,

(4) This way of instruction, as it was in itself imperfect and liable to many disadvantages, so through the weakness, negligence, and wickedness of men,

it proved insufficient to retain the knowledge of God in the world. For under this dispensation the generality of mankind fell into their great apostasy from God, and betook themselves unto the conduct and service of the devil; of the ways, means, and degrees whereof I have discoursed elsewhere.[4] Hereon God also regarded them not, but "suffered all nations to walk in their own ways" (Acts 14:16), giving them up to their own hearts' lusts to "walk in their own counsels," as it is expressed [in] Psalm 81:12. And although this fell not out without the horrible wickedness and ingratitude of the world, yet there being then no certain standard of divine truth whereunto they might repair, they broke off the easier from God through the imperfection of this dispensation. If it shall be said, that since the revelation of the will of God has been committed unto writing men have apostatized from the knowledge of God, as is evident in many nations of the world, which sometimes professed the gospel, but are now overrun with heathenism, Mahometism,[5] and idolatry, I say, this has not come to pass through any defect in the way and means of illumination, or the communication of the truth unto them, but God has given them up to be destroyed for their wickedness and ingratitude; and "except we repent we shall all likewise perish" (Rom. 1:18; 2 Thess. 2:11–12).[6] Otherwise, where the standard of the word is once fixed, there is a constant means of preserving divine revelations. Wherefore,

3. God has gathered up into the Scripture all divine revelations given out by himself from the beginning of the world, and all that ever shall be so to the end thereof, which are of general use unto the church, that it may be thoroughly instructed in the whole mind and will of God, and directed in all that worship of him and obedience unto him which is necessary to give us acceptance with him here, and to bring us unto the eternal enjoyment of him hereafter. For¶

(1) when God first committed the law to writing, with all those things which accompanied it, he obliged the church unto the use of it alone, without additions of any kind. Now, this he would not have done had he not expressed therein, that is [in] the books of Moses, all that was any way needful unto the faith and obedience of the church. For he did not only command them to attend with all diligence unto his word as it was then written for their instruction

---

4   In the margin: *De Natura Theologia*, book 3.—Owen. This is a reference to Owen's Θεολογούμενα Παντοδαπά, *sive*, *De Natura, Ortu, Progressu, et Studio Verae Theologiae, Libri Sex: Quibus Etiam Origines et Processus Veri et Falsi Cultus Religiosi, Casus et Instaurationes Ecclesiae Illustiores ab Ipsis Rerum Primordiis, Enarrantur* (1661).

5   I.e., Islam.

6   This is a quotation from Luke 13:3.

and direction in faith and obedience, annexing all sorts of promises unto their so doing (Deut. 6:6–7), but also expressly forbids them, as was said, to add anything thereunto or to conjoin anything therewith (Deut. 4:2; 12:32), which he would not have done had he omitted other divine revelations, before given, that were any way necessary unto the use of the church. As he added many new ones, so he gathered in all the old from the unfaithful repository of tradition, and fixed them in a writing given by divine inspiration.¶

(2) For all other divine revelations which were given out to the church for its use in general under the Old Testament, they are all comprised in the following books thereof; nor was this, that I know of, ever questioned by any person pretending to sobriety, though some, who would be glad of any pretense against the integrity and perfection of the Scripture, have fruitlessly wrangled about the loss of some books, which they can never prove concerning any one that was certainly of a divine origin.¶

(3) The full revelation of the whole mind of God, whereunto nothing pretending thereunto is ever to be added, was committed unto and perfected by Jesus Christ (Heb. 1:1–2). That the revelations of God made by him, whether in his own person or by his Spirit unto his apostles, were also by divine inspiration committed to writing, is expressly affirmed concerning what he delivered in his own personal ministry (Luke 1:4; Acts 1:1; John 20:31), and may be proved by uncontrollable[7] arguments concerning the rest of them. Hence, as the Scriptures of the Old Testament were shut up with a caution and admonition unto the church to adhere unto the law and testimony, with threatening of a curse unto the contrary (Mal. 4:4–6), so the writings of the New Testament are closed with a curse on any that shall presume to add anything more thereunto (Rev. 22:18). Wherefore,

4. The Scripture is now become the only external means of divine supernatural illumination, because it is the only repository of all divine supernatural revelation (Ps. 19:7–8; Isa. 8:20; 2 Tim. 3:15–17). The pretenses of tradition, as a collateral means of preserving and communicating supernatural revelation, have been so often evicted of falsity that I shall not further press their impeachment. Besides, I intend those in this discourse by whom it is acknowledged that the Bible is, as sufficient and perfect, so the only treasury of divine revelations. And what has been offered by any to weaken or impair its esteem, by taking off from its credibility, perfection, and sufficiency, as unto all its own proper ends, has brought no advantage unto the church, nor benefit unto the faith of believers. But yet,

---

7 I.e., incontrovertible.

5. In asserting the Scripture to be the only external means of divine revelation, I do it not exclusively unto those institutions of God which are subordinate unto it, and appointed as means to make it effectual unto our souls, as

(1) Our own personal endeavors, in reading, studying, and meditating on the Scripture, that we may come unto a right apprehension of the things contained in it, are required unto this purpose. It is known to all how frequently this duty is pressed upon us, and what promises are annexed to the performance of it (see Deut. 6:6–7; 11:18–19; Josh. 1:8; Pss. 1:2; 119; Col. 3:16; 2 Tim. 3:15). Without this it is in vain to expect illumination by the word; and, therefore, we may see multitudes living and walking in extreme darkness when yet the word is everywhere nigh unto them. Bread, which is the staff of life, will yet nourish no man who does not provide it and feed upon it. No more would manna, unless it was gathered and prepared. Our own nature and the nature of divine revelations considered, and what is necessary for the application of the one to the other, make this evident. For God will instruct us in his mind and will, as we are men, in and by the rational faculties of our souls. Nor is an external revelation capable of making any other impression on us but what is so received. Wherefore, when I say that the Scripture is the only external means of our illumination, I include therein all our own personal endeavors to come to the knowledge of the mind of God therein, which shall be afterward spoken unto. And those who, under any pretenses, do keep, drive, or persuade men from reading and meditating on the Scripture, do take an effectual course to keep them in and under the power of darkness.

(2) The mutual instruction of one another in the mind of God out of the Scripture is also required hereunto. For we are obliged by the law of nature to endeavor the good of others in various degrees, as our children, our families, our neighbors, and all with whom we have conversation. And this is the principal good absolutely considered, that we can communicate unto others, namely, to instruct them in the knowledge of the mind of God. This whole duty, in all the degrees of it, is represented in that command, "Thou shalt teach my words diligently unto thy children, and shalt talk of them when thou sittest in thine house, and when thou walkest by the way, and when thou liest down, and when thou risest up" (Deut. 6:7). Thus, when our Savior found his disciples talking of the things of God by the wayside, he, bearing unto them the person of a private man, instructed them in the sense of the Scripture (Luke 24:26–27, 32). And the neglect of this duty in the world, which is so great that the very mention of it, or the least attempt to perform it, is a matter of scorn and reproach, is one cause of that great ignorance and darkness which yet abounds among us. But the nakedness of

this folly, whereby men would be esteemed Christians in the open contempt of all duties of Christianity, will in due time be laid open.

(3) The ministry of the word in the church is that which is principally included in this assertion: the Scripture is the only means of illumination, but it becomes so principally by the application of it unto the minds of men in the ministry of the word (see Matt. 5:14–15; 2 Cor. 5:18–20; Eph. 4:11–15; 1 Tim. 3:15). The church and the ministry of it are the ordinances of God unto this end, that his mind and will, as revealed in the word, may be made known to the children of men, whereby they are enlightened. And that church and ministry whereof this is not the first principal design and work is neither appointed of God nor approved by him. Men will one day find themselves deceived in trusting to empty names; it is duty alone that will be comfort and reward (Dan. 12:3).

6. That the Scripture, which thus contains the whole of divine revelation, may be a sufficient external cause of illumination unto us, two things are required.

(1) That we believe it to be a divine revelation, that is, the word of God, or a declaration of himself, his mind and will, immediately proceeding from him; or that it is of a pure divine origin, proceeding neither from the folly or deceit, nor from the skill or honesty of men (so is it stated [in] 2 Pet. 1:19–21; Heb. 1:1; 2 Tim. 3:16; Isa. 8:20). It tenders no light or instruction under any other notion but as it comes immediately from God, not as the word of man, but as "it is indeed the Word of the living God" (1 Thess. 2:13). And whatever anyone may learn from or by the Scriptures under any other consideration, it belongs not unto the illumination we inquire after (Neh. 8:8; Isa. 28:9; Hos. 14:9; Prov. 1:6; Ps. 119:34; Matt. 15:16; 2 Tim. 2:7; 1 John 5:20).

(2) That we understand the things declared in it, or the mind of God as revealed and expressed therein. For if it be given unto us a sealed book, which we cannot read, either because it is sealed or because we are ignorant and cannot read, whatever visions or means of light it has in it, we shall have no advantage thereby (Isa. 29:11–12). It is not the words themselves of the Scripture only, but our understanding them, that gives us light. פתח דבריך יאיר—the opening the door, "the entrance of thy Word giveth light" (Ps. 119:130). It must be opened, or it will not enlighten. So, the disciples understood not the testimonies of the Scripture concerning the Lord Christ, they were not enlightened by them, until he expounded them unto them (Luke 24:27, 45). And we have the same instance in the eunuch and Philip (Acts 8:31, 35–36). To this very day the nation of the Jews have the Scriptures of the Old Testament and the outward letter of them in such

esteem and veneration that they even adore and worship them, yet are they not enlightened by it. And the same is fallen out among many that are called Christians, or they could never embrace such foolish opinions and practice such idolatries in worship as some of them do, who yet enjoy the letter of the gospel.

ILLUMINATION: BELIEF AND UNDERSTANDING

And this brings me to my design, which we have been thus far making way unto; and it is to show that both these are from the Holy Ghost, namely, that we truly believe the Scripture to be the word of God, and that we understand savingly the mind of God therein; both which belong unto our illumination.

That which I shall first inquire into is the way how, and the ground whereon, we come to believe the Scripture to be the word of God in a due manner. For that this is required of us in a way of duty, namely, that we should believe the Scripture to be the word of God with faith divine and supernatural, I suppose will not be denied, and it shall be afterward proved. And what is the work of the Spirit of God herein will be our first inquiry.

Secondly, whereas we see by experience that all who have or enjoy the Scripture do not yet understand it, or come to a useful, saving knowledge of the mind and will of God therein revealed, our other inquiry shall be, how we may come to understand the word of God aright, and what is the work of the Spirit of God in the assistance which he affords us unto that purpose.

With respect unto the first of these inquiries, whereunto the present discourse is singly designed, I affirm that it is the work of the Holy Spirit to enable us to believe the Scripture to be the word of God, or the supernatural, immediate revelation of his mind unto us, and infallibly to evidence it unto our minds, so as that we may spiritually and savingly acquiesce[8] therein. Some, upon a mistake of this proposition, do seem to suppose that we resolve all faith into private suggestions of the Spirit or deluding pretenses thereof. And some, it may be, will be ready to apprehend that we confound the efficient cause and formal reason of faith or believing, rendering all rational arguments and external testimonies useless. But, indeed, there neither is nor shall be any occasion administered unto these fears or imaginations. For we shall plead nothing in this matter but what is consonant to the faith and judgment of the ancient and present church of God, as shall be fully

---

8   I.e., comply.

evidenced in our progress. I know some have found out other ways whereby the minds of men, as they suppose, may be sufficiently satisfied in the divine authority of the Scripture, but I have tasted of their new wine and desire it not, because I know the old to be better, though what they plead is of use in its proper place.

2

What It Is Infallibly to Believe the Scripture to Be the Word of God, Affirmed

MY DESIGN REQUIRES that I should confine my discourse unto as narrow bounds as possible, and I shall so do, showing,

1. What it is in general infallibly to believe the Scripture to be the word of God, and what is the ground and reason of our so doing. Or, what it is to believe the Scripture to be the word of God, as we are required to believe it so to be in a way of duty.
2. That there are external arguments of the divine origin of the Scripture, which are effectual motives to persuade us to give an unfeigned assent thereunto.
3. That yet, moreover, God requires of us that we believe them to be his word with faith divine, supernatural, and infallible:
4. Evidence the grounds and reasons whereon we do so believe, and ought so to do.

Unto these heads most of what ensues in the first part of this discourse may be reduced.

It is meet[1] that we should clear the foundation whereon we build, and the principles whereon we do proceed, that what we design to prove may be the better understood by all sorts of persons, whose edification we intend. For these things are the equal concern of the learned and unlearned. Wherefore,

---

1 I.e., fitting; proper.

some things must be insisted on which are generally known and granted. And our first inquiry is, what it is to believe the Scripture to be the word of God with faith divine and supernatural, according as it is our duty so to do.

1. And in our believing or our faith, two things are to be considered. (1) What it is that we do believe. And (2) wherefore we do so believe it. The first is the material object of our faith, namely, the things which we do believe; the latter, the formal object of it, or the cause and reason why we do believe them. And these things are distinct. The material object of our faith is the things revealed in the Scripture, declared unto us in propositions of truth. For things must be so proposed unto us, or we cannot believe them. That God is one in three persons, that Jesus Christ is the Son of God, and the like propositions of truth, are the material object of our faith, or the things that we do believe; and the reason why we do believe them is, because they are proposed in the Scripture. Thus, the apostle expresses the whole of what we intend: "I delivered unto you first of all that which I also received, how that Christ died for our sins according to the Scriptures, and that he was buried, and that he rose again the third day according to the Scriptures" (1 Cor. 15:3–4). Christ's death, and burial, and resurrection, are the things proposed unto us to be believed, and so the object of our faith. But the reason why we believe them is, because they are declared in the Scriptures (see Acts 8:28–30). Sometimes, indeed, this expression of "believing the Scriptures," by a metonymy,[2] denotes both the formal and material objects of our faith, the Scriptures themselves as such, and the things contained in them. So "They believed the Scripture, and the word which Jesus said" (John 2:22), or the things delivered in the Scripture, and further declared by Christ, which before they understood not. And they did so believe what was declared in the Scriptures because it was so declared in them. Both are intended in the same expression, "They believed the Scripture," under various considerations (so Acts 26:27). The material object of our faith, therefore, are the articles of our creed, by whose enumeration we answer unto that question, "What we believe?" giving an account of the hope that is in us, as the apostle does (Acts 26:22–23). But if, moreover, we are asked a reason of our faith or hope, or why we believe the things we do profess, as God to be one in three persons, Jesus Christ to be the Son of God, we do not answer, "Because so it is," for this is that which we believe, which were senseless. But we must give some other answer unto that inquiry, whether

---

2 I.e., a figure of speech in which the name of one thing is used for another because an attribute of it is associated with it.

it be made by others or ourselves. The proper answer unto this question contains the formal reason and object of our faith, that which it rests upon and is resolved into. And this is that which we look after.

2. We do not, in this inquiry, intend any kind of persuasion or faith but that which is divine and infallible, both which [are] from its formal reason or objective cause. Men may be able to give some kind of reasons why they believe what they profess so to do, that will not suffice or abide the trial in this case, although they themselves may rest in them. Some, it may be, can give no other account hereof but that they have been so instructed by them whom they have sufficient reason to give credit unto, or that they have so received them by tradition from their fathers. Now, whatever persuasion these reasons may beget in the minds of men that the things which they profess to believe are true, yet if they are alone, it is not divine faith whereby they do believe, but that which is merely human, as being resolved into human testimony only, or an opinion on probable arguments; for no faith can be of any other kind than is the evidence it reflects on or arises from. I say it is so where they are alone; for I doubt not but that some who have never further considered the reason of their believing than the teaching of their instructors have yet that evidence in their own souls of the truth and authority of God in what they believe that with respect thereunto their faith is divine and supernatural. The faith of most has a beginning and progress not unlike that of the Samaritans, as shall be afterward declared (John 4:40–42).

3. When we inquire after faith that is infallible, or believing infallibly, which, as we shall show hereafter, is necessary in this case, we do not intend an inherent quality in the subject, as though he that believes with faith infallible must himself also be infallible; much less do we speak of infallibility absolutely, which is a property of God, who alone, from the perfection of his nature, can neither deceive nor be deceived. But it is that property or adjunct of the assent of our minds unto divine truths or supernatural revelations, whereby it is differenced from all other kinds of assent whatever. And this it has from its formal object, or the evidence whereon we give this assent. For the nature of every assent is given unto it by the nature of the evidence which it proceeds from or relies on. This in divine faith is divine revelation, which, being infallible, renders the faith that rests on it and is resolved into it infallible also. No man can believe that which is false, or which may be false, with divine faith, for that which renders it divine is the divine truth and infallibility of the ground and evidence which it is built upon. But a man may believe that which is true infallibly so, and yet his faith not be infallible. That the Scripture is the word of God is infallibly true, yet the faith whereby a man believes it

so to be may be fallible, for it is such as his evidence is, and no other. He may believe it to be so on tradition, or the testimony of the Church of Rome only, or on outward arguments, all which being fallible, his faith is so also, although the things he assents unto be infallibly true. Wherefore, unto this faith divine and infallible, it is not required that the person in whom it is be infallible, nor is it enough that the thing itself believed be infallibly true, but, moreover, that the evidence whereon he does believe it be infallible also. So it was with them who received divine revelations immediately from God. It was not enough that the things revealed unto them were infallibly true, but they were to have infallible evidence of the revelation itself; then was their faith infallible, though their persons were fallible. With this faith, then, a man can believe nothing but what is divinely true, and therefore it is infallible; and the reason is, because God's veracity, who is the God of truth, is the only object of it. Hence says the prophet, ‏ותאמנו יהוה אלהיכם תאמינו‎[3]—"Believe in the Lord your God, so shall ye be established" (2 Chron. 20:20); or that faith which is in God and his word is fixed on truth, or is infallible. Hence the inquiry in this case is, "What is the reason why we believe anything with this faith divine or supernatural?" Or, "What is it the believing whereof makes our faith divine, infallible, and supernatural?" Wherefore,

4. The authority and veracity of God revealing the material object of our faith, or what it is our duty to believe, are the formal object and reason of our faith, from whence[4] it arises and whereinto it is ultimately resolved. That is, the only reason why we do believe that Jesus Christ is the Son of God, that God is one single essence subsisting in three persons, is because that God who is truth, the "God of truth" (Deut. 32:4), who "cannot lie" (Titus 1:2), and whose "Word is truth" (John 17:17), and the Spirit which gave it out is "truth" (1 John 5:6), has revealed these things to be so. And our believing these things on that ground renders our faith divine and supernatural. Supposing also a respect unto the subjective efficiency of the Holy Ghost, inspiring it into our minds, whereof afterward.[5] For to speak distinctly, our faith is supernatural, with respect unto the production of it in our minds by the Holy Ghost; and infallible, with respect unto the formal reason of it, which is divine revelation; and is divine, in opposition unto what is merely human, on both accounts.

---

3 *Biblia Hebraica Stuttgartensia* reads, ‏הַאֲמִינוּ בַּיהוָה אֱלֹהֵיכֶם וְהֵאָמֵנוּ‎. *Biblia Hebraica Stuttgartensia*, ed. Karl Elliger and Wilhelm Rudolph (Stuttgart: Deutsche Bibelgesellschaft, 1983).

4 I.e., where.

5 This is a reference to the second treatise in this volume, *The Causes, Ways, and Means of Understanding the Mind of God.*

As things are proposed unto us to be believed as true, faith in its assent respects only the truth or veracity of God, but whereas this faith is required of us in a way of obedience, and is considered not only physically, in its nature, but morally also, as our duty, it respects also the authority of God, which I therefore join with the truth of God as the formal reason of our faith (see 2 Sam. 7:28). And these things the Scripture pleads and argues when faith is required of us in the way of obedience. "Thus saith the Lord" is that which is proposed unto us as the reason why we should believe what is spoken, whereunto oftentimes other divine names and titles are added, signifying his authority who requires us to believe: "Thus saith the Lord God, the Holy One of Israel" (Isa. 30:15); "Thus saith the high and lofty One that inhabiteth eternity, whose name is Holy" (Isa. 57:15); "Believe in the Lord your God" (2 Chron. 20:20). "The word of the Lord" precedes most revelations in the prophets, another reason why we should believe, the Scripture proposes none (Heb. 1:1–2). Yea, the interposition of any other authority between the things to be believed and our souls and consciences, besides the authority of God, overthrows the nature of divine faith. I do not say the interposition of any other means whereby we should believe, of which sort God has appointed many, but the interposition of any other authority upon which we should believe, as that pretended in and by the Church of Rome. No men can be lords of our faith, though they may be "helpers of our joy."[6]

5. The authority and truth of God, considered in themselves absolutely, are not the immediate formal object of our faith, though they are the ultimate whereinto it is resolved. For we can believe nothing on their account unless it be evidenced unto us, and this evidence of them is in that revelation which God is pleased to make of himself, for that is the only means whereby our consciences and minds are affected with his truth and authority. We do, therefore, no otherwise rest on the truth and veracity of God in anything than we rest on the revelation which he makes unto us, for that is the only way whereby we are affected with them; not "the Lord is true" absolutely, but, "Thus saith the Lord," and, "the Lord hath spoken," is that which we have immediate regard unto. Hereby alone are our minds affected with the authority and veracity of God, and by what way soever it is made unto us, it is sufficient and able so to affect us. At first, as has been showed, it was given immediately to some persons, and preserved for the use of others in an oral ministry; but now all revelation, as has also been declared, is contained in the Scriptures only.

---

6   2 Cor. 1:24.

6. It follows that our faith, whereby we believe any divine, supernatural truth, is resolved into the Scripture, as the only means of divine revelation, affecting our minds and consciences with the authority and truth of God; or, the Scripture, as the only immediate, divine, infallible revelation of the mind and will of God, is the first immediate formal object of our faith, the sole reason why and ground whereon we do believe the things that are revealed with faith divine, supernatural, and infallible. We do believe Jesus Christ to be the Son of God. Why do we so do? On what ground or reason? It is because of the authority of God commanding us so to do, and the truth of God testifying thereunto. But how or by what means are our minds and consciences affected with the authority and truth of God, so as to believe with respect unto them, which makes our faith divine and supernatural? It is alone the divine, supernatural, infallible revelation that he has made of this sacred truth, and of his will, that we should believe it. But what is this revelation, or where is it to be found? It is the Scripture alone, which contains the entire revelation that God has made of himself, in all things which he will have us to believe or do. Hence—

7. The last inquiry arises, how, or on what grounds, for what reasons, do we believe the Scripture to be a divine revelation, proceeding immediately from God, or to be that word of God which is truth divine and infallible? Whereunto we answer, it is solely on the evidence that the Spirit of God, in and by the Scripture itself, gives unto us that it was given by immediate inspiration from God. Or, the ground and reason whereon we believe the Scripture to be the word of God are the authority and truth of God evidencing themselves in and by it unto the minds and consciences of men. Hereon, as, whatever we assent unto as proposed in the Scripture, our faith rests on and is resolved into the veracity and faithfulness of God, so is it also in this of believing the Scripture itself to be the infallible word of God, seeing we do it on no other grounds but its own evidence that so it is.

This is that which is principally to be proved, and therefore to prepare for it and to remove prejudices, something is to be spoken to prepare the way thereunto.

3

Sundry Convincing External Arguments for Divine Revelation

THERE ARE SUNDRY cogent arguments, which are taken from external considerations of the Scripture, that evince it on rational grounds to be from God. All these are motives of credibility, or effectual persuasives[1] to account and esteem it to be the word of God. And although they neither are, nor is it possible they ever should be, the ground and reason whereon we believe it so to be with faith divine and supernatural, yet are they necessary unto the confirmation of our faith herein against temptations, oppositions, and objections. These arguments have been pleaded by many, and that usefully, and therefore it is not needful for me to insist upon them. And they are the same, for the substance of them, in ancient and modern writers, however managed by some with more learning, dexterity, and force of reasoning than by others. It may not be expected, therefore, that in this short discourse, designed unto another purpose, I should give them much improvement. However, I shall a little touch on those which seem to be most cogent, and that in them wherein, in my apprehension, their strength does lie. And I shall do this to manifest that although we plead that no man can believe the Scriptures to be the word of God with faith divine, supernatural, and infallible, but upon its own internal divine evidence and efficacy, yet we allow and make use of all those external arguments of its sacred truth and divine origin which are pleaded by others, ascribing unto them as much weight and cogency as they can do, acknowledging the persuasion which they beget and effect to be as firm as they can pretend it to be. Only, we do not judge them to contain the

---

1 I.e., persuasions.

whole of the evidence which we have for faith to rest on or to be resolved into; yea, not that at all which renders it divine, supernatural, and infallible.

The rational arguments, we say, which are or may be used in this matter, with the human testimonies whereby they are corroborated, may and ought to be made use of and insisted on. And it is but vainly pretended that their use is superseded by our other assertions, as though, where faith is required, all the subservient use of reason were absolutely discarded, and our faith thereby rendered irrational. And the assent unto the divine origin and authority of the Scriptures, which the mind ought to give upon them, we grant to be of as high a nature as it is pretended to be, namely, a moral certainty. Moreover, the conclusion which unprejudiced reason will make upon these arguments is more firm, better grounded, and more pleadable, than that which is built merely on the sole authority of any church whatever. But this we assert, that there is an assent of another kind unto the divine origin and authority of the Scriptures required of us, namely, that of faith divine and supernatural. Of this none will say that it can be effected by or resolved into the best and most cogent of rational arguments and external testimonies which are absolutely human and fallible. For it does imply a contradiction to believe infallibly upon fallible evidence. Wherefore I shall prove, that beyond all these arguments and their effect upon our minds, there is an assent unto the Scripture as the word of God required of us with faith divine, supernatural, and infallible; and, therefore, there must be a divine evidence which is the formal object and reason of it, which alone it rests on and is resolved into, which shall also be declared and proved. But yet, as was said in the first place, because their property is to level the ground, and to remove the rubbish of objections out of the way, that we may build the safer on the sure foundation, I shall mention some of those which I esteem justly pleadable in this cause. And,

THE ANTIQUITY OF SCRIPTURE

1. The antiquity of these writings, and of the divine revelation contained in them, is pleaded in evidence of their divine origin, and it may be so deservedly. For where it is absolute, it is unquestionable: that which is most ancient in any kind is most true. God himself makes use of this plea against idols: "'Ye are my witnesses,' saith the Lord. 'I, even I, am the Lord; and beside me there is no saviour. I have declared and have saved, and I have showed when there was no strange god among you: therefore ye are my witnesses,' saith the Lord, 'that I am God'" (Isa. 43:10–12). That which he asserts is, that he alone is God, and no other. This he calls the people to testify by this

argument, that he was among them as God, that is, in the church, before any strange god was known or named. And so it is justly pleaded in the behalf of this revelation of the mind of God in the Scripture; it was in the world long before any other thing or writing pretended to be given unto the same end. Whatever, therefore, ensued with the like design must either be set up in competition with it or opposition unto it, above which it has its advantage merely from its antiquity. Whereas, therefore, this writing, in the first books of it, is acknowledged to be ancienter than any other that is extant in the world, or indeed that ever was so, and may be proved so to be, it is beyond all reasonable apprehension that it should be of human origin. For we know how low, weak, and imperfect all human inventions were at the first, how rude and unpolished in every kind, until time, observation, following additions and diminutions, had shaped, formed, and improved them. But this writing coming forth in the world absolutely the first in its kind, directing us in the knowledge of God and ourselves, was at first and at once so absolutely complete and perfect, that no art, industry, or wisdom of man, could ever yet find any just defect in it, or was able to add anything unto it whereby it might be bettered or improved. Neither from the beginning would it ever admit of any additions unto it, but what came from the same fountain of divine revelation and inspiration, clearing itself in all ages from all addition and superfetation[2] of men whatever. This at least puts a singular character upon this book, and represents it with such reverend awe and majesty that it is the highest petulancy[3] not to pay it a sacred respect.

This argument is pursued by many at large, as that which affords a great variety of historical and chronological observations. And it has been so scanned and improved that nothing but the giving of it a new dress remains for present or future diligence. But the real force of it lies in the consideration of the people by and among whom this revelation first commenced in the world, and the time wherein it did so. When some nations had so improved and cultivated the light of nature as greatly to excel others in wisdom and knowledge, they generally looked upon the people of the Jews as ignorant and barbarous. And the more wise any of them conceived themselves, the more they despised them. And, indeed, they were utter strangers unto all those arts and sciences whereby the faculties of men's minds are naturally enlightened and enlarged. Nor did they pretend unto any wisdom whereby to stand in competition with other nations, but only what they received by

---

2   I.e., excessive accumulation.
3   I.e., contemptuous or rude speech or behavior.

divine revelations. This alone God himself had taught them to look upon and esteem as their only wisdom before all the world (Deut. 4:6–8).¶

Now, we shall not need to consider what were the first attempts of other nations in expressing their conceptions concerning things divine, the duty and happiness of man. The Egyptians and Grecians were those who vied for reputation in the improvement of this wisdom, but it is known and confessed that the utmost production of their endeavors were things foolish, irrational, and absurd, contrary to the being and providence of God, to the light of nature, leading mankind into a maze of folly and wickedness. But we may consider what they attained unto in the fullness of time by their utmost improvement of science, wisdom, mutual intelligence, experience, communication, laborious study and observation. When they had added and subducted[4] to and from the inventions of all former ages from time immemorial, when they had used and improved the reason, wisdom, invention, and conjectures of all that went before them in the study of this wisdom, and had discarded whatever they had found by experience unsuited to natural light and the common reason of mankind, yet it must be acknowledged that the apostle passes a just censure on the utmost of their attainments, namely, that they waxed vain in their imaginations, and that the world by wisdom knew not God. Whence, then, was it that in one nation esteemed barbarous, and really so with respect unto that wisdom, those arts and sciences, which ennobled other nations, from that antiquity wherein it is not pretended that reason and wisdom had received any considerable improvement, without converse, communication, learning, or experience, there should at once proceed such a law, doctrine, and instructions concerning God and man, so stable, certain, uniform, as should not only incomparably excel all products of human wisdom unto that purpose, however advantaged by time and experience, but also abide invariable throughout all generations, so as that whatever has been advanced in opposition unto it, or but differing from it, has quickly sunk under the weight of its own unreasonableness and folly? This one consideration, unless men have a mind to be contentious, gives sufficient satisfaction that this book could have no other origin but what it pleads for itself, namely, an immediate emanation from God.

THE PRESERVATION OF SCRIPTURE

2. It is apparent that God in all ages has had a great regard unto it, and acted his power and care in its preservation. Were not the Bible what it pretends

4   I.e., subtracted.

to be, there had been nothing more suitable to the nature of God, and more becoming divine providence, than long since to have blotted it out of the world. For to suffer a book to be in the world, from the beginning of times, falsely pretending his name and authority, seducing so great a portion of mankind into a pernicious and ruinous apostasy from him, as it must do and does if it be not of a divine origin, and exposing inconceivable multitudes of the best, wisest, and soberest among them, unto all sorts of bloody miseries, which they have undergone in the behalf of it, seems not consonant unto that infinite goodness, wisdom, and care wherewith this world is governed from above. But, on the contrary, whereas the malicious craft of Satan and the prevalent power and rage of mankind have combined and been set at work to the ruin and utter suppression of this book, proceeding sometimes so far as that there was no appearing way for its escape, yet, through the watchful care and providence of God, sometimes putting itself forth in miraculous instances, it has been preserved unto this day, and shall be so to the consummation of all things. The event of that which was spoken by our Savior does invincibly prove the divine approbation of this book, as that does its divine origin: "Till heaven and earth pass, one jot or one tittle shall in no wise pass from the law" (Matt. 5:18).¶

God's perpetual care over the Scripture for so many ages that not a letter of it should be utterly lost, nothing that has the least tendency toward its end should perish, is evidence sufficient of his regard unto it. Especially would it be so if we should consider with what remarkable judgments and severe reflections of vengeance on its opposers this care has been managed, instances whereof might easily be multiplied. And if any will not ascribe this preservation of the books of the Bible, not only in their being, but in their purity and integrity, free from the least just suspicion of corruption, or the intermixture of anything human or heterogeneous, unto the care of God, it is incumbent on him to assign some other cause proportionate to such an effect, while it was the interest of heaven and the endeavor of earth and hell to have it corrupted and destroyed. For my part, I cannot but judge that he that sees not a hand of divine providence stretched out in the preservation of this book and all that is in it, its words and syllables for thousands of years, through all the overthrows and deluges of calamities that have befallen the world, with the weakness of the means whereby it has been preserved, and the interest, in some ages, of all those in whose power it was to have it corrupted, as it was of the apostate churches of the Jews and Christians, with the open opposition that has been made unto it, does not believe there is any such thing as divine providence at all.¶

It was first written in the very infancy of the Babylonian empire, with which it afterward contemporized about nine hundred years. By this monarchy, that people, which alone had these oracles of God committed to them, were oppressed, destroyed, and carried into captivity. But this book was then preserved among them while they were absolutely under the power of their enemies, although it condemned them and all their gods and religious worship, wherewith we know how horribly mankind is enraged. Satan had enthroned himself as the object of their worship, and the author of all ways of divine veneration among them. These they adhered unto as their principal interest, as all people do unto that they esteem their religion. In the whole world, there was nothing that judged, condemned, opposed him or them, but this book only, which was now absolutely in their power. If that by any means could have been destroyed, then when it was in the hands of but a few, and those for the most part flagitious[5] in their lives, hating the things contained in it, and wholly under the power of their adversaries, the interest of Satan and the whole world in idolatry had been secured. But, through the mere provision of divine care, it outlived that monarchy, and saw the ruin of its greatest adversaries. So it did also during the continuance of the Persian monarchy, which succeeded, while the people was still under the power of idolaters, against whom this was the only testimony in the world. By some branches of the Grecian monarchy a most fierce and diligent attempt was made to have utterly destroyed it; but still it was snatched by divine power out of the furnace, not one hair of it being singed, or the least detriment brought unto its perfection. The Romans destroyed both the people and place designed until then for its preservation, carrying the ancient copy of the law in triumph to Rome on the conquest of Jerusalem; and while all absolute power and dominion in the whole world, where this book was known or heard of, was in their hands, they exercised a rage against it for sundry ages, with the same success that former enemies had. From the very first, all the endeavors of mankind that professed an open enmity against it have been utterly frustrated.¶

And whereas, also, those unto whom it was outwardly committed, as the Jews first, and the anti-Christian church of apostatized Christians afterward, not only fell into opinions and practices absolutely inconsistent with it, but also built all their present and future interests on those opinions and practices; yet none of them durst[6] ever attempt the corrupting of one line in it, but were

---

5   I.e., villainous.
6   I.e., dared.

forced to attempt their own security by a pretense of additional traditions, and keeping the book itself, as much as they durst, out of the hands and knowledge of all not engaged in the same interest with themselves. Whence could all this proceed but from the watchful care and power of divine providence? And it is brutish folly not to believe that what God does so protect did originally proceed from himself, seeing it pleads and pretends so to do; for every wise man will take more care of a stranger than a bastard falsely imposed on him unto his dishonor.

THE DIVINE CONTENT OF SCRIPTURE

3. The design of the whole, and all the parts of it, has an impress on it of divine wisdom and authority. And hereof there are two parts: first, to reveal God unto men, and secondly, to direct men to come unto the enjoyment of God. That these are the only two great concerns of our nature, of any rational being, were easy to prove, but that it is acknowledged by all those with whom I treat. Now, never did any book or writing in the world, any single or joint endeavors of mankind or invisible spirits, in the way of authority, give out a law, rule, guide, and light for all mankind universally in both these, namely, the knowledge of God and ourselves, but this book only; and if any other, it may be, like the Alcoran,[7] did pretend in the least thereunto, it quickly discovered its own folly, and exposed itself to the contempt of all wise and considerate men. The only question is, How it has discharged itself in this design? For if it has completely and perfectly accomplished it, it is not only evident that it must be from God, but also that it is the greatest benefit and kindness that divine benignity and goodness ever granted unto mankind; for without it all men universally must necessarily wander in an endless maze of uncertainties, without ever attaining light, rest, or blessedness, here or hereafter. Wherefore,

First Design: To Reveal God to Us

(1) As it takes on itself to speak in the name and authority of God, and delivers nothing, commands nothing, but what becomes his infinite holiness, wisdom, and goodness; so it makes that declaration of him, in his nature, being, and subsistence, with the necessary properties and acts thereof, his will, with all his voluntary actings or works, wherein we may be or are concerned, so as that we may know him aright, and entertain true notions and apprehensions

---

7   I.e., Koran.

of him, according to the utmost capacity of our finite, limited understanding. Neither do we urge his authority in this case, but here and elsewhere resort unto the evidence of his reasonings, compared with the event or matter of fact. What horrible darkness, ignorance, and blindness was upon the whole world with respect unto the knowledge of God? What confusion and debasement of our nature ensued thereon, while God "suffered all nations to walk in their own ways, and winked at the times of their ignorance,"[8] the apostle declares at large (Rom. 1:18ff.). The sum is, that the only true God being become unknown to them, as the wisest of them acknowledged (Acts 17:23), and as our apostle proved against them, the devil, that murderer from the beginning, and enemy of mankind, had under various pretenses substituted himself in his room, and was become "the god of this world," as he is called (2 Cor. 4:4), and had appropriated all the religious devotion and worship of the generality of mankind unto himself; for "the things which the Gentiles sacrificed, they sacrificed unto devils, and not unto God," as our apostle affirms (1 Cor. 10:20), and as may easily be evinced; and I have abundantly manifested it elsewhere.¶[9]

It is acknowledged that some few speculative men among the heathen did seek after God in that horrid darkness wherewith they were encompassed, and labored to reduce their conceptions and notions of his being unto what reason could apprehend of infinite perfections, and what the works of creation and providence could suggest unto them; but as they never could come unto any certainty or consistency of notions in their own minds, proceeding but a little beyond conjecture, as is the manner of them who seek after anything in the dark, much less with one another, to propose anything unto the world for the use of mankind in these things by common consent; so they could none of them either ever free themselves from the grossest practical idolatry in worshiping the devil, the head of their apostasy from God, or in the least influence the minds of the generality of mankind with any due apprehensions of the divine nature. This is the subject and substance of the apostle's disputation against them (Rom. 1). In this state of things, what misery and confusion the world lived in for many ages, what an endless labyrinth of foolish, slavish superstitions and idolatries it had cast itself into, I have in another discourse particularly declared.[10] With respect hereunto

---

8   This quotation is a conflation of Acts 14:16 and 17:30.

9   In the margin: *De Natura Theologia.*—Owen. For English translation, see John Owen, *Biblical Theology: The History of Theology from Adam to Christ*, trans. Stephen P. Westcott (Grand Rapids, MI: Soli Deo Gloria, 2014).

10   In the margin: *Ubi supra de Origine & Progressu Idololatria.*—Owen. For English translation, see Owen, *Biblical Theology*.

the Scripture is well called by the apostle Peter, "a light shining in a dark place" (2 Pet. 1:19). It gives unto all men at once a perfect, clear, steady, uniform declaration of God, his being, subsistence, properties, authority, rule, and actings, which evidences itself unto the minds and consciences of all whom the god of this world has not absolutely blinded by the power of prejudices and lusts, confirming them in an enmity unto and hatred of God himself. There is, indeed, no more required to free mankind from this horrible darkness, and enormous conceptions about the nature of God and the worship of idols, but a sedate,[11] unprejudiced consideration of the revelation of these things in the books of the Scripture. We may say, therefore, to all the world, with our prophet, "When they say unto you, 'Seek unto them that have familiar spirits, and unto wizards that peep and mutter; should not a people seek unto their God? For the living to the dead? To the law and to the testimony? If they speak not according to this word, it is because there is no light in them'" (Isa. 8:19–20).¶

And this also plainly manifests the Scripture to be of a divine origin. For if this declaration of God, this revelation of himself and his will, is incomparably the greatest and most excellent benefit that our nature is capable of in this world, more needful for and more useful unto mankind than the sun in the firmament, as to the proper end of their lives and beings, and if none of the wisest men in the world, neither severally nor jointly, could attain unto themselves or make known unto others this knowledge of God, so that we may say with our apostle that "in the wisdom of God the world by wisdom knew not God" (1 Cor. 1:21), and whereas those who attempted any such things yet waxed vain in their imaginations and conjectures, so that no one person in the world dares own the regulation of his mind and understanding by their notions and conceptions absolutely, although they had all advantages of wisdom and the exercise of reason above those, at least the most of them, who wrote and published the books of the Scripture, it cannot, with any pretense of reason, be questioned whether they were given by inspiration from God, as they pretend and plead. There is that done in them which all the world could not do, and without the doing whereof all the world must have been eternally miserable, and who could do this but God? If anyone shall judge that that ignorance of God which was among the heathens of old, or is among the Indians[12] at this day, is not so miserable a matter as we make it, or that there is any way to free them from it but by

---

11 I.e., calm.
12 I.e., Native Americans.

an emanation of light from the Scripture, he dwells out of my present way, upon the confines of atheism, so that I shall not divert unto any converse with him. I shall only add, that whatever notions of truth concerning God and his essence there may be found in those philosophers who lived after the preaching of the gospel in the world, or are at this day to be found among the Mohammedans or other false worshipers in the world, above those of the more ancient pagans, they all derive from the fountain of the Scripture, and were thence by various means traduced.[13]

Second Design: To Direct Us to the Enjoyment of God

(2) The second end of this doctrine is to direct mankind in their proper course of living unto God, and attaining that rest and blessedness whereof they are capable, and which they cannot but desire. These things are necessary to our nature, so that without them it were better not to be; for it is better to have no being in the world, than, while we have it, always to wander, and never to act toward its proper end, seeing all that is really good unto us consists in our tendency thereunto and our attainment of it. Now, as these things were never stated in the minds of the community of mankind, but that they lived in perpetual confusion; so, the inquiries of the philosophers about the chief end of man, the nature of felicity or blessedness, the way of attaining it, are nothing but so many uncertain and fierce digladiations,[14] wherein not any one truth is asserted, nor any one duty prescribed, that is not spoiled and vitiated[15] by its circumstances and ends. Besides, they never rose up so much as to a surmise of or about the most important matters of religion, without which it is demonstrable by reason that it is impossible we should ever attain the end for which we were made, or the blessedness whereof we are capable. No account could they ever give of our apostasy from God, of the depravation of our nature, of the cause, or necessary cure of it. In this lost and wandering condition of mankind, the Scripture presents itself as a light, rule, and guide unto all, to direct them in their whole course unto their end, and to bring them unto the enjoyment of God; and this it does with such clearness and evidence as to dispel all the darkness and put an end unto all the confusion of the minds of men, as the sun with rising does the shades of the night, unless they willfully shut their eyes against it, loving darkness rather than light, because their deeds are evil.¶

13 I.e., criticized; maligned.
14 I.e., fights with swords or hand to hand.
15 I.e., impaired.

For all the confusion of the minds of men, to extricate themselves from whence they found out and immixed[16] themselves in endless questions to no purpose, arose from their ignorance of what we were originally, of what we now are, and how we came so to be, by what way or means we may be delivered or relieved, what are the duties of life, or what is required of us in order to our living to God as our chiefest end, and wherein the blessedness of our nature does consist. All the world was never able to give an answer tolerably satisfactory unto any one of these inquiries, and yet, unless they are all infallibly determined, we are not capable of the least rest or happiness above the beasts that perish. But now all these things are so clearly declared and stated in the Scripture that it comes with an evidence like a light from heaven on the minds and consciences of unprejudiced persons. What was the condition of our nature in its first creation and constitution, with the blessedness and advantage of that condition; how we fell from it; and what was the cause, what is the nature, and what the consequences and effects of our present depravation and apostasy from God; how help and relief is provided for us herein by infinite wisdom, grace, and bounty; what that help is, how we may be interested in it, and made partakers of it; what is that system of duties, or course of obedience unto God, which is required of us, and wherein our eternal felicity does consist—are all of them so plainly and clearly revealed in the Scripture, as in general to leave mankind no ground for doubt, inquiry, or conjecture. Set aside inveterate[17] prejudices from tradition, education, false notions, into the mold whereof the mind is cast, the love of sin, and the conduct of lust, which things have an inconceivable power over the minds, souls, and affections of men, and the light of the Scripture in these things is like that of the sun at noonday, which shuts up the way unto all further inquiry, and efficaciously necessitates unto an acquiescency in it. And, in particular, in that direction which it gives unto the lives of men, in order unto that obedience which they owe to God, and that reward which they expect from him, there is no instance conceivable of anything conducing thereunto, which is not prescribed therein, nor of anything which is contrary unto it that falls not under its prohibition. Those, therefore, whose desire or interest it is that the bounds and differences of good and evil should be unfixed and confounded, who are afraid to know what they were, what they are, or what they shall come unto, who care to know neither God nor themselves, their duty nor their reward, may despise

16 I.e., mixed thoroughly.
17 I.e., well-established.

this book, and deny its divine origin. Others will retain a sacred veneration of it, as of the offspring of God.

THE TESTIMONY OF THE CHURCH

4. The testimony of the church may in like manner be pleaded unto the same purpose. And I shall also insist upon it, partly to manifest wherein its true nature and efficacy do consist, and partly to evince the vanity of the old pretense, that even we also, who are departed from the Church of Rome, do receive the Scripture upon the authority thereof; whence it is further pretended that, on the same ground and reason, we ought to receive whatever else it proposes unto us.

(1) The church is said to be the pillar and ground of truth (1 Tim. 3:15), which is the only text pleaded with any sobriety to give countenance unto the assertion of the authority of the Scripture with respect unto us to depend on the authority of the church. But the weakness of a plea to that purpose from hence has been so fully manifested by many already that it needs no more to be insisted on. In short, it cannot be so the ground and pillar of truth that the truth should be, as it were, built and rest upon it as its foundation; for this is directly contrary to the same apostle, who teaches us that the church itself is "built upon the foundation of the prophets and apostles, Jesus Christ himself being the chief corner-stone" (Eph. 2:20). The church cannot be the ground of truth, and truth the ground of the church, in the same sense or kind. Wherefore, the church is the ground and pillar of truth, in that it holds up and declares the Scriptures and the things contained therein so to be.

(2) In receiving anything from a church, we may consider the authority of it, or its ministry. By the authority of the church in this matter, we intend no more but the weight and importance that is in its testimony, as testimonies do vary according to the worth, gravity, honesty, honor, and reputation of them by whom they are given. For to suppose an authority, properly so called, in any church, or all the churches of the world, whereon our reception of the Scripture should depend, as that which gives it authority toward us, and a sufficient warranty to our faith, is a nice imagination. For the authority and truth of God stand not in need nor are capable of any such attestation from men. All they will admit of from the children of men is, that they do humbly submit unto them, and testify their so doing with the reasons of it. The ministry of the church in this matter is that duty of the church whereby it proposes and declares the Scripture to be the word of God, and that as it has occasion to all the world. And this ministry also may be considered ei-

ther formally, as it is appointed of God unto this end, and blessed by him; or materially only, as the thing is done, though the grounds whereon it is done and the manner of doing it be not divinely approved.

We wholly deny that we receive the Scripture, or ever did, on the authority of the Church of Rome, in any sense whatever, for the reasons that shall be mentioned immediately. But it may be granted that, together with the ministry of other churches in the world, and many other providential means of their preservation and successive communication, we did *de facto*[18] receive the Scriptures by the ministry of the Church of Rome also, seeing they also were in the possession of them. But this ministry we allow only in the latter sense, as an actual means in subserviency unto God's providence, without respect unto any special institution.

And for the authority of the church in this case, in that sense wherein it is allowed, namely, as denoting the weight and importance of a testimony, which, being strengthened by all sorts of circumstances, may be said to have great authority in it, we must be careful unto whom or what church we grant or allow it. For let men assume what names or titles to themselves they please, yet if the generality of them be corrupt or flagitious in their lives, and have great secular advantages, which they highly prize and studiously improve, from what they suppose and profess the Scripture to supply them with, be they called church or what you please, their testimony therein is of very little value, for all men may see that they have an earthly, worldly interest of their own therein. And it will be said that if such persons did know the whole Bible to be a fable, as one pope expressed himself to that purpose, they would not forgo the profession of it, unless they could more advantage themselves in the world another way. Wherefore, whereas it is manifest unto all, that those who have the conduct of the Roman church have made and do make to themselves great earthly, temporal advantages, in honor, power, wealth, and reputation in the world, by their profession of the Scripture, their testimony may rationally be supposed to be so far influenced by self-interest as to be of little validity.

The testimony, therefore, which I intend is that of multitudes of persons of unspotted reputation on all other accounts in the world, free from all possibility of impeachment, as unto any designed evil or conspiracy among themselves, with respect unto any corrupt end, and who, having not the least secular advantage by what they testified unto, were absolutely secured against all exceptions which either common reason or common usage among

18 Lat. "in fact" or "in reality."

mankind can put in unto any witness whatever. And, to evidence the force that is in this consideration, I shall briefly represent, first, who they were that gave and do give this testimony, in some special instances; second, what they gave this testimony unto; third, how, or by what means, they did so.

[1] And, in the first place, the testimony of those by whom the several books of the Scripture were written is to be considered. They all of them, severally and jointly, witnessed that what they wrote was received by inspiration from God. This is pleaded by the apostle Peter in the name of them all:

> For we have not followed cunningly-devised fables, when we made known unto you the power and coming of our Lord Jesus Christ, but were eye-witnesses of his majesty. For he received from God the Father honour and glory, when there came such a voice to him from the excellent glory, "This is my beloved Son, in whom I am well pleased." And this voice which came from heaven we heard, when we were with him in the holy mount. We have also a more sure word of prophecy, whereunto ye do well that ye take heed, as unto a light that shineth in a dark place, until the day dawn, and the day-star arise in your hearts. Knowing this first, that no prophecy of the Scripture is of any private interpretation. For the prophecy came not in old time by the will of man: but holy men of God spake as they were moved by the Holy Ghost. (2 Pet. 1:16–21)

This is the concurrent testimony of the writers both of the Old Testament and the New, namely, that as they had certain knowledge of the things they wrote, so their writing was by inspiration from God. So, in particular, John bears witness unto his Revelation: "These are the true and faithful sayings of God" (Rev. 19:9; 22:6). And what weight is to be laid hereon is declared, "This is the disciple which testifieth of these things, and wrote these things: and we know that his testimony is true" (John 21:24). He testified to the truth of what he wrote; but how was it known to the church there intended ("we know that his testimony is true"), that so it was indeed? He was not absolutely αὐτόπιστος, or one that was to be believed in merely on his own account; yet here it is spoken in the name of the church with the highest assurance, and "we know that his testimony is true." I answer, this assurance of theirs did not arise merely from his moral or natural endowments or holy counsels, but from the evidence they had of his divine inspiration, whereof we shall treat afterward.

The things pleaded to give force unto this testimony in particular are all that such a testimony is capable of, and so many as would require a large discourse by itself to propose, discuss, and confirm them. But supposing the testimony they gave, I shall, in compliance with my own design, reduce the evidences of its truth unto these two considerations: first, of their persons; and, secondly, of the manner of their writing.

{1} As to their persons, they were absolutely removed from all possible suspicion of deceiving or being deceived. The wit of all the atheistical spirits in the world is not able to fix on any one thing that would be a tolerable ground of any such suspicion concerning the integrity of witnesses, could such a testimony be given in any other case. And surmises[19] in things of this nature, which have no pleadable ground for them, are to be looked on as diabolical suggestions or atheistical dreams, or at best the false imaginations of weak and distempered minds. The nature and design of their work; their unconcernment with all secular interests; their unacquaintance with one another; the times and places wherein the things reported by them were done and acted; the facility of convincing them of falsehood if what they wrote in matter of fact, which is the fountain of what else they taught, were not true; the evident certainty that this would have been done, arising from the known desire, ability, will, and interest of their adversaries so to do, had it been possible to be effected, seeing this would have secured them the victory in the conflicts wherein they were violently engaged, and have put an immediate issue unto all that difference and uproar that was in the world about their doctrine; their harmony among themselves, without conspiracy or antecedent agreement; the miseries which they underwent, most of them without hope of relief or recompense in this world, upon the sole account of the doctrine taught by themselves; with all other circumstances innumerable, that are pleadable to evince the sincerity and integrity of any witnesses whatever—do all concur to prove that they did not follow cunningly devised fables in what they declared concerning the mind and will of God as immediately from himself. To confront this evidence with bare surmises, incapable of any rational countenance or confirmation, is only to manifest what brutish impudence, infidelity, and atheism are forced to retreat unto for shelter.

{2} Their style or manner of writing deserves a peculiar consideration. For there are impressed on it all those characters of a divine origin that can be communicated unto such an outward adjunct of divine revelation. Notwithstanding the distance of the ages and seasons wherein they lived, the difference of the languages wherein they wrote, with the great variety of their parts, abilities, education, and other circumstances, yet there is upon the

---

19 I.e., things surmised or speculated.

whole and all the parts of their writing such gravity, majesty, and authority, mixed with plainness of speech, and absolute freedom from all appearance of affectation[20] of esteem or applause, or anything else that derives from human frailty, as must excite an admiration in all that seriously consider them. But I have at large elsewhere insisted on this consideration. And have also, in the same place, showed that there is no other writing extant in the world that ever pretended unto a divine origin, as the apocryphal books under the Old Testament, and some fragments of spurious pieces pretended to be written in the days of the apostles, but they are, not only from their matter, but from the manner of their writing, and the plain footsteps of human artifice and weakness therein, sufficient for their own conviction, and do openly discover their own vain pretensions.[21] So must every thing necessarily do, which being merely human pretends unto an immediate derivation from God. When men have done all they can, these things will have as evident a difference between them as there is between wheat and chaff, between real and painted fire (Jer. 23:28–29).

Unto the testimony of the divine writers themselves, we must add that of those who in all ages have believed in Christ through their word, which is the description which the Lord Jesus Christ gives of his church (John 17:20). This is the church, that is, those who wrote the Scripture, and those who believe in Christ through their word through all ages, which bears witness to the divine origin of the Scripture, and it may be added that we know this witness is true. With these I had rather venture my faith and eternal condition than with any society, any real or pretended church whatever. And among these there is a special consideration to be had of those innumerable multitudes who, in the primitive times, witnessed this confession all the world over. For they had many advantages above us to know the certainty of sundry matters of fact which the verity[22] of our religion depends upon. And we are directed unto a special regard of their testimony, which is signalized by Christ himself. In the great judgment that is to be passed on the world, the first appearance is of the souls of them that were beheaded for "the witness of Jesus, and for the Word of God" (Rev. 20:4). And there is at present a special regard unto them in heaven upon the account of their witness and testimony (Rev. 6:9–11). These were they who, with the loss of their lives by the sword, and other ways of violence, gave testimony unto the truth of the word of God. And to reduce these things unto a natural consideration, who

---

20 I.e., design to impress; artificial.

21 See *Of the Divine Original, Authority, Self-Evidencing Light, and Power of the Scriptures*, chap. 5.

22 I.e., true principle of belief.

can have the least occasion to suspect all those persons of folly, weakness, credulity, wickedness, or conspiracy among themselves, which such a diffuse multitude was absolutely incapable of? Neither can any man undervalue their testimony but he must comply with their adversaries against them, who were known generally to be of the worst of men. And who is there that believes there is a God and an eternal future state that had not rather have his soul with Paul than Nero, with the holy martyrs than their bestial persecutors? Wherefore, this suffrage and testimony, begun from the first writing of the Scripture, and carried on by the best of men in all ages, and made conspicuously glorious in the primitive times of Christianity, must needs be with all wise men unavoidably cogent, at least unto a due and sedate consideration of what they bear witness unto, and sufficient to scatter all such prejudices as atheism or profaneness may raise or suggest.

[2] What it was they gave testimony unto is duly to be considered. And this was not only that the book of the Scripture was good, holy, and true, in all the contents of it, but that the whole and every part of it was given by divine inspiration, as their faith in this matter is expressed (2 Pet. 1:20–21). On this account, and no other, did they themselves receive the Scripture, as also believe and yield obedience unto the things contained in it. Neither would they admit that their testimony was received if the whole world would be content to allow of or obey the Scripture on any other or lower terms. Nor will God himself allow of an assent unto the Scripture under any other conception, but as the word which is immediately spoken by himself. Hence, they who refuse to give credit thereunto are said to "belie the Lord, and say, 'It is not he'" (Jer. 5:12); yea, to "make God a liar" (1 John 5:10). If all mankind should agree together to receive and make use of this book, as that which taught nothing but what is good, useful, and profitable to human society; as that which is a complete directory unto men in all that they need to believe or do toward God; the best means under heaven to bring them to settlement, satisfaction, and assurance of the knowledge of God and themselves; as the safest guide to eternal blessedness; and therefore must needs be written and composed by persons wise, holy, and honest above all comparison, and such as had such knowledge of God and his will as is necessary unto such an undertaking—yet all this answers not the testimony given by the church of believers in all ages unto the Scriptures. It was not lawful for them, it is not for us, so to compound this matter with the world. That the whole Scripture was given by inspiration from God, that it was his word, his true and faithful sayings, was that which, in the first place, they gave testimony unto, and we also are obliged so to do. They never pretended unto any other assurance of the things

they professed, nor any other reason of their faith and obedience, but that the Scripture, wherein all these things are contained, was given immediately from God, or was his word. And, therefore, they were always esteemed no less traitors to Christianity who gave up their Bibles to persecutors than those who denied Jesus Christ.

[3] The manner wherein this testimony was given adds to the importance of it.¶

{1} Many of them, especially in some seasons, gave it in, and with sundry miraculous operations. This our apostle pleads as a corroboration of the witness given by the first preachers of the gospel unto the truths of it (Heb. 2:4), as the same was done by all the apostles together (Acts 5:32). It must be granted that these miracles were not wrought immediately to confirm this single truth, that the Scripture was given by inspiration of God, but that the end of miracles is to be an immediate witness from heaven, or God's attestation to their persons and ministry by whom they were wrought. His presence with them and approbation of their doctrine were publicly declared by them. But the miracles wrought by the Lord Christ and his apostles, whereby God gave immediate testimony unto the divine mission of their persons and infallible truth of their doctrine, might either not have been written, as most of them were not, or they might have been written and their doctrine recorded in books not given by inspiration from God. Besides, as to the miracles wrought by Christ himself, and most of those of the apostles, they were wrought among them by whom the books of the Old Testament were acknowledged as the oracles of God, and before the writing of those of the New, so that they could not be wrought in the immediate confirmation of the one or the other. Neither have we any infallible testimony concerning these miracles but the Scripture itself, wherein they are recorded, whence it is necessary that we should believe the Scripture to be infallibly true, before we can believe on grounds infallible the miracles therein recorded to be so. Wherefore, I grant that the whole force of this consideration lies in this alone, that those who gave testimony to the Scripture to be the word of God had an attestation given unto their ministry by these miraculous operations, concerning which we have good collateral security also.

{2} Many of them confirmed their testimony with their sufferings, being not only witnesses, but martyrs, in the peculiar church notion of that word, grounded on the Scripture (Acts 22:20; Rev. 2:13; 17:6). So far were they from any worldly advantage by the profession they made and the testimony they gave, as that in the confirmation of them they willingly and cheerfully underwent whatever is evil, dreadful, or destructive to human nature, in all its temporary concerns. It is, therefore, unquestionable that they had the highest assurance of the truth in these things which the mind of man is capable of. The management of this argument is the principal design of the apostle in the whole eleventh chapter of the epistle to the Hebrews. For, having declared the nature of faith in general, namely, that it is the "substance of things hoped for, and the evidence of things not seen" (Heb. 11:1)—that is, such an assent unto and confidence of invisible things, things capable of no demonstration from sense or reason, as respects divine revelation only, whereinto alone it is resolved—for our encouragement thereunto and establishment therein, he produces a long catalogue of those who died, suffered, and obtained great things thereby. That which he principally insists upon is the hardships, miseries, cruelties, tortures, and several sorts of deaths, which they underwent, especially from verse 35 to the end. These he calls a "cloud of witnesses," wherewith we are compassed about (Heb. 12:1), giving testimony unto what we do believe, that is, divine revelation, and in a special manner to the promises therein contained, unto our encouragement in the same duty, as he there declares. And certainly, what was thus testified unto by so many great, wise, and holy persons, and that in such a way and manner, has as great an outward evidence of its truth as anything of that nature is capable of in this world.

{3} They gave not their testimony casually, or on some extraordinary occasion only, or by some one solemn act, or in some one certain way, as other testimonies are given, nor can be given otherwise; but they gave their testimony in this cause in their whole course, in all that they thought, spoke, or did in the world, and in the whole disposal of their ways, lives, and actions, as every true believer continues to do at this day. For a man, when he is occasionally called out, to give a verbal testimony unto the divine origin of the Scripture, ordering in the meantime the whole course of his conversation, his hopes, designs, aims, and ends, without any eminent respect or regard unto it, his testimony is of no value, nor can have any influence on the minds of sober and considerate men. But when men do manifest and evince that the declaration of the mind of God in the Scripture has a sovereign divine authority over their souls and consciences, absolutely and in all things, then is their witness cogent and efficacious. There is to me a thousand times more force and weight in the testimony to this purpose of some holy persons, who universally and in all things, with respect unto this world and their future eternal condition, in all their thoughts, words, actions, and ways, do really experiment in themselves, and express to others, the power and authority of this word of God in their souls and consciences, living, doing, suffering, and dying in peace, assurance of mind, and consolation thereon, than in the verbal declaration of the most splendid, numerous church in the world, who evidence not such an inward sense of its power and efficacy. There is, therefore, that force in the real testimony which has been given in all ages, by all this sort of persons, not one excepted, unto the divine authority of the Scripture, that it is highly arrogant for anyone to question the truth of it without evident convictions of its imposture, which no person of any tolerable sobriety did ever yet pretend unto.

THE EFFECT OF SCRIPTURE

5. I shall add, in the last place, the consideration of that success which the doctrine derived solely from the Scripture, and resolved thereinto, has had in the world upon the minds and lives of men, especially upon the first preaching of the gospel. And two things offer themselves hereon immediately unto our consideration: one, the persons by whom this doctrine was successfully carried on in the world, and, two, the way and manner of the propagation of it; both which the Scripture takes notice of in particular, as evidences of that divine power which the word was really accompanied with.

(1) For the persons unto whom this work was committed, I mean the apostles and first evangelists, were, as to their outward condition in the world, poor, low, and every way despised; and as unto the endowments of their minds, destitute of all those abilities and advantages which might give them either reputation or probability of success in such an undertaking. This the Jews marked in them with contempt (Acts 4:13). And the Gentiles also generally despised them on the same account. As they afforded our apostle no better title than that of a "babbler" (Acts 17:18), so for a long time they kept up the public vogue in the world that Christianity was the religion of idiots and men illiterate. But God had another design in this order of things, which our apostle declares upon an admission of the inconsiderable meanness of them unto whom the dispensation of the gospel was committed: "We have this treasure in earthen vessels, that the excellency of the power may be of God, and not of us" (2 Cor. 4:7). The reason why God would make use of such instruments only in so great a work was that through their meanness his own glorious power might be more conspicuous. There is nothing more common among men, or more natural unto them, than to admire the excellencies of those of their own race and kind, and a willingness to have all evidences of a divine, supernatural power clouded and hidden from them. If, therefore, there had been such persons employed as instruments in this work, whose powers, abilities, qualifications, and endowment, might have been probably pretended as sufficient and the immediate causes of such

an effect, there would have been no observation of the divine power or glory of God. But he who is not able to discern them in the bringing about of so mighty a work by means so disproportionate thereunto, is under the power of the unrelievable prejudices intimated by our apostle in this case (2 Cor. 4:3–7).

(2) The means which were to be used unto this end, namely, the subduing of the world unto the faith and obedience of the gospel, so erecting the spiritual kingdom of Christ in the minds of men who before were under the power and dominion of his adversary, must either be force and arms, or eloquence, in plausible, persuasive reasonings. And mighty works have been wrought by the one and the other of them. By the former have empires been set up and established in the world, and the superstition of Mohammed imposed on many nations. And the latter also has had great effects on the minds of many. Wherefore, it might have been expected that those who had engaged themselves in so great a design and work as that mentioned should betake themselves unto the one or other of these means and ways, for the wit of man cannot contrive any way unto such an end but what may be reduced unto one of these two, seeing neither upon the principles of nature nor on the rules of human wisdom or policy can any other be imagined. But even both these ways were abandoned by them, and they declared against the use of either of them. For as outward force, power, and authority, they had none, the use of all carnal weapons being utterly inconsistent with this work and design, so the other way, of persuasive orations, of enticing words, of alluring arts and eloquence, with the like effects of human wisdom and skill, were all of them studiously declined by them in this work, as things extremely prejudicial to the success thereof (1 Cor. 2:4–5). But this alone they betook themselves unto: they went up and down, preaching to Jews and Gentiles "that Jesus Christ died for our sins, and rose again, according to the Scriptures" (1 Cor. 15:3–4). And this they did by virtue of those spiritual gifts which were the hidden powers of the world to come, whose nature, virtue, and power, others were utterly unacquainted with. This preaching of theirs, this preaching of the cross, both for the subject, matter, and manner of it, without art, eloquence, or oratory, was looked on as a marvelous, foolish thing, a sweaty kind of babbling, by all those who had got any reputation of learning or cunning among men. This our apostle at large discourses (1 Cor. 1). In this state of things, everything was under as many improbabilities of success, unto all rational conjectures, as can be conceived.¶

Besides, together with the doctrine of the gospel that they preached, which was new and uncouth unto the world, they taught observances of religious worship in meetings, assemblies, or conventicles to that end, which all the laws in the world did prohibit (Acts 16:21; 18:13). Hereupon, no sooner did the rulers and governors of the world begin to take notice of them and what they did, but they judged that it all tended to sedition, and that commotions would ensue thereon. These things enraged the generality of mankind against them and their converts, who therefore made havoc of them with incredible fury. And yet, notwithstanding all these disadvantages, and against all these oppositions, their doctrine prevailed to subdue the world to the obedience thereof. And there may be added unto all these things one or two considerations from the state of things at that time in the world, which signal the quality of this work, and manifest it to have been of God. As

[1] That in the New Testament, the writers of it do constantly distribute all those with whom they had to do in this world into Jews and Greeks, which we render Gentiles, the other nations of the world coming under that denomination because of their preeminence on various accounts. Now, the Jews at that time were *in solidum*,[23] possessed of all the true religion that was in the world, and this they boasted of as their privilege, bearing up themselves with the thought and reputation of it everywhere and on all occasions, it being at that time their great business to gain proselytes unto it, whereon also their honor and advantage did depend. The Greeks, on the other side, were in as full a possession of arts, sciences, literature, and all that which the world calls "wisdom," as the Jews were of religion; and they had also a religion, received by a long tradition of their fathers, from time immemorial, which they had variously cultivated and dressed with mysteries and ceremonies, unto their own complete satisfaction. Besides, the Romans, who were the ruling part of the Gentiles, did ascribe all their prosperity and the whole raising of their stupendous empire to their gods and the religious worship they gave unto them, so that it was a fundamental maxim in their policy and rule that they should prosper or decay according as they observed or were negligent in the religion they received.¶

As, indeed, not only those who owned the true God and his providence, but, before idolatry and superstition had given place unto atheism, all people did solemnly impute all their achievements and successes unto their gods, as the prophet speaks of the Chaldeans (Hab. 1:11). And he who first undertook to record the exploits of the nations of the world does constantly assign all their good and evil unto their gods, as they were pleased or provoked. The Romans, especially, boasted that their religion was the cause of their prosperity: "in piety, in devotion to religion, and in that special wisdom which consists

---

23 Lat. "in total."

in the recognition of the truth that the world is swayed and directed by divine disposal, we have excelled every race and every nation,"[24] says their great oracle. And Dionysius of Halicarnassus, a great and wise historian, giving an account of the religion of the Romans and the ceremonies of their worship, affirms that he does it unto this end: "that those who have been ignorant of the Roman piety should cease to wonder at their prosperity and successes in all their wars, seeing, by reason of their religion, they had the gods always propitious and succourable unto them."[25] The consideration hereof made them so obstinate in their adherence unto their present religion, that when, after many ages and hundreds of years, some books of Numa, their second king, and principal establisher of their commonwealth, were occasionally found, instead of paying them any respect, they ordered them to be burnt, because one who had perused them took his oath that they were contrary to their present worship and devotion. And this was that which upon the declension of their empire, after the prevalency of the Christian religion, those who were obstinate in their paganism reflected severely upon the Christians; the relinquishment of their old religion they fiercely avowed to be the cause of all their calamities. In answer unto which calumny,[26] principally, Augustine wrote his excellent discourse *De civitate Dei.*[27]

In this state of things, the preachers of the gospel come among them, and not only bring a new doctrine, under all the disadvantages before mentioned, and, moreover, that he who was the head of it was newly crucified by the present powers of the earth for a malefactor,[28] but also such a doctrine as was

24 In the text: *Pietate et religione atque hâc una sapientia, quòd deorum immortalium numine omnia regi gubernarique perspeximus, omnes gentes nationesque superamus* (Orat. de Har. Resp., 9).—Owen. For Latin text and English translation, see Cicero, *Pro Archia. Post reditum in senatu. Post reditum ad quirites. De domo sua. De haruspicum responsis. Pro Plancio,* trans. N. H. Watts, Loeb Classical Library 158 (Cambridge, MA: Harvard University Press, 1923), 340–41. This quotation is drawn from Cicero's *De haruspicum responsis* (56 BC), occasioned by unrest caused from ominous apparitions in central Italy and their interpretation by haruspicy, a form of divination performed by Etruscan priests.

25 In the text: (Antiq. Rom. lib. 2).—Owen. For text and English translation, see Dionysius of Halicarnassus, *Roman Antiquities,* vol. 1, *Books 1–2,* trans. Earnest Cary, Loeb Classical Library 319 (Cambridge, MA: Harvard University Press, 1937), 522–23. Dionysius of Halicarnassus was a first-century BC Greek historian and teacher of rhetoric. He wrote his history of Rome, *Antiquitates Romanae,* from which this quotation is drawn, in order to reconcile Greek civilization to the reality of the Roman empire.

26 I.e., slander.

27 For a modern translation of the referenced discourse, see Augustine, *The City of God against the Pagans,* ed. and trans. R. W. Dyson, Cambridge Texts in the History of Political Thought (Cambridge: Cambridge University Press, 1998).

28 I.e., lawbreaker; felon.

expressly to take away the religion from the Jews, and the wisdom from the Greeks, and the principal maxim of polity from the Romans, whereon they thought they had raised their empire. It was easy to declare how all those sects were engaged in worldly interest, honor, reputation, and principles of safety, to oppose, decry, condemn, and reject this new doctrine. And if a company of sorry craftsmen were able to fill a whole city with tumult and uproar against the gospel, as they did when they apprehended it would bring in a decay of their trade (Acts 19), what can we think was done in all the world by all those who were engaged and enraged by higher provocations? It was as death to the Jews to part with their religion, both on the account of the conviction they had of its truth and the honor they esteemed to accrue to themselves thereby. And for the Greeks to have that wisdom, which they and their forefathers had been laboring in for so many generations, now to be all rejected as an impertinent foolery by the sorry preachments[29] of a few illiterate persons, it raised them unto the highest indignation. And the Romans were wise enough to secure the fundamental maxim of their state. Wherefore the world seemed very sufficiently fortified against the admission of this new and strange doctrine, on the terms whereon it was proposed. There can be no danger, sure, that ever it should obtain any considerable progress. But we know that things fell out quite otherwise; religion, wisdom, and power, with honor, profit, interest, reputation, were all forced to give way to its power and efficacy.

[2] The world was at that time in the highest enjoyment of peace, prosperity, and plenty that ever it attained from the entrance of sin; and it is known how from all these things are usually made provision for the flesh to fulfill the lusts thereof. Whatever the pride, ambition, covetousness, sensuality of any persons could carry them forth to lust after, the world was full of satisfactions for. And most men lived, as in the eager pursuit of their lusts, so in a full supply of what they did require. In this condition, the gospel is preached unto them, requiring at once, and that indispensably, a renunciation of all those worldly lusts which before had been the salt of their lives. If men designed any compliance with it or interest in it, their pride, ambition, luxury, covetousness, sensuality, malice, revenge, must all be mortified and rooted up. Had it only been a new doctrine and religion, declaring that knowledge and worship of God which they had never heard of before, they could not but be very wary in giving it entertainment; but when withal it required, at the first instant, that for its sake they should "pull out their right eyes, and cut off their right hands,"

---

29   I.e., dogmatic instructions and exhortations.

to part with all that was dear and useful unto them, and which had such a prevalent interest in their minds and affections as corrupt lusts are known to have, this could not but invincibly fortify them against its admittance. But yet this also was forced to give place, and all the fortifications of Satan therein were, by the power of the word, cast to the ground, as our apostle expresses it (2 Cor. 10:4–5), where he gives an account of that warfare whereby the world was subdued to Christ by the gospel. Now, a man that has a mind to make himself an instance of conceited folly and pride, may talk as though there was in all this no evidence of divine power giving testimony to the Scripture and the doctrine contained in it, but the characters of it are so legible unto every modest and sedate prospect that they leave no room for doubt or hesitation.

But the force of the whole argument is liable unto one exception of no small moment, which must, therefore, necessarily be taken notice of and removed. For whereas we plead the power, efficacy, and prevalency of the gospel in former days, as a demonstration of its divine origin, it will be inquired whence it is that it is not still accompanied with the same power, nor does produce the same effects? For we see the profession of it is now confined to narrow limits in comparison of what it formerly extended itself unto, neither do we find that it gets ground anywhere in the world, but is rather more and more straitened every day. Wherefore, either the first prevalency that is asserted unto it, and argued as an evidence of its divinity, did indeed proceed from some other accidental causes, in an efficacious though unseen concurrence, and was not by an emanation of power from itself, or the gospel is not at present what it was formerly, seeing it has not the same effect upon or power over the minds of men as that had of old. We may, therefore, suspend the pleading of this argument from what was done by the gospel formerly, lest it reflect disadvantage upon what we profess at present.

Answer 1. Whatever different events may fall out in different seasons, yet the gospel is the same as ever it was from the beginning. There is not another book, containing another doctrine, crept into the world instead of that once delivered unto the saints. And whatever various apprehensions men may have, through their weakness or prejudices, concerning the things taught therein, yet are they in themselves absolutely the same that ever they were, and that without the loss or change of a material word or syllable in the manner of their delivery. This I have proved elsewhere,[30] and it is a thing capable of the most evident demonstration. Wherefore, whatever entertainment this gospel

---

30 Owen is referring to his *Of the Divine Original, Authority, Self-Evidencing Light, and Power of the Scriptures.*

meets with at present in the world, its former prevalency may be pleaded in justification of its divine origin.

Answer 2. The cause of this event lies principally in the sovereign will and pleasure of God. For although the Scripture be his word, and he has testified it so to be by his power, put forth and exerted in dispensations of it unto men, yet is not that divine power included or shut up in the letter of it, so that it must have the same effect wherever it comes. We plead not that there is absolutely in itself, its doctrine, the preaching or preachers thereof, such a power, as it were naturally and physically, to produce the effects mentioned. But it is an instrument in the hand of God unto that work which is his own, and he puts forth his power in it and by it as it seems good unto him. And if he does at any time so put forth his divine power in the administration of it, or in the use of this instrument, as that the great worth and excellency of it shall manifest itself to be from him, he gives a sufficient attestation of it. Wherefore, the times and seasons of the prevalency of the gospel in the world are in the hand and at the sovereign disposal of God. And as he is not obliged ("for who hath known the mind of the Lord, or who hath been his counsellor?")[31] to accompany it with the same power at all times and seasons, so the evidence of his own power going along with it at any time, while under an open claim of a divine origin, is an uncontrollable approbation of it. Thus, at the first preaching of the word, to fulfill the promises made unto the fathers from the foundation of the world, to glorify his Son Jesus Christ, and the gospel itself which he had revealed, he put forth that effectual divine power in its administration, whereby the world was subdued unto the obedience of it. And the time will come when he will revive the same work of power and grace to retrieve the world into a subjection to Jesus Christ. And although he does not in these latter ages cause it to run and prosper among the nations of the world who have not as yet received it as he did formerly, yet, considering the state of things at present among the generality of mankind, the preservation of it in that small remnant by whom it is obeyed in sincerity is a no less glorious evidence of his presence with it and care over it than was its eminent propagation in days of old.

Answer 3. The righteousness of God is in like manner to be considered in these things: for whereas he had granted the inestimable privilege of his word unto many nations, they, through their horrible ingratitude and wickedness, detained the truth in unrighteousness, so that the continuance of the gospel among them was no way to the glory of God, no, nor yet unto their

---

31 Rom. 11:34.

own advantage. For neither nations nor persons will ever be advantaged by an outward profession of the gospel while they live in a contradiction and disobedience to its precepts, yea, nothing can be more pernicious to the souls of men. This impiety God is at this day revenging on the nations of the world, having utterly cast off many of them from the knowledge of the truth, and given up others unto "strong delusions, to believe lies,"[32] though they retain the Scriptures and outward profession of Christianity. How far he may proceed in the same way of righteous vengeance toward other nations also we know not, but ought to tremble in the consideration of it. When God first granted the gospel unto the world, although the generality of mankind had greatly sinned against the light of nature, and had rejected all those supernatural revelations that at any time had been made unto them, yet had they not sinned against the gospel itself nor the grace thereof. It pleased God, therefore, to wink at and pass over that time of their ignorance, so as that his justice should not be provoked by any of their former sins to withhold the efficacy of his divine power in the administration of the gospel from them, whereby he "called them to repentance."[33] But now, after that the gospel has been sufficiently tendered unto all nations, and has, either as unto its profession or as unto its power, with the obedience that it requires, been rejected by the most of them, things are quite otherwise stated. It is from the "righteous judgment of God,"[34] revenging the sins of the world against the gospel itself, that so many nations are deprived of it, and so many left obstinate in its refusal. Wherefore, the present state of things does no way weaken or prejudice the evidence given unto the Scripture by that mighty power of God, which accompanied the administration of it in the world. For what has since fallen out, there are secret reasons of sovereign wisdom, and open causes in divine justice, whereunto it is to be assigned.

These things I have briefly called over, and not as though they were all of this kind that may be pleaded, but only to give some instances of those external arguments whereby the divine authority of the Scripture may be confirmed.

CONCLUSION: COMPELLING EVIDENCE FOR THE RATIONAL AND UNPREJUDICED

Now, these arguments are such as are able of themselves to beget in the minds of men sober, humble, intelligent, and unprejudiced, a firm opinion,

32 2 Thess. 2:11.
33 Acts 17:30.
34 Rom. 2:5.

judgment, and persuasion that the Scripture does proceed from God. Where persons are prepossessed with invincible prejudices, contracted by a course of education, wherein they have imbibed principles opposite and contrary thereunto, and have increased and fortified them by some fixed and hereditary enmity against all those whom they know to own the divinity of the Scripture, as it is with Mohammedans and some of the Indians, these arguments, it may be, will not prevail immediately to work or effect their assent. It is so with respect unto them also who, out of love unto and delight in those ways of vice, sin, and wickedness, which are absolutely and severely condemned in the Scripture, without the least hope of a dispensation unto them that continue under the power of them, will not take these arguments into due consideration. Such persons may talk and discourse of them, but they never weigh them seriously, according as the importance of the cause does require. For if men will examine them as they ought, it must be with a sedate judgment that their eternal condition depends upon a right determination of this inquiry. But for those who can scarce get liberty from the service and power of their lusts seriously to consider what is their condition, or what it is like to be, it is no wonder if they talk of these things, after the manner of these days, without any impression on their minds and affections, or influence on the practical understanding. But our inquiry is after what is a sufficient evidence for the conviction of rational and unprejudiced persons, and the defeating of objections to the contrary, which these and the like arguments do every way answer.

Some think fit here to stay, that is, in these or the like external arguments, or rational motives of faith, such as render the Scriptures so credible as that it is an unreasonable thing not to assent unto them. That certainty which may be attained on these arguments and motives is, as they say, the highest which our minds are capable of with respect unto this object, and therefore includes all the assent which is required of us unto this proposition, that the Scriptures are the word of God, or all the faith whereby we believe them so to be. When I speak of these arguments, I intend not them alone which I have insisted on, but all others also of the same kind, some whereof have been urged and improved by others with great diligence; for in the variety of such arguments as offer themselves in this cause, everyone chooses out what seems to him most cogent, and some amass all that they can think on. Now, these arguments, with the evidence tendered in them, are such as nothing but perverse prejudice can detain men from giving a firm assent unto. And no more is required of us but that, according to the motives that are proposed unto us and the arguments used to that purpose, we come unto a judgment and persuasion, called a moral assurance of the truth of the Scripture, and endeavor to yield obedience unto God accordingly.[35]

And it were to be wished that there were more than it is feared there are who were really so affected with these arguments and motives. For the truth is, tradition and education practically bear the whole sway in this matter. But yet, when all this is done, it will be said that all this is but a mere natural work, whereunto no more is required but the natural exercise and acting of our own reason and understanding; that the arguments and motives used, though strong, are human and fallible, and, therefore, the conclusion we make from them is so also, and wherein we may be deceived; that an assent grounded and resolved into such rational arguments only is not faith in the sense of the Scripture; in brief, that it is required that we believe the Scriptures to be the word of God with faith divine and supernatural, which cannot be deceived. Two things are replied hereunto.

1. That where the things believed are divine and supernatural, so is the faith whereby we believe them or give our assent unto them. Let the motives and arguments whereon we give our assent be of what kind they will, so that the assent be true and real, and the things believed be divine and supernatural, the faith whereby we believe is so also. But this is all one, as if in things natural a man should say, our sight is green when we see that which is so, and blue when we see that which is blue. And this would be so in things moral, if the specification of acts were from their material objects; but it is certain that they are not of the same nature always with the things they are conversant about, nor are they changed thereby from what their nature is in themselves, be it natural or supernatural, human or divine. Now, things divine are only the material object of our faith, as has been showed before; and by an enumeration of them do we answer unto the question, "What is it that you do believe?" But it is the formal object or reason of all our acts from whence they are denominated, or by which they are specified. And the formal reason of our faith, assent, or believing is that which prevails with us to believe, and on whose account we do so, wherewith we answer unto that question, "Why do you believe?" If this be human authority, arguments highly probable but absolutely fallible, motives cogent but only to beget a moral persuasion, whatever we do believe thereon, our faith is human, fallible, and a moral assurance only. Wherefore it is said,

---

35 The growing body of literature referenced here by Owen centered on the idea that the inspiration of the Bible could be definitively proven through rational deductions from objective evidence. Owen, obviously, wants to move beyond such arguments. He does not dismiss them but sees them as incomplete by themselves.

2. That this assent is sufficient, all that is required of us, and contains in it all the assurance which our minds are capable of in this matter. For no further evidence or assurance is in any case to be inquired after than the subject matter will bear. And so is it in this case, where the truth is not exposed to sense, nor capable of a scientific demonstration, but must be received upon such reasons and arguments as carry it above the highest probability, though they leave it beneath science or knowledge, or infallible assurance; if such a persuasion of mind there be.

But yet I must needs say, that although those external arguments, whereby learned and rational men have proved, or may yet further prove, the Scripture to be a divine revelation given of God, and the doctrine contained in it to be a heavenly truth, are of singular use for the strengthening of the faith of them that do believe, by relieving the mind against temptations and objections that will arise to the contrary, as also for the conviction of gainsayers;[36] yet to say that they contain the formal reason of that assent which is required of us unto the Scripture as the word of God, that our faith is the effect and product of them, which it rests upon and is resolved into, is both contrary to the Scripture, destructive of the nature of divine faith, and exclusive of the work of the Holy Ghost in this whole matter.

Wherefore, I shall do these two things before I proceed to our principal argument designed. First, I shall give some few reasons, proving that the faith whereby we believe the Scripture to be the word of God is not a mere firm moral persuasion, built upon external arguments and motives of credibility, but is divine and supernatural, because the formal reason of it is so also. Second, I shall show what is the nature of that faith whereby we do or ought to believe the Scripture to be the word of God, what is the work of the Holy Spirit about it, and what is the proper object of it. In the first I shall be very brief, for my design is to strengthen the faith of all, and not to weaken the opinions of any.

---

36 I.e., those who declare something to be untrue or invalid.

Moral Certainty, the Result of External Arguments, Insufficient

Four Arguments against the Sufficiency of Moral Certainty

1. DIVINE REVELATION is the proper object of divine faith. With such faith we can believe nothing but what is so, and what is so can be received no otherwise by us. If we believe it not with divine faith, we believe it not at all. Such is the Scripture, as the word of God, everywhere proposed unto us, and we are required to believe, that is, first to believe it so to be, and then to believe the things contained in it. For this proposition, that the Scripture is the word of God, is a divine revelation, and so to be believed. But God nowhere requires, nor ever did, that we should believe any divine revelation upon such grounds, much less on such grounds and motives only. They are left unto us as consequential unto our believing, to plead with others in behalf of what we profess, and for the justification of it unto the world. But that which requires our faith and obedience unto, in the receiving of divine revelations, whether immediately given and declared or as recorded in the Scripture, is his own authority and veracity: "I am the Lord"; "Thus saith the high and lofty One"; "Thus saith the Lord"; "To the law and to the testimony"; "This is my beloved Son, hear ye him"; "All Scripture is given by inspiration of God"; "Believe in the Lord and his prophets."[1] This alone is that which he requires us to resolve our faith into. So, when he gave unto us the law of our lives, the eternal and unchangeable rule of our obedience unto him, in the Ten Commandments, he gives no other reason to oblige us thereunto but this only, "I am the Lord thy

---

1   Ex. 20:2; Isa. 57:15; Ex. 9:1; Isa. 8:20; Luke 9:35; 2 Tim. 3:16; 2 Chron. 20:20.

God."[2] The sole formal reason of all our obedience is taken from his own nature and our relation unto him. Nor does he propose any other reason why we should believe him, or the revelation which he makes of his mind and will. And our faith is part of our obedience, the root and principal part of it; therefore, the reason of both is the same.¶

Neither did our Lord Jesus Christ nor his apostles ever make use of such arguments or motives for the ingenerating[3] of faith in the minds of men, nor have they given directions for the use of any such arguments to this end and purpose. But when they were accused to have followed "cunningly-devised fables,"[4] they appealed unto Moses and the prophets, to the revelations they had themselves received, and those that were before recorded. It is true, they wrought miracles in confirmation of their own divine mission and of the doctrine which they taught, but the miracles of our Savior were all of them wrought among those who believed the whole Scripture then given to be the word of God, and those of the apostles were before the writings of the books of the New Testament. Their doctrine, therefore, materially considered, and their warranty to teach it, were sufficiently, yea, abundantly confirmed by them. But divine revelation, formally considered, and as written, was left upon the old foundation of the authority of God who gave it. No such method is prescribed, no such example is proposed unto us in the Scripture, as to make use of these arguments and motives for the conversion of the souls of men unto God, and the ingenerating of faith in them. Yea, in some cases, the use of such means is decried as unprofitable, and the sole authority of God, putting forth his power in and by his word, is appealed unto (1 Cor. 2:4–5, 13; 14:36–37; 2 Cor. 4:7). But yet, in a way of preparation, subservient unto the receiving the Scripture as the word of God, and for the defense of it against gainsayers and their objections, their use has been granted and proved. But from first to last, in the Old and New Testament, the authority and truth of God are constantly and uniformly proposed as the immediate ground and reason of believing his revelations; nor can it be proved that he does accept or approve of any kind of faith or assent but what is built thereon and resolved thereinto.¶

The sum is, we are obliged in a way of duty to believe the Scriptures to be a divine revelation, when they are ministerially or providentially proposed unto us, whereof afterward. The ground whereon we are to receive them is the authority and veracity of God speaking in them; we believe them because

2   Ex. 20:2.
3   I.e., generating or producing.
4   2 Pet. 1:16.

they are the word of God. Now, this faith, whereby we so believe, is divine and supernatural, because the formal reason of it is so, namely, God's truth and authority. Wherefore, we do not, nor ought to believe the Scripture as highly probable, or with a moral persuasion and assurance, built upon arguments absolutely fallible and human only. For if this be the formal reason of faith, namely, the veracity and authority of God, if we believe not with faith divine and supernatural, we believe not at all.

2. The moral certainty treated of is a mere effect of reason. There is no more required unto it but that the reasons proposed for the assent required be such as the mind judges to be convincing and prevalent; from whence an inferior kind of knowledge, or a firm opinion, or some kind of persuasion which has not yet gotten an intelligible name, does necessarily ensue. There is, therefore, on this supposition, no need of any work of the Holy Ghost to enable us to believe or to work faith in us; for no more is required herein but what necessarily arises from a naked exercise of reason. If it be said that the inquiry is not about what is the work of the Spirit of God in us, but concerning the reasons and motives to believing that are proposed unto us, I answer, it is granted; but what we urge herein is that the act which is exerted on such motives, or the persuasion which is begotten in our minds by them, is purely natural, and such as requires no special work of the Holy Ghost in us for the effecting of it. Now this is not faith, nor can we be said in the Scripture sense to believe thereby, and so, in particular, not the Scriptures to be the word of God. For faith is "the gift of God," and is "not of ourselves" (Eph. 2:8). It is "given unto some on the behalf of Christ" (Phil. 1:29), and not unto others (Matt. 11:25; 13:11). But this assent on external arguments and motives is of ourselves, equally common and exposed unto all. "No man can say that Jesus is the Lord, but by the Holy Ghost" (1 Cor. 12:3); but he who believes the Scripture truly, aright, and according to his duty, does say so. No man comes to Christ, but he that has "heard and learned of the Father" (John 6:45). And as this is contrary to the Scripture, so it is expressly condemned by the ancient church, particularly by the second Arausican council:[5] "If anyone says that not only the increase of faith but also its beginning and the very desire for faith, if anyone says that this belongs to us by nature and not by a gift of grace, that is, by the inspiration of the Holy Spirit amending our will and turning it from unbelief to faith and from godlessness to godliness, it is

5   The Second Arausican Council is an alternative designation for the Second Council of Orange, held in 529, which grew out of the controversy between Augustine and Pelagius over the role of God's grace in the work of salvation and decided in favor of Augustinianism.

proof that he is opposed to the teaching of the Apostles."[6] And plainly: "If anyone affirms that we can form any right opinion or make any right choice which relates to the salvation of eternal life, as is expedient for us, or that we can be saved, that is, assent to the preaching of the gospel through our natural powers without the illumination and inspiration of the Holy Spirit, who makes all men gladly assent to and believe in the truth, he is led astray by a heretical spirit."[7]

It is still granted that the arguments intended, that is, all of them which are true indeed and will endure a strict examination, for some are frequently made use of in this cause which will not endure a trial, are of good use in their place and unto their proper end, that is, to beget such an assent unto the truth as they are capable of effecting. For although this be not that which is required of us in a way of duty, but inferior to it, yet the mind is prepared and disposed by them unto the receiving of the truth in its proper evidence.

3. Our assent can be of no other nature than the arguments and motives whereon it is built, or by which it is wrought in us, as in degree it cannot exceed their evidence. Now, these arguments are all human and fallible. Exalt them unto the greatest esteem possible, yet because they are not demonstrations, nor do necessarily beget a certain knowledge in us, which, indeed, if they did, there were no room left for faith or our obedience therein, they produce an opinion only, though in the highest kind of probability, and firm against objections. For we will allow the utmost assurance that can be claimed upon them. But this is exclusive of all divine faith, as to any article, thing, matter, or object to be believed. For instance, a man professes that he believes Jesus Christ to be the Son of God. Demand the reason why he does so, and he will say, "Because God, who cannot lie, has revealed and declared him so

6   In the text: *Si quis sicut augmentum ita etiam initium fidei, ipsumque credulitatis affectum, non per gratiae donum, id est, per inspirationem Spiritus Sancti, corrigentem voluntatem nostram ab infidelitate ad fidem, ab impietate ad pietatem, sed naturaliter nobis inesse dicit, apostolicis dogmatibus adversarius approbator* (Can. 5, 7).—Owen. For a modern Latin edition, see Heinrich Denzinger, *A Compendium of Creeds, Definitions, and Declarations of the Catholic Church,* rev. ed., ed. Peter Hünermann (San Francisco: Ignatius, 2012). For the English translation, see John H. Leith, ed., *Creeds of the Churches: A Reader in Christian Doctrine from the Bible to the Present,* 3rd ed. (Louisville: Westminster John Knox, 1982), 39.

7   In the text: *Si quis per naturae vigorem bonum aliquod quod ad salutem pertinet vitae eternae, cogitare ut expedit, aut eligere, sive salutari, id est, evangelicae praedicationi consentire posse affirmat absque illuminatione et inspiratione Spiritus Sancti, qui dat omnibus suavitatem consentiendo et credendo veritati, haeretico fallitur spiritu* (Can. 7).—Owen. For a modern Latin edition, see Denzinger, *Compendium of Creeds.* For English translation, see Leith, *Creeds of the Churches,* 39–40.

to be." Proceed yet further, and ask him where or how God has revealed and declared this so to be; and he will answer, "In the Scripture, which is his Word." Inquire now further of him, which is necessary, wherefore he believes this Scripture to be the word of God, or an immediate revelation given out from him; for hereunto we must come, and have somewhat that we may ultimately rest in, excluding in its own nature all further inquiries, or we can have neither certainty nor stability in our faith. On this supposition his answer must be, that he has many cogent arguments that render it highly probable so to be, such as have prevailed with him to judge it so to be, and whereon he is fully persuaded as having the highest assurance hereof that the matter will bear, and so does firmly believe it to be the word of God. Yea, but, it will be replied, all these arguments are in their kind or nature human, and therefore fallible, such as it is possible they may be false; for everything may be so that is not immediately from the first essential verity. This assent, therefore, unto the Scriptures as the word of God is human, fallible, and such as wherein we may be deceived. And our assent unto the things revealed can be of no other kind than that we give unto the revelation itself, for there into it is resolved, and thereunto it must be reduced; these waters will rise no higher than their fountain. And thus at length we come to believe Jesus Christ to be the Son of God with a faith human and fallible, and which at last may deceive us; which is to "receive the Word of God as the word of men, and not as it is in truth, the Word of God," contrary to the apostle (1 Thess. 2:13). Wherefore,

4. If I believe the Scripture to be the word of God with a human faith only, I do no otherwise believe whatever is contained in it, which overthrows all faith properly so called. And if I believe whatever is contained in the Scripture with faith divine and supernatural, I cannot but by the same faith believe the Scripture itself, which removes the moral certainty treated of out of our way. And the reason of this is, that we must believe the revelation and the things revealed with the same kind of faith, or we bring confusion on the whole work of believing. No man living can distinguish in his experience between that faith wherewith he believes the Scripture and that wherewith he believes the doctrine of it, or the things contained in it, nor is there any such distinction or difference intimated in the Scripture itself; but all our believing is absolutely resolved into the authority of God revealing. Nor can it be rationally apprehended that our assent unto the things revealed should be of a kind and nature superior unto that which we yield unto the revelation itself. For let the arguments which it is resolved into be never so evident and cogent, let the assent itself be as firm and certain as can be imagined, yet is it human still and natural, and therein is inferior unto that which is divine and supernatural. And

yet, on this supposition, that which is of a superior kind and nature is wholly resolved into that which is of an inferior, and must betake itself on all occasions thereunto for relief and confirmation; for the faith whereby we believe Jesus Christ to be the Son of God is on all occasions absolutely melted down into that whereby we believe the Scriptures to be the word of God.

But none of these things are my present special design, and therefore I have insisted long enough upon them. I am not inquiring what grounds men may have to build an opinion or any kind of human persuasion upon that the Scriptures are the word of God, no, nor yet how we may prove or maintain them so to be unto gainsayers; but what is required hereunto that we may believe them to be so with faith divine and supernatural, and what is the work of the Spirit of God therein.

CERTAINTY UNTO OBEDIENCE

But it may be further said, that these external arguments and motives are not of themselves, and considered separately from the doctrine which they testify unto, the sole ground and reason of our believing. For if it were possible that a thousand arguments of a like cogency with them were offered to confirm any truth or doctrine, if it had not a divine worth and excellency in itself, they could give the mind no assurance of it. Wherefore it is the truth itself, or doctrine contained in the Scripture, which they testify unto, that animates them and gives them their efficacy. For there is such a majesty, holiness, and excellency in the doctrines of the gospel, and, moreover, such a suitableness in them unto unprejudiced reason, and such an answerableness unto all the rational desires and expectations of the soul, as evidence their procedure[8] from the fountain of infinite wisdom and goodness. It cannot but be conceived impossible that such excellent, heavenly mysteries, of such use and benefit unto all mankind, should be the product of any created industry. Let but a man know himself, his state and condition, in any measure, with a desire of that blessedness which his nature is capable of, and which he cannot but design, when the Scripture is proposed unto him in the ministry of the church, attested by the arguments insisted on, there will appear unto him in the truths and doctrines of it, or in the things contained in it, such an evidence of the majesty and authority of God as will prevail with him to believe it to be a divine revelation. And this persuasion is such that the mind is established in its assent unto the truth, so as to yield obedience unto all that

---

8   I.e., procession.

is required of us. And whereas our belief of the Scripture is in order only to the right performance of our duty, or all that obedience which God expects from us, our minds being guided by the precepts and directions, and duly influenced by the promises and threatenings of it thereunto, there is no other faith required of us but what is sufficient to oblige us unto that obedience.

This being, so far as I can apprehend, the substance of what is by some learned men proposed and adhered unto, it shall be briefly examined.[9] And I say here, as on other occasions, that I should rejoice to see more of such a faith in the world as would effectually oblige men unto obedience, out of a conviction of the excellency of the doctrine and the truth of the promises and threatenings of the word, though learned men should never agree about the formal reason of faith. Such notions of truth, when most diligently inquired into, are but as sacrifice compared with obedience. But the truth itself is also to be inquired after diligently.

This opinion, therefore, either supposes what we shall immediately declare, namely, the necessity of an internal, effectual work of the Holy Spirit, in the illumination of our minds, so enabling us to believe with faith divine and supernatural, or it does not. If it does, it will be found, as I suppose, for the substance of it, to be coincident with what we shall afterward assert and prove to be the formal reason of believing. However, as it is usually proposed, I cannot absolutely comply with it, for these two reasons, among others.

1. It belongs unto the nature of faith, of what sort soever it be, that it be built on and resolved into testimony. This is that which distinguished it from any other conception, knowledge, or assent of our minds, on other reasons and causes. And if this testimony be divine, so is that faith whereby we give assent unto it, on the part of the object. But the doctrines contained in the Scripture, or the subject matter of the truth to be believed, have not in them the nature of a testimony, but are the material, not formal, objects of faith, which must always differ. If it be said that these truths or doctrines do so evidence themselves to be from God, as that in and by them we have the witness and authority of God himself proposed unto us to resolve our faith into, I will not further contend about it, but only say that the authority of God, and so his veracity, do manifest themselves primarily in the revelation itself, before they do so in the things revealed, which is that we plead for.

2. The excellency of the doctrine, or things revealed in the Scriptures, respects not so much the truth of them in speculation as their goodness and

---

9   Owen here is interacting with the idea that the reason Christians believe the Bible to be the word of God is external argumentation or the exercise of rational faculties. This may result in moralism, but it is not supernatural faith.

suitableness unto the souls of men as to their present condition and eternal end. Now, things under that consideration respect not so much faith as spiritual sense and experience. Neither can any man have a due apprehension of such a goodness suitable unto our constitution and condition, with absolute usefulness in the truth of the Scriptures, but on a supposition of that antecedent assent of the mind unto them which is believing; which, therefore, cannot be the reason why we do believe.

But if this opinion proceeds not upon the aforesaid supposition, immediately to be proved, but requires no more unto our satisfaction in the truth of the Scriptures, and assent thereon, but the due exercise of reason, or the natural faculties of our minds, about them when proposed unto us, then I suppose it to be most remote from the truth, and that among many other reasons, for these that ensue.

1. On this supposition, the whole work of believing would be a work of reason. Be it so, say some, nor is it meet it should be otherwise conceived. But if so, then the object of it must be things so evident in themselves and their own nature as that the mind is, as it were, compelled by that evidence unto an assent, and cannot do otherwise. If there be such a light and evidence in the things themselves, with respect unto our reason, in the right use and exercise of it, then is the mind thereby necessitated unto its assent; which both overthrows the nature of faith, substituting an assent upon natural evidence in the room thereof, and is absolutely exclusive of the necessity or use of any work of the Holy Ghost in our believing, which sober Christians will scarcely comply with.

2. There are some doctrines revealed in the Scripture, and those of the most importance that are so revealed, which concern and contain things so above our reason that, without some previous supernatural disposition of mind, they carry in them no evidence of truth unto mere reason, nor of suitableness unto our constitution and end. There is required unto such an apprehension both the spiritual elevation of the mind by supernatural illumination, and a divine assent unto the authority of the revelation thereon, before reason can be so much as satisfied in the truth and excellency of such doctrines. Such are those concerning the holy Trinity, or the subsistence of one singular essence in three distinct persons, the incarnation of the Son of God, the resurrection of the dead, and sundry others that are the most proper subjects of divine revelation. There is a heavenly glory in some of these things, which as reason can never thoroughly apprehend, because it is finite and limited, so, as it is in us by nature, it can neither receive them nor delight in them as doctrinally proposed unto us, with all the aids and assistance before mentioned. "Flesh

and blood reveals not these things unto our minds, but our Father which is in heaven."[10] Nor does any man know these mysteries of the kingdom of God, but he unto "whom it is given";[11] nor do any learn these things aright, but those that "are taught of God."[12]

3. Take our reason singly, without the consideration of divine grace and illumination, and it is not only weak and limited, but depraved and corrupted. And the carnal mind cannot subject itself unto the authority of God in any supernatural revelation whatever. Wherefore, the truth is, that the doctrines of the gospel, which are purely and absolutely so, are so far from having a convincing evidence in themselves of their divine truth, excellency, and goodness unto the reason of men as unrenewed by the Holy Ghost, as that they are "foolishness" and most undesirable unto it, as I have elsewhere proved at large.[13] We shall, therefore, proceed.

CERTAINTY WROUGHT BY THE SPIRIT

There are two things considerable with respect unto our believing the Scriptures to be the word of God in a due manner, or according to our duty. The first respects the subject, or the mind of man, how it is enabled thereunto; the other, the object to be believed, with the true reason why we do believe the Scripture with faith divine and supernatural.

The first of these must of necessity fall under our consideration herein, as that without which, whatever reasons, evidences, or motives are proposed unto us, we shall never believe in a due manner. For whereas the mind of man, or the minds of all men, are by nature depraved, corrupt, carnal, and enmity against God, they cannot of themselves, or by virtue of any innate ability of their own, understand or assent unto spiritual things in a spiritual manner, which we have sufficiently proved and confirmed before.[14] Wherefore, that assent which is wrought in us by mere external arguments, consisting in the rational conclusion and judgment which we make upon their truth and evidence, is not that faith wherewith we ought to believe the word of God.

Wherefore, that we may believe the Scriptures to be the word of God according to our duty, as God requires it of us, in a useful, profitable, and saving manner, above and beyond that natural, human faith and assent which is the

10 Matt. 16:17.
11 Matt. 13:11.
12 Isa. 54:13.
13 Owen is likely referring to Πνευματολογια, or, A Discourse concerning the Holy Spirit, bk. 3.
14 Πνευματολογια, or, A Discourse concerning the Holy Spirit, bk. 3, chap. 3.

effect of the arguments and motives of credibility before insisted on, with all others of the like kind, there is and must be wrought in us, by the power of the Holy Ghost, faith supernatural and divine, whereby we are enabled so to do, or rather whereby we do so. This work of the Spirit of God, as it is distinct from, so in order of nature it is antecedent unto, all divine objective evidence of the Scriptures being the word of God, or the formal reason moving us to believe it. Wherefore, without it, whatever arguments or motives are proposed unto us, we cannot believe the Scriptures to be the word of God in a due manner, and as it is in duty required of us.

Some, it may be, will suppose these things ἀπροσδιόνυσα,[15] and impertinent unto our present purpose. For while we are inquiring on what grounds we believe the Scripture to be the word of God, we seem to flee to the work of the Holy Ghost in our own minds, which is irrational. But we must not be ashamed of the gospel, nor of the truth of it, because some do not understand or will not duly consider what is proposed. It is necessary that we should return unto the work of the Holy Spirit, not with peculiar respect unto the Scriptures that are to be believed, but unto our own minds and that faith wherewith they are to be believed. For it is not the reason why we believe the Scriptures, but the power whereby we are enabled so to do, which at present we inquire after.

That the faith whereby we believe the Scripture to be the word of God is wrought in us by the Holy Ghost can be denied only on two principles or suppositions. One, that it is not faith divine and supernatural whereby we believe them so to be, but only we have other moral assurance thereof. Two, that this faith divine and supernatural is of ourselves, and is not wrought in us by the Holy Ghost. The first of these has been already disproved, and shall be further evicted afterward, and, it may be, they are very few who are of that judgment. For generally, whatever men suppose the prime object, principal motive, and formal reason of that faith to be, yet that it is divine and supernatural they all acknowledge. And as to the second, what is so, it is of the operation of the Spirit of God. For to say it is divine and supernatural is to say that it is not of ourselves, but that it is the grace and gift of the Spirit of God, wrought in us by his divine and supernatural power. And those of the Church of Rome, who would resolve our faith in this matter objectively into the authority of their church, yet subjectively acknowledge the work of the Holy Spirit ingenerating faith in us, and that work to be necessary to our believing the Scripture in a due manner. "All external and human persua-

15 Gk. "out of place."

sions are not sufficient causes of faith; however, the things of faith may be sufficiently proposed by men. But an internal cause is necessary, that is, a certain divine light inciting to belief, or certain internal eyes to see, given to us by the grace of God," says Canus.[16] Nor is there any of the divines of that church which dissent herein. We do not, therefore, assert any such divine formal reason of believing, as that the mind should not stand in need of supernatural assistance enabling it to assent thereunto. Nay, we affirm that without this there is in no man any true faith at all, let the arguments and motives whereon he believes be as forcible and pregnant with evidence as can be imagined. It is in this case as in things natural; neither the light of the sun, nor any persuasive arguments unto men to look up unto it, will enable them to discern it unless they are endued with a due visive[17] faculty.

And this the Scripture is express in beyond all possibility of contradiction. Neither is it, that I know of, by any as yet in express terms denied. For indeed, that all which is properly called faith, with respect unto divine revelation, and is accepted with God as such, is the work of the Spirit of God in us, or is bestowed on us by him, cannot be questioned by any who own the gospel. I have also proved it elsewhere so fully and largely as that I shall give it at present no other confirmation but what will necessarily fall in with the description of the nature of that faith whereby we do believe, and the way or manner of its being wrought in us.

The work of the Holy Ghost unto this purpose consists in the saving illumination of the mind, and the effect of it is a supernatural light, whereby the mind is renewed (see Rom. 12:2; Eph. 1:18–19; 3:16–19). It is called a "heart to understand, eyes to see, ears to hear" (Deut. 29:4). The "opening of the eyes of our understanding" (Eph. 1:18). The "giving of an understanding" (1 John 5:20). Hereby we are enabled to discern the evidences of the divine origin and authority of the Scripture that are in itself, as well as assent unto the truth contained in it; and without it we cannot do so. For "the natural man receiveth not the things of the Spirit of God, for they are foolishness unto him, neither can he know them, because they are spiritually discerned"

---

16 In the text: *Externae omnes et humanae persuasiones non sunt satis ad credendum, quantumcunque ab hominibus competenter ea quae sunt fidei proponantur. Sed necessaria est insuper causa interior, hoc est divinum quoddam lumen incitans ad credendum, et oculi quidam interni Dei beneficio ad videndum dati* (Loc. Theol., lib. ii. cap. 8).—Owen. This is a citation and Owen's translation of Cano's *De locis theologicis* (Lovani, 1564). For the Latin text, see Melchor Cano, *De locis theologicis*, ed. Juan Belda Plans (Madrid: Biblioteca de Autores Cristianos, 2006), 33–34. No English translation exists. Cano (1509–1560) was a Spanish Benedictine theologian, and this was an influential treatise on theological method.

17 I.e., visual.

(1 Cor. 2:14). And unto this end it is written in the prophets that "we shall be all taught of God" (John 6:45). That there is a divine and heavenly excellency in the Scripture cannot be denied by any who, on any grounds or motives whatever, do own its divine origin. For all the works of God do set forth his praise, and it is impossible that anything should proceed immediately from him but that there will be express characters of divine excellencies upon it; and as to the communication of these characters of himself, he has "magnified his Word above all his name."[18] But these we cannot discern, be they in themselves never so illustrious, without the effectual communication of the light mentioned unto our minds; that is, without divine, supernatural illumination.

Herein he who commanded "light to shine out of darkness shineth in our hearts, to give the light of the knowledge of the glory of God in the face of Jesus Christ" (2 Cor. 4:6). He irradiates[19] the mind with a spiritual light, whereby it is enabled to discern the glory of spiritual things. This they cannot do "in whom the god of this world hath blinded the eyes of them that believe not, lest the light of the glorious gospel of Christ, who is the image of God, should shine into them" (2 Cor. 4:4). Those who are under the power of their natural darkness and blindness, especially where there are in them also superadded[20] prejudices, begotten and increased by the craft of Satan, as there are in the whole world of unbelievers, cannot see or discern that divine excellency in the Scripture, without an apprehension whereof no man can believe it aright to be the word of God. Such persons may assent unto the truth of the Scripture and its divine origin upon external arguments and rational motives, but believe it with faith divine and supernatural, on those arguments and motives only, they cannot.

There are two things which hinder or disenable men from believing with faith divine and supernatural, when any divine revelation is objectively proposed unto them. First, the natural blindness and darkness of their minds, which are come upon all by the fall, and the depravation of their nature that ensued thereon. Secondly, the prejudices that, through the craft of Satan, the god of this world, their minds are possessed with, by traditions, education, and converse in the world. This last obstruction or hindrance may be so far removed by external arguments and motives of credibility, as that men may upon them attain unto a moral persuasion concerning the divine origin of the Scripture. But these arguments cannot remove or take away the native blindness of the mind, which is removed by their renovation and divine

18 Ps. 138:2.
19 I.e., illuminates.
20 I.e., increased in a compounding way.

illumination alone. Wherefore, none, I think, will positively affirm that we can believe the Scripture to be the word of God, in the way and manner which God requires, without a supernatural work of the Holy Spirit upon our minds in the illumination of them. So, David prays that God would "open his eyes, that he might behold wondrous things out of the law" (Ps. 119:18); that he would "make him understand the way of his precepts" (Ps. 119:27); that he would "give him understanding, and he should keep the law" (Ps. 119:34). So, the Lord Christ also "opened the understanding of his disciples, that they might understand the Scriptures" (Luke 24:45); as he had affirmed before that it was given unto some to know the mysteries of the kingdom of God, and not unto others (Matt. 11:25; 13:11). And neither are these things spoken in vain, nor is the grace intended in them needless.

The communication of this light unto us the Scripture calls revealing and revelation: "Thou hast hid these things from the wise and prudent, and hast revealed them unto babes" (Matt. 11:25); that is, given them to understand the mysteries of the kingdom of heaven, when they were preached unto them. And "no man knoweth the Father, but he to whom the Son will reveal him" (Matt. 11:27). So the apostle prays for the Ephesians, "that God would give them the Spirit of wisdom and revelation in the knowledge of Christ, that, the eyes of their understanding being enlightened, they might know," etc. (Eph. 1:17–19). It is true, these Ephesians were already believers, or considered by the apostle as such; but if he judged it necessary to pray for them that they might have "the Spirit of wisdom and revelation to enlighten the eyes of their understanding," with respect unto farther degrees of faith and knowledge, or, as he speaks in another place, that they might come unto "the full assurance of understanding, to the acknowledgment of the mystery of God" (Col. 2:2), then it is much more necessary to make them believers who before were not so, but utter strangers unto the faith.

But as a pretense hereof has been abused, as we shall see afterward, so the pleading of it is liable to be mistaken. For some are ready to apprehend that this retreat unto a Spirit of revelation is but a pretense to discard all rational arguments, and to introduce enthusiasm into their room. Now, although the charge be grievous, yet, because it is groundless, we must not forgo what the Scripture plainly affirms and instructs us in, thereby to avoid it. Scripture testimonies may be expounded according to the analogy of faith,[21] but denied

---

21 The "analogy of faith" is a general sense of the meaning of Scripture, constructed from the clear or unambiguous passages, used as the basis for interpreting difficult texts. For more on the analogy of faith, see Andrew S. Ballitch, *The Gloss and the Text: William Perkins on Interpreting Scripture with Scripture*, Studies in Historical and Systematic Theology (Bellingham, WA:

or despised, seem they never so contrary unto our apprehension of things, they must not be. Some, I confess, seem to disregard both the objective work of the Holy Spirit in this matter, whereof we shall treat afterward, and his subjective work also in our minds, that all things may be reduced unto sense and reason. But we must grant that a "Spirit of wisdom and revelation"[22] to open the eyes of our understanding is needful to enable us to believe the Scripture to be the word of God in a due manner, or forgo the gospel; and our duty it is to pray continually for that Spirit, if we intend to be established in the faith thereof.

But yet we plead not for external immediate revelations, such as were granted unto the prophets, apostles, and other penmen of the Scripture. The revelation we intend differs from them both in its special subject and formal reason or nature, that is, in the whole kind. For, one, the subject matter of divine, prophetic revelation by a θεοπνευστία, or "immediate divine inspiration," are things not made known before. Things they were "hid in God," or the counsels of his will, and "revealed unto the apostles and prophets by the Spirit" (Eph. 3:5, 9–10). Whether they were doctrines or things, they were, at least as unto their present circumstances, made known from the counsels of God by their revelation. But the matter and subject of the revelation we treat of is nothing but what is already revealed. It is an internal revelation of that which is outward and antecedent unto it; beyond the bounds thereof it is not to be extended. And if any pretend unto immediate revelations of things not before revealed, we have no concern in their pretenses.

They differ likewise in their nature or kind. For immediate, divine, prophetical revelation, consisted in an immediate inspiration or afflatus,[23] or in visions and voices from heaven, with a power of the Holy Ghost transiently affecting their minds and guiding their tongues and hands to whom they were granted, whereby they received and represented divine impressions, as an instrument of music does the skill of the hand whereby it is moved; the nature of which revelation I have more fully discoursed elsewhere.[24] But this revelation of the Spirit consists in his effectual operation, freeing our minds from darkness, ignorance, and prejudice, enabling them to discern spiritual

---

Lexham, 2020), 66–68; Richard A. Muller, *Dictionary of Latin and Greek Theological Terms: Drawn Principally from Protestant Scholastic Theology* (Grand Rapids, MI: Baker Academic, 1985), 33.

22 Eph. 1:17.

23 I.e., revelation.

24 Owen is likely referring either to *Of the Divine Original, Authority, Self-Evidencing Light, and Power of the Scriptures* or to Πνευματολογια, or, *A Discourse concerning the Holy Spirit.*

things in a due manner. And such a Spirit of revelation is necessary unto them who would believe aright the Scripture, or anything else that is divine and supernatural contained therein. And if men who, through the power of temptations and prejudices, are in the dark, or at a loss as to the great and fundamental principle of all religion, namely, the divine origin and authority of the Scripture, will absolutely lean unto their own understandings, and have the whole difference determined by the natural powers and faculties of their own souls, without seeking after divine aid and assistance, or earnest prayer for the Spirit of wisdom and revelation to open the eyes of their understandings, they must be content to abide in their uncertainties, or to come off from them without any advantage to their souls. Not that I would deny unto men, or take them off from, the use of their reason in this matter; for what is their reason given unto them for, unless it be to use it in those things which are of the greatest importance unto them? Only, I must crave leave to say that it is not sufficient of itself to enable us to the performance of this duty, without the immediate aid and assistance of the Holy Spirit of God.

If anyone, upon these principles, shall now ask us wherefore we believe the Scripture to be the word of God, we do not answer, "It is because the Holy Ghost has enlightened our minds, wrought faith in us, and enabled us to believe it." Without this, we say indeed, did not the Spirit of God so work in us and upon us, we neither should nor could believe with faith divine and supernatural. If God had not opened the heart of Lydia, she would not have attended unto the things preached by Paul, so as to have received them. And without it the light oftentimes shines in darkness, but the darkness comprehends it not. But this neither is nor can be the formal object of our faith, or the reason why we believe the Scripture to be of God, or anything else; neither do we nor can we rationally answer by it unto this question, why we do believe. This reason must be something external and evidently proposed unto us. For whatever ability of spiritual assent there be in the understanding, which is thus wrought in it by the Holy Ghost, yet the understanding cannot assent unto anything with any kind of assent, natural or supernatural, but what is outwardly proposed unto it as true, and that with sufficient evidence that it is so. That, therefore, which proposes anything unto us as true, with evidence of that truth, is the formal object of our faith, or the reason why we do believe, and what is so proposed must be evidenced to be true, or we cannot believe it; and according to the nature of that evidence such is our faith—human if that be human, and divine if that be so. Now, nothing of this is done by that saving light which is infused into our minds, and is, therefore, not the reason why we believe what we do so.

Whereas, therefore, some, who seem to conceive that the only general ground of believing the Scripture to be the word of God does consist in rational arguments and motives of credibility, do grant that private persons may have their assurance hereof from the illumination of the Holy Ghost, though it be not pleadable to others; they grant what is not, that I know of, desired by any, and which in itself is not true. For this work consisting solely in enabling the mind unto that kind of assent which is faith divine and supernatural, on supposition of an external formal reason of it duly proposed, is not the reason why any do believe, nor the ground whereinto their faith is resolved.

INTERNAL TESTIMONY IS NOT THE REASON OF FAITH

It remains only that we inquire whether our faith in this matter be not resolved into an immediate internal testimony of the Holy Ghost, assuring us of the divine origin and authority of the Scripture, distinct from the work of spiritual illumination, before described. For it is the common opinion of Protestant divines that the testimony of the Holy Ghost is the ground whereon we believe the Scripture to be the word of God, and in what sense it is so shall be immediately declared. But hereon are they generally charged, by those of the Church of Rome and others, that they resolve all the ground and assurance of faith into their own particular spirits, or the spirit of everyone that will pretend thereunto. And this is looked upon as a sufficient warranty to reproach them with giving countenance unto enthusiasms, and exposing the minds of men to endless delusions. Wherefore, this matter must be a little further inquired into.

And by an internal testimony of the Spirit, an extraordinary afflatus, or new immediate revelation may be intended. Men may suppose they have, or ought to have, an internal particular testimony that the Scripture is the word of God, whereby, and whereby alone, they may be infallibly assured that so it is. And this is supposed to be of the same nature with the revelation made unto the prophets and penmen of the Scripture; for it is neither an external proposition of truth nor an internal ability to assent unto such a proposition, and besides these there is no divine operation in this kind but an immediate prophetical inspiration or revelation. Wherefore, as such a revelation or immediate testimony of the Spirit is the only reason why we do believe, so it is that alone which our faith rests on and is resolved into.

This is that which is commonly imputed unto those who deny either the authority of the church, or any other external arguments or motives of credibility, to be the formal reason of our faith. Howbeit there is no one of them, that I know of, who ever asserted any such thing. And I do, therefore, deny that our faith is resolved into any such private testimony, immediate revelation, or inspiration of the Holy Ghost, and that for the ensuing reasons.

1. Since the finishing of the canon of the Scripture, the church is not under that conduct as to stand in need of such new extraordinary revelations. It does, indeed, live upon the internal gracious operations of the Spirit, enabling us to understand, believe, and obey the perfect, complete revelation of the will of God already made; but new revelations it has neither need nor use of. And to suppose them, or a necessity of them, not only overthrows the perfection of the Scripture, but also leaves us uncertain whether we know all that is to be believed in order unto salvation, or our whole duty, or when we may do so. For it would be our duty to live all our days in expectation of new revelations, wherewith neither peace, assurance, nor consolation is consistent.

2. Those who are to believe will not be able, on this supposition, to secure themselves from delusion, and from being imposed on by the deceits of Satan. For this new revelation is to be tried by the Scripture, or it is not. If it [is] to be tried and examined by the Scripture, then does it acknowledge a superior rule, judgment, and testimony, and so cannot be that which our faith is ultimately resolved into. If it be exempted from that rule of trying the spirits, then first, it must produce the grant of this exemption, seeing the rule is extended generally unto all things and doctrines that relate unto faith or obedience. Second, it must declare what are the grounds and evidences of its own αὐτοπιστία, or "self-credibility," and how it may be infallibly or assuredly distinguished from all delusions; which can never be done. And if any tolerable countenance could be given unto these things, yet we shall show immediately that no such private testimony, though real, can be the formal object of faith or reason of believing.

3. It has so fallen out, in the providence of God, that generally all who have given up themselves, in any things concerning faith or obedience, unto the pretended conduct of immediate revelations, although they have pleaded a respect unto the Scripture also, have been seduced into opinions and practices directly repugnant unto it. And this, with all persons of sobriety, is sufficient to discard this pretense.

TESTIMONY AS EFFICACIOUS PERSUASION

But this internal testimony of the Spirit is by others explained quite in another way. For they say that besides the work of the Holy Ghost before insisted on, whereby he takes away our natural blindness, and, enlightening our minds, enables us to discern the divine excellencies that are in the Scripture, there is another internal efficiency of his, whereby we are moved, persuaded, and enabled to believe. Hereby we are taught of God, so as that, finding the glory and majesty of God in the word, our hearts do, by an ineffable[25] power, assent unto the truth without any hesitation. And this work of the Spirit carries its own evidence in itself, producing an assurance above all human judgment, and such as stands in need of no further arguments or testimonies; this faith rests on and is resolved into. And this some learned men seem to embrace, because they suppose that the objective evidence which is given in the Scripture itself is only moral, or such as can give only a moral assurance.[26] Whereas, therefore, faith ought to be divine and supernatural, so must that be whereinto it is resolved, yea, it is so alone from the formal reason of it. And they can apprehend nothing in this work that is immediately divine but only this internal testimony of the Spirit, wherein God himself speaks unto our hearts.

But yet neither, as it is so explained, can we allow it to be the formal object of faith, nor that wherein it does acquiesce.¶

1. For it has not the proper nature of a divine testimony. A divine work it may be, but a divine testimony it is not; but it is of the nature of faith to be built on an external testimony. However, therefore, our minds may be established, and enabled to believe firmly and steadfastly, by an ineffable internal work of the Holy Ghost, whereof also we may have a certain experience, yet neither that work nor the effect of it can be the reason why we do believe nor whereby we are moved to believe, but only that whereby we do believe.

2. That which is the formal object of faith, or reason whereon we believe, is the same, and common unto all that do believe. For our inquiry is not how or by what means this or that man came to believe, but why anyone or everyone ought so to do unto whom the Scripture is proposed. The object proposed unto all to be believed is the same; and the faith required of all in a way of duty is the same, or of the same kind and nature, and therefore the reason why we believe must be the same also. But, on this supposition, there must be as many distinct reasons of believing as there are believers.

3. On this supposition, it cannot be the duty of anyone to believe the Scripture to be the word of God who has not received this internal testimony of the Spirit. For where the true formal reason of believing is not proposed

---

25 I.e., unspeakable.

26 Owen is once again interacting with the idea that the reason Christians believe the Bible to be the word of God is external argumentation or the exercise of rational faculties.

unto us, there it is not our duty to believe. Wherefore, although the Scripture be proposed as the word of God, yet is it not our duty to believe it so to be until we have this work of the Spirit in our hearts, in case that be the formal reason of believing. But not to press any further how it is possible men may be deceived and deluded in their apprehensions of such an internal testimony of the Spirit, especially if it be not to be tried by the Scripture, which if it be, it loses its αὐτοπιστία, or "self-credibility," or if it be, it casts us into a circle, which the Papists charge us with, it cannot be admitted as the formal object of our faith, because it would divert us from that which is public, proper, every way certain and infallible.

However, that work of the Spirit which may be called an internal real testimony is to be granted as that which belongs unto the stability and assurance of faith. For if he did no otherwise work in us or upon us but by the communication of spiritual light unto our minds, enabling us to discern the evidences that are in the Scripture of its own divine origin, we should often be shaken in our assent and moved from our stability. For whereas our spiritual darkness is removed but in part, and at best, while we are here, we see things but darkly, as in a glass, all things believed having some sort of inevidence or obscurity attending them; and whereas temptations will frequently shake and disturb the due respect of the faculty unto the object, or interpose mists and clouds between them, we can have no assurance in believing unless our minds are further established by the Holy Ghost. He does, therefore, two ways assist us in believing, and ascertain our minds of the things believed, so as that we may hold fast the beginning of our confidence firm and steadfast unto the end.

For (1) he gives unto believers a spiritual sense of the power and reality of the things believed, whereby their faith is greatly established. And although the divine witness, whereunto our faith is ultimately resolved, does not consist herein, yet it is the greatest corroborating testimony whereof we are capable. This is that which brings us unto the "riches of the full assurance of understanding" (Col. 2:2; as also 1 Thess. 1:5). And on the account of this spiritual experience is our perception of spiritual things so often expressed by acts of sense, as tasting, seeing, feeling, and the like means of assurance in things natural. And when believers have attained hereunto, they do find the divine wisdom, goodness, and authority of God so present unto them as that they need neither argument, nor motive, nor anything else, to persuade them unto or confirm them in believing. And whereas this spiritual experience, which believers obtain through the Holy Ghost, is such as cannot rationally be contended about, seeing those who have received it cannot fully express it, and those who have not cannot understand it, nor the efficacy which it has to secure and establish the mind, it is left to be determined on by them alone who have their "senses exercised to discern good and evil."[27] And this belongs unto the internal subjective testimony of the Holy Ghost.

(2) He assists, helps, and relieves us, against temptations to the contrary, so as that they shall not be prevalent. Our first prime assent unto the divine authority of the Scripture, upon its proper grounds and reasons, will not secure us against future objections and temptations unto the contrary, from all manner of causes and occasions. David's faith was so assaulted by them as that he said in his haste "that all men were liars."[28] And Abraham himself, after he had received the promise that in his seed all nations should be blessed, was reduced unto that anxious inquiry, "Lord God, what wilt thou give me, seeing I go childless?" (Gen. 15:2). And Peter was so winnowed[29] by Satan, that although his faith failed not, yet he greatly failed and fainted in its exercise. And we all know what fears from within, what fightings from without, we are exposed unto in this matter. And of this sort are all those atheistical objections against the Scripture which these days abound with, which the devil uses as fiery darts to inflame the souls of men and to destroy their faith; and, indeed, this is that work which the powers of hell are principally engaged in at this day. Having lopped off many branches, they now lay their axe to the root of faith, and hence, in the midst of the profession of Christian religion, there is no greater controversy than whether the Scriptures are the word of God or not. Against all these temptations does the Holy Ghost give in such a continual supply of spiritual strength and assistance unto believers as that they shall at no time prevail, nor their faith totally fail. In such cases the Lord Christ intercedes for us that our faith fail not, and God's grace is sufficient against the buffetings of these temptations. And herein the fruit of Christ's intercession, with the grace of God and its efficiency, are communicated unto us by the Holy Ghost. What are those internal aids whereby he establishes and assures our minds against the force and prevalency of objections and temptations against the divine authority of the Scripture, how they are communicated unto us and received by us, this is no place to declare in particular. It is in vain for any to pretend unto the name of Christians by whom they are denied. And these also have the nature of an internal, real testimony, whereby faith is established.

27 Heb. 5:14.
28 Ps. 116:11.
29 I.e., separated desirable and undesirable elements; sifted.

INCREASED OPPOSITION TO THE
AUTHORITY OF SCRIPTURE

And because it is somewhat strange that, after a long, quiet possession of the professed faith, and assent of the generality of the minds of men thereunto, there should now arise among us such an open opposition unto the divine authority of the Scriptures as we find there is by experience, it may not be amiss in our passage[30] to name the principal causes or occasions thereof; for if we should bring them all into one reckoning, as justly we may, who either openly oppose it and reject it, or who use it or neglect it at their pleasure, or who set up other guides in competition with it or above it, or otherwise declare that they have no sense of the immediate authority of God therein, we shall find them to be like the Moors[31] or slaves in some countries or plantations: they are so great in number and force above their rulers and other inhabitants, that it is only want of communication, with confidence, and some distinct interests, that keep them from casting off their yoke and restraint. I shall name three causes only of this surprising and perilous event.

1. A long-continued outward profession of the truth of the Scripture, without an inward experience of its power, betrays men at length to question the truth itself, at least not to regard it as divine. The owning of the Scripture to be the word of God bespeaks a divine majesty, authority, and power, to be present in it and with it. Wherefore, after men who have for a long time so professed do find that they never had any real experience of such a divine presence in it by any effects upon their own minds, they grow insensibly regardless of it, or allow it a very common place in their thoughts. When they have worn off the impressions that were on their minds from tradition, education, and custom, they do for the future rather not oppose it than in any way believe it. And when once a reverence unto the word of God on the account of its authority is lost, an assent unto it on the account of its truth will not long abide. And all such persons, under a concurrence of temptations and outward occasions, will either reject it or prefer other guides before it.

2. The power of lust, rising up unto a resolution of living in those sins whereunto the Scripture does unavoidably annex eternal ruin, has prevailed with many to cast off its authority. For while they are resolved to live in an outrage of sin, to allow a divine truth and power in the Scripture is to cast themselves under a present torment, as well as to ascertain their future misery; for no other can be his condition who is perpetually sensible that God

---

30 "Our passage" is simply a reference to Owen's argument or line of reasoning.
31 I.e., Muslim inhabitants of the Iberian Peninsula.

always condemns him in all that he does, and will assuredly take vengeance on him, which is the constant language of the Scripture concerning such persons. Wherefore, although they will not immediately fall into an open atheistical opposition unto it, as that which, it may be, is not consistent with their interest and reputation in the world, yet, looking upon it as the devils did on Jesus Christ, as that which "comes to torment them before the time,"[32] they keep it at the greatest distance from their thoughts and minds, until they have habituated themselves unto a contempt of it. There being, therefore, an utter impossibility of giving any pretense of reconciliation between the owning of the Scripture to be the word of God, and a resolution to live in an excess of known sin, multitudes suffer their minds to be bribed by their corrupt affections to a relinquishment of any regard unto it.

3. The scandalous quarrels and disputations of those of the Church of Rome against the Scripture and its authority have contributed much unto the ruin of the faith of many. Their great design is by all means to secure the power, authority, and infallibility of their church. Of these they say continually, as the apostle in another case of the mariners, "unless these stay in the ship, we cannot be saved."[33] Without an acknowledgment of these things, they would have it that men can neither at present believe nor be saved hereafter. To secure this interest, the authority of the Scripture must be by all means questioned and impaired. A divine authority in itself they will allow it, but with respect unto us it has none but what it obtains by the suffrage and testimony of their church. But whereas authority is ἐκ τῶν πρός τὶ,[34] and consists essentially in the relation and respect which it has unto others, or those that are to be subject unto it, to say that it has an authority in itself but none toward us, is not only to deny that it has any authority at all, but also to reproach it with an empty name. They deal with it as the soldiers did with Christ: they put a crown on his head, and clothed him with a purple robe, and bowing the knee before him mocked him, saying, "Hail, king of the Jews!"[35] They ascribe unto it the crown and robe of divine authority in itself, but not toward any one person in the world. So, if they please, God shall be God, and his word be of some credit among men. Herein they seek continually to entangle those of the weaker sort by urging them vehemently with this question, "How do you know the Scripture to be the word of God?" and have in continual readiness a number of sophistical artifices to weaken all evidences that shall be pleaded

---

32 Matt. 8:29.
33 Acts 27:31.
34 Gk. "from them to something" or "from them to anything."
35 Mark 15:18.

in its behalf. Nor is that all, but on all occasions they insinuate such objections against it, from its obscurity, imperfection, want of order, difficulties, and seeming contradictions in it, as are suited to take off the minds of men from a firm assent unto it or reliance on it; as if a company of men should conspire, by crafty multiplied insinuations, divulged on all advantages, to weaken the reputation of a chaste and sober matron, although they cannot deprive her of her virtue, yet, unless the world were wiser than for the most part it appears to be, they will insensibly take off from her due esteem. And this is as bold an attempt as can well be made in any case, for the first tendency of these courses is to make men atheists, after which success it is left an uncertain hazard whether they will be Papists or not.¶

Wherefore, as there can be no greater nor more dishonorable reflection made on Christian religion than that it has no other evidence or testimony of its truth but the authority and witness of those by whom it is at present professed, and who have notable worldly advantages thereby, so the minds of multitudes are secretly influenced by the poison of these disputes to think it no way necessary to believe the Scripture to be the word of God, or at least are shaken off from the grounds whereon they have professed it so to be. And the like disservice is done unto faith and the souls of men by such as advance a light within, or immediate inspiration into competition with it or the room of it. For as such imaginations take place and prevail in the minds of men, so their respect unto the Scripture and all sense of its divine authority do decay, as experience does openly manifest.

It is, I say, from an unusual concurrence of these and the like causes and occasions that there is at present among us such a decay in, relinquishment of, and opposition unto the belief of the Scripture, as, it may be, former ages could not parallel. But against all these objections and temptations the minds of true believers are secured, by supplies of spiritual light, wisdom, and grace from the Holy Ghost.

CONCLUSION

There are several other special gracious actings of the Holy Spirit on the minds of believers, which belong also unto this internal real testimony whereby their faith is established. Such are his anointing and sealing of them, his witnessing with them, and his being an earnest in them, all which must be elsewhere spoken unto. Hereby is our faith every day more and more increased and established. Wherefore, although no internal work of the Spirit can be the formal reason of our faith, or that which it is resolved into, yet is it such as without it we can never sincerely believe as we ought, nor be established in believing against temptations and objections.

And with respect unto this work of the Holy Ghost, it is that [which] divines at the first Reformation did generally resolve our faith of the divine authority of the Scripture into the testimony of the Holy Spirit. But this they did not do exclusively unto the proper use of external arguments and motives of credibility, whose store indeed is great, and whose fountain is inexhaustible. For they arise from all the undubitable[36] notions that we have of God or ourselves, in reference unto our present duty or future happiness. Much less did they exclude that evidence thereof which the Holy Ghost gives unto it in and by itself. Their judgment is well expressed in the excellent words of one of them. "Let this point therefore stand" says he,

> that those whom the Holy Spirit has inwardly taught truly rest upon Scripture, and that Scripture indeed is self-authenticated; therefore it is not right to subject it to proof and reasoning. And the certainty it deserves with us, it attains by the testimony of the Spirit. For even if it wins reverence for itself by its own majesty, it seriously affects us only when it is sealed upon our hearts through the Spirit. Therefore, illumined by his power, we believe neither by our own nor by anyone else's judgment that Scripture is from God; but above human judgment we affirm with utter certainty (just as if we were gazing upon the majesty of God himself) that it has flowed to us from the very mouth of God by the ministry of men. We seek no proofs, no marks of genuineness upon which our judgment may lean; but we subject our judgment and wit to it as to a thing far beyond any guesswork. . . . Nor do we do this as those miserable men who habitually bind over their minds to the thralldom of superstition; but we feel that the undoubted power of his divine majesty lives and breathes there. By this power we are drawn and inflamed, knowingly and willingly, to obey him, yet also more vitally and more effectively than by mere human willing or knowing. . . . Such, then, is a conviction that requires no reasons; such, a knowledge with which the best reason agrees—in which the mind truly reposes more securely and constantly than in any reasons; such, finally, a feeling that can be born only of heavenly revelation. I speak of nothing other than what each believer experiences within himself—though my words fall far beneath a just explanation of the matter.[37]

36 I.e., undoubtable; unquestionable.
37 In the text: *Maneat ergo,* says he, *hoc fixum, quos Spiritus sanctus intus docuit, solidè acquiescere in Scriptura, et hanc quidem esse* αὐτόπιστον, *neque demonstrationi et rationibus subjici eam*

And we may here briefly call over what we have attained or passed through. For (1) we have showed, in general, both what is the nature of divine revelation and divine illumination, with their mutual respect unto one another. (2) What are the principal external arguments or motives of credibility whereby the Scripture may be proved to be of a divine origin. (3) What kind of persuasion is the effect of them, or what is the assent which we give unto the truth of the Scriptures on their account. (4) What objective evidence there is unto reason in the doctrine of the Scriptures to induce the mind to assent unto them. (5) What is the nature of that faith whereby we believe the Scripture to be the word of God, and how it is wrought in us by the Holy Ghost. (6) What is that internal testimony which is given unto the divine authority of the Scriptures by the Holy Spirit, and what is the force and use thereof. The principal part of our work does yet remain.

fas esse: quam tamen meretur apud nos certitudinem Spiritus testimonio consequi. Etsi enim reverentiam sua sibi ultro majestate conciliat, tunc tamen demum serià nos afficit, quum per Spiritum obsignata est cordibus nostris. Illius ergo veritate illuminati, jam non aut nostro, aut aliorum judicio credimus a Deo esse Scripturam; sed supra humanum judicium, certo certius constituimus (non secus ac si ipsius Dei numen illic intueremur) hominum ministerio, ab ipsissimo Dei ore ad nos fluxisse. Non argumenta, non verisimilitudines quaerimus, quibus judicium nostrum incumbit; sed ut rei extra aestimandi aleam positae, judicium ingeniumque nostrum subjicimus. . . . Neque qualiter superstitionibus solent miseri homines captivam mentem addicere: sed quia non dubiam vim numinis illic sentimus vigere ac spirare, qua ad parendum, scientes ac volentes, vividius tamen et efficacius quam pro humana aut volunte aut scientia trahimur et accendimur. . . . Talis ergo est persuasio quae rationes non requirat: talis notitia, cui optima ratio constet, nempe, in qua securius constantiusque mens quiescit quam in ullis rationibus: talis denique sensus, qui nisi ex coelesti revelatione nasci nequeat. Non aliud loquor quam quod apud se experitur fidelium unusquisque, nisi quod longe infra justam rei explicationem verba subsidunt (Calv. Instit., lib. i. cap. 7, sec. 5).—Owen. John Calvin, *Joannis Calvini opera selecta*, vol. 3, *Institutionis christianae religionis 1559, libros I et II continens*, ed. Petrus Barth and Guilelmus Niesel (1928; repr. Eugene, OR: Wipf and Stock, 2010), 1.7.5. For the English translation, see John Calvin, *Institutes of the Christian Religion*, ed. John T. McNeill, trans. Ford Lewis Battles (Philadelphia: Westminster, 1960), 1.7.5.

5

Divine Revelation Itself the Only Foundation and Reason of Faith

THAT WHICH WE HAVE thus far made way for, and which is now our only remaining inquiry is, What is the work of the Holy Ghost with respect unto the objective evidence which we have concerning the Scripture, that it is the word of God, which is the formal reason of our faith, and whereinto it is resolved? That is, we come to inquire and to give a direct answer unto that question, why we believe the Scripture to be the word of God? What it is that our faith rests upon herein? And what it is that makes it the duty of every man to believe it so to be unto whom it is proposed? And the reason why I shall be the briefer herein is, because I have long since, in another discourse, cleared this argument, and I shall not here again call over anything that was delivered therein, because what has been unto this day gainsaid unto it or excepted against it has been of little weight or consideration.[1] Unto this great inquiry, therefore, I say,

We believe the Scripture to be the word of God with divine faith for its own sake only; or, our faith is resolved into the authority and truth of God only as revealing himself unto us therein and thereby. And this authority and veracity of God do infallibly manifest or evince themselves unto our faith, or our minds in the exercise of it, by the revelation itself in the Scripture, and no otherwise. Or, "Thus saith the Lord," is the reason why we ought to believe, and why we do so; why we believe at all in general, and why we believe anything in particular. And this we call the formal object or reason of faith.

1 See *Of the Divine Original, Authority, Self-Evidencing Light, and Power of The Scriptures.*

And it is evident that this is not God himself absolutely considered; for so he is only the material object of our faith: "He that cometh to God must believe that he is" (Heb. 11:6). Nor is it the truth of God absolutely; for that we believe as we do other essential properties of his nature. But it is the truth of God revealing himself, his mind and will unto us in the Scripture. This is the sole reason why we believe anything with divine faith.

It is or may be inquired, Wherefore we do believe Jesus Christ to be the Son of God, or that God is one in nature, subsisting in three persons, the Father, Son, and Holy Spirit? I answer, it is because God himself, the first truth, who cannot lie, has revealed and declared these things so to be, and he who is our all requires us so to believe. If it be asked how, wherein, or whereby God has revealed or declared these things so to be, or what is that revelation which God has made hereof? I answer, it is the Scripture, and that only. And if it be asked how I know this Scripture to be a divine revelation, to be the word of God? I answer, (1) I do not know it demonstratively, upon rational, scientifical principles, because such a divine revelation is not capable of such a demonstration (1 Cor. 2:9). (2) I do not assent unto it, or think it to be so, only upon arguments and motives highly probable, or morally uncontrollable only, as I am assuredly persuaded of many other things whereof I can have no certain demonstration (1 Thess. 2:13). (3) But I believe it so to be with faith divine and supernatural, resting on and resolved into the authority and veracity of God himself, evidencing themselves unto my mind, my soul, and conscience by this revelation itself, and not otherwise.

Here we rest, and deny that we believe the Scripture to be the word of God formally for any other reason but itself, which assures us of its divine authority. And if we rest not here, we must run on the rock of a moral certainty only, which shakes the foundation of all divine faith, or fall into the gulf and labyrinth of an endless circle in proving two things mutually by one another, as the church by the Scripture and the Scripture by the church, in an everlasting rotation. Unless we intend so to wander, we must come to something wherein we may rest for its own sake, and that not with a strong and firm opinion, but with divine faith. And nothing can rationally pretend unto this privilege but the truth of God manifesting itself in the Scripture. And, therefore, those who will not allow it hereunto do some of them wisely deny that the Scripture's being the word of God is the object of divine faith directly, but only of a moral persuasion from external arguments and considerations. And I do believe that they will grant, that if the Scripture be so to be believed, it must be for its own sake. For those who would have us to believe the Scripture to be the word of God upon the authority of the church, proposing it unto us and witnessing it so to be, though they make a fair appearance of a ready and easy way for the exercise of faith, yet when things come to be sifted and tried, they do so confound all sorts of things that they know not where to stand or abide. But it is not now my business to examine their pretenses, I have done it elsewhere.[2] I shall therefore prove and establish the assertion laid down, after I have made way to it by one or two previous observations.

1. We suppose herein all the motives of credibility before mentioned, that is, all the arguments *ab extra*,[3] which vehemently persuade the Scripture to be the word of God, and wherewith it may be protected against objections and temptations to the contrary. They have all of them their use, and may in their proper place be insisted on. Especially ought they to be pleaded when the Scripture is attacked by an atheism arising from the love and practice of those lusts and sins which are severely condemned therein, and threatened with the utmost vengeance. With others, they may be considered as previous inducements unto believing, or concomitant[4] means of strengthening faith in them that do believe.¶

In the first way, I confess, to the best of my observation of things past and present, their use is not great, nor ever has been in the church of God. For assuredly the most that do sincerely believe the divine origin and authority of the Scripture do it without any great consideration of them or being much influenced by them. And there are many who, as Augustine speaks, are saved *simplicitate credendi*,[5] and not *subtilitate disputandi*,[6] that are not able to inquire much into them, nor yet to apprehend much of their force and efficacy, when they are proposed unto them. Most persons, therefore, are effectually converted to God, and have saving faith, whereby they believe the Scripture, and virtually all that is contained in it, before they have ever once considered them. And God forbid we should think that none believe the Scriptures aright but those who are able to apprehend and manage the subtle arguments of learned men produced in their confirmation! Yea, we affirm, on the contrary, that those who believe them on no other grounds have, indeed, no true divine faith at all. Hence, they were not of old insisted on for the ingenerating of faith in them to whom the word was preached, nor ordinarily are so to this day by any who understand what is their work

---

2   Owen is referring to *Of the Divine Original, Authority, Self-Evidencing Light, and Power of the Scriptures*.
3   Lat. "from the outside."
4   I.e., accompanying.
5   Lat. "in simplicity of belief."
6   Lat. "by subtlety of examination."

and duty. But in the second way, wherever there is occasion from objections, oppositions, or temptations, they may be pleaded to good use and purpose. And they may do well to be furnished with them who are unavoidably exposed unto trials of that nature. For as for that course which some take, in all places and at all times, to be disputing about the Scriptures and their authority, it is a practice giving countenance unto atheism, and is to be abhorred of all that fear God, and the consequents of it are sufficiently manifest.

2. The ministry of the church, as it is the ground and pillar of truth, holding it up and declaring it, is in an ordinary way previously necessary unto believing; for "faith cometh by hearing, and hearing by the Word of God."[7] We believe the Scripture to be the word of God for itself alone, but not by itself alone. The ministry of the word is the means which God has appointed for the declaration and making known the testimony which the Holy Spirit gives in the Scripture unto its divine origin. And this is the ordinary way whereby men are brought to believe the Scripture to be the word of God. The church in its ministry, owning, witnessing, and avowing it so to be, instructing all sorts of persons out of it, there is, together with a sense and apprehension of the truth and power of the things taught and revealed in it, faith in itself as the word of God ingenerated in them.

3. We do also here suppose the internal effectual work of the Spirit begetting faith in us, as was before declared, without which we can believe neither the Scriptures nor anything else with faith divine, not for want of evidence in them, but of faith in ourselves.

These things being supposed, we do affirm, that it is the authority and truth of God, as manifesting themselves in the supernatural revelation made in the Scripture, that our faith arises from and is resolved into. And herein consists that testimony which the Spirit gives unto the word of God that it is so; for it is the Spirit that bears witness, because the Spirit is truth. The Holy Ghost being the immediate author of the whole Scripture, does therein and thereby give testimony unto the divine truth and origin of it, by the characters of divine authority and veracity impressed on it, and evidencing themselves in its power and efficacy. And let it be observed, that what we assert respects the revelation itself, the Scripture, "the writing," τὴν γραφήν, and not merely the things written or contained in it. The arguments produced by some to prove the truth of the doctrines of the Scripture reach not the cause in hand. For our inquiry is not about believing the truths revealed, but about believing the revelation itself, the Scripture itself, to be divine. And this we do only

7   Rom. 10:17.

because of the authority and veracity of the revealer, that is, of God himself, manifesting themselves therein.

To manifest this fully I shall do these things.

First, prove that our faith is so resolved into the Scripture as a divine revelation, and not into anything else; that is, we believe the Scripture to be the word of God for its own sake, and not for the sake of anything else, either external arguments or authoritative testimony of men whatever.

Second, show how or by what means the Scripture does evidence its own divine origin, or that the authority of God is so evidenced in it and by it as that we need no other formal cause or reason of our faith, whatever motives or means of believing we may make use of. And as to the first of these.[8]

FAITH RESOLVED INTO SCRIPTURE AS DIVINE REVELATION

That is the formal reason whereon we do believe, which the Scripture proposes as the only reason why we should so do, why it is our duty to do so, and whereunto it requires our assent. Now, this is to itself as it is the word of God, and because it is so. Or it proposes the authority of God in itself, and that alone, which we are to acquiesce in, and the truth of God, and that alone, which our faith is to rest on and is resolved into. It does not require us to believe it upon the testimony of any church, or on any other arguments that it gives us to prove that it is from God, but speaks unto us immediately in his name, and thereon requires faith and obedience.

Some, it may be, will ask whether this proves the Scripture to be the word of God, because it says so of itself, when any other writing may say the same? But we are not now giving arguments to prove unto others the Scripture to be the word of God, but only proving and showing what our own faith rests on and is resolved into, or, at least, ought so to be. How it evidences itself unto our faith to be the word of God we shall afterward declare. It is sufficient unto our present purpose that God requires us to believe the Scripture for no other reason but because it is his word, or a divine revelation from him; and if so, his authority and truth are the formal reason why we believe the Scripture or anything contained in it. To this purpose do testimonies abound in particular, besides that general attestation which is given unto it in that sole preface of divine revelations, "Thus saith the Lord" and therefore they are to be believed. Some of them we must mention.

---

8 This second point is picked up in chap. 6.

THE BIBLICAL ARGUMENT

> When all Israel is come to appear before the Lord thy God in the place
> which he shall choose, thou shalt read this law before all Israel in their
> hearing. Gather the people together, men, and women, and children, and
> thy stranger that is within thy gates, that they may hear, and that they may
> learn, and fear the Lord your God, and observe to do all the words of this
> law, and that their children, which have not known anything, may hear, and
> learn to fear the Lord your God. (Deut. 31:11–13)

It is plain that God here requires faith and obedience of the whole people,
men, women, and children. The inquiry is, what he requires it unto? It is to
this law, to this law written in the books of Moses, which was to be read unto
them out of the book, at the hearing of which they were obliged to believe and
obey. To evidence that law to be his, he proposes nothing but itself. But it will
be said, "That generation was sufficiently convinced that the law was from
God by the miracles which they beheld in the giving of it"; but, moreover,
it is ordered to be proposed unto children of future generations, who knew
nothing, that they may hear, and learn to fear the Lord.

That which, by the appointment of God, is to be proposed unto them that
know nothing, that they may believe, that is unto them the formal reason of
their believing. But this is the written word: "Thou shalt read this law unto
them which have not known anything, that they may hear and learn," etc.
Whatever use, therefore, there may be of other motives or testimonies to
commend the law unto us, of the ministry of the church especially, which is
here required unto the proposal of the word unto men, it is the law itself, or
the written word, which is the object of our faith, and which we believe for
its own sake. See also Deuteronomy 29:29, where "revealed things" are said
to "belong unto us and our children, that we might do them," that is, receive
them on the account of their divine revelation.

> When they shall say unto you, Seek unto them that have familiar spirits,
> and unto wizards that peep and that mutter; should not a people seek unto
> their God? For the living to the dead? To the law and to the testimony;
> if they speak not according to this word, it is because there is no light in
> them. (Isa. 8:19–20)

The inquiry is, by what means men may come to satisfaction in their minds
and consciences, or what their faith or trust is in. Two things are proposed unto

this end. One, immediate diabolical revelations, real or pretended. Two, the written word of God, "the law and the testimony." Hereunto are we sent, and that upon the account of its own authority alone, in opposition unto all other pretenses of assurance or security. And the sole reason why anyone does not acquiesce by faith in the written word is because he has no mornings or light of truth shining on him. But how shall we know the law and testimony, this written word, to be the word of God, and believe it so to be, and distinguish it from every other pretended divine revelation that is not so? This is declared,

"The prophet that hath a dream, let him tell a dream; and he that hath my word, let him speak my word faithfully. 'What is the chaff to the wheat?' saith the Lord. 'Is not my word like as a fire?' saith the Lord, 'and like a hammer that breaketh the rock in pieces?'" (Jer. 23:28–29). It is supposed that there are two persons in reputation for divine revelations, esteemed "prophets," one of them only pretends so to be, and declares the dreams of his own fancy, or the divinations of his own mind, as the word of God. The other has the word of God, and declares it faithfully from him. Yea, but how shall we know the one from the other? Even as men know wheat from chaff, by their different natures and effects. For as false, pretended revelations are but as chaff, which every wind will scatter, so the true word of God is like a fire and like a hammer, is accompanied with such light, efficacy, and power that it manifests itself unto the consciences of men so to be. Hereon does God call us to rest our faith on it, in opposition unto all other pretenses whatever.

But is it of this authority and efficacy in itself? See Luke 16:27–31, "Then he said," the rich man in hell, "I pray thee therefore, father, that thou wouldest send him," Lazarus, who was dead, "unto my father's house, for I have five brethren, that he may testify unto them lest they also come into this place of torment. Abraham saith unto him, 'They have Moses and the prophets, let them hear them.' And he said, 'Nay, father Abraham, but if one went unto them from the dead, they will repent.' And he said unto him, 'If they hear not Moses and the prophets, neither will they be persuaded, though one rose from the dead.'" The question here between Abraham and the rich man in this parable, indeed between the wisdom of God and the superstitious contrivances of men, is about the way and means of bringing those who are unbelievers and impenitent unto faith and repentance. He who was in hell apprehended that nothing would make them believe but a miracle, one rising from the dead and speaking unto them; which, or the like marvelous operations, many at this day think would have mighty power and influence upon them to settle their minds and change their lives. Should they see one "rise from the dead," and come and converse with them, this would convince them of the immortality of the soul, of future rewards and punishments, as giving them sufficient evidence thereof, so that they would assuredly repent and change their lives; but as things are stated, they have no sufficient evidence of these things, so that they doubt so far about them as that they are not really influenced by them; give them but one real miracle, and you shall have them forever. This, I say, was the opinion and judgment of him who was represented as in hell, as it is of many who are posting thither apace. He who was in heaven thought otherwise, wherein we have the immediate judgment of Jesus Christ given in this matter, determining this controversy. The question is about sufficient evidence and efficacy to cause us to believe things divine and supernatural; and this he determines to be in the written word, "Moses and the prophets." If he that will not believe on the single evidence of the written word to be from God, or a divine revelation of his will, will never believe upon the evidence of miracles nor any other motives, then that written word contains in itself the entire formal reason of faith, or all that evidence of the authority and truth of God in it, which faith divine and supernatural rests upon; that is, it is to be believed for its own sake. But says our Lord Jesus Christ himself, "If men will not hear," that is, believe, "Moses and the prophets, neither will they be persuaded, though one rose from the dead," and come and preach unto them, a greater miracle than which they could not desire. Now, this could not be spoken if the Scripture did not contain in itself the whole entire formal reason of believing; for if it have not this, something necessary unto believing would be wanting, though that were enjoyed. And this is directly affirmed,

"And many other signs truly did Jesus in the presence of his disciples, which are not written in this book. But these are written, that ye might believe that Jesus is the Christ, the Son of God, and that believing ye might have life through his name" (John 20:30–31). The signs which Christ wrought did evidence him to be the Son of God. But how come we to know and believe these signs? What is the way and means thereof? Says the blessed apostle, "These things are written, that ye might believe"; this writing of them by divine inspiration is so far sufficient to beget and assure faith in you, as that thereby you may have eternal life through Jesus Christ. For if the writing of divine things and revelations be the means appointed of God to cause men to believe unto eternal life, then it must, as such, carry along with it sufficient reason why we should believe, and grounds whereon we should do so. And in like manner is this matter determined by the apostle Peter,

For we have not followed cunningly-devised fables, when we made known unto you the power and coming of our Lord Jesus Christ, but were eye-witnesses of his majesty. For he received from God the Father honour and glory, when there came such a voice to him from the excellent glory, "This is my beloved Son, in whom I am well pleased." And this voice which came from heaven we heard, when we were with him in the holy mount. We have also a more sure word of prophecy, whereunto ye do well that ye take heed, as unto a light that shineth in a dark place, until the day dawn, and the day-star arise in your hearts. Knowing this first, that no prophecy of the Scripture is of any private interpretation. For the prophecy came not in old time by the will of man; but holy men of God spake as they were moved by the Holy Ghost. (2 Pet. 1:16–21)

The question is about the gospel, or the declaration of the powerful coming of Jesus Christ, whether it were to be believed or no? And if it were, upon what grounds? Some said it was a "cunningly-devised fable"; others, that it was a fanatical story of madmen, as Festus thought of it when preached by Paul (Acts 26:24), and very many are of the same mind still.¶

The apostles, on the contrary, averred that what was spoken concerning him were "words of truth and soberness,"[9] yea, "faithful sayings, and worthy of all acceptation" (1 Tim. 1:15), that is, to be believed for its worth and truth. The grounds and reasons hereof are two. (1) The testimony of the apostles, who not only conversed with Jesus Christ and were "eyewitnesses of his majesty," beholding his glory, "the glory as of the only-begotten of the Father, full of grace and truth" (John 1:14), which they gave in evidence of the truth of the gospel (1 John 1:1), but also heard a miraculous testimony given unto him immediately from God in heaven (2 Pet. 1:17–18). This gave them, indeed, sufficient assurance; but whereinto shall they resolve their faith who heard not this testimony? (2) Why, they have "a more sure," that is, a most sure, "word of prophecy," that is, the written word of God, that is sufficient of itself to secure their faith in this matter, especially as confirmed by the testimony of the apostles, whereby the church comes to be built in its faith "on the foundation of the apostles and prophets" (Eph. 2:20). But why should we believe this word of prophecy? May not that also be a "cunningly-devised fable," and the whole Scripture be but the suggestions of men's private spirits, as is objected (2 Pet. 1:20)? All is finally resolved into this, that the writers of it were immediately "moved" or acted "by the Holy Ghost," from which divine origin it carries along its own evidence with it. Plainly, that which the apostle teaches us is that we believe all other divine truths for the Scripture's sake, or because they are declared therein; but the Scripture we believe for its own sake, or because "holy men of God" wrote it "as they were moved by the Holy Ghost."

9 Acts 26:25.

So is the whole object of faith proposed by the same apostle: "The words which were spoken before by the holy prophets, and of the commandment of the apostles of the Lord and Saviour" (2 Pet. 3:2). And because our faith is resolved into them, we are said to be "built upon the foundation of the apostles and prophets," as was said (Eph. 2:20), that is, our faith rests solely, as on its proper foundation, which bears the weight of it, on the authority and truth of God in their writings. Hereunto we may add that of Paul.

"According to the revelation of the mystery which was kept secret since the world began, but now is made manifest, and by the scriptures of the prophets, according to the commandment of the everlasting God, made known to all nations for the obedience of faith" (Rom. 16:25–26). The matter to be believed is the mystery of the gospel, which was kept secret since the world began, or from the giving of the first promise, not absolutely, but with respect unto that full manifestation which it has now received. This God commands to be believed, the everlasting God, he who has sovereign authority over all, requires faith in a way of obedience hereunto. But what ground or reason have we to believe it? This alone is proposed, namely, the divine revelation made in the preaching of the apostles and writings of the prophets; for "faith cometh by hearing, and hearing by the Word of God" (Rom. 10:17). This course, and no other, did our Savior, even after his resurrection, take to beget and confirm faith in the disciples (Luke 24:25–27). That great testimony to this purpose, 2 Timothy 3:15–17, I do not plead in particular, because I have so fully insisted on it in another discourse.[10]

From these and many other testimonies to the same purpose which might be produced, it is evident,

1. That it is the Scripture itself, the word or will of God as revealed or written, which is proposed unto us as the object of our faith and obedience, which we are to receive and believe with faith divine and supernatural.

2. That no other reason is proposed unto us either as a motive to encourage us, or as an argument to assure us that we shall not be mistaken, but only its own divine origin and authority, making our duty necessary and securing our faith infallibly. And those testimonies are with me of more weight a thousand times than the plausible reasonings of any to the contrary. With some, indeed, it is grown a matter of contempt to quote or cite the Scripture in our writings, such reverence have they for the ancient fathers, some of whose writings are nothing else but a perpetual contexture[11] of Scripture. But

---

10 *Of the Divine Original, Authority, Self-Evidencing Light, and Power of The Scriptures*, chap. 3.
11 I.e., weaving; linking together.

for such who pretend to despise those testimonies in this case, it is because either they do not understand what they are produced to confirm or cannot answer the proof that is in them. For it is not unlikely but that some persons, well-conceited of their own understanding in things wherein they are most ignorant, will pride and please themselves in the ridiculousness of proving the Scripture to be the word of God by testimonies taken out of it. But, as was said, we must not forgo the truth because either they will not or cannot understand what we discourse about.

The Example of the Prophets and Apostles

Our assertion is confirmed by the uniform practice of the prophets and apostles, and all the penmen of the Scripture, in proposing those divine revelations which they received by immediate inspiration from God. For that which was the reason of their faith unto whom they first declared those divine revelations, is the reason of our faith now they are recorded in the Scripture. For the writing of it being by God's appointment, it comes into the room and supplies the place of their oral ministry. On what ground soever men were obliged to receive and believe divine revelations when made unto them by the prophets and apostles, on the same are we obliged to receive and believe them now they are made unto us in the Scripture, the writing being by divine inspiration, and appointed as the means and cause of our faith. It is true, God was pleased sometimes to bear witness unto their personal ministry by miracles or signs and wonders, as, "God bearing them witness" (Heb. 2:4). But this was only at some seasons, and with some of them. That which they universally insisted on, whether they wrought any miracles or not, was, that the word which they preached, declared, wrote, was not the word of man, came not by any private suggestion, or from any invention of their own, but was indeed the word of God (1 Thess. 2:13), and declared by them as they were acted by the Holy Ghost (2 Pet. 1:21).

Under the Old Testament, although the prophets sometimes referred persons unto the word already written, as that which their faith was to acquiesce in (Isa. 8:20; Mal. 4:4), setting out its power and excellency for all the ends of faith and obedience (Pss. 19:7–9; 119), and not to anything else, nor to any other motives or arguments to beget and require faith, but its own authority only; yet as to their own special messages and revelations, they laid the foundation of all the faith and obedience which they required in this alone, "Thus saith the Lord, the God of truth." And under the New Testament, the infallible preachers and writers thereof do in the first place propose the writings of the Old Testament to be received for their own sake, or on the account of their divine origin (see John 1:45; Luke 16:29, 31; Matt. 21:42; Acts 18:24–25, 28; 24:14; 26:22; 2 Pet. 1:21). Hence are they called "The oracles of God" (Rom. 3:2). And oracles always required an assent for their own sake, and other evidence they pleaded none. And for the revelations which they superadded, they pleaded that they had them immediately from God "by Jesus Christ" (Gal. 1:1). And this was accompanied with such an infallible assurance in them that received them as to be preferred above a supposition of the highest miracle to confirm anything to the contrary (Gal. 1:8). For if an angel from heaven should have preached any other doctrine than what they revealed and proposed in the name and authority of God, they were to esteem him accursed. For this cause they still insisted on their apostolical authority and mission, which included infallible inspiration and direction, as the reason of the faith of them unto whom they preached and wrote. And as for those who were not themselves divinely inspired, or wherein those that were so did not act by immediate inspiration, they proved the truth of what they delivered by its consonancy unto the Scriptures already written, referring the minds and consciences of men unto them for their ultimate satisfaction (Acts 18:28; 28:23).

The Obligation to Believe

It was before granted that there is required, as subservient unto believing, as a means of it, or for the resolution of our faith into the authority of God in the Scriptures, the ministerial proposal of the Scriptures and the truths contained in them, with the command of God for obedience unto them (Rom. 16:25–26). This ministry of the church, either extraordinary or ordinary, God has appointed unto this end, and ordinarily it is indispensable thereunto: "How shall they believe in him of whom they have not heard? And how shall they hear without a preacher? And how shall they preach, except they be sent?" (Rom. 10:14–15). Without this, ordinarily we cannot believe the Scripture to be the word of God, nor the things contained in it to be from him, though we do not believe either the one or the other for it. I do grant that in extraordinary cases outward providences may supply the room of this ministerial proposal; for it is all one, as unto our duty, by what means the Scripture is brought unto us. But upon a supposition of this ministerial proposal of the word, which ordinarily includes the whole duty of the church in its testimony and declaration of the truth, I desire to know whether those unto whom it is proposed are obliged, without further external evidence, to receive it as the word of God, to rest their faith on it, and submit their consciences unto it? The rule seems plain, that they are obliged so to do

(Mark 16:16). We may consider this under the distinct ways of its proposal, extraordinary and ordinary.

Upon the preaching of any of the prophets by immediate inspiration of the Holy Ghost, or on their declaration of any new revelation they had from God, by preaching or writing, suppose Isaiah or Jeremiah, I desire to know whether or not all persons were bound to receive their doctrine as from God, to believe and submit unto the authority of God in the revelation made by him, without any external motives or arguments, or the testimony or authority of the church witnessing thereunto? If they were not, then were they all excused as guiltless who refused to believe the message they declared in the name of God, and in despising the warnings and instructions which they gave them. For external motives they used not, and the present church mostly condemned them and their ministry, as is plain in the case of Jeremiah. Now, it is impious to imagine that those to whom they spoke in the name of God were not obliged to believe them, and it tends to the overthrow of all religion. If we shall say that they were obliged to believe them, and that under the penalty of divine displeasure, and so to receive the revelation made by them, on their declaration of it, as the word of God, then it must contain in it the formal reason of believing, or the full and entire cause, reason, and ground why they ought to believe with faith divine and supernatural. Or let another ground of faith in this case be assigned.

Suppose the proposal be made in the ordinary ministry of the church. Hereby the Scripture is declared unto men to be the word of God; they are acquainted with it, and with what God requires of them therein, and they are charged in the name of God to receive and believe it. Does any obligation unto believing hence arise? It may be some will say that immediately there is not; only they will grant that men are bound hereon to inquire into such reasons and motives as are proposed unto them for its reception and admission. I say there is no doubt but that men are obliged to consider all things of that nature which are proposed unto them, and not to receive it with brutish, implicit belief. For the receiving of it is to be an act of men's own minds or understandings, on the best grounds and evidences which the nature of the thing proposed is capable of. But supposing men to do their duty in their diligent inquiries into the whole matter, I desire to know whether, by the proposal mentioned, there come upon men an obligation to believe? If there do not, then are all men perfectly innocent who refuse to receive the gospel in the preaching of it, as to any respect unto that preaching; which to say is to overthrow the whole dispensation of the ministry. If they are obliged to believe upon the preaching of it, then has the word in itself those evidences of its divine origin and authority which are a sufficient ground of faith or reason of believing; for what God requires us to believe upon has so always.

As the issue of this whole discourse, it is affirmed that our faith is built on and resolved into the Scripture itself, which carries with it its own evidence of being a divine revelation; and therefore does that faith ultimately rest on the truth and authority of God alone, and not on any human testimony, such as is that of the church, nor on any rational arguments or motives that are absolutely fallible.

6

The Nature of Divine Revelations

Their Self-Evidencing Power Considered, Particularly
That of the Scriptures as the Word of God

IT MAY BE SAID that if the Scripture thus evidences itself to be the word of God, as the sun manifests itself by light and fire by heat, or as the first principles of reason are evident in themselves without farther proof or testimony, then everyone, and all men, upon the proposal of the Scripture unto them, and its own bare assertion that it is the word of God, would necessarily, on that evidence alone, assent thereunto, and believe it so to be. But this is not so, all experience lies against it; nor is there any pleadable ground of reason that so it is, or that so it ought to be.

In answer unto this objection I shall do these two things:

First, I shall show what it is, what power, what faculty in the minds of men, whereunto this revelation is proposed, and whereby we assent unto the truth of it; wherein the mistakes whereon this objection proceeds will be discovered.

Second, I shall mention some of those things whereby the Holy Ghost testifies and gives evidence unto the Scripture in and by itself, so as that our faith may be immediately resolved into the veracity of God alone.

EPISTEMOLOGICAL CONSIDERATIONS

And, in the first place, we may consider that there are three ways whereby we assent unto anything that is proposed unto us as true, and receive it as such.

1. By inbred principles of natural light, and the first rational actings of our minds. This in reason answers instinct in irrational creatures. Hence God complains that his people did neglect and sin against their own natural

light and first dictates of reason, whereas brute creatures would not forsake the conduct of the instinct of their natures (Isa. 1:3). In general, the mind is necessarily determined to an assent unto the proper objects of these principles; it cannot do otherwise. It cannot but assent unto the prime dictates of the light of nature, yea, those dictates are nothing but its assent. Its first apprehension of the things which the light of nature embraces, without either express reasonings or further consideration, is this assent. Thus does the mind embrace in itself the general notions of moral good and evil, with the difference between them, however, it practically complies not with what they guide unto (Jude 10). And so does it assent unto many principles of reason, as that the whole is greater than the part, without admitting any debate about them.

2. By rational consideration of things externally proposed unto us. Herein the mind exercises its discursive faculty, gathering one thing out of another, and concluding one thing from another. And hereon is it able to assent unto what is proposed unto it in various degrees of certainty, according unto the nature and degree of the evidence it proceeds upon. Hence it has a certain knowledge of some things, of others, an opinion or persuasion prevalent against the objections to the contrary, which it knows, and whose force it understands, which may be true or false.

3. By faith. This respects that power of our minds whereby we are able to assent unto anything as true which we have no first principles concerning, no inbred notions of, nor can from more known principles make unto ourselves any certain rational conclusions concerning them. This is our assent upon testimony, whereon we believe many things which no sense, inbred principles, nor reasonings of our own, could either give us an acquaintance with or an assurance of. And this assent also has not only various degrees, but is also of divers kinds, according as the testimony is which it arises from and rests on; as being human if that be human, and divine if that be so also.

According to these distinct faculties and powers of our souls, God is pleased to reveal or make known himself, his mind or will, three ways unto us. For he has implanted no power in our minds, but the principal use and exercise of it are to be with respect unto himself and our living unto him, which is the end of them all. And a neglect of the improvement of them unto this end is the highest aggravation of sin. It is an aggravation of sin when men use the creatures of God otherwise than he has appointed, or in not using them to his glory; when they take his corn, and wine, and oil, and spend them on their lusts (Hos. 2:8). It is a higher aggravation when men in sinning abuse and dishonor their own bodies; for these are the principal external workmanship of God, being made for eternity, and whose preservation unto his glory is committed unto us in a special manner. This the apostle declares to be the peculiar aggravation of the sin of fornication, and uncleanness of any kind (1 Cor. 6:18–19). But the height of impiety consists in the abuse of the faculties and powers of the soul, wherewith we are endowed purposely and immediately for the glorifying of God. Hence proceed unbelief, profaneness, blasphemy, atheism, and the like pollutions of the spirit or mind. And these are sins of the highest provocation. For the powers and faculties of our minds being given us only to enable us to live unto God, the diverting of their principal exercise unto other ends is an act of enmity against him and affront unto him.

SELF-AUTHENTICATING REVELATION

1. He makes himself known unto us by the innate principles of our nature, unto which he has communicated, as a power of apprehending, so an indelible sense of his being, his authority, and his will, so far as our natural dependence on him and moral subjection unto him do require. For whereas there are two things in this natural light and these first dictates of reason: first, a power of conceiving, discerning, and assenting, and, secondly, a power of judging and determining upon the things so discerned and assented unto; by the one God makes known his being and essential properties, and by the other his sovereign authority over all.

As to the first, the apostle affirms that τὸ γνωστὸν τοῦ θεοῦ φανερόν ἐστιν ἐν αὐτοῖς, "that which may be known of God," his essence, being, subsistence, his natural, necessary, essential properties, "is manifest in them" (Rom. 1:19); that is, it has a self-evidencing power, acting itself in the minds of all men endued with natural light and reason.

And as unto his sovereign authority, he does evidence it in and by the consciences of men; which are the judgment that they make, and cannot but make, of themselves and their actions, with respect unto the authority and judgment of God (Rom. 2:14–15). And thus the mind does assent unto the principles of God's being and authority, antecedently unto any actual exercise of the discursive faculty of reason, or other testimony whatever.

2. He does it unto our reason in its exercise, by proposing such things unto its consideration as from whence it may and cannot but conclude in an assent unto the truth of what God intends to reveal unto us that way. This he does by the works of creation and providence, which present themselves unavoidably unto reason in its exercise, to instruct us in the nature, being, and properties of God.

Thus "the heavens declare the glory of God, and the firmament showeth his handywork. Day unto day uttereth speech, and night unto night showeth knowledge. There is no speech nor language, where their voice is not heard" (Ps. 19:1–3). But yet they do not thus declare, evidence, and reveal the glory of God unto the first principles and notions of natural light without the actual exercise of reason. They only do so "when we consider his heavens, the work of his fingers, the moon and the stars, which he hath ordained," as the same psalmist speaks (Ps. 8:3). A rational consideration of them, their greatness, order, beauty, and use is required unto that testimony and evidence which God gives in them and by them unto himself, his glorious being [and] power. To this purpose the apostle discourses at large concerning the works of creation (Rom. 1:20–21), as also of those of providence (Acts 14:15–17; 17:24–28), and the rational use we are to make of them (Rom. 1:29). So, God calls unto men for the exercise of their reason about these things, reproaching them with stupidity and brutishness where they are wanting therein (Isa. 46:5–8; 44:18–20).

3. God reveals himself unto our faith, or that power of our souls whereby we are able to assent unto the truth of what is proposed unto us upon testimony. And this he does by his word, or the Scriptures, proposed unto us in the manner and way before expressed.

He does not reveal himself by his word unto the principles of natural light, nor unto reason in its exercise. But yet these principles, and reason itself, with all the faculties of our minds, are consequentially affected with that revelation, and are drawn forth into their proper exercise by it. But in the gospel the "righteousness of God is revealed from faith to faith" (Rom. 1:17), not to natural light, sense, or reason in the first place. And it is faith that is the evidence of things not seen, as revealed in the word (Heb. 11:1). Unto this kind of revelation, "Thus saith the Lord" is the only ground and reason of our assent; and that assent is the assent of faith, because it is resolved into testimony alone.

The Consonance of Revelation

And concerning these several ways of the communication or revelation of the knowledge of God, it must be always observed that there is a perfect consonancy in the things revealed by them all. If anything pretends from the one what is absolutely contradictory unto the other, or our senses as the means of them, it is not to be received.

The foundation of the whole, as of all the actings of our souls, is in the inbred principles of natural light, or first necessary dictates of our intellectual, rational nature. This, so far as it extends, is a rule unto our apprehension in all that follows. Wherefore, if any pretend, in the exercise of reason, to conclude unto anything concerning the nature, being, or will of God, that is directly contradictory unto those principles and dictates, it is no divine revelation unto our reason, but a paralogism[1] from the defect of reason in its exercise. This is that which the apostle charges on and vehemently urges against the heathen philosophers. Inbred notions they had in themselves of the being and eternal power of God; and these were so manifest in them thereby that they could not but own them. Hereon they set their rational, discursive faculty at work in the consideration of God and his being. But herein were they so vain and foolish as to draw conclusions directly contrary unto the first principles of natural light, and the unavoidable notions which they had of the eternal being of God (Rom. 1:21–25). And many, upon their pretended rational consideration of the promiscuous event of things in the world, have foolishly concluded that all things had a fortuitous beginning, and have fortuitous events, or such as, from a concatenation[2] of antecedent causes, are fatally necessary, and are not disposed by an infinitely wise, unerring, holy providence. And this also is directly contradictory unto the first principles and notions of natural light, whereby it openly proclaims itself not to be an effect of reason in its due exercise, but a mere delusion.

So, if any pretend unto revelations by faith which are contradictory unto the first principles of natural light or reason, in its proper exercise about its proper objects, it is a delusion. On this ground, the Roman doctrine of transubstantiation is justly rejected; for it proposes that as a revelation by faith, which is expressly contradictory unto our sense and reason in their proper exercise about their proper objects. And a supposition of the possibility of any such thing would make the ways whereby God reveals and makes known himself to cross and interfere one with another; which would leave us no certainty in anything, divine or human.

The Priority of Special Revelation

But yet as these means of divine revelation do harmonize and perfectly agree one with the other, so they are not objectively equal, or equally extensive, nor are they coordinate, but subordinate unto one another. Wherefore, there are many things discernible by reason in its exercise which do not appear unto the first principles of natural light. So the sober philosophers of old

---

1   I.e., illogical or fallacious reasoning or argument.
2   I.e., a series of interconnected things or events.

attained unto many true and great conceptions of God and the excellencies of his nature, above what they arrived unto who either did not or could not cultivate and improve the principles of natural light in the same manner as they did. It is, therefore, folly to pretend that things so made known of God are not infallibly true and certain, because they are not obvious unto the first conceptions of natural light, without the due exercise of reason, provided they are not contradictory thereunto. And there are many things revealed unto faith that are above and beyond the comprehension of reason in the best and utmost of its most proper exercise. Such are all the principal mysteries of Christian religion. And it is the height of folly to reject them, as some do, because they are not discernible and comprehensible by reason, seeing they are not contradictory thereunto. Wherefore, these ways of God's revelation of himself are not equally extensive or commensurate, but are so subordinate one unto another that what is wanting unto the one is supposed by the other, unto the accomplishment of the whole and entire end of divine revelation; and the truth of God is the same in them all.

1. The revelation which God makes of himself in the first way, by the inbred principles of natural light, does sufficiently and infallibly evidence itself to be from him; it does it in, unto, and by those principles themselves. This revelation of God is infallible, the assent unto it is infallible, which the infallible evidence it gives of itself makes to be so. We dispute not now what a few atheistical skeptics pretend unto, whose folly has been sufficiently detected by others. All the sobriety that is in the world consents in this, that the light of the knowledge of God, in and by the inbred principles of our minds and consciences, does sufficiently, uncontrollably, and infallibly manifest itself to be from him, and that the mind neither is nor can be possibly imposed on in its apprehensions of that nature. And if the first dictates of reason concerning God do not evidence themselves to be from God, they are neither of any use nor force; for they are not capable of being confirmed by external arguments, and what is written about them is to show their force and evidence, not to give them any. Wherefore, this first way of God's revelation of himself unto us is infallible, and infallibly evidences itself in our minds, according to the capacity of our natures.

2. The revelation that God makes of himself by the works of creation and providence unto our reason in exercise, or the faculties of our souls as discursive, concluding rationally one thing from another, does sufficiently, yea, infallibly, evidence and demonstrate itself to be from him, so that it is impossible we should be deceived therein. It does not do so unto the inbred principles of natural light, unless they are engaged in a rational exercise about

the means of the revelation made; that is, we must rationally consider the works of God, both of creation and providence, or we cannot learn by them what God intends to reveal of himself. And in our doing so we cannot be deceived: for "the invisible things of God from the creation of the world are clearly seen, being understood by the things that are made, even his eternal power and Godhead" (Rom. 1:20). They are clearly seen, and therefore may be perfectly understood as to what they teach of God, without any possibility of mistake. And wherever men do not receive the revelation intended in the way intended, that is, do not certainly conclude that what God teaches by his works of creation and providence, namely, his eternal power and Godhead, with the essential properties thereof, infinite wisdom, goodness, righteousness, and the like, is certainly and infallibly so, believing it accordingly, it is not from any defect in the revelation, or its self-evidencing efficacy, but only from the depraved, vicious habits of their minds, their enmity against God, and dislike of him. And so the apostle says that they who rejected or improved not the revelation of God did it "because they did not like to retain God in their knowledge" (Rom. 1:28). For which cause God did so severely revenge their natural unbelief, as is there expressed (see Isa. 46:8; 44:19–20). That which I principally insist on from hence is, that the revelation which God makes of himself, by the works of creation and providence, does not evince itself unto the first principles of natural light, so as that an assent should be given thereunto, without the actual exercise of reason, or the discursive faculty of our minds about them, but thereunto it does infallibly evidence itself. So may the Scripture have, and has, a self-evidencing efficacy, though this appear not unto the light of first natural principles, no, nor to bare reason in its exercise. For,

3. Unto our faith God reveals himself by the Scripture, or his word, which he has magnified above all his name (Ps. 138:2), that is, implanted in it more characters of himself and his properties than in any other way whereby he reveals or makes himself known unto us. And this revelation of God by his word, we confess, is not sufficient nor suited to evidence itself unto the light of nature, or the first principles of our understanding, so that, by bare proposal of it to be from God, we should by virtue of them immediately assent unto it, as men assent unto self-evident natural principles, as that the part is less than the whole, or the like. Nor does it evidence itself unto our reason, in its mere natural exercise, as that by virtue thereof we can demonstratively conclude that it is from God, and that what is declared therein is certainly and infallibly true. It has, indeed, such external evidences accompanying it as make a great impression on reason itself. But the power of our souls whereunto it

is proposed is that whereby we can give an assent unto the truth upon the testimony of the proposer, whereof we have no other evidence. And this is the principal and most noble faculty and power of our nature. There is an instinct in brute creatures that has some resemblance unto our inbred natural principles, and they will act that instinct, improved by experience, into a great likeness of reason in its exercise, although it be not so. But as unto the power or faculty of giving an assent unto things on witness or testimony, there is nothing in the nature of irrational creatures that has the least shadow of it or likeness unto it. And if our souls did want but this one faculty of assenting unto truth upon testimony, all that remains would not be sufficient to conduct us through the affairs of this natural life. This, therefore, being the most noble faculty of our minds is that whereunto the highest way of divine revelation is proposed.

That our minds, in this special case, to make our assent to be according unto the mind of God, and such as is required of us in a way of duty, are to be prepared and assisted by the Holy Ghost, we have declared and proved before. On this supposition, the revelation which God makes of himself by his word does no less evidence itself unto our minds, in the exercise of faith, to be from him, or gives no less infallible evidence as a ground and reason why we should believe it to be from him, than his revelation of himself by the works of creation and providence does manifest itself unto our minds in the exercise of reason to be from him, nor with less assurance than what we assent unto, in and by the dictates of natural light. And when God reveals himself, that is, his "eternal power and Godhead," by "the things that are made,"[3] the works of creation, "the heavens declaring his glory, and the firmament showing his handywork,"[4] the reason of men, stirred up and brought into exercise thereby, does infallibly conclude, upon the evidence that is in that revelation, that there is a God, and he eternally powerful and wise, without any further arguments to prove the revelation to be true. So, when God by his word reveals himself unto the minds of men, thereby exciting and bringing forth faith into exercise, or the power of the soul to assent unto truth upon testimony, that revelation does no less infallibly evidence itself to be divine or from God, without any external arguments to prove it so to be.¶

If I shall say unto a man that the sun is risen and shines on the earth, if he question or deny it, and ask how I shall prove it, it is a sufficient answer

---

3 Rom. 1:20.
4 Ps. 19:1.

to say that it manifests itself in and by its own light. And if he adds that this is no proof to him, for he does not discern it; suppose that to be so, it is a satisfactory answer to tell him that he is blind; and if he be not so, that it is to no purpose to argue with him who contradicts his own sense, for he leaves no rule whereby what is spoken may be tried or judged on. And if I tell a man that the "heavens declare the glory of God, and the firmament showeth his handywork,"[5] or that the "invisible things of God from the creation of the world are clearly seen, being understood by the things that are made,"[6] and he shall demand how I prove it, it is a sufficient answer to say that these things, in and by themselves, do manifest unto the reason of every man, in its due and proper exercise, that there is an eternal, infinitely wise and powerful Being, by whom they were caused, produced, and made, so as that whosoever knows how to use and exercise his reasonable faculty in the consideration of them, their origin, order, nature, and use, must necessarily conclude that so it is. If he shall say that it does not so appear unto him that the being of God is so revealed by them, it is a sufficient reply, in case he be so indeed, to say he is phrenetic,[7] and has not the use of his reason; and if he be not so, that he argues in express contradiction unto his own reason, as may be demonstrated. This the heathen philosophers granted. Cicero says, "For when we gaze upward to the sky and contemplate the heavenly bodies, what can be so obvious and so manifest as that there must exist some power possessing transcendent intelligence by whom these things are ruled? . . . If a man doubts this, I really cannot see why he should not also be capable of doubting the existence of the sun."[8] And if I declare unto anyone that the Scripture is the word of God, a divine revelation, and that it does evidence and manifest itself so to be. If he shall say that he has the use and exercise of his sense and reason as well as others and yet it does not appear unto him so to be, it is, as unto the present inquiry, a sufficient reply, for the security of the authority of the Scriptures, though other means may be used for his

---

5 Ps. 19:1.
6 Rom. 1:20.
7 I.e., an archaic form of frenetic; frenzied, frantic.
8 In the text: *Quid enim potest*, says Cicero, *esse tam apertum, tamque perspicuum, cùm coelum suspeximus, coelestiaque contemplati sumus, quàm esse aliquod numen praestantissimae mentis, quo haec regantur? . . . Quod qui dubitet, haud sane intelligo cur non idem, sol sit, an nullus sit, dubitare possit* (De Natura Deor. lib. ii. 2).—Owen. For the Latin text and English translation, see Cicero, *On the Nature of the Gods. Academics*, trans. H. Rackham, Loeb Classical Library 268 (Cambridge, MA: Harvard University Press, 1933), 125–27. Cicero's *De natura deorum* (45 BC), or *On the Nature of the Gods*, is a philosophical dialogue that examines theological topics from skeptical, Stoic, and Epicurean perspectives.

176 THE REASON OF FAITH

conviction, to say that "all men have not faith,"[9] by which alone the evidence of the divine authority of the Scripture is discoverable, in the light whereof alone we can read those characters of its divine extract which are impressed on it and communicated unto it.

If it be not so, seeing it is a divine revelation, and it is our duty to believe it so to be, it must be either because our faith is not fitted, suited, nor able to receive such an evidence, suppose God would give it unto the revelation of himself by his word, as he has done unto those by the light of nature and works of providence, or because God would not or could not give such an evidence unto his word as might manifest itself so to be. And neither of these can be affirmed without a high reflection on the wisdom and goodness of God.

That our faith is capable of giving such an assent is evident from hence, because God works it in us and bestows it upon us for this very end. And God requires of us that we should infallibly believe what he proposes unto us, at least when we have infallible evidence that it is from him. And as he appoints faith unto this end, and approves of its exercise, so he does both judge and condemn them who fail therein (2 Chron. 20:20; Isa. 7:9; Mark 16:16). Yea, our faith is capable of giving an assent, though of another kind, more firm, and accompanied with more assurance, than any given by reason in the best of its conclusions. And the reason is, because the power of the mind to give assent upon testimony, which is its most noble faculty, is elevated and strengthened by the divine supernatural work of the Holy Ghost, before described.

To say that God either could not or would not give such a power unto the revelation of himself by his word as to evidence itself to be so is exceedingly prejudicial unto his honor and glory, seeing the everlasting welfare of the souls of men is incomparably more concerned therein than in the other ways mentioned. And what reason could be assigned why he should implant a less evidence of his divine authority on this than on them, seeing he designed far greater and more glorious ends in this than in them? If anyone shall say the reason is because this kind of divine revelation is not capable of receiving such evidences, it must be either because there cannot be evident characters of divine authority, goodness, wisdom, power, implanted in it or mixed with it, or because an efficacy to manifest them cannot be communicated unto it. That both these are otherwise shall be demonstrated in the last part of this discourse, which I shall now enter upon.

---

9 2 Thess. 3:2.

HOW SCRIPTURE EVIDENCES ITS DIVINE
ORIGIN AND AUTHORITY

It has been already declared that it is the authority and veracity of God, revealing themselves in the Scripture and by it, that is the formal reason of our faith, or supernatural assent unto it as it is the word of God.

It remains only that we inquire, in the second place, into the way and means whereby they evidence themselves unto us, and the Scripture thereby to be the word of God, so as that we may undoubtedly and infallibly believe it so to be. Now, because faith, as we have showed, is an assent upon testimony, and consequently divine faith is an assent upon divine testimony, there must be some testimony or witness in this case whereon faith does rest. And this we say is the testimony of the Holy Ghost, the author of the Scriptures, given unto them, in them, and by them. And this work or testimony of the Spirit may be reduced unto two heads, which may be distinctly insisted on.

Divine Excellency

The impressions or characters which are subjectively left in the Scripture and upon it by the Holy Spirit, its author, of all the divine excellencies or properties of the divine nature, are the first means evidencing that testimony of the Spirit which our faith rests upon, or they do give the first evidence of its divine origin and authority, whereon we do believe it. The way whereby we learn the eternal power and deity of God from the works of creation is no otherwise but by those marks, tokens, and impressions of his divine power, wisdom, and goodness, that are upon them. For from the consideration of their subsistence, greatness, order, and use, reason does necessarily conclude an infinite subsisting Being, of whose power and wisdom these things are the manifest effects. These are clearly seen and understood by the things that are made. We need no other arguments to prove that God made the world but itself. It carries in it and upon it the infallible tokens of its origin. See to this purpose the blessed meditation of the psalmist (Ps. 104 throughout).¶

Now, there are greater and more evident impressions of divine excellencies left on the written word, from the infinite wisdom of the Author of it, than any that are communicated unto the works of God, of what sort soever. Hence David, comparing the works and the word of God, as to their instructive efficacy in declaring God and his glory, although he ascribes much unto the works of creation, yet does he prefer the word incomparably before them (Pss. 19:1–3, 7–9; 147:8–9, etc., 19–20). And these do manifest the word unto our faith to be his more clearly than the others do the works to be his unto our reason. As yet I do not know that it is denied by any, or the contrary asserted, namely, that God, as the immediate author of the Scripture, has left in the very word itself evident tokens and impressions of his wisdom, prescience, omniscience, power, goodness, holiness, truth, and other divine, infinite excellencies, sufficiently evidenced unto the enlightened minds of believers. Some, I confess, speak suspiciously herein, but until they will directly deny it, I shall not need further to confirm it than I have done long since in another treatise.[10] And I leave it to be considered whether, morally speaking, it be possible that God should immediately by himself, from the eternal counsels of his will, reveal himself, his mind, the thoughts and purposes of his heart, which had been hidden in himself from eternity, on purpose that we should believe them and yield obedience unto him, according to the declaration of himself so made, and yet not give with it or leave upon it any τεκμήριον, any "infallible token," evidencing him to be the author of that revelation. Men who are not ashamed of their Christianity will not be so to profess and seal that profession with their blood, and to rest their eternal concerns on that security herein which they have attained, namely, that there is that manifestation made of the glorious properties of God in and by the Scripture, as it is a divine revelation, which incomparably excels in evidence all that their reason receives concerning his power from the works of creation.

This is that whereon we believe the Scripture to be the word of God with faith divine and supernatural, if we believe it so at all. There is in itself that evidence of its divine origin, from the characters of divine excellencies left upon it by its author, the Holy Ghost, as faith quietly rests in and is resolved into. And this evidence is manifest unto the meanest and most unlearned, no less than unto the wisest philosophers. And the truth is, if rational arguments and external motives were the sole ground of receiving the Scripture to be the word of God, it could not be but that learned men and philosophers would have always been the most forward and most ready to admit it, and most firmly to adhere unto it and its profession. For whereas all such arguments do prevail on the minds of men according as they are able aright to discern their force and judge of them, learned philosophers would have had the advantage incomparably above others. And so some have of late affirmed that it was the wise, rational, and learned men who at first most readily received the gospel;[11] an assertion which nothing but gross ignorance of the Scripture

---

10   Owen is referring to *Of the Divine Original, Authority, Self-Evidencing Light, and Power of the Scriptures.*

11   Owen seems to be again combating the idea that the reason Christians believe the Bible to be the word of God is external argumentation or the exercise of rational faculties.

itself, and of all the writings concerning the origin of Christianity, whether of Christians or heathens, could give the least countenance unto (1 Cor. 1:23, 26). From hence is the Scripture so often compared unto light, called light, "a light shining in a dark place,"[12] which will evidence itself unto all who are not blind, nor do willfully shut their eyes, nor have their eyes blinded by the god of this world, lest the light of the glorious gospel of Christ, who is the image of God, should shine unto them; which consideration I have handled at large elsewhere.[13]

Divine Efficacy

The Spirit of God evidences the divine origin and authority of the Scripture by the power and authority which he puts forth in it and by it over the minds and consciences of men, with its operation of divine effects thereon. This the apostle expressly affirms to be the reason and cause of faith: "If all prophesy, and there come in one that believeth not, or one unlearned, he is convinced of all, he is judged of all. And thus are the secrets of his heart made manifest, and so falling down on his face he will worship God, and report that God is in you of a truth" (1 Cor. 14:24–25). The acknowledgment and confession of God to be in them, or among them, is a profession of faith in the word administered by them. Such persons assent unto its divine authority, or believe it to be the word of God. And on what evidence or ground of credibility they did so is expressly declared. It was not upon the force of any external arguments produced and pleaded unto that purpose. It was not upon the testimony of this or that or any church whatever; nor was it upon a conviction of any miracles which they saw wrought in its confirmation. Yea, the ground of the faith and confession declared is opposed unto the efficacy and use of the miraculous gifts of tongues (1 Cor. 14:23–24). Wherefore, the only evidence whereon they received the word, and acknowledged it to be of God, was that divine power and efficacy whereof they found and felt the experience in themselves. "He is convinced of all, judged of all, and thus are the secrets of his heart made manifest," whereon he falls down before it with an acknowledgment of its divine authority, finding the word to come upon his conscience with an irresistible power of conviction and judgment thereon. "He is convinced of all, judged of all," he cannot but grant that there is θεῖόν τι, "a divine efficacy" in it or accompanying of it. Especially his mind is influenced by this, that the "secrets of his heart are made manifest" by it.

---

12 2 Pet. 1:19.
13 *Of the Divine Original, Authority, Self-Evidencing Light, and Power of the Scriptures*, chap. 4.

For all men must acknowledge this to be an effect of divine power, seeing God alone is καρδιογνώστης, "he who searches, knows, and judges the heart."¶

And if the woman of Samaria believed that Jesus was the Christ because he "told her all things that ever she did" (John 4:29), there is reason to believe that word to be from God which makes manifest even the secrets of our hearts. And although I do conceive that by "The Word of God" (Heb. 4:12), the living and eternal Word is principally intended, yet the power and efficacy there ascribed to him is that which he puts forth by the word of the gospel. And so that word also, in its place and use, "pierceth even to the dividing asunder of soul and spirit, and of the joints and marrow, and is a discerner," or passes a critical judgment on "the thoughts and intents of the heart,"[14] or makes manifest the secrets of men's hearts, as it is here expressed.¶

Hereby, then, does the Holy Ghost so evidence the divine authority of the word, namely, by that divine power which it has upon our souls and consciences, that we do assuredly acquiesce in it to be from God. So, the Thessalonians are commended that they "received the Word not as the word of men, but as it is in truth, the Word of God, which effectually worketh in them that believe" (1 Thess. 2:13). It distinguishes itself from the word of men, and evidences itself to be indeed the word of God, by its effectual operation in them that believe. And he who has this testimony in himself has a higher and more firm assurance of the truth than what can be attained by the force of external arguments or the credit of human testimony. Wherefore, I say in general, that the Holy Spirit gives testimony unto and evinces the divine authority of the word by its powerful operations and divine effects on the souls of them that do believe. So that although it be weakness and foolishness unto others, yet, as is Christ himself unto them that are called, it is the power of God and the wisdom of God.

And I must say, that although a man be furnished with external arguments of all sorts concerning the divine origin and authority of the Scriptures, although he esteem his motives of credibility to be effectually persuasive, and have the authority of any or all the churches in the world to confirm his persuasion, yet if he has no experience in himself of its divine power, authority, and efficacy, he neither does nor can believe it to be the word of God in a due manner, with faith divine and supernatural. But he that has this experience has that testimony in himself which will never fail.

14 Heb. 4:12. In his commentary on Heb. 4:12, Owen clearly understands the Word of God to be Christ. See *An Exposition on the Third, Fourth, and Fifth Chapters of the Epistle of Paul the Apostle to the Hebrews* (London, 1674), 272–75.

This will be the more manifest if we consider some few of those many instances wherein it exerts its power, or the effects which are produced thereby.

The Principal Effect: Conversion

The principal divine effect of the word of God is in the conversion of the souls of sinners unto God. The greatness and glory of this work we have elsewhere declared at large.[15] And all those who are acquainted with it, as it is declared in the Scripture, and have any experience of it in their own hearts, do constantly give it as an instance of the exceeding greatness of the power of God. It may be they speak not improperly who prefer the work of the new creation before the work of the old, for the express evidences of almighty power contained in it, as some of the ancients do. Now, of this great and glorious effect the word is the only instrumental cause, whereby the divine power operates and is expressive of itself. For we are "born again," born of God, "not of corruptible seed, but of incorruptible, by the Word of God, which liveth and abideth forever" (1 Pet. 1:23). For "of his own will doth God beget us with the Word of truth" (James 1:18). The word is the seed of the new creature in us, that whereby our whole natures, our souls and all their faculties, are changed and renewed into the image and likeness of God. And by the same word is this new nature kept and preserved (1 Pet. 2:2), and the whole soul carried on unto the enjoyment of God. It is unto believers "an ingrafted Word, which is able to save their souls" (James 1:21). The "Word of God's grace, which is able to build us up, and give us an inheritance among all them which are sanctified" (Acts 20:32); and that because it is the "power of God unto salvation unto everyone that believeth" (Rom. 1:16).¶

All the power which God puts forth and exerts, in the communication of that grace and mercy unto believers whereby they are gradually carried on and prepared unto salvation, he does it by the word. Therein, in a special manner, is the divine authority of the word evidenced, by the divine power and efficacy given unto it by the Holy Ghost. The work which is effected by it, in the regeneration, conversion, and sanctification of the souls of believers does evidence infallibly unto their consciences that it is not the word of man, but of God. It will be said, "This testimony is private in the minds only of them on whom this work is wrought," and therefore do I press it no further, but "he that believeth hath the witness in himself" (1 John 5:10). Let it be granted that all who are really converted unto God by the power of the word have that infallible evidence and testimony of its divine origin, authority, and

15 Πνευματολογια, or, A Discourse concerning the Holy Spirit, bk. 3.

power in their own souls and consciences, that they thereon believe it with faith divine and supernatural, in conjunction with the other evidences before mentioned, as parts of the same divine testimony, and it is all I aim at herein.

But yet, although this testimony be privately received, for in itself it is not so, but common unto all believers, it is ministerially pleadable in the church as a principal motive unto believing. A declaration of the divine power which some have found by experience in the word is an ordinance of God to convince others and to bring them unto the faith. Yea, of all the external arguments that are or may be pleaded to justify the divine authority of the Scripture, there is none more prevalent nor cogent than this of its mighty efficacy in all ages on the souls of men, to change, convert, and renew them into the image and likeness of God, which has been visible and manifest.

Moreover, there are yet other particular effects of the divine power of the word on the minds and consciences of men, belonging unto this general work, either preceding or following it, which are clearly sensible, and enlarge the evidence. As,

Conviction

The work of conviction of sin on those who expected it not, who desired it not, and who would avoid it if by any means possible they could. The world is filled with instances of this nature. While men have been full of love to their sins, at peace in them, enjoying benefit and advantage by them, the word coming upon them in its power has awed, disquieted, and terrified them, taken away their peace, destroyed their hopes, and made them, as it were, whether they would or not—that is, contrary to their desires, inclinations, and carnal affections—to conclude that if they comply not with what is proposed unto them in that word, which before they took no notice of nor had any regard unto, they must be presently or eternally miserable.

Conscience is the territory or dominion of God in man, which he has so reserved unto himself that no human power can possibly enter into it or dispose of it in any wise. But in this work of conviction of sin, the word of God, the Scripture, enters into the conscience of the sinner, takes possession of it, disposes it unto peace or trouble, by its laws or rules, and no otherwise. Where it gives disquietment, all the world cannot give it peace; and where it speaks peace, there is none can give it trouble. Were not this the word of God, how should it come thus to speak in his name and to act his authority in the consciences of men as it does? When once it begins this work, conscience immediately owns a new rule, a new law, a new government, in order to the judgment of God upon it and all its actions. And it is contrary to the nature of conscience to take this upon itself, nor would it do so but that it sensibly finds God speaking and acting in it and by it (see 1 Cor. 14:24–25). An invasion may be made on the outward duties that conscience disposes unto, but none can be so upon its internal actings. No power under heaven can cause conscience to think, act, or judge otherwise than it does by its immediate respect unto God. For it is the mind's self-judging with respect unto God, and what is not so is no act of conscience. Wherefore, to force an act of conscience implies a contradiction. However, it may be defiled, bribed, seared, and at length utterly debauched, admit of a superior power, a power above or over itself, under God, it cannot.

I know conscience may be prepossessed with prejudices, and, by education, with the insinuation of traditions, take on itself the power of false, corrupt, superstitious principles and errors, as means of conveying unto it a sense of divine authority; so is it with the Mohammedans and other false worshipers in the world. But the power of those divine convictions whereof we treat is manifestly different from such prejudicate[16] opinions. For where these are not imposed on men by artifices and delusions easily discoverable, they prepossess their minds and inclinations by traditions, antecedently unto any right judgment they can make of themselves or other things, and they are generally wrapped up and condited[17] in their secular interests. The convictions we treat of come from without upon the minds of men, and that with a sensible power, prevailing over all their previous thoughts and inclinations. Those first affect, deceive, and delude the notional part of the soul, whereby conscience is insensibly influenced and diverted into improper respects, and is deceived as to its judging of the voice of God; these immediately principle the practical understanding and self-judging power of the soul. Wherefore, such opinions and persuasions are gradually insinuated into the mind, and are admitted insensibly without opposition or reluctancy, being never accompanied at their first admission with any secular disadvantage. But these divine convictions by the word befall men, some when they think of nothing less and desire nothing less; some when they design other things, as the pleasing of their ears or the entertainment of their company; and some that go on purpose to deride and scoff at what should be spoken unto them from it. It might also be added unto the same purpose how confirmed some have been in their carnal peace and security by love of sin, with innumerable inveterate prejudices; what losses and ruin to their outward concerns many have fallen

16   I.e., biased; preconceived.
17   I.e., preserved.

into by admitting of their convictions; what force, diligence, and artifices have been used to defeat them, what contribution of aid and assistance there has been from Satan unto this purpose; and yet against all has the divine power of the word absolutely prevailed and accomplished its whole designed effect (see 2 Cor. 10:4–5; Jer. 23:29; Zech. 1:6).

It does it by the light that is in it, and that spiritual illuminating efficacy wherewith it is accompanied. Hence it is called a "light shining in a dark place" (2 Pet. 1:19). That light whereby God "shines in the hearts" and minds of men (2 Cor. 4:4, 6). Without the Scripture all the world is in darkness: "Darkness covers the earth, and gross darkness the people" (Isa. 60:2). It is the kingdom of Satan, filled with darkness and confusion. Superstition, idolatry, lying vanities, wherein men know not at all what they do nor whither they go, fill the whole world, even as it is at this day. And the minds of men are naturally in darkness; there is a blindness upon them that they cannot see nor discern spiritual things, no, not when they are externally proposed unto them, as I have at large evinced elsewhere.[18] And no man can give a greater evidence that it is so than he who denies it so to be. With respect unto both these kinds of darkness the Scripture is a light, and accompanied with a spiritual illuminating efficacy, thereby evidencing itself to be a divine revelation. For what but divine truth could recall the minds of men from all their wanderings in error, superstition, and other effects of darkness, which of themselves they love more than truth? All things being filled with vanity, error, confusion, misapprehensions about God and ourselves, our duty and end, our misery and blessedness, the Scripture, where it is communicated by the providence of God, comes in as a light into a dark place, discovering all things clearly and steadily that concern either God or ourselves, our present or future condition, causing all the ghosts and false images of things which men had framed and fancied unto themselves in the dark to vanish and disappear. *Digitus Dei!*[19] This is none other but the power of God. But principally it evinces this its divine efficacy by that spiritual saving light which it conveys into and implants on the minds of believers.¶

Hence there is none of them who have gained any experience by the observation of God's dealings with them but shall, although they know not the ways and methods of the Spirit's operations by the word, yea, can say, with the man unto whom the Lord Jesus restored his sight, "One thing I know, that, whereas I was blind, now I see."[20] This power of the word, as the instrument of

---

18 Πνευματολογια, *or, A Discourse concerning the Holy Spirit*, bk. 3.
19 Lat. "it is the finger of God."
20 John 9:25.

the Spirit of God for the communication of saving light and knowledge unto the minds of men, the apostle declares (2 Cor. 3:18; 4:4, 6). By the efficacy of this power does he evidence the Scripture to be the word of God. Those who believe find by it a glorious, supernatural light introduced into their minds, whereby they who before saw nothing in a distinct, affecting manner in spiritual [things], do now clearly discern the truth, the glory, the beauty, and excellency of heavenly mysteries, and have their minds transformed into their image and likeness. And there is no person who has the witness in himself of the kindling of this heavenly light in his mind by the word but has also the evidence in himself of its divine origin.

Awe and Wonder

It does, in like manner, evidence its divine authority by the awe which it puts on the minds of the generality of mankind unto whom it is made known, so that they dare not absolutely reject it. Multitudes there are unto whom the word is declared who hate all its precepts, despise all its promises, abhor all its threatenings, like nothing, approve of nothing, of what it declares or proposes, and yet dare not absolutely refuse or reject it. They deal with it as they do with God himself, whom they hate also, according to the revelation which he has made of himself in his word. They wish he were not, sometimes they hope he is not, would be glad to be free of his rule, but yet dare not, cannot absolutely deny and disown him, because of that testimony for himself which he keeps alive in them whether they will or not. The same is the frame of their hearts and minds toward the Scripture, and that for no other reason but because it is the word of God, and manifests itself so to be. They hate it, wish it were not, hope it is not true, but are not by any means able to shake off a disquiet in the sense of its divine authority. This testimony it has fixed in the hearts of multitudes of its enemies (Ps. 45:5).

Consolation

It evidences its divine power in administering strong consolations in the deepest and most unrelievable distresses. Some such there are, and such many men fall into, wherein all means and hopes of relief may be utterly removed and taken away. So is it when the miseries of men are not known unto any that will so much as pity them or wish them relief; or if they have been known, and there has been an eye to pity them, yet there has been no hand to help them. Such has been the condition of innumerable souls, as on other accounts, so in particular under the power of persecutors, when they have been shut up in filthy and nasty dungeons, not to be brought out but unto death, by the most exquisite tortures that the malice of hell could invent or the bloody cruelty of man inflict. Yet in these and the like distresses does the word of God, by its divine power and efficacy, break through all interposing difficulties, all dark and discouraging circumstances, supporting, refreshing, and comforting such poor distressed sufferers, yea, commonly filling them under overwhelming calamities with "joy unspeakable and full of glory."[21] Though they are in bonds, yet is the word of God not bound; neither can all the power of hell, nor all the diligence or fury of men, keep out the word from entering into prisons, dungeons, flames, to administer strong consolations against all fears, pains, wants, dangers, deaths, or whatever we may in this mortal life be exposed unto. And sundry other instances of the like nature might be pleaded, wherein the word gives evident demonstration unto the minds and consciences of men of its own divine power and authority, which is the second way whereby the Holy Ghost, its author, gives testimony unto its origin.

But it is not merely the grounds and reasons whereon we believe the Scripture to be the word of God which we designed to declare; the whole work of the Holy Spirit enabling us to believe them so to be was proposed unto consideration. And beyond what we have insisted on, there is yet a further peculiar work of his, whereby he effectually ascertains our minds of the Scriptures being the word of God, whereby we are ultimately established in the faith thereof. And I cannot but both admire and bewail that this should be denied by any that would be esteemed Christians. Wherefore, if there be any necessity thereof, I shall take occasion in the second part of this discourse further to confirm this part of the truth, thus far debated, namely, that God by his Holy Spirit does secretly and effectually persuade and satisfy the minds and souls of believers in the divine truth and authority of the Scriptures, whereby he infallibly secures their faith against all objections and temptations whatsoever; so that they can safely and comfortably dispose of their souls in all their concerns, with respect unto this life and eternity, according unto the undeceivable truth and guidance of it. But I shall no further insist on these things at present.

[21] 1 Pet. 1:8.

Inferences from the Whole

Some Objections Answered

THREE THINGS do offer themselves unto consideration from what has been discoursed.

1. What is the ground and reason why the meanest and most unlearned sort of believers do assent unto this truth, that the Scriptures are the word of God, with no less firmness, certainty, and assurance of mind, than do the wisest and most learned of them. Yea, oftentimes the faith of the former sort herein is of the best growth and firmest consistency against oppositions and temptations. Now, no assent of the mind can be accompanied with any more assurance than the evidence whose effect it is, and which it is resolved into, will afford. Nor does any evidence of truth beget an assent unto it in the mind but as it is apprehended and understood. Wherefore, the evidence of this truth, wherein soever it consists, must be that which is perceived, apprehended, and understood by the meanest and most unlearned sort of true believers. For, as was said, they do no less firmly assent and adhere unto it than the wisest and most learned of them. It cannot, therefore, consist in such subtle and learned arguments, whose sense they cannot understand or comprehend. But the things we have pleaded are of another nature. For those characters of divine wisdom, goodness, holiness, grace, and sovereign authority, which are implanted in the Scripture by the Holy Ghost, are as legible unto the faith of the meanest as of the most learned believer. And they also are no less capable of an experimental understanding of the divine power and efficacy of the Scripture, in all its spiritual operations, than those who are more wise and skillful in discerning the force of external arguments and motives of credibility. It must, therefore, of necessity be granted, that the

formal reason of faith consists in those things whereof the evidence is equally obvious unto all sorts of believers.

2. Whence it is that the assent of faith, whereby we believe the Scriptures to be the word of God, is usually affirmed to be accompanied with more assurance than any assent which is the effect of science upon the most demonstrative principles. They who affirm this do not consider faith as it is in this or that individual person, or in all that do sincerely believe, but in its own nature and essence, and what it is meet and able to produce. And the schoolmen[1] do distinguish between a certainty or assurance of evidence and an assurance of adherence. In the latter, they say, the certainty of faith does exceed that of science; but it is less in respect of the former. But it is not easily to be conceived how the certainty of adherence should exceed the certainty of evidence, with respect unto any object whatsoever. That which seems to render a difference in this case is, that the evidence which we have in things scientific is speculative and affects the mind only; but the evidence which we have by faith effectually works on the will also, because of the goodness and excellency of the things that are believed. And hence it is that the whole soul does more firmly adhere unto the objects of faith upon that evidence which it has of them, than unto other things whereof it has clearer evidence, wherein the will and affections are little or not at all concerned. And Bonaventure gives a reason of no small weight why faith is more certain than science, not with the certainty of speculation, but of adherence:

> Faithful Christians cannot be induced or convinced by argument, torture, or promise of reward to deny—even with empty words—the truth that they believe. No one who is well versed in any field of knowledge would behave this way, if (for example) he were compelled by the harshest torments to repudiate his own understanding concerning some point of geometry or arithmetic. Only the most reckless and absurd mathematician would dare risk his life on such grounds, unless it were in obedience to a faith which forbids him to lie.[2]

1 "Schoolmen" is a reference to medieval scholastic theologians.
2 In the text: *Quoniam fideles Christiani, nec argumentis, nec tormentis, nec blandimentis adduci possunt, vel inclinari, ut veritatem quam credunt vel ore tenus negent; quod nemo peritus alicujus scientiae faceret, si acerrimis tormentis cogeretur scientiam suam de conclusione aliqua geometrica vel arithmetica retractare. Stultus enim et ridiculus esset geometra, qui pro sua scientia in controversiis geometricis mortem auderet subire, nisi in quantum dictat fides, non esse mentiendum.*—Owen. For the Latin text, albeit slightly different, see *S. Bonaventurae opera omnia*, vol. 3, ed. PP. College A S. Bonaventura (Florence: Collegii S. Bonaventurae, 1887), 481–82.

And whatever may be said of this distinction, I think it cannot modestly be denied that there is a greater assurance in faith than is in any scientific conclusions, until as many good and wise men will part with all their worldly concerns and their lives, by the most exquisite tortures, in the confirmation of any truth which they have received, merely on the ground of reason acting in human sciences, as have so done on the certainty which they had by faith that the Scripture is a divine revelation. For in bearing testimony hereunto have innumerable multitudes of the best, the holiest, and the wisest men that ever were in the world, cheerfully and joyfully sacrificed all their temporal and adventured all their eternal concerns. For they did it under a full satisfaction that in parting with all temporary things, they should be eternally blessed or eternally miserable, according as their persuasion in faith proved true or false. Wherefore, unto the firmitude[3] and constancy which we have in the assurance of faith, three things do concur—

(1) That this ability of assent upon testimony is the highest and most noble power or faculty of our rational souls; and, therefore, where it has the highest evidence whereof it is capable, which it has in the testimony of God, it gives us the highest certainty of assurance whereof in this world we are capable.

(2) Unto the assent of divine faith there is required a special internal operation of the Holy Ghost. This renders it of another nature than any mere natural act and operation of our minds. And, therefore, if the assurance of it may not properly be said to exceed the assurance of science in degree, it is only because it is of a more excellent kind, and so is not capable of comparison unto it as to degrees.

(3) That the revelation which God makes of himself, his mind and will, by his word, is more excellent, and accompanied with greater evidence of his infinitely glorious properties, wherein alone the mind can find absolute rest and satisfaction, which is its assurance, than any other discovery of truth, of what sort soever, is capable of. Neither is the assurance of the mind absolutely perfect in anything beneath the enjoyment of God. Wherefore, the soul by faith making the nearest approaches whereof in this life it is capable, unto the eternal spring of being, truth, and goodness, it has the highest rest, satisfaction, and assurance therein, that in this life it can attain unto.

3. It follows from hence that those that would deny either of these two things, or would so separate between them as to exclude the necessity of either unto the duty of believing, namely, the internal work of the Holy Spirit

---

No English translation of this source exists. Bonaventure (1221–1274), a Franciscan from Italy, was an influential scholastic theologian and philosopher.

3 I.e., strength; stability.

on the minds of men, enabling them to believe, and the external work of the same Holy Spirit, giving evidence in and by the Scripture unto its own divine origin, do endeavor to expel all true divine faith out of the world, and to substitute a probable persuasion in the room thereof.

For a close unto this discourse, which has now been drawn forth unto a greater length than was at first intended, I shall consider some objections that are usually pleaded in opposition unto the truth asserted and vindicated.

1. It is, therefore, objected, in the first place, that the plea hitherto insisted on cannot be managed without great disadvantage to Christian religion. For if we take away the rational grounds on which we believe the doctrine of Christ to be true and divine, and the whole evidence of the truth of it be laid on things not only derided by men of atheistical spirits, but in themselves such as cannot be discerned by any but such as do believe, on what grounds can we proceed to convince an unbeliever?

Answer 1. By the way, it is one thing to prove and believe the doctrine of Christ to be true and divine; another, to prove and believe the Scripture to be given by inspiration of God, or the divine authority of the Scripture, which alone was proposed unto consideration. A doctrine true and divine may be written in and proposed unto us by writings that were not divinely and infallibly inspired; and so might the doctrine of Christ have been, but not without the unspeakable disadvantage of the church. And there are sundry arguments which forcibly and effectually prove the doctrine of Christ to have been true and divine, which are not of any efficacy to prove the divine authority of the Scriptures; though, on the other hand, whatever does prove the divine authority of the Scriptures does equally prove the divine truth of the doctrine of Christ.

Answer 2. There are two ways of convincing unbelievers: the one insisted on by the apostles and their followers, the other by some learned men since their days. The way principally insisted on by the apostles was, by preaching the word itself unto them in the evidence and demonstration of the Spirit, by the power whereof, manifesting the authority of God in it, they were convinced, and falling down acknowledged God to be in it of a truth (1 Cor. 2:4–5; 14:24–25). It is likely that in this their proposal of the gospel, the doctrine and truths contained in it, unto unbelievers, those of atheistical spirits would both deride them and it; and so, indeed, it came to pass, many esteeming themselves to be babblers and their doctrine to be errant folly. But yet they desisted not from pursuing their work in the same way, whereunto God gave success. The other way is, to prove unto unbelievers that the Scripture is true and divine by rational arguments, wherein some learned persons have labored, especially in these last ages, to very good purpose. And certainly their labors are greatly to be commended, while they attend unto these rules.¶

First, that they produce no arguments but such as are cogent, and not liable unto just exceptions. For if, to manifest their own skill or learning, they plead such reasons as are capable of an answer and solution, they exceedingly prejudice the truth, by subjecting it unto dubious disputations, whereas in itself it is clear, firm, and sacred. Second, that they do not pretend their rational grounds and arguments to be the sole foundation that faith has to rest upon, or which it is resolved into. For this were the ready way to set up an opinion, instead of faith supernatural and divine. Accept but of these two limitations, and it is acknowledged that the rational grounds and arguments intended may be rationally pleaded, and ought so to be, unto the conviction of gainsayers. For no man does so plead the self-evidencing power of the Scripture as to deny that the use of other external motives and arguments is necessary to stop the mouths of atheists, as also unto the further establishment of them who do believe. These things are subordinate, and no way inconsistent.

The truth is, if we will attend unto our own and the experience of the whole church of God, the way whereby we come to believe the Scripture to be the word of God ordinarily is this, and no other. God having first given his word as the foundation of our faith and obedience, has appointed the ministry of men, at first extraordinary, afterward ordinary, to propose unto us the doctrines, truths, precepts, promises, and threatenings contained therein. Together with this proposition of them, they are appointed to declare that these things are not from themselves, nor of their own invention (2 Tim. 3:14–17). And this is done variously. Unto some the word of God in this ministry thus comes, or is thus proposed, preached, or declared, while they are in a condition not only utterly unacquainted with the mysteries of it, but filled with contrary apprehensions, and consequently prejudices against it. Thus, it came of old unto the pagan world, and must do so unto such persons and nations as are yet in the same state with them. Unto these the first preachers of the gospel did not produce the book of the Scriptures, and tell them that it was the word of God, and that it would evidence itself unto them so to be. For this had been to despise the wisdom and authority of God in their own ministry. But they preached the doctrines of it unto them, grounding themselves on the divine revelation contained therein. And this proposition of the truth or preaching of the gospel was not left of God to work itself into the reason of men by the suitableness of it thereunto; but being his own institution for their illumination and conversion, he accompanied it with divine power, and made it effectual unto the ends designed (Rom. 1:16).¶

And the event hereof among mankind was that by some this new doctrine was derided and scorned, by others, whose hearts God opened to attend unto it, it was embraced and submitted unto. Among those who, after the propagation of the gospel, are born, as they say, within the pale of the church, the same doctrine is variously instilled into persons, according unto the several duties and concerns of others to instruct them. Principally, the ministry of the word is ordained of God unto that end, whereon the church is the pillar and ground of truth. Those of both sorts unto whom the doctrine mentioned is preached or proposed are directed unto the Scriptures as the sacred repository thereof. For they are told that these things come by revelation from God, and that that revelation is contained in the Bible, which is his word. Upon this proposal, with inquiry into it and consideration of it, God cooperating by his Spirit, there is such evidence of its divine origin communicated unto their minds through its power and efficacy, with the characters of divine wisdom and holiness implanted on it, which they are now enabled to discern, that they believe it and rest in it as the immediate word of God. Thus was it in the case of the woman of Samaria and the inhabitants of Sychar with respect unto their faith in Christ Jesus (John 4:42). This is the way whereby men ordinarily are brought to believe the word of God (Rom. 10:14–15), and that neither by external arguments nor motives, which no one soul was ever converted unto God by, nor by any mere naked proposal and offer of the book unto them, nor by miracles, nor by immediate revelation or private subjective testimony of the Spirit; nor is their faith a persuasion of mind that they can give no reason of, but only that they are so persuaded.

2. But it will be yet further objected, that if there be such clear evidence in the thing itself, that is, in the divine origin and authority of the Scriptures, that none who freely use their reason can deny it, then it lies either in the naked proposal of the thing unto the understanding—and if so, then everyone that assents unto this proposition, "that the whole is greater than the part," must likewise assent unto this, "that the Scripture is the word of God"—or the evidence must not lie in the naked proposal, but in the efficacy of the Spirit of God in the minds of them unto whom it is proposed.

Answer 1. I know no divine, ancient or modern, Popish or Protestant, who does not assert that there is a work of the Holy Ghost on the minds of men necessary unto a due belief of the Scripture to be the word of God. And the consideration hereof ought not by any Christian to be excluded. But they say not that this is the objective testimony or evidence on which we believe the Scripture to be the word of God, concerning which alone is our inquiry.

Answer 2. We do not dispute how far or by what means this proposition, "the Scripture is the word of God," may be evidenced merely unto our reason, but unto our understanding as capable of giving an assent upon testimony. It is not said that this is a first principle of reason, though it be of faith, nor that it is capable of a mathematical demonstration. That the whole is greater than the part is self-evident unto our reason upon its first proposal, but such none pretends to be in the Scripture, because it is a subject not capable of it. Nor do those who deny the self-evidence of the Scripture pretend by their arguments for its divine authority to give such an evidence of it unto reason as is in first principles or mathematical demonstrations, but content themselves with that which they call a moral certainty. But it is by faith we are obliged to receive the truth of this proposition, which respects the power of our minds to assent unto truth upon testimony, infallibly on that which is infallible. And hereunto it evidences its own truth, not with the same, but with an evidence and certainty of a higher nature and nobler kind than that of the strictest demonstration in things natural or the most forcible argument in things moral.

3. It will be objected, that if this be so, then none can be obliged to receive the Scripture as the word of God who has not faith, and none have faith but those in whom it is wrought by the Spirit of God, and thereinto all will be resolved at last.

Answer 1. Indeed, there is no room for this objection, for the whole work of the Spirit is pleaded only as he is the efficient cause of believing, and not the objective, or reason why we do believe. But

Answer 2. We must not be ashamed to resolve all we do well, spiritually and in obedience to the command of God, unto the efficacious operation of the Holy Ghost in us, unless we intend to be ashamed of the gospel. But this still makes his internal operation to be the efficient, and not his internal testimony to be the formal, reason of our faith.

Answer 3. It is another question, whether all obligation unto duty is and must be proportionate unto our own strength without divine assistance; which we deny, and affirm that we are obliged unto many things by virtue of God's command which we have no power to answer but by virtue of his grace.

Answer 4. Where the proposal of the Scripture is made in the way before described, those unto whom it is proposed are obliged to receive it as the word of God, upon the evidence which it gives of itself so to be. Yea, every real, true, divine revelation made unto men, or every proposal of the Scripture by divine providence, has that evidence of its being from God accompanying it as is sufficient to oblige them unto whom it was made to believe it, on pain of his displeasure. If this were otherwise, then either were God obliged to confirm every particular divine revelation with a miracle, which, as to its obligation unto believing, wants not its difficulty, which he did not, as in many of the prophets, nor does at this day at the first proposal of the gospel to the heathen, or else, when he requires faith and obedience in such ways as in his wisdom he judges meet, that is, in the ordinary ministry of the word, they are not obliged thereby, nor is it their sin to refuse a compliance with his will.

Answer 5. If this difficulty can be no otherwise avoided but by affirming that the faith which God requires of us with respect unto his word is nothing but a natural assent unto it upon rational arguments and considerations, which we have an ability for, without any spiritual aid of the Holy Ghost, or respect unto his testimony, as before described, which overthrows all faith, especially that which is divine, I shall rather ten thousand times allow of all the just consequences that can follow on the supposition mentioned than admit of this relief. But of those consequences this is none, that any unto whom the Scripture is proposed are exempted from an obligation unto believing.

4. In like manner, there is no difficulty in the usual objection which respects particular books of the Scripture, why we receive them as canonical and reject others; as, namely, the book of Proverbs, and not of Wisdom, of Ecclesiastes, and not Ecclesiasticus.[4] For,

Answer 1. As to the books of the Old Testament, we have the canon of them given us in the New, where it is affirmed that unto the church of the Jews were committed the oracles of God, which both confirms all that we receive and excludes all that we exclude. And unto the New there are no pretenders, nor ever were, to the least exercise of the faith of any.

Answer 2. All books whatever that have either themselves pretended unto a divine origin, or have been pleaded by others to be of that extract, have been, and may be from themselves, without further help, evicted of falsehood in that pretense. They have all of them hitherto, in matter or manner, in plain confessions or other sufficient evidence, manifested themselves to be of a human origin. And much danger is not to be feared from any that for the future shall be set forth with the same pretense.

---

4 Wisdom and Ecclesiasticus are books included in the Apocrypha. The question of whether the Apocrypha is Holy Scripture was one of the many issues that divided the Church of Rome and Protestants. For a contemporary source, note article 6 of the Thirty-Nine Articles of the Church of England. See also Edmon L. Gallagher and John D. Meade, *The Biblical Canon Lists from Early Christianity: Texts and Analysis* (Oxford: Oxford University Press, 2017).

Answer 3. We are not bound to refuse the ministry of the church, or the advantages of providence whereby the Scripture is brought unto us, with the testimonies which, either directly or collaterally, any one part of it gives unto another. Although the Scripture is to be believed for itself, yet it is not ordinarily to be believed by itself, without the help of other means.

Answer 4. On these suppositions I fear not to affirm that there are on every individual book of the Scripture, particularly those named, those divine characters and criteria which are sufficient to differentiate them from all other writings whatever, and to testify their divine authority unto the minds and consciences of believers. I say of believers, for we inquire not on what ground unbelievers, or those who do not believe, do believe the word of God, nor yet directly on what outward motives such persons may be induced so to do. But our sole inquiry at present is, what the faith of them who do believe is resolved into. It is not, therefore, said that when our Lord Jesus Christ—for we acknowledge that there is the same reason of the first giving out of divine revelations as is of the Scripture—came and preached unto the Jews, that those mere words, "I am the light of the world,"[5] or the like, had all this evidence in them or with them; for nothing he said of that kind may be separated from its circumstances. But supposing the testimonies given in the Scripture beforehand to his person, work, time, and manner of coming, with the evidence of the presence of God with him in the declaration that he made of his doctrine and himself to be the Messiah, the Jews were bound to believe what he taught, and himself to be the Son of God, the Savior of the world, and so did many of them upon his preaching only (John 4:42). And in like manner they were bound to believe the doctrine of John Baptist, and to submit unto his institutions, although he wrought no miracle, and those who did not, rejected the counsel of God for their good, and perished in their unbelief. But although our Lord Jesus Christ wrought no miracles to prove the Scripture then extant to be the word of God, seeing he wrought them among such only as by whom that was firmly believed, yet the wisdom of God saw it necessary to confirm his personal ministry by them. And without a sense of the power and efficacy of the divine truth of the doctrine proposed, miracles themselves will be despised; so they were by some who were afterward converted by the preaching of the word (Acts 2:13),[6] or they will produce only a false faith, or a ravished assent upon an amazement, that will not abide (Acts 3:7–8; 8:13, 21).

---

5   John 8:12.
6   Acts 2:13 does not seem to be the correct reference. Acts 2:41 is a possible referent.

Appendix

A SUMMARY REPRESENTATION of the nature and reason of that faith wherewith we believe the Scripture to be the word of God, with some attestations given unto the substance of what has been delivered concerning it, shall give a close to this discourse. As to the first part of this design, the things that follow are proposed.

PRESUPPOSITIONS OF THE DISCOURSE

Unto the inquiry, on what grounds, or for what reason, we believe the Scripture to be the word of God, many things are supposed, as on all hands agreed upon, whose demonstration or proof belongs not unto our present work. Such are,

1. The being of God and his self-subsistence, with all the essential properties of his nature.

2. Our relation unto him and dependence on him, as our creator, benefactor, preserver, judge, and rewarder, both as unto things temporal and eternal. Wherefore,

3. The τὸ γνωστὸν τοῦ θεοῦ, "whatever may be known of God"[1] by the light of nature, whatever is manifest in or from the works of creation and providence, and necessary actings of conscience, as to the being, rule, and authority of God, are supposed as acknowledged in this inquiry.

4. That beyond the conduct and guidance of the light of nature, that men may live unto God, believe and put their trust in him, according to their duty, in that obedience which he requires of them, so as to come unto the enjoyment of him, a supernatural revelation of his mind and will unto them, especially in that condition wherein all mankind are since the entrance of sin, is necessary.

1 Rom. 1:19.

5. That all those unto whom God has granted divine revelations immediately from himself, for their own use, and that of all other men unto whom they were to be communicated, were infallibly assured that they came from God, and that their minds were no way imposed on in them.

6. That all these divine revelations, so far as they are any way necessary to guide and instruct men in the true knowledge of God and that obedience which is acceptable unto him, are now contained in the Scriptures, or those books of the Old and New Testament which are commonly received and owned among all sorts of Christians.

ARGUMENT SUMMARY IN FIFTEEN POINTS

These things, I say, are supposed unto our present inquiry, and taken for granted; so that the reader is not to look for any direct proof of them in the preceding discourse. But on these suppositions it is alleged and proved,

1. That all men unto whom it is duly proposed as such are bound to believe this Scripture, these books of the Old and New Testament, to be the word of God, that is, to contain and exhibit an immediate, divine, supernatural revelation of his mind and will, so far as is any way needful that they may live unto him, and that nothing is contained in them but what is of the same divine origin.

2. The obligation of this duty of thus believing the Scripture to be the word of God arises partly from the nature of the thing itself, and partly from the special command of God. For it being that revelation of the will of God without the knowledge whereof and assent whereunto we cannot live unto God as we ought, nor come unto the enjoyment of him, it is necessary that we should believe it unto these ends, and God requires it of us that so we should do.

3. We cannot thus believe it in a way of duty, but upon a sufficient evidence and prevalent testimony that so it is.

4. There are many cogent arguments, testimonies, and motives to persuade, convince, and satisfy unprejudiced persons, that the Scripture is the word of God or a divine revelation, and every way sufficient to stop the mouths of gainsayers, proceeding on such principles of reason as are owned and approved by the generality of mankind. And arguments of this nature may be taken from almost all considerations of the properties of God and his government of the world, of our relation unto him, of what belongs unto our present peace and future happiness.

5. From the arguments and testimonies of this nature, a firm persuasion of mind, defensible against all objections, that the Scripture is the word of God,

may be attained, and that such, as that those who live not in contradiction unto their own light and reason, through the power of their lusts, cannot but judge it their wisdom, duty, and interest to yield obedience unto his will as revealed therein.

6. But yet that persuasion of mind which may be thus attained, and which rests wholly upon these arguments and testimonies, is not entirely that faith wherewith we are obliged to believe the Scripture to be the word of God in a way of duty. For it is not to be merely human, how firm soever the persuasion in it may be, but divine and supernatural, of the same kind with that whereby we believe the things themselves contained in the Scripture.

7. We cannot thus believe the Scripture to be the word of God, nor any divine truth therein contained, without the effectual illumination of our minds by the Holy Ghost. And to exclude the consideration of his work herein is to cast the whole inquiry out of the limits of Christian religion.

8. Yet is not this work of the Holy Spirit in the illumination of our minds, whereby we are enabled to believe in a way of duty with faith supernatural and divine, the ground and reason why we do believe, or the evidence whereon we do so, nor is our faith resolved thereinto.

9. Whereas, also, there are sundry other acts of the Holy Spirit in and upon our minds, establishing this faith against temptations unto the contrary, and further ascertaining us of the divine origin of the Scripture, or testifying it unto us, yet are they none of them severally, nor all of them jointly, the formal reason of our faith, nor the ground which we believe upon. Yet are they such as that without the first work of divine illumination, we cannot believe at all in a due manner; so without his other consequent operations, we cannot believe steadfastly against temptations and oppositions. Wherefore,

10. Those only can believe the Scripture aright to be the word of God, in a way of duty, whose minds are enlightened, and who are enabled to believe by the Holy Ghost.

11. Those who believe not are of two sorts, for they are either such as oppose and gainsay the word as a cunningly devised fable, or such as are willing without prejudice to attend unto the consideration of it. The former sort may be resisted, opposed, and rebuked by external arguments, and such moral considerations as vehemently persuade the divine origin of the Scripture, and from the same principles may their mouths be stopped as to their cavils and exceptions against it. The other sort are to be led on unto believing by the ministry of the church in the dispensation of the word itself, which is the ordinance of God unto that purpose. But,

12. Neither sort do ever come truly to believe, either merely induced thereunto by force of moral arguments only, or upon the authority of that church by whose ministry the Scripture is proposed unto them to be believed. Wherefore,

13. The formal reason of faith divine and supernatural, whereby we believe the Scripture to be the word of God in the way of duty, and as it is required of us, is the authority and veracity of God alone, evidencing themselves unto our minds and consciences in and by the Scripture itself. And herein consists that divine testimony of the Holy Ghost, which, as it is a testimony, gives our assent unto the Scriptures the general nature of faith, and as it is a divine testimony gives it the special nature of faith divine and supernatural.

14. This divine testimony given unto the divine origin of the Scripture in and by itself, whereinto our faith is ultimately resolved, is evidenced and made known, as by the characters of the infinite perfections of the divine nature that are in it and upon it, so by the authority, power, and efficacy, over and upon the souls and consciences of men, and the satisfactory excellency of the truths contained therein, wherewith it is accompanied.

15. Wherefore, although there be many cogent external arguments whereby a moral, steadfast persuasion of the divine authority of the Scriptures may be attained, and although it be the principal duty of the true church in all ages to give testimony thereunto, which it has done successively at all times since first it was entrusted with it, and although there be many other means whereby we are induced, persuaded, and enabled to believe it, yet is it for its own sake only, efficaciously manifesting itself to be the word of God, or upon the divine testimony that is given in it and by it thereunto, that we believe it to be so with faith divine and supernatural.

Therefore, those who either deny the necessity of an internal subjective work of the Holy Ghost enabling us to believe, or the objective testimony of the Holy Spirit given unto the Scripture in and by itself, or do deny their joint concurrence in and unto our believing, do deny all faith properly divine and supernatural.

AGREEMENT OF ANCIENT AND MODERN AUTHORS

This being the substance of what is declared and pleaded for in the preceding treatise, to prevent the obloquy[2] of some and confirm the judgment of

---

2   I.e., strong public criticism or verbal abuse.

others, I shall add the suffrage of ancient and modern writers given unto the principal parts of it, and whereon all other things asserted in it do depend.

Clement of Alexandria discourses at large unto this purpose, "We have the Lord himself for the principle or beginning of doctrine, who by the prophets, the gospel, and blessed apostles, in various manners and by divers degrees, goes before us, or leads us unto knowledge."[3] This is that which we lay down as the reason and ground of faith, namely, the authority of the Lord himself instructing us by the Scriptures. ¶

So he adds: "And if anyone suppose that he needs any other principle, the principle will not be kept," that is, if we need any other principle whereinto to resolve our faith, the word of God is no more a principle unto us,

> But he who is faithful from himself is worthy to be believed in his sovereign writing and voice; which, as it appears is administered by the Lord for the benefit of men. And certainly we use it as a rule of judging for the invention of things. But whatever is judged is not credible, or to be believed, until it is judged; and that is no principle which stands in need to be judged.[4]

The intention of his words is, that God, who alone is to be believed for himself, has given us his word as the rule whereby we are to judge of all things. And this word is so to be believed as not to be subject unto any other judgment; because if it be so, it cannot be either a principle or a rule. ¶

And so he proceeds: "Wherefore, it is meet that, embracing by faith the most sufficient, indemonstrable principle, and taking the demonstrations of the

---

3 In the text: Ἔχομεν γὰρ τὴν ἀρχὴν τῆς πίστεως τὸν Κύριον, διά τε προφητῶν, διά τε τοῦ εὐαγγελίου, καὶ διὰ τῶν μακαρίων ἀποστόλων, πολυτρόπως καὶ πολυμερῶς ἐξ ἀρχῆς εἰς τέλος ἡγούμενον τῆς γνώσεως (Strom, 7).—Owen. For critical editions of Clement's *Stromata*, see Clemens Alexandrinus, *Stromata Buch I-VI*, Herausgegeben von Otto Stählin (Berlin: Akademie-Verlag, 1960), and Clement of Alexandria, *Miscellanies, Book VII: The Greek Text with Introduction, Translation, Notes, Dissertations, and Indices*, trans. Fenton John Anthony Hort and Joseph B. Mayor (London: Macmillan, 1902). For an English translation, see Clement of Alexandria, *Stromateis: Books 1-3*, trans. John Ferguson, Fathers of the Church 85 (Washington, DC: Catholic University of America Press, 1991). This is a citation and Owen's translation of Clement of Alexandria's *Stromata*, bk. 7, chap. 16. Clement (ca. 150–ca. 215) was a theologian who taught at the catechetical school of Alexandria and tried to win favor for Christianity among the educated classes. He is a controversial figure due to the extent of his appropriation of Hellenistic philosophy.

4 In the text: Τὴν ἀρχὴν δε εἴτις ἕτερον δεῖθαι ὑπολάβοι, οὐκέτ ἄν ὄντως ἀρχὴ φυλαχθείη. Ὁ μὲν οὖν ἐξ ἑαυτοῦ πίστος, τῇ κυριαχῇ γραφῇ τε καὶ φωνῇ ἀξιόπιστος εἰκότως ἄν διὰ τοῦ Κυρίου πρὸς τὴν τῶν ἀνθρώπων εὐερνεσίαν ἐνεργουμένη· ἀμέλει πρὸς τὴν τῶν πραγμάτων εὕρεσιν, αὐτῇ χρώμεθα κριτηρίου· τὸ κρινόμενον δὲ πᾶν ἔτι ἄπιστον πρὶν χριθῆναι ὥς οὐδ' ἀρχὴ τὸ κρίσεως δεόμενου.—Owen. The English translation is Owen's.

principle from the principle itself, we are instructed by the voice of the Lord himself unto the acknowledgment of the truth."[5] In few words he declares the substance of what we have pleaded for. No more do we maintain in this cause but what Clement does here assert, namely, that we believe the Scripture for itself, as that which needs no antecedent or external demonstration, but all the evidence and demonstration of its divine origin is to be taken from itself alone; which yet he further confirms: "For we would not attend or give credit simply to the definitions of men, seeing we have right also to define in contradiction unto them. And seeing it is not sufficient merely to say or assert what appears to be truth, but to beget a belief also of what is spoken, we expect not the testimony of men, but confirm that which is inquired about with the voice of the Lord, which is more full and firm than any demonstration, yea, which rather is the only demonstration. Thus we, taking our demonstrations of the Scripture out of the Scripture, are assured by faith as by demonstration."[6] And in other places, as *Stromata*, book 4, he plainly affirms that the way of Christians was to prove the Scripture by itself, and all other things by the Scripture.

Basilius speaks to the same purpose on Psalm 115: "Faith, which draws the soul to assent above all methods of reasonings, faith, which is not the effect of geometrical demonstrations, but of the efficacy of the Spirit."[7] The nature, cause, and efficacy of that faith whereby we believe the Scripture to be the word of God, are asserted by him.

Nemesius: "The doctrine of the divine oracles hath its credibility from itself, because of its divine inspiration."[8]

---

5   In the text: Εἰκότως τοίνυν πίστει περιβαλόντες ἀναπάλεικλον τὴν ἀρχὴν ἐκ περιουσίας, καὶ τὰς ἀποδείξεις παρ᾽ αὐτῆς τῆς ἀρχῆς λαβόντες φωνῇ Κυρίου παιδευόμεθα πρὸς τὴν ἐπίγνωσιν τῆς ἀληθείας.—Owen. The English translation is Owen's.

6   In the text: Οὐ γὰρ ἁπλῶς ἀποφαινομένοις ἀνθρώποις προσέχομεν, οἷς καὶ ἀνταποφαίνεσθαι ἐπ᾽ ἴσης ἔξεστιν. Εἰ δ᾽ οὐκ ἀρκεῖ μόνον ἁπλῶς εἰπεῖν τὸ δόξαν, ἀλλὰ πιστώσασθαι δεῖ τὸ λεχθέν, οὐ τὴν ἐξ ἀνθρώπων ἀναμένομεν μαρτυρίαν, ἀλλὰ τῇ τοῦ κυρίου φωνῇ πιστούμεθα τὸ ζητούμενον. Ἡ πασῶν ἀποδείξεων ἐχεγγυωτέρα μᾶλλον δὲ ἣ μόνη ἀπόδειξις οὖσα τυγχάνει. Οὕτως οὖν καὶ ἡμεῖς ἀπ᾽ αὐτῶν τῶν γραφῶν τελείως ἀποδεικνύτες, ἐκ πίστεως πιθόμεθα [corr. πειθόμεθα] ἀποδεικτικῶς.—Owen. The English translation is Owen's.

7   In the text: Πίστις ἡ ὑπὲρ τὰς λογικὰς μεθόδους τὴν ψυχὴν εἰς συνκατάβασιν ἕλκουσα. Πίστις οὐχ ἡ γεωμετρικαῖς ἀνάγκαις, ἀλλ᾽ ἡ ταῖς τοῦ πνεύματος ἐνεργείαις ἐκκινομένη.—Owen. This is a reference to and Owen's translation of Basil the Great's homily on Ps. 115. For a Greek edition, see Basil the Great, "Homilia in psalmum cxv," in *Opera omnia*, ed. J. P. Migne, Patrologia Graeca 30 (Paris: Migne, 1888), 103–14. For an English translation, see Basil the Great, *On Christian Doctrine and Practice*, trans. Mark DelCogliano, Popular Patristics 47 (Yonkers, NY: St. Vladimir's Seminary, 2012), 218–26. Basil (ca. 330–379) is known as one of the Cappadocian Fathers and a champion of orthodoxy during the late fourth-century Trinitarian controversy.

8   In the text: Ἡ τῶν θείων λογικων διδασκαλία, τὸ πιστὸν ἀφ᾽ ἑαυτῆς ἔχει διὰ τὸ θεόπνευστον εἶναι (De Homin., cap. ii.).—Owen. This is a citation and Owen's translation of Nemesius of

The words of Augustine, though taken notice of by all, yet may here be again reported:

I would hear, I would understand how you made the heaven and the earth. Moses wrote this, he wrote it, and is gone hence to thee, for he is not now before me; for if he were, I would hold him, and ask him, and beseech him for thy sake, that he would open these things unto me, and I would apply the ears of my body to the sounds breaking forth from his mouth. But if he should use the Hebrew language, in vain should he affect my sense, for he would not at all touch my mind. If he should speak Latin, I should know what he said. But whence should I know that he spoke the truth? and if I should know this also, should I know it of him? Within me, in the habitation of my own thoughts, truth, neither in Hebrew, Greek, Latin, nor any barbarous language, without the organs of mouth or tongue, without the noise of syllables, would say, 'He speaks the truth;' and I, being immediately assured or certain of it, would say unto that servant of thine, 'Thou speakest truth.' Whereas, therefore, I cannot ask him, I ask thee, O Truth, with which he being filled spoke the things that are true; O my God, I ask of thee; pardon my sins; and thou who gavest unto this thy servant to speak these things, give unto me to understand them.[9]

Emesa's *De natura hominis*, chap. 2. For the Greek text, see Nemesius Emesenus, *Nemesii Emeseni de natura hominis*, ed. Moreno Morani, Bibliotheca Scriptorum Graecorum et Romanorum Teubneriana (Leipzig: BSB B. G. Teubner Verlagsgesellschaft, 1987). For an English translation, see Nemesius, *On the Nature of Man*, trans. R. W. Sharples and P. J. van der Eijk, Translated Texts for Historians 49 (Liverpool: Liverpool University Press, 2008). Nemesius was a fourth-century bishop whose work was an attempt to devise a system of anthropology on the basis of Christian philosophy.

9   In the text: *Audiam et intelligam quo modo fecisti caelum et terram. Scripsit hoc Moses, scripsit et abiit, transivit hinc ad te; Neque enim nunc ante me est. Nam si esset, tenerem eum, et rogarem eum, et per te obsecrarem, ut mihi ista panderet, et praeberem aures corporis mei, sonis erumpentibus ex ore ejus. At si Hebraea voce loqueretur, frustra pulsaret sensum meum, nec indementem meam quidquam tangeret. Si autem Latinè, scirem quid diceret, sed unde scirem an verum diceret? quod si et hoc scirem num et ab illo scirem? Intus utique mihi, intus in domicilio cogitationis, nec Hebraea, nec Graeca, nec Latina, nee barbara veritas, sine oris et linguae organis, sine strepitu syllabarum diceret, Verum dicit; at ego statim erectus confidenter illi homini tuo dicerem, Verum dicis. Cum ergo ilium interrogare non possim, te quo plenus vera dixit, Veritas, te Deus meus rogo, parce peccatis meis, et qui illi servo tuo dedisti haec dicere, da et mihi haec intelligere* (Confess., lib. xi. cap. 3).—Owen. This is a citation and Owen's translation of Augustine's *Confessiones*, bk. 11, chap. 3. For the Latin text, see James J. O'Donnell, *Augustine, "Confessions,"* vol. 1, *Introduction and Text* (Oxford: Oxford University Press, 2012). For an English translation, see Saint Augustine, *Confessions*, trans. Gary Wills (New York: Penguin, 2006).

That which is most remarkable in these words is, that he plainly affirms that faith would not ensue on the declaration of the prophets themselves if they were present with us, unless there be an internal work of the Holy Spirit upon our minds to enable us, and persuade them thereunto. And, indeed, he seems to place all assurance of the truth of divine revelations in the inward assurance which God gives us of them by his Spirit; which we have before considered.

The Second Arausican Council gives full testimony unto the necessity of the internal grace of the Spirit that we may believe: "If anyone assent to the preaching of the gospel through our natural powers without the illumination and inspiration of the Holy Spirit, he is led away by a heretical spirit"[10]

To descend unto later times, wherein these things have been much disputed, yet the truth has beamed such light into the eyes of many as to enforce an acknowledgment from them when they have examined themselves about it. The words of Baptista Mantuanus are remarkable:

I have often thought with myself whence the Scripture itself is so persuasive, from whence it doth so powerfully influence the minds of its hearers, that it inclines or leads them not only to receive an opinion, but surely to believe. This is not to be imputed to the evidence of reasons, which it does not produce, nor unto the industry of art, with words smooth and fit to persuade, which it uses not. See, then, if this be not the cause of it, that we are persuaded that it comes from the first Truth or Verity. But whence are we so persuaded, but from itself alone? As if its own authority should effectually draw us to believe it. But whence, I pray, has it this authority? We saw not God preaching, writing, or teaching of it; but yet, as if we had seen him, we believe and firmly hold that the things which we read proceeded from the Holy Ghost. It may be this is the reason why we so firmly adhere unto it, that truth is more solid in it, though not more clear, than in other writings; for all truth has a persuasive power, the greater truth the greater power, and that which is greatest the greatest efficacy of all. But why, then, do not all believe the gospel? Answer. Because all are not drawn of God.

10 In the text: *Siquis evangelicae praedicationi consentire posse confirmat absque illuminatione et inspiratione Spiritus Sancti, haeretico fallitur spiritu* (Can. 7).—Owen. This is a reference to the Second Council of Orange (529), Canon 7. For the Latin text, see Heinrich Denzinger, *A Compendium of Creeds, Definitions, and Declarations of the Catholic Church*, rev. ed., ed. Peter Hünermann (San Francisco: Ignatius, 2012). For the English translation, see John H. Leith, *Creeds of the Churches: A Reader in Christian Doctrine from the Bible to the Present*, 3rd ed. (Louisville: Westminster John Knox, 1982), 39–40.

But what need is there of any long disputation? We therefore firmly believe the Scriptures, because we have received a divine inspiration assuring us.[11]

And in what sense this is allowed has been declared in the preceding discourse.

I shall close the whole with the testimony of them by whom the truth which we assert is most vehemently opposed, when it rises in opposition unto a special interest of their own.

Two things there are which are principally excepted against in the doctrine of Protestants concerning our belief of the Scripture. The first is with respect unto the Holy Spirit as the efficient cause of faith, for whereas they teach that no man can believe the Scripture to be the word of God in a due manner, and according unto his duty, without the real internal aid and operation of the Holy Ghost, however it be proposed unto him, and with what arguments soever the truth of its divine origin be confirmed, this is charged on them as an error and a crime. And, secondly, whereas they also affirm that there is an inward testimony or witness of the Holy Spirit, whereby he assures and confirms the minds of men in the faith of the Scriptures with an efficacy exceeding all the persuasive evidence of outward arguments and motives, this also by some they are traduced for. And yet those of the Roman church who are looked on as most averse from that resolution of faith which most Protestants acquiesce in, do expressly maintain both these assertions.

The design of Stapleton, *De principiis fidei*, is to prove "that it is impossible to produce any act of faith, or to believe with faith rightly so called, without special grace, and the divine infusion of the gift of faith," which he

---

11 In the text: *Saepe mecum cogitavi unde tam suadibilis sit ipsa Scriptura, unde tam potenter influat in animos auditorum, unde tantum habeat energiae, ut non ad opinandum tantum, sed ad solide credendum omnes inflectat? Non est hoc imputandum rationum evidentiae, quas non adducit; non artis industriae aut verbis suavibus ad persuadendum accommodatis quibus non utitur. Sed vide an id in causa sit quod persuasi sumus earn a prima veritate fluxisse? Sed unde sumus it a persuasi nisi ab ipsa? quasi ad ei credendum nos suiipsius contrahat authoritas. Sed unde oro hanc authoritatem sibi vendicavit? Neque enim vidimus nos Deum concionantem, scribentem, docentem, tamen, ac si vidissemus, credimus et tenemus a Spiritu Sancto fluxisse quae legimus; forsan fuerit haec ratio firmiter adhaerendi, quod in ea veritas sit solidior, quamvis non clarior; habet enim omnis veritas vim inclinativam, et major majorem, et maxima maximam. Sed cur ergo non omnes credunt evangelio? Respond. Quod non omnes trahuntur a Deo. Sed longa opus est disputatione? Firmiter sacris Scripturis ideo credimus quod divinam inspirationem intus accepimus* (De Patient., lib. iii. cap. 2).—Owen. This is a citation and Owen's translation of bk. 3, chap. 2 of *De patientia* (Basel, 1499), by Baptista of Mantua (1447–1516), a Carmelite reformer, humanist, and poet. The cited work is a discourse on both physical and spiritual illness. No modern edition or English translation exists.

there proves with sundry arguments.[12] And Bellarmine speaks to the same purpose: "The arguments which render the articles of our faith credible are not such as produce an undoubted faith, unless the mind be divinely assisted."[13]

Melchor Cano, disputes expressly to this purpose: "This is firmly to be held, that human authority and all the motives before mentioned, or any other which may be used by him who proposes the object of faith to be believed, are not sufficient causes of believing as we are obliged to believe; but there is, moreover, necessary an internal efficient cause moving us to believe, which is the special help or aid of God."[14] And a little after he speaks yet more plainly, "Wherefore, all external human persuasions or arguments are not sufficient causes of faith, however the things of faith may be sufficiently proposed by men; there is, moreover, necessary an internal cause, that is, a certain divine light, inciting to believe, or certain internal eyes to see, given us by the grace of God."[15] Yea, all other learned men of the same profession do speak to the same purpose.

The other assertion, also, they do no less comply with: "The secret testimony of the Spirit is altogether necessary, that a man may believe the testimony and judgment of the church about the Scriptures," says Stapleton.[16] And the words of Gregory de Valentia are remarkable: "Whereas," says he,

12 In the text: *impossibile esse sine speciali gratia, ac dono fidei divinitùs infuso, actum verae fidei producere, aut ex veri nominis fide credere* (controver. 4, lib. viii. cap. 1).—Owen. This is a citation and Owen's translation of Thomas Stapleton's *De principiis fidei doctrinalibus* (Paris, 1579), controv. 4, bk. 8, chap. 1, of which no modern edition or English translation exists. Stapleton (1534–1598) was a famous English Roman Catholic polemicist.

13 In the text: *Argumenta quae articulos fidei nostrae credibiles faciunt non talia sunt ut fidem omnino indubitatam reddant, nisi mens divinitùs adjuvetur* (De Grat. et Lib. Arbit., lib. iv. cap. 3).—Owen. This is a citation and Owen's translation of bk. 4, chap. 3 of *De gratia et libero arbitrio* by Bellarmine (1542–1621), an Italian Jesuit and Cardinal, who was the chief apologist for Tridentine Catholicism. For the Latin text, see Robert Bellarmine's *Opera omnia* (Paris: Ludovicum Vivès, 1874). No English translation exists.

14 In the text: *Id statuendum est, authoritatem humanam et incitamenta omnia ilia praedicta, sive alia quaecunque adhibita ab eo qui proponit fidem, non esse sufficientes causas ad credendum ut credere tenemur, sed praeterea opus esse interiori causa efficiente, id est, Dei speciali auxilio moventis ad credendum* (Loc. Theol., lib. ii. cap. 8).—Owen. This is a citation and Owen's translation of Melchor Cano's (1509–1560) *De locis theologicis* (Lovani, 1564), 52–53. No English translation exists.

15 In the text: *Externae igitur omnes et humanae persuasiones non sunt satis ad credendum, quantumcunque ab hominibus competenter ea quae sunt fidei proponantur; sed necessaria est insuper causa interior, hoc est, divinum quoddam lumen, incitans ad credendum, et oculi quidam interiores Dei beneficio ad videndum dati.*—Owen. The English translation is Owen's.

16 In the text: *Arcanum divini Spiritus testimonium prorsus necessarium est, ut quis ecclesiae testimonio ac judicio circa Scripturarum approbationem credat.*—Owen. Owen does not provide a

we have hitherto pleaded arguments for the authority of Christian doctrine, which even by themselves ought to suffice prudent persons to induce their minds to belief, yet I know not whether there be not an argument greater than they all, namely, that those who are truly Christians do find or feel by experience their minds so affected in this matter of faith, that they are moved, and obliged, firmly to believe, neither for any argument that we have used, nor for any of the like sort that can be found out by reason, but for somewhat else which persuades our minds in another manner, and far more effectually than any arguments whatever.[17]

Let any man compare these words with those of Calvin,[18] which, as I remember, I have cited before, and he will know from whence the sense of them was taken.[19] And to show what [Gregory] means by this internal argument and persuasion, he affirms elsewhere that "it is God himself who, by the voice of his revelation, and by a certain internal instinct and impulse, witnesses unto the minds of men the truth of Christian doctrine or of the Holy Scripture."[20]

These few testimonies have I produced among the many that might be urged to the same purpose, not to confirm the truth which we have pleaded for, which stands on far surer foundations, but only to obviate[21] prejudices in the minds of some, who, being not much conversant in things of this nature, are ready to charge what has been delivered unto this purpose with singularity.

---

citation, but the quotation likely comes from *De principiis fidei doctrinalibus*, from which he previously quoted. The English translation is his own.

17   In the text: *Cum hactenus ejusmodi argumenta pro authoritate Christianae doctrinae fecerimus, quae per seipsa satis prudentibus esse debeant, ut animum inducant velle credere; tamen nescio an non sit argumentum iis omnibus majus, quod qui vere Christiani sunt, ita se animo affectos esse, quod ad fidem attinet, sentiunt, ut praecipue quidem propter nullum argumentum, quod vel hactenus fecimus vel ratione similiter excogitari possit, sed propter aliud nescio quid, quod alio quodam modo et longe fortius quam ulla argumenta persuadet, ut ad firmiter credendum se intelligant* (tom. iii. in Thom., disp. 7, qu. 1, punc. 4, sect. 2).—Owen. This is a citation and Owen's translation of the third volume of Gregory of Valencia's *Commentariorum theologicorum* (Ingolstadt, 1603). No modern edition or English translation exists. Gregory (d. 1603) was a Jesuit professor at the University of Ingolstadt, and his work is both a system of theology and commentary on the *Summa theologica* of Thomas Aquinas, specifically, disp. 7, q. 1, pt. 4, sec. 2.

18   In the text: (*Institut* lib. 1., cap. 7, sect. 5).—Owen. See John Calvin, *Institutes of the Christian Religion*, ed. John T. McNeill, trans. Ford Lewis Battles (Philadelphia: Westminster, 1960), 1.7.5.

19   He cited the lengthy Latin paragraph in his conclusion to chap. 4.

20   In the text: *Deus ipse imprimis est, qui, Christianam doctrinam atque adeo Scripturam sacram veram esse, voce revelationis suae et interno quodam instinctu et impulsu, humanis mentibus contestatur.*—Owen. Owen does not note his citation of Gregory, merely saying it is from "elsewhere." The English translation is his own.

21   I.e., anticipate; prevent.

ΣΥΝΕΣΙΣ
ΠΝΕΥΜΑΤΙΚΗ

or,

The Causes, Ways, and Means
of Understanding the Mind of God
as Revealed in His Word,
with Assurance Therein.
And
a Declaration of the Perspicuity of
the Scriptures, with the External Means
of the Interpretation of Them.

By John Owen, D.D.

———

Open thou mine eyes, that I may behold
wondrous things out of thy law.

PSALM 119:18

Give me understanding, and I shall live.

PSALM 119:144

———

London, Printed for N Ponder at
the Peacock in the Poultry
over against the Stocks-Market: 1678.

The Causes, Ways, and Means of Understanding the Mind of God

Contents

Preface   *213*

1   Introduction   *219*

Usurpation of the Church of Rome with Reference unto the Interpretation of the Scripture, or Right Understanding of the Mind of God Therein. Right and Ability of All Believers as to Their Own Duty Herein Asserted. Importance of the Truth Proposed. The Main Question Stated. The Principal Efficient Cause of the Understanding Which Believers Have in the Mind and Will of God as Revealed in the Scriptures, the Spirit of God Himself. General Assertions to Be Proved. Declared in Sundry Particulars. Inferences from Them.

2   The Holy Spirit as the Principal Efficient Cause of Understanding Scripture: Part 1—The Biblical Evidence   *227*

The General Assertion Confirmed with Testimonies of the Scripture. Psalm 119:18 Opened at Large. Objections Answered, 2 Corinthians 3:13–18. Explained, Isaiah 25:7; Luke 24:44–45. Opened, Ephesians 1:17–19. Explained and Pleaded in Confirmation of the Truth, Hosea 14:9.

3   The Holy Spirit as the Principal Efficient Cause of Understanding Scripture: Part 2—More Biblical Evidence and the Contrast of False Knowledge   *243*

Other Testimonies Pleaded in Confirmation of the Same Truth. John 16:13 Opened. How Far All True Believers Are Infallibly Led into All Truth Declared, and the Manner How They Are So. 1 John 2:20, 27 Explained. What Assurance of the Truth They Have Who Are Taught of God, Ephesians 4:14; Job 36:22; John 6:45. Practical Truths Inferred from the Assertion Proved.

4   The Nature and Effects of Illumination   *265*

The Special Work of the Holy Spirit in the Illumination of Our Minds unto the Understanding of the Scripture Declared and Vindicated. Objections Proposed and Answered. The Nature of the Work Asserted. Psalm 119:18; Ephesians 1:18; Luke 24:45; 1 Peter 2:9; Colossians 1:13; 1 John 5:20 Opened and Vindicated.

5   Ignorance: Causes and Remedies   *279*

Causes of the Ignorance of the Mind of God Revealed in the Scripture; and of Errors about It; What They Are; and How They Are Removed.

6   Inspiration and Perspicuity   *295*

The Work of the Holy Spirit in the Composing and Disposal of the Scripture as a Means of Sacred Illumination; the Perspicuity of the Scripture unto the Understanding of the Mind of God Declared and Vindicated.

7   Biblical Interpretation   *309*

Means to Be Used for the Right Understanding of the Mind of God in the Scripture. Those Which Are Prescribed in a Way of Duty.

8   Rules for Biblical Interpretation   *321*

The Second Sort of Means for the Interpretation of the Scripture, Which Are Disciplinarian.

9   Biblical Interpretation and the Church   *341*

Helps Ecclesiastical in the Interpretation of the Scripture.

Short chapter titles have been added by the editor; Owen's original titles are in italics.

Preface

I SHALL IN A FEW WORDS give the reader an account of the occasion and design of the small ensuing discourse. Some while since I published a treatise about the *Reason of Faith, or the Grounds Whereon We Believe the Scripture to Be the Word of God*, with that faith which is our duty, and prerequired unto all other acceptable obedience. But although this be the first fundamental principle of supernatural religion, yet is it not sufficient unto any of the ends thereof, that we believe the Scripture to be a divine revelation, unless we understand the mind and will of God therein revealed. At least the knowledge and understanding of those things wherein our present duty and future state of blessedness or misery are immediately concerned, are no less indispensably necessary unto us, than is the belief of the Scripture to be the word of God. To declare the way and means whereby we may assuredly attain that understanding is the design of the ensuing discourse, as those whereby we come infallibly to believe the Scripture with faith divine and supernatural are the subject of the former.¶[1]

My principal scope in both has been to manifest that such is the abundant goodness, wisdom, and grace of God in granting unto us the inestimable benefit of his Word, that no persons whatever shall or can come short of the advantage intended by it but through their own sinful negligence and ingratitude, the highest crimes in things of a spiritual and eternal concern. For he has given such convincing evidences of the procedure or emanation of the Scripture from himself, by the divine inspiration of the penmen thereof, and so plainly declared his mind and will therein as unto the faith and obedience which he requires of any or all sorts of persons in their various circumstances, that everyone who takes care of his own present and eternal welfare may and shall, in the due use of the means by him appointed, and discharge of the

---

1   The ¶ symbol indicates that a paragraph break has been added to Owen's original text.

duties by him prescribed unto that end, with a due dependence on the aid and assistance which he will not withhold from any who diligently seek him, infallibly attain such measure of the knowledge of his mind and will, with full assurance therein, as will be sufficient to guide him unto eternal blessedness.¶

The same measure of divine knowledge is not required in all and everyone, that they may live unto God and come unto the enjoyment of him. The dispensation of God toward mankind, in nature, providence, and grace, is an invincible spring of such variety among them, as will not allow a prescription of the same measures of knowledge unto all who have a consistency with divine wisdom and goodness; and a supposition of it would bring confusion into all the order of things and persons which is of divine constitution. Nor is it pretended that any one man may or can have, in the use of any means whatever, a full comprehension of all divine revelations in this life, nor perhaps of any one of them; or that all men, in the use of the same means prescribed unto them, shall have the same conceptions of all things revealed. The Scripture was given for the use of the whole church, and that in all ages, states, and conditions, with respect unto that inconceivable variety of circumstances which all sorts of causes do distribute the whole multitude of them into. Wherefore, the wisdom of God therein has suited itself unto the instruction of every individual believer, unto the moment of his entrance into eternity. That any one of them, that any society of them, should have a perfect comprehension of the entire revelation of God, or a perfect understanding of the whole Scripture, and every part of it, with all that is contained therein, was never required of them in a way of duty, nor ever designed unto them in a way of privilege. For besides that he has replenished it with unfathomable stores, unsearchable treasures of divine mysteries, wherein we cannot find out the Almighty unto perfection, and has provided another state for the comprehension of that by sight which is the object of adoration and admiration in believing, such knowledge is not necessary unto any that they may lead the life of faith, and discharge the duties thereof, in all holy obedience unto God. Yea, such a knowledge and comprehension would be inconsistent with that state and condition wherein we are to walk with God, according to the tenor of the covenant of grace, and during the continuance thereof. But the substance of what we plead for is, that such is the wisdom, goodness, and love of God toward mankind, in the grant that he has made unto them of the revelation of himself, his mind and will, in the Scripture, as that no one person does or can fail of attaining all that understanding in it and of it which is any way needful for his guidance to live unto God in his circumstances and relations, so as to come unto the blessed enjoyment of him, but by the sinful neglect of the means and duties prescribed by him for the attainment of that understanding, and want of a due dependence on those spiritual aids and assistances which he has prepared for that end.¶

By what ways and means he has thus provided for the assurance and security of all men, in things of their eternal concern, and what are those acts of his wisdom, power, and grace, which he exerts for that end, namely, that they may both believe the Scripture to be his word, and understand his mind revealed therein, both according unto what is required of them in a way of duty, so as in both they may be accepted with him, is the design of this and the other forementioned discourse to declare. And they are both of them principally intended for the use of the ordinary sort of Christians, who know it their concern to be established in the truth of those things wherein they have been instructed. For they are frequently attacked with those questions, "How do you know the Scriptures to be the word of God? And what assurance have you that you understand anything contained in them, seeing all sorts of persons are divided about their sense and meaning, nor do you pretend unto any immediate inspiration to give you assurance?" And if, on these ensnaring inquiries, they are cast under any doubts or perplexities in their minds, as it often falls out among them who have not diligently weighed the principles of their own profession, the next insinuation is that they ought to betake themselves either to some other present guide, as their own light and reason, or make a complete resignation of themselves and the conduct of their souls unto the pretended authority and guidance of other men. To give assurance and security unto their minds that they neither are nor can be deceived in the belief of the Scriptures to be the word of God, and the understanding of his mind and will therein, so far as their present obedience and eternal happiness are concerned, and that unto this end they need not be beholding unto any, nor depend on any but God himself, in the use of known and obvious means or duties, is designed in these small treatises.¶

And upon the principles evinced[2] and confirmed in them, I have yet proposed a further inquiry, namely, what conduct, in these times of great contests about the assurance of faith, and the causes of it, everyone that takes care of his own salvation ought to betake himself unto, that he may not be deceived nor miscarry in the end? And this is designed with special respect unto the Church of Rome, which vehemently pretends unto the sole infallible conduct in these things. But probably the near approach of the daily expected and earnestly desired hour of my discharge from all further service in this world

2 I.e., provided evidence for.

will prevent the accomplishment of that intention. In the continual prospect hereof do I yet live and rejoice, which, among other advantages unspeakable, has already given me a lack of concern in those oppositions which the passions or interests of men engage them in, of a very near alliance unto, and scarce distinguishable from, that which the grave will afford.¶

I have but one thing more to acquaint the reader with, wherewith[3] I shall close this preface, and it is the same with that wherewith the preface unto the former discourse is concluded. This also belongs unto the second part of my discourse concerning the dispensation and operations of the Holy Spirit. The first volume on that subject, some years since published, having found good acceptance among them that are godly and learned, both at home and abroad, I have been desired to give out what yet remained for the complete accomplishment of what I had designed thereon in this way of lesser discourses, that may have their use before the whole be finished, or whether ever it be so or no.[4]

---

3 I.e., by which.

4 Πνευματολογια, or, A Discourse concerning the Holy Spirit: Wherein an Account Is Given of His Name, Nature, Personality, Dispensation, Operations, and Effects; His Whole Work in the Old and New Creation Is Explained; the Doctrine concerning It Vindicated from Oppositions and Reproaches. The Nature also and Necessity of Gospel Holiness; the Difference between Grace and Morality, or a Spiritual Life unto God in Evangelical Obedience and a Course of Moral Virtues, Are Stated and Declared (1674).

Συνεσις Πνευματικη

Introduction

Usurpation of the Church of Rome with Reference unto the
Interpretation of the Scripture, or Right Understanding of the Mind
of God Therein. Right and Ability of All Believers as to Their Own
Duty Herein Asserted. Importance of the Truth Proposed. The Main
Question Stated. The Principal Efficient Cause of the Understanding
Which Believers Have in the Mind and Will of God as Revealed in
the Scriptures, the Spirit of God Himself. General Assertions to Be
Proved. Declared in Sundry Particulars. Inferences from Them.[1]

OUR BELIEF OF THE SCRIPTURES to be the word of God, or a divine revelation, and our understanding of the mind and will of God as revealed in them, are the two springs of all our interest in Christian religion. From them are all those streams of light and truth derived whereby our souls are watered, refreshed, and made fruitful unto God. It therefore concerns us greatly to look well to those springs, that they be neither stopped nor defiled, and so rendered useless unto us. Though a man may have pleasant streams running by his habitation and watering his inheritance, yet if the springs of them be in the power of others, who can either divert their course or poison their waters, on their pleasure he must always depend for the benefit of them.

Thus has it fallen out in the world in this matter; so has the Church of Rome endeavored to deal with all Christians. Their main endeavor is to seize those springs of religion into their own power. The Scripture itself, they tell us, cannot be believed to be the word of God with faith divine but

---

[1] Short chapter titles have been added by the editor; Owen's original titles are in italics.

upon the proposal and testimony of their Church; thereby is one spring secured. And when it is believed so to be, it ought not to be interpreted, it cannot be understood, but according to the mind, judgment, and exposition of the same Church; which in like manner secures the other. And having of old possessed these springs of Christian religion, they have dealt with them according as might be expected from unjust invaders of other men's rights and *malae fidei possessoribus*.[2] So when the Philistines contended for the wells which Abraham and Isaac had dug, when they had got possession of them they stopped them up. And when the scribes and Pharisees had gotten the key of knowledge, they would neither enter into the kingdom of God themselves, nor suffer those that would so to do, as our Savior tells us. For the one of these springs, which is the letter of the Scripture itself, when it ought to have gone forth like the waters of the sanctuary, to refresh the church and make it fruitful unto God, they partly stopped it up and partly diverted its course, by shutting it up in an unknown tongue and debarring the people from the use of it. And in the exercise of their pretended right unto the other spring, or the sole interpretation of the Scripture, they have poisoned the streams with all manner of errors and delusions, so as that they became not only useless, but noxious and pernicious unto the souls of men. For under the pretense hereof, namely, that their Church has the sole power of interpreting the Scriptures, and cannot err therein, have they obtruded all their errors, with all their abominations in worship and practice, on the minds and consciences of men.[3]

The first of these springs I have in a former discourse on this subject taken out of their hand, so far as we ourselves are concerned therein, or I have vindicated the just right of all Christians thereunto, and given them possession thereof. This I did by declaring the true grounds and reasons whereon we do, and whereon any can, truly believe the Scripture to be the word of God with faith divine and supernatural.[4] For besides other advantages wherewith

---

2 Lat. "occupants of bad faith."

3 In this paragraph, Owen highlights several features of contemporary Roman Catholic theology: the primacy of the Vulgate, church tradition as the basis for biblical authority, and the authoritative biblical interpretation of the Curia. These positions were canonized in the Council of Trent (1545–1563). See H. J. Schroeder, trans. *The Canons and Decrees of the Council of Trent* (London: B. Herder, 1941).

4 See *The Reason of Faith, or, An Answer unto That Inquiry, "Wherefore We Believe the Scripture to Be the Word of God." With the Causes and Nature of That Faith Wherewith We Do So. Wherein the Grounds Whereon the Holy Scripture Is Believed to Be the Word of God with Faith Divine and Supernatural, Are Declared and Vindicated* (1677), the first treatise in this volume.

the knowledge of that truth is accompanied, it dispossesses the Romanists of their claim unto this fountain of religion, by evidencing that we do and ought thus to believe the divine origin of the Scripture, without any regard to the testimony or authority of their Church.

That which now lies before us is the vindication of the right of all believers unto the other spring also, or a right understanding of the mind and will of God as revealed in the Scripture, suitably unto the duty that God requires of them in their several capacities and conditions.

What is necessary unto the interpretation of difficult places and passages in the Scripture, and what measure of understanding of the mind and will of God as revealed therein is required of persons in their various conditions, as they are teachers of others or among the number of them that are to be taught, shall, among other things, be afterward spoken unto. My principal design is to manifest that *every believer may, in the due use of the means appointed of God for that end, attain unto such a full assurance of understanding in the truth, or all that knowledge of the mind and will of God revealed in the Scripture, which is sufficient to direct him in the life of God, to deliver him from the dangers of ignorance, darkness, and error, and to conduct him unto blessedness.*[5] Wherefore, as unto the belief of the Scripture itself, so as unto the understanding, knowledge, and faith of the things contained therein, we do not depend on the authoritative interpretation of any church or person whatever. And although ordinary believers are obliged to make diligent and conscientious use of the ministry of the church, among other things, as a means appointed of God to lead, guide, and instruct them in the knowledge of his mind and will revealed in the Scripture, which is the principal end of that ordinance, yet is not their understanding of the truth, their apprehension of it, and faith in it, to rest upon or to be resolved into their authority, who are not appointed of God to be lords of their faith, but helpers of their joy. And thereon depends all our interest in that great promise, that we shall be all taught of God. For we are not so unless we do learn from him and by him the things which he has revealed in his word.

And there is not any truth of greater importance for men to be established in. For unless they have a full assurance of understanding in themselves, unless they hold their persuasion of the sense of Scripture revelations from God alone, if their spiritual judgment of truth and falsehood depend on the authority of men, they will never be able to undergo any suffering for

---

5 Italics in this treatise are in the original.

the truth or to perform any duty unto God in a right manner. The truths of the gospel and the ways of religious worship, for which any believer may be called to suffer in this world, are such as about whose sense and revelation in the Scripture there is great difference and controversy among men. And if there be not an assured, yea, infallible way and means of communicating unto all believers a knowledge of the mind and will of God in the Scripture concerning those things so controverted, the grounds whereof are fixed in their own minds, but that they do wholly depend on the expositions and interpretations of other men, be they who they will, they cannot suffer for them either cheerfully or honorably, so as to give glory to God, or to obtain any solid peace and comfort in their own souls. For if a man under his sufferings for his profession can give himself no other account but this, that what he suffers for is the truth of God revealed in the Scripture, because such or such whom he has in veneration or esteem do so affirm and have so instructed him, or because this is the doctrine of this or that church, the papal or the Reformed church, which it has prescribed unto him, he will have little joy of his suffering in the end. Yea, there is that which is yet worse in this matter as things are stated at this day in the world. Truth and error are promiscuously persecuted, according unto the judgment, interest, and inclinations of them that are in power. Yea, sometimes both truth and error are persecuted in the same place and at the same time, upon errors differing from both. Dissent is grown almost all that is criminal in Christian religion all the world over. But in this state of things, unless we grant men an immediate understanding of their own in the mind and will of God, yea, a full assurance therein, there will be nothing whereby a man who suffers for the most important truths of the gospel can in his own soul and conscience distinguish himself from those who suffer in giving testimony unto the most pernicious errors; for all outward means of confidence which he has, they may have also.

It therefore behooves all those who may possibly be called to suffer for the truth in any season, or on any occasion, to assure their minds in this fundamental truth: that they may have in themselves a certain undeceiving understanding of the mind and will of God, as revealed in the Scripture, independent of the authority of any church or persons whatsoever; the use of whose ministry herein we do yet freely and fully allow.

Nor, indeed, without a supposition hereof, can any man perform any duty to God in an acceptable manner, so as that his obedience may be the obedience of faith, nor can upon good grounds die in peace, since the just shall live by his own faith alone.

THE PRIMARY QUESTION STATED

Wherefore, our present inquiry is:

How believers, or any men whatever, may attain a right understanding in their own minds of the meaning and sense of the Scriptures, as to the doctrine or truths contained in them, in answer unto the design of God, as unto what he would have us know or believe; or,

How they may attain a right perception of the mind of God in the Scripture, and what he intends in the revelation of it, in opposition unto ignorance, errors, mistakes, and all false apprehensions, and so in a right manner to perform the duties which by it we are instructed in.

In answer unto the inquiry proposed concerning the knowledge and understanding of believers in the mind of God as revealed in the Scriptures, I shall consider—

First, the principal efficient cause; and, secondly, all the means, internal and external, which are appointed of God thereunto.

SUMMARY OF ARGUMENT

As to the first of these, or the principal efficient cause of the due knowledge and understanding of the will of God in the Scripture, it is the Holy Spirit of God himself alone. For,

There is a special work of the Spirit of God on the minds of men, communicating spiritual wisdom, light, and understanding unto them, necessary unto their discerning and apprehending aright the mind of God in his word, and the understanding of the mysteries of heavenly truth contained therein. And I shall add hereunto, that among all the false and foolish imaginations that ever Christian religion was attacked or disturbed with, there never was any, there is none more pernicious than this, that the mysteries of the gospel are so exposed unto the common reason and understanding of men as that they may know them and comprehend them in a useful manner, and according to their duty, without the effectual aid and assistance of the Spirit of God.

It is the fondest thing in the world to imagine that the Holy Ghost does any way teach us but in and by our own reasons and understandings. We renounce all enthusiasms[6] in this matter, and plead not for any immediate prophetical inspirations. Those who would prohibit us the use of our reason in the things of religion would deal with us as the Philistines did with Samson: first put out our eyes, and then make us grind in their mill. Whatever we know, be it of what

---

6   I.e., claims of receiving extrabiblical, external, immediate revelations after the close of the canon.

sort it will, we know it in and by the use of our reason; and what we conceive, we do it by our own understanding. Only the inquiry is, whether there be not a special work of the Holy Spirit of God, enlightening our minds and enabling our understandings to perceive and apprehend his mind and will as revealed in the Scripture, and without which we cannot so do. The substance, therefore, of the ensuing discourse may be reduced unto these heads.

1. That we stand not in need of any new divine afflations,[7] or immediate prophetical inspirations, to enable us to understand the Scripture, or the mind and will of God as revealed therein. Neither did the prophets or holy penmen of the Scripture learn the mind of God in the revelations made unto them, and by them unto the church, merely from the divine inspiration of them. Those immediate inspirations unto them were in the stead and place of the written word, and no otherwise. After they did receive them, they were by the same means to inquire into the mind and will of God in them as we do it in and by the written word (1 Pet. 1:10–11).

2. That as to the right understanding of the mind of God in the Scripture, or our coming unto the riches of the full assurance of understanding in the acknowledgment of the mystery of God, we do not, nor need to depend on the authoritative instruction or interpretation of the Scripture by any church whatever, or all of them in the world, though there be great use of the true ministry of the church unto that end.

3. That in the mere exercise of our own natural reason and understanding, with the help of external means, we cannot attain that knowledge of the mind and will of God in the Scripture, of the sense and meaning of the Holy Ghost therein, which is required of us in a way of duty, without the special aid and assistance of the Holy Spirit of God. Wherefore, principally, it is asserted,

4. That there is a special work of the Holy Spirit, in the supernatural illumination of our minds, needed unto the end proposed, namely, that we may aright, and according unto our duty, understand the mind of God in the Scripture ourselves, or interpret it unto others.

5. That hereby alone is that full assurance of understanding in the knowledge of the mystery of God, his truth and grace, to be obtained, whereby any man may answer the mind and will of God, or comply with his own duty in all that he may be called to do or suffer in this world in his special circumstances. Wherefore,

6. The certainty and assurance that we may have and ought to have of our right understanding the mind of God in the Scripture, either in general or

---

7 I.e., breathing into; inspiration.

as to any special doctrine, does not depend upon, is not resolved into, any immediate inspiration or enthusiasm; it does not depend upon nor is resolved into the authority of any church in the world; nor is it the result of our reason and understanding merely in their natural actings, but as they are elevated, enlightened, guided, conducted, by an internal efficacious work of the Spirit of God upon them.

7. That whereas the means of the right interpretation of the Scripture, and understanding of the mind of God therein, are of two sorts: first, such as are prescribed unto us in a way of duty, as prayer, meditation on the word itself, and the like; and, secondly, disciplinary, in the accommodation of arts and sciences, with all kind of learning, unto that work. The first sort of them does entirely depend on a supposition of the spiritual aids mentioned, without which they are of no use; and the latter is not only consistent therewith, but singularly subservient thereunto. Wherefore, the nature and use of all these means shall be afterward declared.

This being the substance of what is designed in the ensuing discourse, it is evident that the positions before laid down concerning the special work of the Spirit on the minds of men, in communicating spiritual wisdom, light, and knowledge unto them, is in the first place and principally to be confirmed, as that whereon all the other assertions do absolutely depend.

It is the Scripture itself alone from whence[8] the truth in this matter can be learned, and by which alone what is proposed concerning it must be tried; therefore, as unto this first part of this work, I shall do little more than plead the express testimonies thereof. When we come to consider the way and manner of the communication of these spiritual aids unto us, the whole matter will be more fully stated, and such objections as may be laid against our assertion removed out of the way.

And there are two ends designed in this undertaking.

First, that which the evangelist Luke proposed in his writing the Gospel unto Theophilus, namely, "That he might know the certainty of the things wherein he had been instructed" (Luke 1:4). When we have been instructed in the truth of the gospel, and do give our assent thereunto, yet it is needful that we should examine the grounds and reasons of what we do believe thereon, that we may have a certainty or full assurance of them. This, therefore, we shall direct, namely, how a man may come to an undeceiving persuasion and full assurance that the things wherein he has been instructed, and which he knows, are true and according to the mind of God, so as that he may thereon

---

8 I.e., where.

be "no more tossed to and fro with every wind of doctrine,"[9] by the sleight of men, and cunning craftiness, whereby they lie in wait to deceive.

Secondly, we design to inquire what conduct unto this end a man that takes care of his salvation, and who is convinced that he must give an account of himself unto God, ought in this matter, as to the right understanding of the mind and will of God in the Scripture, to betake himself unto. And as I shall show that there is no safety in depending on enthusiasms, or immediate pretended infallible inspirations, nor on the pretended infallibility of any church, so the Holy Spirit of God, enlightening our minds in the exercise of our own reason or understanding, and in use of the means appointed of God unto that end, is the only safe guide to bring us unto the full assurance of the mind and will of God as revealed in the Scripture.

Wherefore, the whole foundation of this work lies in these two things. One, that there is such a special work of the Holy Spirit on our minds, enabling them to understand the Scriptures in a right manner, or to know the mind of God in them. Two, in showing what is the special nature of this work, what are the effects of it upon our minds, and how it differs from all enthusiastic inspirations, and what is the true exercise of our minds in compliance therewith. And these things we shall first inquire into.

---

9 Eph. 4:14.

2

The Holy Spirit as the Principal Efficient Cause of Understanding Scripture

Part 1—The Biblical Evidence

The General Assertion Confirmed with Testimonies of the Scripture. Psalm 119:18 Opened at Large. Objections Answered, 2 Corinthians 3:13–18. Explained, Isaiah 25:7; Luke 24:44–45. Opened, Ephesians 1:17–19. Explained and Pleaded in Confirmation of the Truth, Hosea 14:9.

PSALM 119:18

The whole of our assertion is comprised in the prayer of the psalmist, גל עיני ואביטה נפלאות מתורתך—"Open thou mine eyes, that I may behold wondrous things out of thy law" (Ps. 119:18). The same request, for the substance of it, is repeated sundry times in the same Psalm (Ps. 119:33–34; etc.). Thus he prayed. That it may be esteemed our duty to pray in like manner is the substance of what we plead for. What we pray for from God, that we have not in and of ourselves; as the ancient church constantly pleaded against the Pelagians.[1] And what we pray for according to the mind of God, that we do receive. Wherefore, our discerning, our understanding, of the wonderful

---

[1] Pelagians are those who hold to the heterodox teachings of Pelagius (ca. 354–418), who denied original sin and believed that human beings had the free will to achieve perfection without the aid of divine grace.

227

things of the law, is not of ourselves; it is that which is given us, that which we receive from God.

But that the force of our argument from this testimony may be the more evident, the words or terms of it must be explained, that we may see whether they be equivalent unto, or of the same signification with, those laid down in our assertion.

1. That which is the object of the understanding prayed for, that in the knowledge whereof the psalmist would be illuminated, is תורה.[2] The word signifies instruction; and being referred unto God, it is his teaching or instruction of us by the revelation of himself, the same which we intend by the Scripture. When the books of the Old Testament were completed, they were, for distinction's sake, distributed into תורה, כתובים, and נביאים, or, the "Law," the "Psalms," and the "Prophets" (Luke 24:44).[3] Under that distribution Torah signifies the five books of Moses. But whereas these books of Moses were, as it were, the foundation of all future revelations under the Old Testament, which were given in the explication thereof, all the writings of it are usually called "the Law" (Isa. 8:20). By the law, therefore, in this place, the psalmist understands all the books that were then given unto the church by revelation for the rule of its faith and obedience. And that by the law, in the psalms, the written law is intended, is evident from the first of them, wherein he is declared blessed who "meditateth therein day and night" (Ps. 1:2). Which has respect unto the command of reading and meditating on the books thereof in that manner (Josh. 1:8). That, therefore, which is intended by this word is the entire revelation of the will of God, given unto the church for the rule of its faith and obedience, that is, the Holy Scripture.

2. In this law there are נפלאות, "wonderful things." פלא signifies to be "wonderful," to be "hidden," to be "great" and "high," that which men by the use of reason cannot attain unto or understand, hence נפלאות are things that have such an impression of divine wisdom and power upon them as that they are justly the object of our admiration. That which is too hard for us; as Deuteronomy 17:8, כי יפלא ממך דבר—"If a matter be too hard for thee," hid from thee. And it is the name whereby the miraculous works of God are expressed (Pss. 77:11; 78:11). Wherefore, these "wonderful things of the law" are those expressions and effects of divine wisdom in the Scripture which are above the natural reason and understandings of men to find out and comprehend. Such are the mysteries of divine truth in the Scripture, especially because Christ is

---

2 Heb. "the Law," "Torah," or "instruction."

3 Owen understands כתובים to be "Psalms," although it is better translated as "Writings," the third part of the division of the Old Testament along with the "Law" and the "Prophets."

in them, whose name is פלא, or "Wonderful" (Isa. 9:6). For all the great and marvelous effects of infinite wisdom meet in him. These things and doctrines God calls רבי תורת—I have written to him the "great things of my law," and they were counted by them כמו זר, as a "strange thing" (Hos. 8:12). Because they were "wonderful" in themselves, they neglected and despised them, as that which was foreign and alien from them, which belonged not unto them. So deal many with the mysteries of the gospel at this day; because they are heavenly, spiritual, in themselves marvelous, hidden, and above the understanding of the natural reason of men, that is, they are נפלאות, they reject and despise them as things alien and foreign unto their religion. Wherefore, the "wonderful things" of the Scripture are those mysteries of divine truth, wisdom, and grace, that are revealed and contained therein, with their special respect unto Jesus Christ.

3. Three things are supposed in the words concerning these wonderful things:

(1) That they are recorded, laid up, or treasured, in the law or Scripture, and nowhere else, so as that from there alone are they to be learned and received. "Behold wondrous things out of thy law." That alone is the sacred παρακαταθήκη, or "repository" of them. There are wondrous things in the works of nature and providence, and much of them is contained in the treasury of reason, wherein it may be discerned. But these are stored in the law only, and nowhere else.

(2) That it is our duty to behold, to discern, to understand them, to have an inspection into them, and our great privilege when we are enabled so to do. This makes the psalmist pray so frequently, so fervently, that he may have the discerning of them, or come to an acquaintance with them. Those, therefore, by whom they are neglected do both despise their duty and forsake their own mercy.

(3) That we are not able of ourselves thus to discern them without divine aid and assistance. For the psalmist, who was wiser than the wisest of us, and who had so earnest a desire after these things, yet would not trust unto his own reason, wisdom, ability, and diligence, for the understanding of them, but takes himself unto God by prayer, acknowledging therein that it is the special work of God by his Spirit to enable us to understand his mind and will as revealed in the Scripture.

4. There is expressed in the words the act of God toward us, whereby he enables us to behold, discern, and understand the wonderful effects of divine wisdom, which are treasured up in the Scripture, which the psalmist prays for. This is called his "opening of our eyes," גל עני: Reveal mine eyes,

uncover, unveil mine eyes. There is a light in the word; all truth is light, and sacred truth is sacred light. Yea, the word of God is expressly called "light" (Pss. 36:9; 43:3; 119:105). But there is by nature a covering, a veil, on the eyes of the understandings of all men, so that they are not able of themselves to behold this light, nor to discern anything by it in a due manner. With respect hereunto the psalmist prays that God would "reveal his eyes." *Revelare* is *velamentum levare*, "to reveal is to take off the veil or covering." And this veil is that of our natural darkness, blindness, and ignorance; whereof we have treated elsewhere.[4]

I see not what is wanting unto the explanation or confirmation of the position before laid down. The communication of spiritual light from God is the peculiar work of the Holy Ghost. He is the immediate author of all spiritual illumination. But hereby alone, or by virtue hereof, can we know or understand the mind of God in the Scripture, in such a manner as God requires us to do; and whosoever has received the grace of this divine illumination may do so, so far as he is concerned, in point of faith or obedience.

The law is the Scripture, the written word of God. Therein are "wonderful things," or mysteries of divine wisdom, contained and revealed. To behold these things, is to discern and understand them aright with respect unto our own faith and obedience. This we cannot do without a supernatural act of the Spirit of God upon our minds, enabling them to discern them and understand them; these things are in the text ἀναντιῤῥήτως, "indisputably." And we hence further argue, that which is our duty to pray for spiritual, supernatural aid to enable us to do, that of ourselves we are not able to do without that aid and assistance, at least we may do it by virtue of that aid and assistance; which includes the substance, by just consequence, of what is pleaded for. But such aid it is our duty to pray for, that we may understand aright the revelations of the mind and will of God in the Scriptures, the only thing to be proved.

There is but one thing which I can foresee that may with any pretense of reason be objected unto this testimony of the psalmist in particular. And this is, that he speaks of the times and writings of the Old Testament. Now, it is confessed that there was in them a darkness and obscurity, and such as needed new revelations for the understanding of them. But since all things are brought to light by the gospel, there is no need of any special aid or assistance of the Holy Spirit, by supernatural illumination, for the understanding of them. In answer hereunto I shall consider the discourse of the apostle wherein

---

4 Owen is likely referring to his Πνευματολογια, *or, A Discourse concerning the Holy Spirit*, bk. 3.

he states this whole matter: "And not as Moses, who put a veil over his face, that the children of Israel could not steadfastly look to the end of that which is abolished. But their minds were blinded: for until this day remaineth the same veil untaken away, in the reading of the Old Testament; which is done away in Christ. . . . Nevertheless, when it shall turn to the Lord" (or, they be turned unto the Lord) "the veil shall be taken away. Now the Lord is that Spirit; and where the Spirit of the Lord is, there is liberty. But we all with open face behold as in a glass the glory of the Lord" (2 Cor. 3:13–14, 16–18).

When Moses had received the revelation of the law from God, "his face shone" (Ex. 34:29). For there were wonderful things contained in that revelation with respect unto Jesus Christ; he was in them all, and the end of them all. The whole ministry of Moses was but a testimony given unto the things that were afterward to be spoken concerning him, as the apostle declares (Heb. 3:5).

On the receipt of this revelation "his face shone," because there was a light, a luster, a glory, in the things revealed unto him, and by them reflected on his ministry, which was so represented. Nevertheless, this light did not shine immediately into the hearts and minds of the people. They did not see or discern the glorious and "wonderful things" that were in the law. For there was a double veil or covering that hindered them. One that was put on Moses' face, another that was on their own hearts. Some dark apprehensions and glances of light they had, but they could not look steadfastly unto the end of that which was to be abolished; they could not comprehend the truth concerning Christ, which was the substance and end of the law.

The first veil, that which was on the face of Moses, was the obscurity of the instructions given them, as wrapped up in types, shadows, and dark parables. This they could not see through as clearly to discern the "wonderful things" contained in and under them. This veil is quite taken off in the revelation or doctrine of the gospel, wherein life and immortality are brought to light, and the wonderful things of the mystery of God in Christ are fully declared and plainly expressed. Herein, therefore, it is acknowledged that there is a great difference between those under the Old Testament and those under the New.

But, says the apostle, there is another veil, a veil upon the heart. And hereof he declares two things. First, that this veil is done away only in Christ; and two, that therefore it is not taken away from any but those who are converted unto God. This is the covering of ignorance, darkness, blindness, that is on men by nature. The former veil is taken away by the doctrine of the gospel. This latter is to be removed only by an effectual work of the Spirit of Christ, in the conversion of the souls of men unto God.

And two things do ensue on the removal of this double veil. First, that as unto the doctrine itself concerning the mystery of God in Christ, it is no more represented unto us in types, shadows, and dark parables, but in the clear glass of the gospel, whereon the glory of Christ is reflected. Hereby the veil is taken off from the face of Moses. Second, that we have πρόσωπον ἀνακεκαλυμμένον, an "open, uncovered face," or, as the Syriac reads it, a "revealed eye," whereby we are enabled to discern the wonderful mysteries of God so revealed. This ensues on the taking away of the second veil of darkness and blindness, which is on the hearts of all by nature.

The removal and destruction of this double veil by the Spirit and grace of the gospel is that which is prophesied of, "And he will destroy in this mountain the face," חלט חלוט[5]—"the covering, covered, or the double veil," "that is on the face of all people"; and הַמַּסֵּכָה הַנְּסוּכָה—"the veil veiled over all nations" (Isa. 25:7).

This being the design of the discourse of the apostle, it is evident that although there be a difference between them under the Old Testament and us as to the veil that was on the face of Moses, which is destroyed and removed by the doctrine of the gospel, yet there is none as to the veil which is on the hearts of all by nature, which must be removed by the Holy Spirit, or we cannot "with open face behold the glory of the Lord,"[6] the thing which the psalmist prays for in the place insisted on. That is, that God by his Spirit would more and more renew his mind, and take away his natural darkness and ignorance, that he might be able to behold, perceive, and understand the mind of God as revealed in the Scripture. And if any shall suppose or say, that for their part they need no such special aid and assistance to enable them to understand the mind of God in the Scripture, which is sufficiently exposed to the common reason of all mankind, I shall only say at present, I am afraid they do not understand those places of Scripture where this aid and assistance is so expressly affirmed to be necessary thereunto.

LUKE 24:44–45

But the meaning of the psalmist will the better appear if we consider the communication of the grace which he prayed for unto others. This is expressed, "Then opened he their understanding, that they might understand the Scriptures" (Luke 24:45). A needless work if some men may be believed. But our Lord Jesus Christ thought not so. The truths concerning him were

---

5   *Biblia Hebraica Stuttgartensia* reads, הַלּוֹט הַלּוֹט. *Biblia Hebraica Stuttgartensia*, ed. Karl Elliger and Wilhelm Rudolph (Stuttgart: Deutsche Bibelgesellschaft, 1983); hereafter cited as *BHS*.
6   2 Cor. 3:18.

revealed in the Scripture, that is, in the law, and the prophets, and the Psalms (Luke 24:44). These they read, these they were instructed in, these were preached unto them every day. And probably they were as well skilled in the literal sense of Scripture propositions as those who pretend highest among us so to be. Howbeit they could not understand those "wonderful things" in a way of duty, and as they ought to do, until the Lord Christ "opened their understandings." There was needful unto them an immediate gracious act of his divine power on their minds to enable them thereunto. And I cannot yet much value those men's understanding of the Scripture whose understandings are not opened by the Spirit of Christ.

If we need the openings of our understandings by an act of the power and grace of Christ, that we may understand the Scriptures, then without it we cannot so do, namely, so as to believe and yield obedience, according unto our duty. The consequence is evident, for if we could, there was no need of this act of Christ toward these disciples, who were not destitute of any rational abilities required in us thereunto. And the act of Christ in "opening their understandings" is openly distinguished from the proposition of the doctrine of the Scripture unto them. This was made two ways: first, in the Scripture itself; secondly, in the oral discourse of our Savior upon it. Distinct from both these is that act of his whereby he "opened their understanding, that they might understand the Scripture." Wherefore, nothing but a real internal act of grace, in the illumination of their minds, can be intended thereby; the nature whereof shall be further explained afterward.

EPHESIANS 1:17–19

But there is an eminent place that must be pleaded distinctly to this purpose:

> That the God of our Lord Jesus Christ, the Father of glory, may give unto you the Spirit of wisdom and revelation in the knowledge of him: the eyes of your understanding being enlightened, that you may know what is the hope of his calling, and what the riches of the glory of his inheritance in the saints, and what is the exceeding greatness of his power to us-ward who believe. (Eph. 1:17–19)

This is the whole of what we would assert, and nothing else. And if men would acquiesce[7] by faith in what is here declared, we need to plead this

---

7 I.e., accept; submit.

cause no further, for the words and expressions of the truth here used are more emphatic unto a spiritual understanding than any others we can find out. And I shall only show in the opening of them how our position and sense are contained in them.¶

What the apostle does here for others, it is unquestionably our duty to do for ourselves. We are, then, to pray that God would enable us by his Spirit to know and understand his mind and will as revealed in the Scripture. This, therefore, without special aid and assistance from him by his Spirit, we cannot do. And the aid he gives us consists in the effectual illumination of our minds, or the enlightening of the eyes of our understandings. These things are plain, and not liable, as I suppose, to any exception. And these are all we plead for. Let them be granted without any other distinctions or limitations but what the Scripture will justify, and there is an end of this difference. But some particular passages in the words may be considered, for the better understanding and further confirmation of the truth contained therein—

1. It is a revelation that the apostle prays for, or a Spirit of revelation to be given unto them. This greatly offends some at first hearing, but wholly without cause; for he understands not a new immediate external revelation from God. Believers are not directed to look after such revelations for their guide. Ever since the Scripture was written, the generality of the church was obliged to attend thereunto alone, as their only rule of faith and obedience. And although God reserved unto himself a liberty under the Old Testament, and until the completing of all the books of the New, to add new revelations as he pleased, yet he always bound up the faith and obedience of the present church unto what he had already revealed. And he has now, by the Spirit of his Son, put an end unto all expectation of any new, of any other revelations, wherein the faith or obedience of the church should be concerned. At least we take it for granted in this inquiry, that infallible inspirations in the discovery of things not before revealed are ceased in the church. Nor do the Papists extend their infallibility thereunto, but only unto things already revealed in the Scripture or tradition. What some among ourselves do ascribe of this nature unto their light,[8] I do not well know, nor shall now inquire.

But there is an internal subjective revelation, whereby no new things are revealed unto our minds, or are not outwardly revealed anew, but our minds are enabled to discern the things that are revealed already. All the things here mentioned by the apostle, which he desires they might understand, were already revealed in the Scriptures of the Old Testament, and the New that were

---

8 This is likely a reference to the Quakers.

then written, and the infallible declaration of the gospel in the preaching of the apostles. But there was a new work of revelation required in and unto every person that would understand and comprehend these things in a due manner. For ἀποκάλυψις, or "revelation," is the discovery of anything, whether by the proposal of it unto us, or the enabling of us to discern it when it is so proposed. In the first sense it is used: Romans 16:25; 2 Corinthians 12:1, 7; Galatians 1:12, 2:2. In the latter: Luke 2:32; Ephesians 1:17–18. As when God opened the eyes of the servant of Elisha, on the prayer of his master, to see the horses and chariots of fire that were round about him (2 Kings 6:17). They were not brought thither by the opening of his eyes, only he was enabled to discern them, which before he could not do. Or as when anyone makes use of a telescope to behold things afar off, no object is presented unto him but what was really in the same place before, only his visive[9] faculty is assisted to discern them at that distance, which without that assistance it could not reach unto. And the Holy Spirit is here called the Spirit of revelation, causally, as he is the author or principal efficient cause of it. So, in his communication unto the Lord Christ himself, he is called "The Spirit of wisdom and understanding, the Spirit of counsel and might, the Spirit of knowledge and of the fear of the Lord; that should make him of quick understanding in the fear of the Lord" (Isa. 11:2–3).

2. What the psalmist, in the place before insisted on, calls in general נפלאוה, "wonderful things," the apostle expresses in particular, and distributes them under sundry heads as they were more clearly revealed in the gospel. Such are, "The hope of God's calling," "The riches of his glory," and "The exceeding greatness of his power" in them that do believe. These are some of the principal and most important mysteries of the gospel. No other understanding can we have of these things but only as they are revealed therein, or of the revelation of them. And in the manner of his expression he declares these things to be "wonderful," as the psalmist speaks. For there is in them πλοῦτος τῆς δόξης, "the riches of glory," which is beyond our comprehension. So he expressly affirms that it is ἀνεξιχνίαστος, "past all investigation" (Eph. 3:8), or search; the same word that he uses to set forth the ways of God, when his design is to declare them wonderful, or the object of our admiration: "O the depth of the riches of the wisdom and knowledge of God, how unsearchable are his ways, and his judgements past finding out" (Rom. 11:33). And there is in them ὑπερβαλλον μέγεθος, "an exceeding" or inexpressible "greatness of power."

9 I.e., visual.

Such are the things that are proposed unto us in the Scripture. And the principal reason why some men judge it so easy a matter to understand and comprehend by the innate abilities of their own minds the revelations that are made in the word of God unto us, is because they do not apprehend that there is anything wonderful, or truly great and glorious in them. And, therefore, because they cannot raise their minds unto a comprehension of these mysteries as they are in themselves, they corrupt and debase them to suit them unto their own low, carnal apprehensions, which is the principle that works effectually in the whole of Socinianism.[10] For grant that there are such "wonderful things," such mysteries, in the gospel as we plead, and the men of that persuasion will not deny but that our minds do stand in need of a heavenly assistance to comprehend them aright, for they deny them for no other reason but because their reason cannot comprehend them.

3. Concerning these things so revealed in the word, the apostle prays for these Ephesians that they might know them; as also, he expresses the way whereby alone they might be enabled so to do: Εἰς τὸ εἰδέναι ὑμᾶς, "That they might have a sight, perception, or understanding of them." This he denies a natural man to have, or that he can have; he "cannot know them" (1 Cor. 2:14). It is true, it may be said he cannot know them unless they are clearly and fairly proposed unto him; no, nor then neither by the light and power of his own natural faculties. He cannot do so by the use of any outward means alone. It is futile to imagine that the apostle intends only that a natural man cannot know things that are never proposed unto him, which is neither weakness nor discommendation. For neither can the spiritual man so know anything.

Because it is thus with men by nature, therefore does the apostle so earnestly pray that these Ephesians might be enabled to understand and know these things, and he does it with an unusual solemnity, invoking the "God and Father of our Lord Jesus Christ, the Father of glory," which argues both a great intension of spirit in him, and great weight laid upon the matter of his request.

But what reason is there for this earnestness? What is wanting unto these Ephesians? What would he yet have for them? Were they not rational men, that had their eyes in their heads as well as others? Nay, were not many of them learned men, and skilled in all the curious arts of those days? For here it was that so many upon their first conversion burnt their books to the value of "fifty thousand pieces of silver" (Acts 19:19). Probably they were many of them very knowing in the new and old philosophy. Had they not the Scripture

---

10 See the introduction on Socinianism.

also; that is, all the books of the Old Testament, and those of the New which were then written? Did not the apostle and others preach the doctrine of the gospel unto them, and therein the things which he here mentions? He declares and expressly testifies that he did (Acts 20:20, 27). Speaking unto these very persons, that is, the leaders of them, he says, "I have kept back nothing that was profitable unto you [. . .] but declared unto you all the counsel of God," namely, what is the hope of his calling, and what the greatness of his power. Were not these things sufficiently revealed, and clearly proposed unto them? If they were not, it was because the apostle could not so reveal and propose them, or because he would not. If he could not, then he prays that that might be revealed unto them which was not so to him, or that they might learn what he could not teach them, which is foolish and impious to imagine. If he would not, then he prays that they may know that which he would not teach them, but which he could easily have so done, which is equally foolish to suppose. What, therefore, do they yet lack? What is yet further needed that they might know and understand these things? For we must know that we understand no more of the mind of God in the revelations that he makes unto us than we understand of the things themselves that are revealed by him.

I am persuaded that these Ephesians were generally as wise, and some of them as learned, as any in our days, let them have what conceit of themselves they please. Yet grant some of ours but thus much, that they have their wits about them and the use of their reason, and let them have the things of the gospel, or the doctrines of it, rationally proposed unto them, as they are in the Scripture, and they defy the world to think that they yet want anything to enable them to know and rightly to understand them. To fancy anything else to be necessary hereunto is fanatical madness. For what would men have? What should ail them? Are not the doctrines of the gospel highly rational? Are not the things of it eminently suited unto the reason of mankind? Are not the books of the Scripture written in a style and language intelligible? Is there anything more required unto the understanding of the mind of any author but to conceive the grammatical sense of the words that he uses, and the nature of his propositions and arguings? And although St. Paul, as some say, be one of the obscurest writers they ever met with, yet surely by these means some good shift may be made with his writings also. It is, therefore, canting and nonsense, a reproach to reason and Christian religion itself, to think that this is not enough to enable men to understand the mind of God in the Scriptures.

Well be it so, at present, as unto the highly rational abilities of some persons. It cannot be denied, but that the apostle judged it necessary that these

Ephesians should have the special aid of the Spirit of God unto this end, which he prays for. And we may be excused if we dare not think ourselves better than they, nor to have a sufficiency of learning, wisdom, and reason above others, or less to need prayers of this nature than they did. And we find that the apostle renews his prayer for them again unto the same purpose with great fervency (Eph. 3:14–19). All the difference arises from hence, that the apostle judges that over and above the utmost exercise of our natural faculties and abilities, in the use of outward means, that we may know the mind of God in the Scripture, wherein these Ephesians were not wanting, it is necessary that the "eyes of our understanding" should be spiritually opened and enlightened; but other men, it seems, think not so.

But if men should be allowed to suppose that our minds were no way vitiated,[11] depraved, or darkened by the fall, which supposition is the sole foundation of these assertions, yet it is most irrational to imagine that we can comprehend and understand the mysteries of the gospel without special spiritual illumination. For the original light and abilities of our minds were not suited or prepared for the receiving and understanding of them. For neither their being nor revelation was consistent with the state of integrity. Wherefore, although our minds should be allowed to be as wise and perspicacious[12] with respect unto that natural knowledge of God and all that belongs unto it which was proposed unto us, or necessary for us in the state of nature, yet would it not follow that we are able to discern the mysteries of grace when proposed unto us. The truth is, if our minds be not corrupted or depraved, there is no need of the gospel or its grace; and if they are, we cannot understand the mind of God therein without special illumination.

But it may be said, that these things are consistent. For notwithstanding men's rational abilities and the use of means, yet it is meet[13] that they should both pray for themselves, and that others, whose duty it is, should pray for them also. It is so, that they may be diligent in their inquiries, and obtain the blessing of God upon their diligence. But this does not prove at all that they are not able of themselves to apprehend and know the mind and things of God in the Scripture, or that anything is wanting in them or to them which is absolutely necessary thereunto.

I answer, that on these suppositions there is indeed nothing wanting but that which the apostle moreover prays for, which is none of them. And if that be not also requisite unto this end, his prayer is vain and useless. That men

11   I.e., impaired.
12   I.e., ready with insight and understanding.
13   I.e., fitting, proper.

be diligent in the discharge of their duty herein, and that they may have the special blessing of God thereon, are here supposed, and we shall speak unto them afterward. These are not the things that the apostle here prays for, but that God would give them the "Spirit of wisdom and revelation, to enlighten the eyes of their understanding," that they may know them, as shall be immediately declared. And, indeed, I understand not how this prayer can be suited unto the principles of any who deny the necessity of this internal spiritual aid.

For they cannot but think it strange to pray for a "Spirit of wisdom and revelation" to be given unto their whole congregations, which were a dangerous way, fitted to make them wiser than their teachers. And for themselves, besides using diligence, and praying for a blessing on their diligence, they disavow any further concern in this matter.

4. The thing especially prayed for, in order unto the end proposed, is, that the "eyes of our understandings may be enlightened." This is the same which the psalmist prays for in the place before insisted on, that "God would open his eyes."[14] And it is the internal work of illumination that is intended. Now, although the main force of the argument depends on these words, yet shall I not insist here upon them, because I must speak somewhat more in particular unto the nature of this work afterward. Besides, what is that darkness which is here supposed to be on our minds or understandings, what is its nature, efficacy, and power, how it is taken away and removed, what is the nature of that spiritual light which is communicated unto us in and for the removal thereof, I have at large elsewhere declared.[15] All that at present I shall observe from these words is, in general, that there is a special work of the Spirit of God, in the enlightening the eyes of our understandings, necessary unto our discerning of the mysteries of the gospel in a due manner; which was to be proved.

5. What is declared concerning the author of this work in us, or the principal efficient cause of it, does further confirm the same truth. And this is the Holy Spirit, "That he would give unto you the Spirit of wisdom and revelation." That the Holy Spirit is the immediate author of all supernatural effects and operations in us has been elsewhere proved at large.[16] And what he is promised or given in the gospel so to effect is not anything that is in our own power. Wherefore, the ascription of the communication of this ability unto the Holy Ghost is a sufficient evidence that we want it in ourselves. And all things here affirmed concerning the manner of his communication unto

---

14 Ps. 119:18.

15 Πνευματολογια, or, A Discourse concerning the Holy Spirit, bk. 3.

16 Πνευματολογια, or, A Discourse concerning the Holy Spirit.

us, and his properties as communicated, do evidence the nature and evince the truth of the work ascribed unto him.¶

As for the first, it is by the grant, donation, or free gift of God the Father: "That the God of our Lord Jesus Christ, the Father of glory, would give unto you" (Eph. 1:17). God is called "the King of glory" (Ps. 24:7–8), and "the God of glory" (Acts 7:2), with respect unto his own glorious majesty. But he is "the Father of glory" as he is the eternal spring and cause of all glory unto the church. And these titles are prefixed unto this grant or the request of it, "the God of our Lord Jesus Christ, the Father of glory," to intimate that it proceeds from his relation unto us in Christ, with that love and bounty wherein he is the cause of all grace and glory unto us. Wherefore, receiving this Spirit by free donation, as we do (Luke 11:13), all that we receive from him and by him, we have it by the way of free gift or donation also. Therefore is this ability of understanding the Scripture, and the mysteries of the truth contained therein, a mere free gift of God, which he bestows on whom he will. So our Savior told his disciples, "Unto you it is given to know the mysteries of the kingdom of heaven, but to them," to others, "it is not given" (Matt. 13:11), who yet heard his words and understood the literal sense of the propositions used by him as well as the disciples did. Whoever, therefore, has this ability to know the mysteries of the gospel, he has it by free gift or donation from God. He has received it, and may not boast as if it were from himself, and that he had not received it, as the apostle speaks (1 Cor. 4:7). Again, the properties ascribed unto him, as thus communicated for this end, are "wisdom and revelation."

He is the "Spirit of wisdom." So in the communication of him in all fullness unto the Lord Jesus Christ, the head of the church, he is called "the Spirit of wisdom and understanding" (Isa. 11:2), and that because he was to make him of "quick understanding in the fear of the Lord" (Isa. 11:3). He is a "Spirit of wisdom" essentially in himself, and causally or efficiently unto others; and these things do mutually demonstrate each other. That he is the cause of all wisdom in others, is a demonstration that he is essentially wise in himself. For "he that planted the ear, shall he not hear? He that formed the eye, shall he not see?"[17] And because he is essentially wise, he must be the author of all wisdom unto others. For all good must come from that which is infinitely, eternally, unchangeably so (James 1:17). He is, therefore, called "The Spirit of wisdom" on both these accounts: as he is essentially so in himself, and as he is the efficient cause of all wisdom unto others. And it is in the latter way immediately that he is here so termed. And this property is peculiarly

17 Ps. 94:9.

ascribed unto him as thus given unto us to "open our eyes," with respect unto the work which he is to do. For wisdom is required hereunto, that wisdom which may deliver us from being really fools ourselves, and from judging the things of God to be folly.

There is a wisdom required hereunto: "Who is wise, and he shall understand these things? Prudent, and he shall know them? For the ways of the Lord are right, and the just shall walk in them; but the transgressors shall fall therein" (Hos. 14:9). Want of this wisdom is the cause that wicked men take offense at and dislike the ways of God, because they do not spiritually understand them, and so cast themselves into destruction. And it is of the same things that the prophet affirms, that "none of the wicked shall understand, but the wise shall understand" (Dan. 12:10). And it is called "the wisdom of the just" (Luke 1:17).

This wisdom is not in us by nature. Men are naturally wise in their own conceit; which if continued in is a hopeless frame of mind (Prov. 26:12). And in nothing does it more evidence itself than in apprehensions of their own ability to comprehend spiritual things, and in their contempt of what they do not so [comprehend] as folly (1 Cor. 1:18, 23). And with respect hereunto does the apostle give that advice unto us as our duty, "Let no man deceive himself, if any man among you seemeth to be wise in this world, let him become a fool, that he may be wise" (1 Cor. 3:18). This is a matter wherein men are very apt to deceive themselves, even to conceit themselves wise, and to trust thereunto in the things of God, whereof alone he there treats. Whereas, therefore, the special promise of God is to teach the meek and the humble, there is nothing that sets men at a greater distance from divine instruction than a proud conceit of their own wisdom, wit, parts, and abilities. Wherefore, this wisdom, which is the daughter of natural darkness and the mother of proud spiritual ignorance, the Spirit of wisdom frees the minds of believers from, in the way that shall be afterward declared; and therein is he unto us a "Spirit of wisdom." Moreover, he gives us that "wisdom which is from above," which we are directed to ask of God (James 1:5).[18] Without this wisdom, which he works in us, no man can understand the wisdom of God in the mystery of the gospel; whoso is thus made wise shall understand these things, and none else. There is, therefore, a gift of spiritual wisdom and understanding necessary hereunto, that we may discern the "wonderful things" that are in the word of God. To whom this is not given, they know not the mysteries of the kingdom of heaven. Let

---

18 While James 1:5 speaks of divine wisdom, the Scripture quotation matches James 3:17.

men please or pride themselves while they will in their own wisdom and learning, and explode the consideration of these things in our inquiries after the mind of God, the meanest believer who has received this wisdom from above, according unto the measure of the gift of Christ, knows more of the mind of God in a due manner than they do.

When our Lord Jesus Christ affirmed that he came into the world "that they which see not, might see," or to communicate spiritual, saving light unto the minds of men, the Pharisees, who had great apprehensions of their own wisdom and understanding in the law, replied with scorn: "Are we blind also?" (John 9:39–40). I proved no otherwise, and that to their eternal ruin, yet do I not judge all them to be practically blind who do not doctrinally own the receiving of this wisdom and light from above. For although we make not ourselves to differ from others, nor have anything in a way of spiritual ability but what we have received, yet are some apt to glory as if they had not received, as the apostle intimates (1 Cor. 4:7). Wherefore, the Holy Spirit, as given unto us, is said to be a "Spirit of wisdom," because he makes us wise, or works wisdom in us. This wisdom we have not of ourselves; for to suppose it, renders the word of God of none effect. And this spiritual wisdom, thus to be bestowed upon us, thus to be wrought in us, is necessary, that we may know the mysteries of the gospel, or understand the mind of God therein; which is all that we plead for.

I have insisted the longer upon this testimony, because the whole of what we assert in general, in the nature, causes, and effects of it, is fully declared therein. And this was the way whereby they of old came to understand divine revelations, or the mind of God as revealed in the Scripture. If others, who seem to scorn all mention of the teaching of the Holy Ghost, have found out a course more expedite unto the same end, it is what I understand not, nor do desire to participate in.[19]

19 This could be a reference to the rationalism of Socinianism, but more likely it referred to the overweighted appeal to reason that was growing in the established Church of England.

3

The Holy Spirit as the
Principal Efficient Cause of
Understanding Scripture

Part 2—More Biblical Evidence and
the Contrast of False Knowledge

Other Testimonies Pleaded in Confirmation of the Same Truth.
John 16:13 Opened. How Far All True Believers Are Infallibly
Led into All Truth Declared, and the Manner How They Are So.
1 John 2:20, 27 Explained. What Assurance of the Truth They
Have Who Are Taught of God, Ephesians 4:14; Job 36:22; John
6:45. Practical Truths Inferred from the Assertion Proved.

JOHN 16:13

There are yet other testimonies which may be pleaded unto the same purpose; for unto this end is the Holy Ghost promised unto all believers: "When the Spirit of truth is come, he shall guide you into all truth" (John 16:13).

The Holy Spirit is called "the Spirit of truth" principally on the same account as God absolutely is called "the God of truth,"[1] he is so essentially. He is the first, absolute, divine, eternal verity.[2] So, he is originally called "the Holy Spirit" on the account of his essential holiness. But it is not on that account solely that he is here called "the Spirit of truth." He is so as he is the revealer

1 Isa. 65:16.
2 I.e., true principle of belief.

of all divine, supernatural truth unto the church. As he is also called the "Holy Spirit," as he is author of all holiness in others; therefore is he here promised unto the church, as it is his work to lead us into all truth.

And two things are considerable in this promise: First, what is intended by all truth. Second, how the Holy Spirit guides or leads us into it.

1. With respect unto the object, it is not all truth absolutely that is intended. There is truth in things natural and civil, and stories of things that are past; nothing of this nature is comprised in this promise. We see believers of all sorts as ignorant of, as unacquainted with, many of these things as any other sort of men whatever. Yet does not one word of the promise of Christ fall unto the ground. Wherefore all that truth, or all truth of that nature whereof our Savior there speaks, is alone intended. The mysteries of the gospel, of the kingdom of heaven, the counsel of God about the salvation of the church by Christ, and concerning their faith and obedience, are the truth which he is promised to guide us into. This the apostle calls "all the counsel of God" (Acts 20:27), namely, which respects all the ends of our faith and obedience (Acts 20:21).

It admits of a limitation with respect unto the diversity of subjects, or the persons unto whom this truth is to be communicated. They are not all of them, as to the degrees of light and knowledge, equally to be led into all truth. Everyone unto whom he is thus promised shall be so far led into the knowledge of it as is necessary unto his own estate and condition, his duty and his work. For "unto every one of us is given grace according to the measure of the gift of Christ" (Eph. 4:7). It is Christ alone who, in the free gift of all grace, assigns the measures wherein everyone shall be made partaker of it. In his sovereign will he has allotted the measures of grace, light, and knowledge unto all the members of the church. And there is no less difference in these measures than in the knowledge of the most glorious apostle and that of the meanest believer in the world. The duty, work, and obedience of everyone, is the rule of the measure of his receiving these gifts of Christ. None shall want anything that is necessary unto him; none shall receive anything that he is not to use and improve in a way of duty.

2. Our second inquiry is, how the Spirit does thus lead us into all truth. The external revelation of truth is herein supposed. This he is promised to instruct us in the knowledge of in a spiritual manner, whereby I understand no more but so as it is required of us in a way of duty. To clear the truth hereof, some things must be observed. As,

(1) The promises concerning the mission of the Holy Spirit in these chapters of the Gospel [of John], 14–16, are not to be confined unto the apostles, nor

unto the first age or ages of the church. To do so is expressly contradictory unto the discourse and whole design of our Lord Jesus Christ unto that purpose. For he promises him in opposition unto his own temporary abode in the world, namely, that this [presence] of the Spirit should be forever (John 14:16), ἕως τῆς συντελείας τοῦ αἰῶνος, that is, "until the end of the age" (Matt. 28:20), unto the consummation of the whole state of the church here below. And to suppose the contrary is to overthrow the foundation of all truth and comfort in the church. For their preservation in the one, and the administration of the other unto them, depend on the accomplishment of this promise alone. And so also do all the benefits of the intercession of Christ, which are no otherwise communicated unto us but by the Holy Spirit, as given in pursuit of this promise. For what herein he prayed for his apostles, he prayed for all them that should believe in him through their word unto the end of the world (John 17:20).

(2) It is granted that sundry things in the promises of the Holy Ghost were peculiar unto the apostles, and had their accomplishment on the day of Pentecost, when he descended on them in that glorious, visible manner (Acts 2:1–4). For as they were commanded by our Savior to wait for this his coming before they engaged in the discharge of that office whereunto he had called them (Acts 1:4), so now they were fully empowered and enabled unto all that belonged thereunto. But their peculiar interest in these promises respected only things that were peculiar unto their office; such as that mentioned in this place is not.

(3) It is not an external guidance into the truth by the objective revelation of it that is intended, for such revelations are not granted unto all believers unto whom this promise is made, nor are they to look for them. And the revelation of truth, in the ministerial proposal of it, is common unto all the world unto whom the word is preached, and so is not the subject of a special promise.

(4) Wherefore, it is the internal teaching of the Holy Ghost, giving an understanding of the mind of God, of all sacred truths as revealed, that is intended. For [1], it is the same with that other promise, we "shall be all taught of God."[3] For we are thus taught of God by the Spirit's leading us into all truth, and not otherwise. [2] This the word enforces. "The Spirit of truth," ὁδηγήσει ὑμᾶς, "shall lead and guide you" in the right way to the knowledge of the truth. So, when Philip asked the eunuch whether he understood the things which he read out of the prophet Isaiah, he replied, "How can I," ἐὰς[4] μὴ τὶς ὁδηγήσῃ με, "'unless one lead me' to the sense of it?" That is, "by his

---

3 John 6:45.

4 *Novum Testamentum Graece* reads, ἐὰν. *Novum Testamentum Graece*, ed. B. Aland et al., 28th rev. ed. (Stuttgart: Deutsche Bibelgesellschaft, 2012).

interpretation give me an understanding of it" (Acts 8:31). Thus the Holy Spirit leads us into all truth, by giving us that understanding of it which of ourselves we are not able to attain. And other interpretations the words will not admit. It is, therefore, his work to give us a useful, saving understanding of all sacred truth, or the mind of God as revealed in the Scripture. All spiritual, divine, supernatural truth is revealed in the Scripture. Herein all are agreed. The knowledge, the right understanding, of this truth as so revealed, is the duty of all, according unto the means which they enjoy and the duties that are required of them. Neither can this be denied. Unto this end, that they may do so, the Holy Spirit is here promised unto them that do believe. His divine aid and assistance is, therefore, necessary hereunto. And this we are to pray for, as it is promised. Wherefore, of ourselves, without his special assistance and guidance, we cannot attain a due knowledge of and understanding in the truth revealed in the Scripture. As unto the special nature of this assistance, it shall be spoken unto afterward.

1 JOHN 2:20, 27

This is again affirmed concerning all believers: "You have an unction from the Holy One, and you know all things. [. . .] The anointing which ye have received of him abideth in you, and ye need not that any man teach you, but as the same anointing teacheth you of all things, and is truth, and is no lie, and even as it hath taught you, ye shall abide in it" (1 John 2:20, 27).

1. That by the unction and anointing in this place, the Spirit of God and his work, with respect unto the end mentioned, are intended is not questioned by any that are conversant about these things with sobriety. And it is plain in the text. For (1), that the Holy Spirit in his special operations is called an unction, or is said to anoint us, is evident in many places of the Scripture (see Heb. 1:9; 2 Cor. 1:21–22). Neither is a spiritual unction ascribed unto anything else in the whole Scripture. (2) That expression, "which you have from the Holy One" ([cf.] Acts 3:14; Rev. 3:7), that is, Jesus Christ, does expressly answer unto the promise of Christ to send his Holy Spirit unto us, and that for the end here mentioned, namely, to teach us, and lead us into all truth; whence he is called "the Spirit of the Lord," or "of Christ" (2 Cor. 3:17–18; Eph. 3:16; Phil. 1:19; etc.). (3) That, also, of his "abiding in us" is nothing but an expression of the same promise of Christ that he shall "abide with us forever" (John 14:16). (4) The work here assigned unto this unction is expressly assigned unto the Holy Spirit: "The Spirit of truth will guide you into all truth" (John 16:13). (5) What is said of it, namely, not only that it is

true, and not false, but that it is "truth, and no lie," does plainly intimate his essential verity.¶

And I cannot but wonder that any persons should, against this open and plain evidence, ascribe the things here mentioned unto anything else, and not exclusively unto the Holy Ghost. For so do some contend,[5] that by this unction the doctrine of the gospel only is intended. It is true that the doctrine of the gospel, in the preaching of it, is the means or instrumental cause of this teaching by the Holy Ghost. And on that account what is spoken of the teaching of the Spirit of God may be spoken, in its place, of the doctrine of the gospel, because he teaches us thereby. But here it is spoken of objectively, as what we are to be taught, and not efficiently, as what it is that teaches us. And to say, as they do, it is the instruction which we have by the gospel that is intended, is to assert the effect only, and to exclude the cause. For that signifies no more but the effect of the unction here ascribed unto believers, as that which they had received from the Holy One. Didymus, an ancient learned writer, interprets this unction to be the illuminating grace of the Spirit, and the Holy One to be the Spirit himself.[6] But the other interpretation is more proper and consonant unto the use of the Scripture. The expression is taken from the institution of God under the Old Testament whereby kings and priests were anointed with oil, to signify the gifts of the Spirit communicated unto them for the discharge of their office. And, as a consequence, believers, who are real partakers of the internal unction in the graces and gifts of the Holy Ghost, are said to be "made kings and priests unto God."[7] It is, therefore, the work of the Holy Spirit that is here described. He alone, and his gifts, graces, and privileges that ensue thereon are so expressed, here or anywhere else in the whole Scripture.

5   In the text: (Episcop. in loc. after Socin. on the same place).—Owen. For the first reference, see Simon Episcopius, "Lectiones sacra in i. epistolam catholicam Joannis," in *Opera theologica*, vol. 1 (Roterodami, 1665), 173–428, or pt. 1, chap. 3. No modern edition exists. Simon Episcopius (1583–1643), a Dutch Remonstrant theologian, played a significant role at the Synod of Dort in 1618. For the second reference, see Faustus Socinus, "Explicatio in primam epistolam Johannis," in *Fausti Socini Senensis opera omnia in duos tomos distincta, quorum prior continet ejus opera exegetica et didactica, posterior opera ejusdem polemica comprehendit: accesserunt quaedam hactenus inedita, quorum catalogum versa pagina exhibet*, vol. 1 (Irenopoli, 1656), 157–264. No modern edition exists. Faustus Socinus (1539–1604) was an Italian anti-Trinitarian theologian, from whom Socinianism draws its name.

6   In the text: (lib. ii. de Spir. Sanc).—Owen. This is a citation of bk. 2 of Didymus the Blind's *On the Holy Spirit*. See *Works on the Holy Spirit: Athanasius the Great and Didymus the Blind*, trans. Mark DelCogliano, Andrew Radde-Gallwitz, and Lewis Ayres, Popular Patristics 43 (Yonkers, NY: St. Vladimir's Seminary, 2011). Dydimus (ca. 313–398) was an Alexandrian theologian and defender of Trinitarianism. His *On the Holy Spirit* is an orthodox defense of the divinity of the third person of the Godhead.

7   Rev. 1:6.

2. Two things are to be observed in what is here ascribed unto this unction. First, what is the effect of his work in believers. Secondly, what is the nature of it, or how he produces that effect.

(1) For the first, there is a double expression of it: One, that they "know all things." Two, that they "need not that any should teach them"; both which expressions admit of, yea require, their limitations.

[1] The "all things" intended come under a double restriction: the first taken from the nature of the things themselves, the other from the scope and circumstances of the place; or, the one from the general end, the other from the special design proposed.

{1} The general end proposed is, our abiding in Christ: So "ye shall abide in him"; which the apostle expresses, by "continuing in the Son, and in the Father" (1 John 2:24). Wherefore, the all things here mentioned are all things necessary unto our engrafting into and continuance in Christ. Such are all the fundamental, yea, important truths of the gospel. Whatever is needful unto our communion with Christ and our obedience to him, this all true believers are taught. However, they may mistake in things of lesser moment, and be ignorant in the doctrine of some truths, or have but mean degrees of knowledge in anything, yet shall they all know the mind and will of God as revealed in the Scripture, in all those things and truths which are necessary that they may believe unto righteousness and make confession unto salvation.

{2} The special end under consideration is, preservation and deliverance from the antichrists and seducers of those days, with the errors, lies, and false doctrines which they divulged concerning Christ and the gospel. The only way and means whereby we may be so preserved from the poisons and infections of such pernicious opinions and ways is, the assured knowledge of the truths of the gospel as they are revealed in the Scripture. All those truths which were any way needful to secure their faith and preserve them from mortal seductions, they were taught and did know. And where any man knows the truths which are required unto his implantation into Christ, and his continuance with him in faith and obedience, as also all those which may preserve him from the danger of seduction into pernicious errors, however he may fail and be mistaken in some things of less importance, yet is he secured as unto his present acceptable obedience and future blessedness. And to speak of it by the way, this gives us the rule of our special communion and love. Where any are taught these things, where they have the knowledge and make confession of that truth, or those articles of faith, whereby they may "abide in Christ,"[8]

8   John 15:4.

and are preserved from pernicious seductions, although they may differ from us and the truth in some things of less moment, we are obliged not only to forbearance of them, but communion with them. For who shall refuse them whom Christ has received? Or does Christ refuse any to whom he gives his Spirit, who have the unction from the Holy One? This, and no other, is the rule of our evangelical love and communion among ourselves. Whatever we require more of any as a necessary condition of our Christian society, in point of doctrine, is an unwarrantable imposition on their consciences or practice, or both.

[2] It is said that they so know these things as that they "need not that any should teach them," which also requires a limitation or exposition. For,

{1} It is only the things as before declared that respect is had unto. Now, besides these, there are many other things which believers stand in need to be taught continually, and whose knowledge belongs unto their edification. Many things are very useful unto us that are not absolutely necessary. In natural things, and such as belong unto this present life, men would be very unwilling to be without or part with sundry things, without which yet life might be preserved, because they value them, as of use unto themselves, so enabling them to be useful unto others. And they who understand the nature, use, and benefit of evangelical truths will not be contented that their knowledge in them should be confined only unto those which are of absolute necessity unto the being of spiritual life. Yea, they cannot be well supposed to know those truths themselves who pretend such a satisfaction in them as to look no farther. For all who are sincere in faith and knowledge do aim at that "perfect man in Christ," which all the ordinances of God are designed to bring us unto (Eph. 4:13). Wherefore, notwithstanding the knowledge of these things, there is still use and need of further ministerial teaching in the church.

{2} It is spoken of the things themselves absolutely, and not with respect unto the degrees of the knowledge of them. They did so know them as that there was no need that any man should teach them unto them, as unto their initial knowledge and substance of the things themselves; and so it may be said of all believers. But yet there are degrees of knowledge with respect unto those very things, which they may and ought to be carried on unto, as the apostle speaks (Heb. 6:1). And therefore does the holy apostle himself who writes these things further instruct them in them. And herein consists the principal part of the ministry of the church, even to carry on believers unto perfection in those things wherein, for the substance of them, they have been already instructed.

{3} That which is principally intended is that they need not that any should teach them, so as that they should depend on the light and authority of their instruction. Others may be helpers of their joy, but none can be lords of their faith. You need no such teaching, because of the unction which you have received.

(2) For the general nature of the work here ascribed unto this unction, that is, the Holy Spirit, it is teaching: "The unction teacheth you." There are but two ways whereby the Spirit teaches us, nor can any other be conceived. The one is by objective, the other by subjective revelations. For he teaches us as a "Spirit of wisdom and revelation."[9] The first way of his teaching is by immediate inspiration, communicating new sacred truths from God immediately unto the minds of men. So he taught the prophets and apostles, and all the penmen of the Scripture. By him the word of the Lord came unto them, and they spoke as they were acted by him (1 Pet. 1:11–12; 2 Pet. 1:21). This is not the way of teaching here intended, for the end of this teaching of the Holy Ghost is only to make men teachers of others, which is not here intended. Nor does the apostle discourse unto any such purpose, as though God would grant new revelations unto men to preserve them from errors and seductions, which he has made sufficient provision for in the word (Isa. 8:20; 2 Pet. 1:19). By this word were they to try all doctrines and pretended revelations, yea, those which were so really before they received them (1 John 4:1). Besides, what is here affirmed is ascribed unto all sorts of believers, under the distribution which they are cast into by the apostle, namely, of "old men," "young men," and "babes," which had not all of them received the Spirit of immediate revelation.

His other way of teaching is that which we have insisted on, namely, his enabling us to discern, know, and understand the mind and will of God as revealed in the Scripture, or as declared in any divine revelation. This alone is or can be here intended. Wherefore, this is the design of the apostle in these words: *All divine truths necessary to be known and to be believed, that we may live unto God in faith and obedience, or come unto and abide in Christ, as also be preserved from seducers, are contained in the Scripture, or proposed unto us in divine revelations. These of ourselves we cannot understand unto the ends mentioned; for if we could, there would be no need that we should be taught them by the Holy Spirit. But this is so, he teaches us all these things, enabling us to discern, comprehend, and acknowledge them.* And this is the whole of what we plead for.

---

9 Eph. 1:17.

For a close of our considerations on these words of the apostle, I shall only observe what assurance a man that is thus taught the truth may have that it is the truth which he is taught, and that he is not deceived in his apprehensions of it. For hereon depends the use of this instruction, especially in times of trial, indeed, at all times and on all occasions. It is not enough that we know the truth, but we must be assured that so we do (see Eph. 4:14; Col. 2:2). And there was never a greater artifice in the world than that whereby the Roman church has imposed an impregnable, obstinate credulity on all that adhere thereunto. For it does first fix this in their minds, that it cannot err, and therefore whatever is by her authority proposed unto them is infallibly true. Hence it comes to pass that they will abide obstinate against all convictions and the highest evidence of truth in all particular instances, while this principle is firmly fixed in their minds, that the church which proposes these things unto them cannot err nor be mistaken. Yea, while this persuasion abides with them, they may be, and indeed accordingly are, obliged to believe contradictions, things most irrational and absurd, inconsistent with Christian piety and the peace of human society. However, they say well in this, that it is necessary that a man should have good assurance of the truth which he does profess, or of his own understanding of it and conception about it. This the apostle calls, "the riches of the full assurance of understanding" (Col. 2:2), whereof we shall speak afterward.

Wherefore, whereas the assurance of mind in other teachings depends much on the authority of them by whom they are taught, on a supposition that believers are taught the mind of God in the Scripture by the Holy Spirit, or are by him enabled to discern and know it, the inquiry is, how or by what means they have an assurance that they have a right understanding of the things which they are so taught, so as to abide in them and the profession of them against all opposition whatever, and so as to venture the eternal condition of their souls on that assurance they have of the truth; which everyone must do whether he will or not. And this in the text is referred unto the author of this teaching: "The anointing is truth, and is no lie"; it is true, and infallibly so. There is no fear of, no possibility for, any man being deceived in what he is taught by this unction. And an assurance hereof arises in our minds partly from the manner of his teachings, and partly from the evidence of the things themselves that we are taught. The manner and way of his teaching us in and by the Scripture evidences unto us that what we are taught "is truth, and is no lie." He gives a secret witness unto what he teaches in his teachings: "for it is the Spirit that beareth witness, because the Spirit is truth" (1 John 5:6). And with respect unto the evidence which is so given us of the truth, it is said that the unction whereby we are taught "is truth, and is no lie"; that is, it is impossible anyone should be deceived who is so taught. This will more fully appear when we have declared the whole of his work herein; something only may now be spoken, on occasion of this testimony.

There is a peculiar power accompanying the teaching of God by his Spirit: "Behold, God exalteth by his power, who teacheth like him?" (Job 36:22). So, our Savior expounds that promise, "They shall be all taught of God; every man," he says, "therefore that hath heard and hath learned of the Father, cometh unto me" (John 6:45). There is such an efficacy accompanying God's teaching, that whosoever is so taught does certainly believe the things that he is taught, as having the evidence of the truth of them in himself.

When the Holy Ghost gave new revelations of old unto the prophets and penmen of the Scripture by immediate inspiration, he did therein and therewith communicate unto them an infallible evidence that they were from God. And when he does illuminate our minds in the knowledge of what is revealed, he does therein himself bear witness unto, and assure us of, the truth which we do understand. Hereby do we come to that which the apostle calls the "full assurance of understanding, in the acknowledgment of the mystery of God."[10] He not only enables our minds to apprehend the truth, but he shines into our hearts, the seat of spiritual experience, to give us the "knowledge of the glory of God in the face of Jesus Christ."[11] And the assurance which believers have thereby is above that which any other evidence or demonstration whatever can give. And the meanest believer has from this teaching a greater rest, satisfaction, and assurance in the knowledge of the mind of God, than any that can be attained by the most raised notions or profound disputations: "for he that believeth hath the witness in himself" (1 John 5:10). And why should others think it strange that there should be such evidence of truth in the teaching of the Spirit, by the illumination of our minds in the knowledge of the Scripture, as to give us an assurance of the highest nature, seeing there is none that teaches like him?

Want hereof is that which makes men to fluctuate in their conceptions of spiritual things, and so ready on every occasion to part with what they have received. The Church of Rome has, as we observed, rather craftily than wisely, provided against any inconvenience herein. The doctrines which it teaches are many of them false, and so the things contained in them can give no evidence unto themselves in the minds of men. For there is nothing but

10 Col. 2:2.
11 2 Cor. 4:6.

imagination in error, there is nothing of substance in it. And their way of teaching is not accompanied with any special advantage; yea, it is the most vain that ever was in the world. They would have men suppose that they may advance at once in the true belief of a hundred things whereof they have no evidence, merely resting on the infallibility of the church, by which, they say, they are proposed. Wherefore, they teach men that although they receive no evidencing light in this way of their instruction, nor have any experience of the power or efficacy of truth in what they are taught, yet they may rest assuredly in the infallibility of the church. Hence the assurance they have of anything they suppose truth is not an act of the mind in the embracing of the truth from any evidence that it gives of itself, but a presumption in general that the church is infallible by which these things are proposed unto them. The design is to prevail with men to suppose that they believe all things, when, indeed, they believe nothing; that they understand the mind and will of God, when, indeed, they understand nothing at all of them. For a man believes nothing but what is accompanied with an evidence whereon it ought to be believed. But this they pretend not unto, at least not such that should give them that assurance of the truth of it which is requisite; and therefore are all men by them referred for that unto the infallibility of the Church. Persons weak, ignorant, credulous,[12] or superstitious, either for interest or by the craft of seducers, may be prevailed on to make their resort unto this relief. Those who will not forgo the rational conduct of their own souls, and leave themselves unto the guidance of others, knowing that it is they alone who must give an account of themselves to God, will not easily be induced thereunto.

Others will resolve all into their own rational conceptions of things, without any respect unto a superior infallible teacher. And the minds of many influenced by this notion, that they have themselves alone to trust unto, are come unto the utmost uncertainty and instability in all things of religion; nor can it otherwise be. For as the mind of man is in itself indifferent and undetermined unto anything, as true or false, unless it be in its first notions of the common principles of reason, beyond the evidence that is proposed unto it; so also is it various, unsteady, and apt to fluctuate from one thing to another. And there are but two ways whereby it may be naturally ascertained and determined in its conceptions and assent. The first is by the use of the external senses, which will not deceive it. However, it cannot but receive, believe, and comply with what it comprehends by its senses; as what it sees, hears, and feels. The other is by reason, whereby it deduces certain conclusions from propositions

12 I.e., overly ready to believe.

of necessary truth, that is, by demonstration. But by neither of these ways can the mind be brought unto a stability and assurance in or about things spiritual or supernatural. For they are neither the objects of natural sense nor capable of a scientific demonstration.[13] Wherefore, a man can have nothing but a probability or conjectural knowledge concerning them, unless he has some certain, infallible teaching wherein he can acquiesce. And such is that of this "unction," which "is truth, and is no lie." In and by his teaching of us, namely, the mind of God as revealed in the Scripture, there is such evidence of truth communicated unto our minds and hearts as gives us an immovable assurance of them, or the "full assurance of understanding." For God therein shines in our hearts, to give us the light of the knowledge of his glory in the face of Jesus Christ.

Again, there is an evidence in the things themselves, unto spiritual sense and judgment (Phil. 1:9; Heb. 5:14). This is that which gives the mind the highest assurance of the truth of what it does believe that it is capable of in this world. For when it finds in itself the power and efficacy of the truth wherein it is instructed, that it works, effects, and implants the things themselves upon it, giving and ascertaining unto it all the benefits and comforts which they promise or express, and is thereby united unto the soul, or has a real, permanent, efficacious subsistence in it, then, I say, has the mind the utmost assurance in the truth of it which it does or can desire in the things of this nature. But this belongs not unto our present design.

TAUGHT OF GOD

The testimonies pleaded are sufficient for the confirmation of our first general assertion, namely, *that it is the Holy Spirit who teaches us to understand aright the mind and will of God in the Scripture, without whose aid and assistance we can never do so usefully nor profitably unto our own souls.* Sundry others that speak unto the same purpose will be afterward on various occasions insisted on.

I might add unto these testimonies the faith and profession of the church in all ages. They all believed and professed that the Scriptures could not be understood and interpreted without his assistance and inspiration by whom they were indited,[14] but it is not necessary so to do. For those who profess to

---

13 Owen is here dealing with rationalism and empiricism, the twin themes of the Enlightenment. See Desmond M. Clarke and Catherine Wilson, eds., *The Oxford Handbook of Philosophy in Early Modern Europe* (Oxford: Oxford University Press, 2011).

14 I.e., written or composed.

trust unto their own reason and understanding only, cannot be so ignorant as not to know that they have no countenance given unto their persuasion in antiquity, unless it were by the Pelagians. But whereas there is no profitable handling of sacred truths on any pretense but with an eye unto the guidance of Christian practice, and when that is manifest, it gives a great confirmation in our minds unto the truth itself, I shall, before I proceed unto the consideration of the special ways of the teaching of the Holy Spirit in this matter, and the special duties required of us in compliance with them, that they may be effectual, divert a little unto some such considerations of that nature as derive from this general assertion.

It is the great promise of the New Testament that all believers shall be διδακτοὶ τοῦ θεοῦ, "taught of God," which our Savior himself pleads as the only ground of their believing (John 6:45). And so the apostle tells the Thessalonians that they were θεοδίδακτοι, "taught of God" (1 Thess. 4:9). No man is αὐτόδιδακτος, "taught of himself," his own teacher and guide in sacred things. Neither can any man have a worse master, if he trusts thereunto alone. The diligent use of all outward means appointed of God unto this end, that through the knowledge of the Scripture we may be made wise unto salvation, we always suppose. Among them the ministry of the church has the first and chiefest place (Eph. 4:12–15). For they are with me of no account who think it not worth the utmost of their diligence to attain the knowledge of those "wonderful things"[15] that are in the word. Yea, I should greatly admire at their stupidity who will not give so much credit unto the Scripture testifying of itself, and the suffrage of all good men with it, that there are "wonderful things" contained in it, so far as to inquire with their utmost diligence whether it be so or not, but that I know the reasons and causes of it. But a supreme teacher there must be, on whose wisdom, power, and authority, we ought principally to depend, as unto this end of being taught of God. And hereunto the use of our own reason, the utmost improvement of the rational abilities of our minds, is required. Those who would take away the use of our reason in spiritual things would deal with us, as we said before, as the Philistines did with Samson: first put out our eyes, and then make us grind in their mill.¶

The Scripture we own as the only rule of our faith, as the only treasury of all sacred truths. The knowledge we aim at is, the "full assurance of understanding" in the mind and will of God, revealed therein. The sole inquiry is whether this supreme teacher be the Spirit of God instructing us in and by the Scripture, or whether it be the authority of this or that, any or all of the

15 Ps. 119:18.

churches in the world, which either are so or pretend to be so. Which of these will it be our wisdom to choose and adhere unto? That the Holy Spirit has taken this work upon himself we have already proved, and shall afterward further demonstrate. Some churches, especially that of Rome, assume this office unto themselves. But it is too well known to the most to be trusted herein, and a great prejudice there lies in this cause against that Church at first. The Holy Spirit leaves unto us, yea, requires of us, the diligent use of the Scripture and exercise of our own reason, in subserviency unto his teaching. But this Church requires us to renounce them both, in compliance with herself. And can it stand in competition with him? He is infallible, the unction "is truth, and is no lie";[16] the Spirit is truth. This also, indeed, that Church pretends unto, but with such an open affront unto all evidence of truth as the world never underwent from any of its people before. He is absolutely, infinitely, eternally free from any design but the glory of God, the present and eternal good of them that are instructed by him. It will be very difficult for those of Rome to pretend hereunto. Yea, it is apparent that all the exercise of their instructing authority lies in a subserviency unto their own interest. When I see that men by a pretense hereof have gotten unto themselves wealth, power, principalities, dominions, with great revenues, and do use them all unto their own advantage, and mostly to the satisfaction of their lusts, pleasures, pride, ambition, and the like inordinate affections, I confess I cannot be free to deliver up blindfolded the conduct of my soul unto them. He is full of divine love and care of the souls of them whom he does instruct; is it so with them, or can any creature participate in his love and care? He is infinitely wise, and "knoweth all things, yea, the deep things of God," and can make known what he pleases of them unto us, as the apostle discourses (1 Cor. 2). They who preside in that Church are ignorant themselves, as all men are, and the less they know it the more ignorant they are; yea, for the most part, as unto sacred things, they are comparatively so with respect unto other ordinary men. As a late pope, when some of their divines waited for an infallible determination of a theological controversy among them, confessed that he had not studied those things, nor had the knowledge of them been his profession.

But yet, notwithstanding these and several other differences between these teachers, it is marvelous to consider how many take themselves unto the latter of them, and how few unto the former. And the reason is, because of the different methods they take in teaching, and the different qualifications they

---

16 1 John 2:27.

require in them that are to be taught. For as unto them whom the Spirit of God undertakes to instruct, he requires that they be meek and humble, that they give themselves unto continual prayer, meditation, and study in the word day and night; above all, that they endeavor a conformity in their whole souls and lives unto the truths that he instructs them in. These are hard conditions unto flesh and blood; few there are who like them, and therefore few they are who apply themselves unto the school of God. We may be admitted scholars by the other teacher on far cheaper and easier rates. Men may be made "good Catholics," as to faith and understanding, without the least cost in self-denial, or much trouble unto the flesh in any other duty. There is no qualification required for the admission of a man into the Catholic schools, and barely to be there is to be wise and knowing enough. Wherefore, although all advantages imaginable as unto the teachers lie on the one hand, yet the pretended easy way of learning casts the multitude on the other. For it requires more wisdom than we have of ourselves to be at all that charge and pains in spiritual duty, and diligence in the use of all means for the right understanding of the mind of God, which is required in and of all them who will advantageously partake of the teaching of the Holy Spirit, when it is supposed we may have all the ends which we aim at thereby in an easy and naked assent unto the proposals of the Church, without the least further charge or trouble. But these are the measures of slothful and carnal minds, who prefer their ease, their lusts, and pleasures, before their souls. There is difficulty in all things that are excellent; neither can we partake of the excellency of anything unless we will undertake its difficulty. But although the ways whereby we may come unto a participation of the teaching of the Holy Ghost seem at first rough and uneasy, yet unto all that engage in them they will be found to be ways of pleasantness and paths of peace.

It may be said, that it is evident in common experience that many men do attain a great knowledge and skill in the things revealed in the Scripture, without any of that internal teaching by the illumination of their minds which is pleaded for, especially if it is to be obtained by the means now intimated, and afterward more fully to be declared. For they themselves do renounce the necessity of any such teaching, and esteem all that is spoken of it a vain imagination; and not only so, but live, some of them, in an open defiance of all those qualifications and duties which are required unto a participation of these teachings. Yet it is foolish to pretend they are not skilled in the knowledge of divinity, seeing it is plain that they excel most other men therein; and therefore do sufficiently despise all them who pretend unto any benefit by the supernatural illumination contended for.

FALSE KNOWLEDGE

I answer briefly in this place: it is true there are, and ever were, some, yea many, who profess that they know God, but in works deny him, being abominable and disobedient. The knowledge which such men may attain, and which they make profession of, belongs not unto our inquiry; and we may easily discern both what it is in itself, and wherein it differs from that true knowledge of God which it is our duty to have. For,

1. There is in the Scripture, with respect unto the mind and will of God revealed therein, with the mysteries of truth and grace, mention of γνῶσις and ἐπίγνωσις, "knowledge" and "acknowledgment." The former, if it be alone, affects only the speculative part of the mind with notions of truth. And it is of very little use, but subject unto the highest abuse: Ἡ γνῶσις φυσιοῖ, "knowledge puffs up" (1 Cor. 8:1). It is that which puffs up men into all their proud contentions about religion, which the world is filled with. The other gives the mind an experience of the power and efficacy of the truth known or discovered, so as to transform the soul and all its affections into it, and thereby to give a "full assurance of understanding" unto the mind itself (Phil. 1:9; Luke 1:4; Col. 1:6, 9–10; 2:2; 3:10; Rom. 10:2; Eph. 1:17; 4:13; 1 Tim. 2:4; 2 Tim. 2:25; 3:7; Titus 1:1; 2 Pet. 1:2–3, 8; 2:20). It is not worth disputing at all what knowledge of the first kind, or what degree therein, men, any men, the worst of men, may attain by their industry and skill in other common arts and sciences. For what if they should make such a proficiency therein as to be filled with pride in themselves, and to confound others with their subtle disputations, will any real profit redound[17] hence unto themselves, or the world, or the church of God? It does not, therefore, deserve the least contention about it. But that acknowledgment of the truth which affects the heart, and conforms the soul unto the will of God revealed, is not attainable in any degree without the saving illumination of the Spirit of God.

2. Men may have a knowledge of words, and the meaning of propositions in the Scripture, who have no knowledge of the things themselves designed in them. The things revealed in the Scripture are expressed in propositions whose words and terms are intelligible unto the common reason of mankind. Every rational man, especially if he be skilled in those common sciences and arts which all writings refer unto, may, without any special aid of the Holy Ghost, know the meaning of the propositions that are laid down in, or drawn from the Scripture. Yea, they can do so who believe not one word of it to be true, and they do so, as well as the best of

---

17 I.e., overflow.

them, who have no other help in the understanding of the Scripture but their own reason, let them profess to believe what they will. And whatever men understand of the meaning of the words, expressions, and propositions in the Scripture, if they believe not the things which they declare, they do not in any sense know the mind and will of God in them. For to know a thing as the mind of God, and not to assent unto its truth, implies a contradiction. I shall never grant that a man understands the Scripture aright who understands the words of it only, and not the things which are the mind of God in them. For instance, the Jews understand the words of the Scripture of the Old Testament in its own original language, and they are able to perceive the grammatical sense and construction of the propositions contained in it, they are unacquainted with them and their writings who will not acknowledge their skill, subtlety, and accuracy in these things, yet will not any Christian say they understand the mind of God in the Old Testament. The apostle shows the contrary, and gives the reason for it in the place before insisted on (2 Cor. 3). Such a knowledge of the Scripture no wise man will value, let it be attained how it will.

3. This knowledge that may be thus attained does only inform the mind in the way of an artificial science, but does not really illuminate it. And to this end men have turned divinity into an art, like other common human arts and sciences, and so they learn it, instead of a spiritual wisdom and understanding of divine mysteries. It is true that the knowledge of common learned arts and sciences is of great use unto the understanding of the Scriptures, as unto what they have in common with other writings, and what they refer unto that is of human cognizance; but to bring in all the terms, notions, and rules of those arts and sciences into divinity, and by the mixture of them with it to compose a scheme of divine knowledge, is all one, as if a man should design to make up his house of the scaffolds which he only uses in the building of it. Such is that knowledge of the mind of God in the Scripture which many aim at and content themselves with. And it may be attained, as any other art or science may, without any supernatural aid of the Holy Spirit, and is sufficient to drive a trade with, which, as things are stated in the world, men may use and exercise unto their great advantage. But, as was said before, it is not that which we inquire after. That wisdom in the mystery of the gospel, that knowledge of the mind and will of God in the Scripture, which affects the heart, and transforms the mind in the renovation of it unto the approbation of the "good, and acceptable, and perfect will of God," as the apostle speaks (Rom. 12:2), is alone valuable and desirable, as unto all spiritual and eternal ends.

4. It does not give πάντα πλοῦτον τῆς πληροφορίας τῆς συνέσεως εἰς ἐπίγνωσιν τοῦ μυστηρίου τοῦ θεοῦ—"all riches of the full assurance of understanding, to the acknowledgment of the mystery of God," as the apostle speaks (Col. 2:2). It gives unto men no other assurance of mind in the things that they know but what they have from acknowledged principles, and conclusions drawn from them, in any other science. But that knowledge which men have of the mysteries of the gospel by the teaching and illumination of the Holy Spirit gives them "the riches of assurance of understanding" of a higher nature, even the assurance of faith. That assurance, I say, which believers have in spiritual things is of another nature and kind than can be attained out of conclusions that are only rationally derived from the most evident principles. And therefore, does it produce effects of another nature, both in doing and in suffering. For this is that which effectually and infallibly puts them on all those duties and that obedience in self-denial and the mortification of sin, which the world either knows not or despises. For "he that hath this hope in him purifieth himself, even as Christ is pure" (1 John 3:3). And this also enables them cheerfully and joyfully to suffer all that the world can inflict on them for the profession of those truths whereof they have that assurance. But nothing of this ensues on that common knowledge which men may have from themselves of sacred things. For,

5. It does not enable men to trust in God, and adhere firmly unto him by love. The psalmist, speaking unto God, says, "They that know thy name will put their trust in thee" (Ps. 9:10). To "know the name of God," is to know the revelations that he has made of himself, his mind and his will, in the Scripture. They that have this knowledge, he affirms, "will put their trust in him." Therefore, it is certain that those who put not their trust in God have not the knowledge of him. There is a γνῶσις ψευδόνυμος,[18] a "knowledge falsely so called," which has nothing of real spiritual knowledge but the name. And it is generally much given to disputing, or the maintaining of antitheses, or oppositions unto the truth (1 Tim. 6:20). But it is falsely called knowledge, inasmuch as those in whom it is do neither trust in God nor adhere unto him in love. And we shall not much inquire by what means such a knowledge may be acquired.

CONCLUSION

It remains, therefore, notwithstanding this objection, that all real useful knowledge of the "wonderful things" that are in the Scripture is an effect of God's opening our eyes by the illuminating grace of his Holy Spirit.

---

18 The correct spelling is ψευδώνυμος.

1. And this will enable us to "try the spirits,"[19] as we are commanded, of many among us. For some there are who at once have cast off a due respect unto their rule and guide, the Scripture and Holy Spirit of God. Some formerly have pretended unto such a guidance by the Spirit as that they have neglected or rejected the written word. And some pretend such an adherence unto the word, and such an ability in their own minds and reasons to understand it, as to despise the teaching of the Spirit. Others reject both the one and the other, taking themselves unto another rule and guide, whereunto they ascribe all that belongs unto either or both of them. But a wandering light it has proved unto them, that has led them into a bog of many vain imaginations and corrupt opinions. And it is fallen out with them as might be expected. For although the Holy Spirit be promised to lead us into all truth, yet is he so in a special manner as unto those which concern the person, offices, and grace of our Lord Jesus Christ immediately, whose Spirit he is (see John 16:13–15; 1 John 2:27).¶

Those, therefore, who renounce a dependence on him for instruction out of the word are either left unto palpable ignorance about these things, or unto foolish, corrupt imaginations concerning them. Hence some of them openly deny, some faintly grant, but evidently corrupt, the truth concerning the person of Christ; and unto his offices and grace they seem to have little regard. And what else can be expected from such, who despise the teaching of that Spirit of Christ who is promised to lead us into all truth concerning him? Nor will the loudest pretenses of some unto the Spirit in this matter relieve them. For we inquire not after every spirit that anyone who will may make his boast of, but of that Spirit alone which instructs us in and by the written word.[20]¶

Until such men will return unto the only rule and guide of Christians, until they will own it their duty to seek for the knowledge of truth from the Scripture alone, and in their so doing depend not on anything in themselves, but on the saving instructions of the Spirit of God, it is in vain to contend with them. For they and we build on divers foundations, and their faith and ours are resolved into divers principles, ours into the Scripture, theirs into a light of their own. There are, therefore, no common acknowledged principles between us whereon we may convince each other. And this is the cause that disputes with such persons are generally fruitless, especially as immixed[21]

---

19 1 John 4:1.
20 The parties referred to here are the Quakers and radical sectarians, proponents of a rational faith, especially in the Church of England, and Roman Catholics, respectively. See the introduction for how these groups provide the historical context for Owen's arguments.
21 I.e., mixed thoroughly.

with that intemperancy of reviling other men wherein they exceed. For if that be a way either of learning or teaching of the truth, it is what the Scripture has not instructed us in. When the veil shall be taken from their eyes, and they turned unto the Lord, they will learn more modesty and humility. In the meantime, the issue between these men and us is this and no other: we persuade men to take the Scripture as the only rule, and the holy promised Spirit of God, sought by ardent prayers and supplications, in the use of all means appointed by Christ for that end, for their guide. They deal with men to turn into themselves, and to attend unto the light within them.¶

While we build on these most distant principles, the difference between us is irreconcilable, and will be eternal. Could we come to an agreement here, other things would fall away of themselves. If we shall renounce the Scripture, and the instruction given out of it unto the church by the Spirit of God, taking ourselves unto our own light, we are sure it will teach us nothing but either what they profess, or other things altogether as corrupt. And if they, on the other hand, will forgo their attendance to their pretended light, to hearken unto the voice of God in the Scripture only, and to beg sincerely the guidance of the Holy Spirit therein, they will learn from there no other thing but what we profess. Until, therefore, they return unto the law and testimony, without which, whatsoever is pretended, there is no light in any, we have no more to do but, laboring to preserve the flock of Christ in the profession of the "truth once delivered unto the saints,"[22] to commit the difference between the word and Spirit on the one hand, and the light within on the other, unto the decision of Jesus Christ at the last day.

2. It is from no other root that the contempt of the mysteries of the gospel, and the preferring of other doctrines before them, is sprung up into so much bitter fruit among us. It is by the "Spirit of wisdom and revelation"[23] alone that our minds are enlightened to know what is the hope of God's calling, and what are the riches of his glorious grace. What is his work herein upon our minds, and what upon the word itself, shall be afterward declared. At present, from what has been proved, it is sufficiently evident that without his special gracious aid and assistance, no man can discern, like, or approve of the mysteries of the gospel. And is it any wonder if persons who avowedly deny most of his blessed operations should be either unacquainted with or dislike those mysteries, so as to prefer that which is more suited unto their natural understanding and reason above them? For why should men esteem

22 Jude 3.
23 Eph. 1:17.

of those things which they do not understand, at least as they ought, nor will make use of the means whereby they may be enabled so to do?¶

Wherefore, if there be persons of such a pride and profaneness as to undertake an inquiry into the Scriptures, to know the mind of God in them, and teach it unto others, without prayers and supplications for the teaching, leading, guidance, and assistance of the Holy Spirit, or, which is worse, who condemn and despise all those things as enthusiastic, it may not be expected that they should ever understand or approve of the mysteries that are contained therein. Is it not hence that both teachers and hearers make so slow a progress in the knowledge of the mysteries of the gospel, or grow so little in the knowledge of our Lord and Savior Jesus Christ? How many are there among us who, for the time and outward means, are become as babes, and have need of milk, and not of strong meat? Whence is it that so many teachers do so little endeavor to go on to perfection, but content themselves to dwell on the rudiments or first principles of our profession? Is there not great studying, and little profiting? Great teaching, and little learning? Much hearing, and little thriving? Do we abide in prayer, and abound in prayer as we ought, for that Spirit who alone can lead us into all truth? For that unction which teaches us all things with assurance and experience? I fear here lies our defect. However, this I shall say, that there is no duty which in this world we perform unto God that is more acceptable unto him than fervent prayers for a right understanding of his mind and will in his word. For herein all the glory we give unto him, and the due performance of all our obedience, do depend.

4

The Nature and Effects
of Illumination

The Special Work of the Holy Spirit in the Illumination of Our
Minds unto the Understanding of the Scripture Declared and
Vindicated. Objections Proposed and Answered. The Nature of
the Work Asserted. Psalm 119:18; Ephesians 1:18; Luke 24:45;
1 Peter 2:9; Colossians 1:13; 1 John 5:20 Opened and Vindicated.

WE HAVE, AS I SUPPOSE, sufficiently confirmed our first general assertion, concerning the necessity of a special work of the Holy Ghost in the illumination of our minds, to make us understand the mind of God as revealed in the Scripture.

That which we proceed unto is to show the special nature of his work herein. And I shall take occasion thereunto from the consideration of an objection that is laid against the whole of what we affirm, which was touched on before.

For it is said that there is no need of this endeavor: All men do acknowledge that the aid of the Spirit of God is necessary unto the study and interpretation of the Scripture. And so it is unto all other undertakings that are good and lawful. And herein consists the blessing of God upon man's own diligence and endeavors. If this be that which is intended, namely, the blessing of God upon our endeavors in the use of means, it is granted. But if anything else be designed, it is nothing but to take off all industry in the use of means, to reject all helps of reason and learning, which is in the end to reduce into perfect enthusiasms.

HUMAN RESPONSIBILITY

Answer 1. Whether, by the assignation[1] of his own work unto the Spirit of God, we take away or weaken the use of the other means for the right interpretation of the Scriptures will be tried when we come unto the examination of those ways and means. At present I shall only say that we establish them. For by assigning unto them their proper place and use, we do manifest their worth and necessity. But those by whom they, or any of them, are advanced into the place and unto the exclusion of the operation of the Holy Spirit, do destroy them, or render them unacceptable unto God, and useless unto the souls of men. We shall, therefore, manifest that the assignations which we make in this matter unto the Holy Spirit do render all our use of proper means for the right interpretation of the Scripture in a way of duty indispensably necessary; and the principal reason, so far as I can understand, why some deny the necessity of the work of the Holy Spirit herein, is because they like not those means whose necessary use does arise from an admission thereof.

But thus it has fallen out in other things. Those who have declared anything either of the doctrine or of the power of the grace of the gospel have been traduced[2] as opposing the principles of morality and reason, whereas on their grounds alone their true value can be discovered and their proper use directed. So the apostle, preaching faith in Christ, with righteousness and justification thereby, was accused to have made void the law, whereas without his doctrine the law would have been void, or of no use to the souls of men. So he pleads, "Do we then make void the law through faith? God forbid, yea, we establish the law" (Rom. 3:31). So to this day, justification by the imputation of the righteousness of Christ, and the necessity of our own obedience, the efficacy of divine grace in conversion, and the liberty of our own wills, the stability of God's promises, and our diligent use of means are supposed inconsistent. So, it is here also. The necessity of the communication of spiritual light unto our minds to enable us to understand the Scriptures, and the exercise of our own reason in the use of external means, are looked on as irreconcilable. But, as the apostle says, "Do we make void the law through faith? Yea, we establish it"; though he did it not in that place, nor unto those ends that the Jews would have had and used it. So we may say, do we, by asserting the righteousness of Christ, make void our own obedience? By the efficacy of grace, destroy the liberty of our wills? By the necessity of spiritual illumination, take away the use of reason? Yea, we establish them. We do it not, it may be, in such

---

1   I.e., the allocation or attribution of someone or something as belonging to something; assigning.
2   I.e., falsely shamed or blamed.

a way or in such a manner as some would fancy, and which would render them all on our part really useless, but in a clear consistency with and proper subserviency unto the work of God's Spirit and grace.

ILLUMINATION AS DESCRIBED IN SCRIPTURE

Answer 2. That in particular which lies before us, is to remove that pretense of some that we need no other assistance of the Spirit of God for the right understanding of the Scripture, but only his blessing in general on our own endeavors. To this end two things are to be inquired into: First, what description is given of this work in the Scripture, and what are the effects of it in our minds in general. Second, what is the nature of it in particular.

The Effect of the Spirit's Work

The work itself is variously expressed in the Scripture. And it is that which, whether we will or no, we must be determined by in things of this kind. And the variety of expression serves both unto the confirmation of its truth and illustration of its nature.

1. It is declared by "opening of our eyes" (Ps. 119:18), the "enlightening of the eyes of our understanding" (Eph. 1:18). This opening of our eyes consists in the communication of spiritual light unto our minds by the preaching of the word, as it is declared (Acts 26:17–18). And the expression, though in part metaphorical, is eminently instructive in the nature of this work. For suppose the nearest and best-disposed proposition of any object unto our bodily eyes, with an external light properly suited unto the discovery of it, yet if our eyes be blind, or are closed beyond our own power to open them, we cannot discern it aright. Wherefore, on a supposition of the proposal unto our minds of the divine truths of supernatural revelation, and that in ways and by means suited unto the conveyance of it unto them, which is done in the Scripture and by the ministry of the church, with other outward means, yet without this work of the Spirit of God, called the "opening of our eyes," we cannot discern it in a due manner. And if this be not intended in this expression, it is no way instructive, but rather suited to lead us into a misunderstanding of what is declared and of our own duty. So it is plainly expressed: "Then opened he their understanding, that they might understand the Scriptures" (Luke 24:45).¶

None, I suppose, will deny but that it is the work of the Spirit of God thus to open our eyes, or to enlighten our understandings, for this were to deny the express testimonies of the Scripture, and those frequently reiterated. But some say, he does this by the word only, and the preaching of it. No other work of his, they affirm, is necessary hereunto, or to make us rightly to discern the mind of God in the Scripture, but that it be proposed unto us in a due manner, provided we purge our minds from prejudices and corrupt affections. And this is the work of the Spirit, in that he is the author of the Scriptures, which he makes use of for our illumination.[3] And it is granted that the Scripture is the only external means of our illumination. But in these testimonies, it is considered only as the object thereof. They express a work of the Spirit or grace of God upon our minds, with respect unto the Scripture as its object: "Open my eyes, that I may behold wondrous things out of thy law."[4] The law, or the Scripture, with the "wonderful things" contained therein, are the things to be known, to be discovered and understood. But the means enabling us thereunto, is an internal work upon our minds themselves, which is plainly expressed in distinction from the things to be known. This is the sum of what we plead: there is an efficacious work of the Spirit of God opening our eyes, enlightening our understandings or minds, to understand the things contained in the Scripture, distinct from the objective proposition of them in the Scripture itself, which the testimonies urged do fully confirm.

2. It is expressed as a translation out of darkness into light: "He hath called us out of darkness into [his] marvellous light" (1 Pet. 2:9), "delivered us from the power of darkness" (Col. 1:13), whereby we who were "darkness become light in the Lord" (Eph. 5:8). That in these and the like testimonies, the removal of the inward darkness of our minds, by the communication of spiritual light unto them, and not merely the objective revelation of truth in the Scripture, is intended, I have proved at large elsewhere, and therefore shall not again insist thereon.[5]

3. It is directly called, "the giving of us an understanding; we know that the Son of God is come, and hath given us an understanding, that we may know him that is true" (1 John 5:20). The object of our understanding, or that which we know, is "he that is true." God himself, even the Father, is primarily intended in this expression, for in the following words there is mention of "his Son Jesus Christ," who is in like manner said to be "true," because of his unity in essence with the Father. And, therefore, it is added, "That this is the true God" (1 John 5:20). But we are to know also what concerns our being "in him," and to know him as he is "eternal life." And these things contain

---

3   Here Owen seems to be refuting a theology that confuses inspiration with illumination in the mind, which in essence negates the latter.

4   Ps. 119:18.

5   Owen is likely referring to his Πνευματολογια, or, *A Discourse concerning the Holy Spirit*, bk. 3.

the substance of all evangelical revelations, which, one way or other, depend upon them, and are resolved into them (John 17:3). To know the Father, "the only true God," and the Son as "the true God" also, in the unity of the same essence, to know that eternal life which was with the Father as unto the eternal counsel and preparation of it (1 John 1:2), and is in the Son for its actual communication unto us, and to know our being in him by a participation thereof, the things we mentioned, is to know the mind of God as revealed in the Scripture. Especially these things are intended, which are "foolishness" unto corrupted reason, and as such are rejected by it (1 Cor. 1:23–24; 2:14).

And two things we are to inquire into with reference unto this knowledge. What we are to have to enable us unto it, and that is an *understanding*. How we come by it, it is *given us by the Son of God*.

(1) That which we have is διανοια; this word in all other places of the New Testament does constantly denote the essential faculty of our souls, which we call "understanding" (Matt. 22:37; Mark 12:30; Luke 10:27; Eph. 1:18; 2:3; 4:18; Col. 1:21; Heb. 8:10; 1 Pet. 1:13; 2 Pet. 3:1). And it seems in the Scripture to be distinguished from the mind, by respect unto actual exercise only. The mind in its exercise is our understanding. But it cannot be the natural and essential faculty of our souls that is here intended; for although our natures are corrupted by sin, and not repaired but by Jesus Christ, yet does not that corruption nor reparation denote the destroying or new creation of this being, or the nature of those faculties, which continue the same in both estates. Wherefore, the understanding here mentioned is no more but a power and ability of mind with respect unto what is proposed unto us, to receive and apprehend it in a due manner. We are not able of ourselves to know him that is true, and the eternal life that is in him, but he has enabled us thereunto; for this understanding is given us unto that end, that we may so know him. Wherefore, whatever is proposed unto us in the gospel, or in any divine revelation, concerning these things, we cannot know them, at least as we ought, unless we have the understanding here mentioned given unto us, for so alone do we come by it.

(2) It is given us. That a real and effectual communication unto us of the thing said to be given is intended in this word, of giving from God, is evident from every place in the Scripture where it is used. Some contend that God is said to give things unto us when he does what lies in him that we may enjoy them, though we are never made partakers of them. But the assignation of this way and manner of God's doing what lies in him, where the effect designed does not ensue, not strictly restrained unto outward means, is scandalous, and fit to be exploded out of Christian theology. God says, "What could have been

done more to my vineyard, that I have not done?" (Isa. 5:4). But the expression has plainly a double limitation. One, unto the use of outward means only, concerning which God speaks in that place, and from which he elsewhere plainly distinguishes his giving them a new heart and a new spirit, that they shall all know him and be all taught of him. Two, unto the use of those outward means that were then established, as the only way for the season; for even in respect unto them, he did more for his vineyard when he granted the gospel unto it.¶

But is it possible that any man should think or believe that God cannot really collate grace and mercy on the souls of men when he pleases? Is it not as easy with him, on our restoration by Christ, to implant habits of grace in our souls, as it was at first to create us in original rectitude and righteousness? Wherefore, although we may inquire what God does, and has done, in this matter, according as he has revealed it in his word, yet to say that he does in anything what lies in him though the things which he affirms himself to do be not effected, is defective both in truth and piety. When he says he has done such a thing, or will do so, for us to say, "No, he has not done so, or he will not do so; but he has done, or will do, what lies in him that it may be so, though it never be so, nor have so been," is to make him altogether like ourselves.¶

But on this ground, some pretend that the Son of God is said to have given men understanding, because he has done what is requisite on his part, in the declaration of the gospel, that we may have it, whether ever we have it or not.¶

But [1] what he is said to have done, he had at least a design to do, and if he had so, why does it not take effect? "It is," they say, "because of the unwillingness of men to turn unto him, and other vicious habits of their minds, which hinder them from receiving instruction." But if it be so, then {1} it is supposed that men also in their teachings can give us an understanding as well as the Son of God; for they may teach men the knowledge of the gospel if they are willing to learn, and have no darling lusts or vicious habits of mind to hinder them from learning. {2} Seeing he has taken this work on himself, and designs its accomplishment, cannot the Son of God by his grace remove those vicious habits of the minds of men, that they may have an understanding of these things? If he cannot, why does he take that on him which he cannot effect? If he will not, why does he promise to do that which can never be done without doing what he will not do? And why is he said to do, as he is according to this interpretation of the words, which he has not done, which he will not or cannot do?¶

[2] The giving of an understanding is in this place plainly distinguished from the proposition of the things to be understood; that consists in the doctrine of the gospel, this in an ability to comprehend and know it.

[3] Again, the words here used, of giving understanding, may indeed express the actings or operations of men toward others, when an external proposal of things to be understood, with the due use of means, is intended. But yet if under their teaching men do not learn or comprehend the things wherein they are instructed by them, they cannot properly be said to have given them an understanding of it, with respect unto their moral operation unto that end, but only to have endeavored so to do. But when this phrase of speech is used to express a divine operation, which questionless[6] may be really physical, and so absolutely efficacious, to interpret it concerning an endeavor that may or may not succeed, is not suitable unto those thoughts that become us concerning divine operations. Nor was there any reason why the apostle should emphatically assign this work unto the Son of God, and that as he is the true God and eternal life, if no more be intended but a work of the same nature and kind with what a man might do. And if this be the sense of the words, it is from ourselves, and not from the Son of God, that there is any truth in them, as unto the event. For he might do, it seems, what lies in him to give an understanding, and yet no one man in the world ever had an understanding of the nature designed; for if it may be so with any unto whom he is said to give an understanding, as it is professedly with the most, it may be so with all. Not further to debate these things at present, whereas so excellent a grace and mercy toward the souls of men is here expressly at-tributed unto the Son of God, as the author of it, namely, that he gives us an understanding that we may know him which is true, I cannot think that they interpret the Scripture unto his glory whose exposition of this place consists in nothing but endeavors to prove that indeed he does not so do.

4. It is expressed by teaching, leading, and guiding into the truth (John 6:45; 16:13; 1 John 2:20, 27)—the places have been opened before. And two things are supposed in this expression of teaching.¶

(1) A mind capable of instruction, leading, and conduct. The nature must be rational, and comprehensive of the means of instruction, which can be so taught. Wherefore, we do not only grant herein the use of the rational faculties of the soul, but require their exercise and utmost improvement. If God teach, we are to learn, and we cannot learn but in the exercise of our minds. And it is in vain pretended that God's communication of a supernatural ability unto our minds, and our exercise of them in a way of duty, are inconsistent, whereas indeed they are inseparable in all that we are taught of God. For at the same time that he infuses a gracious ability into our minds, he proposes

---

6 I.e., without question.

the truth unto us whereon that ability is to be exercised. And if these things are inconsistent, the whole real efficacy of God in the souls of men must be denied, which is to despoil him of his sovereignty. But we speak now of natural ability to receive instruction, to be taught, with the exercise of it in learning; for these are supposed in the expression of the communication of a spiritual ability by teaching.¶

(2) A teaching suited unto that ability is promised or asserted. Three ways of this teaching are pleaded: [1] That it consists in a θεοπνευστία, "an immediate infallible inspiration and afflatus,"[7] of the same nature with that of the prophets and apostles of old. But first, this takes away the distinction between the extraordinary and ordinary gifts of the Spirit, so fully asserted in the Scripture, as we shall elsewhere declare. And if it were so, God did not place in the church "some prophets," seeing all were so, and were always to be so. Second, it brings in a neglect of the Scripture, and a leveling it into the same state and condition with the conceptions of everyone that will pretend unto this inspiration. Third, the pretense visibly confutes itself in the manifold mutual contradictions of them that pretend unto it. And would, fourth, thereon be a principle, first of confusion, then of infidelity, and so lead unto atheism. Fifth, the prophets themselves had not the knowledge and understanding of the mind and will of God which we inquire after by their immediate inspirations, which were unto them as the written word unto us, but had it by the same means as we have (1 Pet. 1:10–11). Hence, they so frequently and fervently prayed for understanding, as we have seen in the instance of David.

Wherefore, [2] some say this teaching consists only in the outward preaching of the word, in the ministry of the church, and other external means of its application unto our minds. But there is not one of the testimonies insisted on wherein this promised teaching of God is not distinguished from the proposition of the word in the outward dispensation of it, as has been proved. Besides, everyone that enjoys this teaching, that is, who is taught of God, does really believe and come to Christ thereby: "It is written in the prophets, 'And they shall be all taught of God. Every man therefore that hath heard, and hath learned of the Father, cometh unto me,'" says our blessed Savior (John 6:45). But it is not thus with all, nor ever was, toward whom the most powerful and cogent means of outward instruction have been or are used.

Wherefore, [3] this teaching is an internal work of the Spirit, giving light, wisdom, understanding, unto our minds; so is spoken of and promised in a

---

7   I.e., revelation.

special manner, distinct from the outward work of the dispensation of the word, and all the efficacy of it singly considered. One testimony will serve to this purpose, which has been pleaded and vindicated already. It is by an unction that we are thus taught (1 John 2:20, 27). But the unction consists in a real communication of supernatural gifts and graces, whereof supernatural light is that which is peculiarly necessary unto this end. The communication of them all in all fullness unto Jesus Christ, the head of the church, was his unction (Heb. 1:9; Isa. 61:1). Wherefore, in the real participation of them in our measure does our unction, whereby we are taught, consist.

It is granted that this teaching is such as regards our own industry, in the use of means appointed unto this end, that we may know the mind of God in the Scripture. But yet it is such as includes an inward effectual operation of the Holy Spirit, concomitant[8] with the outward means of teaching and learning. When the eunuch read the prophecy of Isaiah, he affirmed he could not understand it unless someone did guide him. Hereon Philip opened the Scripture unto him. But it was the Holy Ghost that opened his heart, that he might understand it; for so he did the heart of Lydia, without which she would not have understood the preaching of Paul (Acts 16:14). Wherefore, in our learning, under the conduct or teaching of the Spirit, the utmost diligence in the exercise of our own minds is required of us. And where men are defective herein, they are said to be νωθροὶ ταῖς ἀκοαῖς, "dull in hearing" (Heb. 5:11), or slow in the improvement of the instruction given them. And it is a senseless thing to imagine that men should be diverted from the exercise of the faculties of their minds merely because they are enabled to use them unto good purpose or successfully, which is the effect of this internal teaching.

5. It is expressed by shining into our hearts: "God, who commanded the light to shine out of darkness, hath shined in our hearts, to give the light of the knowledge of the glory of God in the face of Jesus Christ" (2 Cor. 4:6). Jesus Christ is the "image of the invisible God, the brightness of his glory, and the express image of his person."[9] And that because of the illustrious representation of all divine excellencies that is made both in his person and his mediation. The person of the Father is the eternal fountain of infinitely divine glorious perfections; and they are all communicated unto the Son by eternal generation. In his person absolutely, as the Son of God, they are all of them essentially; in his person as God-man, as vested with his offices, they are substantially, in opposition unto all types and shadows; and in the glass

---

8   I.e., accompanying.
9   Col. 1:15; Heb. 1:3.

of the gospel they are accidentally, by revelation—really, but not substantially, for Christ himself is the body, the substance of all.[10] As the image of God, so is he represented unto us in the glass of the gospel, and therein are we called to behold the glory of God in him (2 Cor. 3:18). The meaning is, that the truth and doctrine concerning Jesus Christ, his person and mediation, is so delivered and taught in the gospel as that the glory of God is eminently represented thereby, or therein is revealed what we are to know of God, his mind and his will, as he is declared by and in Jesus Christ. But why is it, then, that all do not thus behold "the glory of God in the face of Jesus Christ" unto whom the gospel is preached? Or whence is it that all unto whom the gospel is preached or declared do not apprehend and understand the truth, and reality, and glory of the things revealed or proposed? That is, why do they not understand the mind and will of God as revealed in the gospel? The apostle assigns two reasons hereof: one, from what hinders it in many; two, from what is necessary unto any that so they may do.

(1) The first is the efficacy of the temptations and suggestions of Satan, whereby their minds are filled with prejudices against the gospel and the doctrine of it, being blinded hereby, they can see nothing of beauty and glory in it, and so certainly do not apprehend it aright: "The god of this world hath blinded the minds of them which believe not, lest the light of the glorious gospel of Christ, who is the image of God, should shine into them" (2 Cor. 4:4). This is acknowledged by all to be an obstacle against the right understanding of the gospel. Unless the mind be freed from such prejudices as are the effects of such blinding efficacy of the suggestions of Satan, men cannot attain unto the true knowledge of the mind of God therein. How these prejudices are removed we shall show afterward. But if the mind be free, or freed from them, then it is supposed by some that there is need of no more but the due exercise of its faculties with diligence for that end, nor is anything else required thereunto. It is true, in the ordinary dispensation of divine grace, this is required of us. But the apostle adds,

(2) That there must, moreover, be a divine light shining into our hearts, to enable us hereunto. At least he does so that this was granted unto them who then did believe. And if we have it not as well as they, I fear we do not believe in the same manner as they did. Wherefore, although there be in the gospel and the doctrine of it an illustrious representation of the glory of God

---

10 This is classic Trinitarianism as consistently expressed in Aristotelian or scholastic categories in the post-Reformation Reformed tradition. See Richard A. Muller, *The Triunity of God*, vol. 4 of *Post-Reformation Reformed Dogmatics: The Rise and Development of Reformed Orthodoxy, ca. 1520 to ca. 1725* (Grand Rapids, MI: Baker Academic, 2003).

in Christ, yet are we not able of ourselves to discern it, until the Holy Spirit by an act of his almighty power does irradiate[11] our minds, and implant a light in them suited thereunto. He that does not behold "the glory of God in the face of Jesus Christ" in the gospel does not understand the mind and will of God as revealed therein in a due manner. I suppose this will be granted, seeing both these things are but one and the same, diversely expressed. But this of ourselves we cannot do. For there is an internal work of God upon our minds necessary thereunto. This also is expressed in the words. It is his shining into our hearts, to give the light of this knowledge unto us. There is a light in the gospel, "the light of the glorious gospel of Christ" (2 Cor. 4:4). But there must be a light also in our hearts, or we cannot discern it. And this is no natural light, or a light that is common unto all; but it is a light that, in a way of grace, is given unto them that do believe. And it is wrought in us by the same kind of efficiency as God created light with at the beginning of the world, namely, by a productive act of power. It is evident, therefore, that the light in our hearts which God communicates unto us, that we may have the true knowledge of his mind and will in the gospel, is distinct from that light of truth which is in the gospel itself. The one is subjective, the other is objective only; the one is wrought in us, the other is proposed unto us; the one is an act of divine power in us, the other an act of divine grace and mercy toward us.

Other ways there are whereby this operation of the Holy Spirit in the illumination of our minds is expressed. The instances given and testimonies considered are sufficient unto our purpose. That which we are in the proof of is, that there is more required unto a useful apprehension and understanding of the mind of God in the Scripture than the mere objective proposal of it unto us, and our diligent use of outward means to come to the knowledge of it; which yet, as we shall show, is from the Holy Spirit also. And as the denial hereof does, by just consequence, make void the principal means whereby we may come unto such an understanding, namely, frequent and fervent prayers for the aid and assistance of the Holy Spirit; so no tolerable account can be given of the mind of God and the meaning of the Scripture in the places insisted on. And certainly, if we cannot understand the way and manner of the operation of the Holy Spirit herein, it would be much better to captivate our understanding unto the obedience of faith than to wrest and pervert the Scripture, or debase the spiritual sense of it unto a compliance with our conceptions and apprehensions. But as we have herein the suffrage of them that do believe, in their own experience, who both value and acknowledge this

11 I.e., illuminate.

grace and privilege unto the glory of God, so we have multiplied instances of such as, being destitute of that skill which should enable them to make use of sundry external means, which are in their proper place of great advantage, who yet, by virtue of this divine teaching, are wise in the things of God beyond what some others with all their skill can attain unto.

The Nature of the Spirit's Work

Moreover, the effect of this work of the Holy Spirit on the minds of men does evidence of what nature it is. And this, also, is variously expressed. As,

1. It is called light: "Ye were sometimes darkness, but now are ye light in the Lord" (Eph. 5:8). The introduction of light into the mind is the proper effect of illumination. Men in their natural estate are said to be darkness, the abstract for the concrete, to express how deeply the mind is affected with it; for, as our Savior says, "If the light that is in any be darkness," as it is in them who are darkness, "how great is that darkness!" (Matt. 6:23). And because men are subject to mistake herein, and to suppose themselves, with the Pharisees, to see when they are blind, he gives that caution, "Take heed therefore that the light which is in thee be not darkness" (Luke 11:35). For men are very apt to please themselves with the working and improvement of their natural light, which yet, in the issue, with respect unto spiritual things, will prove but darkness. And while they are under the power of this darkness, that is, while their minds are deeply affected with their natural ignorance, they cannot perceive spiritual things (1 Cor. 2:14), no, not when they are most evidently proposed unto them. For although "the light shineth in darkness," or casts out its beams in the evidence and glory of spiritual truth, yet "the darkness comprehendeth it not" (John 1:5). But by this work of the Holy Spirit we are made "light in the Lord."[12] Light in the mind is a spiritual ability to discern and know spiritual things, as is declared (2 Cor. 4:6). This is bestowed upon us and communicated unto us by the Holy Spirit. There is a real difference between light and darkness. And it is our minds that are affected with them (Luke 11:35). The removal of the one and the introduction of the other are things not absolutely in our own power; he who is "darkness" cannot make himself "light in the Lord." Whatever he may do in way of disposition or preparation, in way of duty and diligence, in the utmost improvement of the natural faculties of his mind, which no man will ever rise unto who is under the power of this darkness, because of the insuperable[13] prejudices and corrupt

---

12 Eph. 5:8.

13 I.e., insurmountable; overwhelming.

affections that it fills the mind with, yet the introduction of this light is an act of him who opens the eyes of our understandings and shines into our hearts. Without this light, no man can understand the Scripture as he ought; and I shall not contend about what they see or behold who are in darkness.

The expulsion of spiritual darkness out of our minds, and the introduction of spiritual light into them, a work so great that they who were "darkness," whose "light was darkness," are made "light in the Lord" thereby, is an effect of the immediate power of the Spirit of God. To ascribe other low and metaphorical senses unto the words is to corrupt the Scripture and to deny the testimony of God. For this light he produces in us by the same power and the same manner of operation whereby he brought light out of darkness at the creation of all things. But by this way and means it is that we attain the "knowledge of God in the face of Jesus Christ,"[14] or the revelation of his mind and will in the gospel.

2. It is called understanding. So the psalmist prays, "Give me understanding, and I shall keep thy law" (Ps. 119:34). So the apostle speaks to Timothy, "Consider what I say, and the Lord give thee understanding in all things" (2 Tim. 2:7). Besides his own consideration of what was proposed unto him, which includes the due and diligent use of all outward means, it was moreover necessary that God should give him understanding by an inward effectual work of his Spirit, that he might comprehend the things wherein he was instructed. And the desire hereof, as of that without which there can be no saving knowledge of the word, nor advantage by it, the psalmist expresses emphatically with great fervency of spirit: "The righteousness of thy testimonies is everlasting. O give me understanding and I shall live" (Ps. 119:144). Without this he knew that he could have no benefit by the everlasting righteousness of the testimonies of God. All understanding, indeed, however it be abused by the most, is the work and effect of the Holy Ghost. For "the inspiration of the Almighty giveth understanding" (Job 32:8). So is this spiritual understanding in a special manner. And in this understanding both the ability of our minds and the due exercise of it is included. And this one consideration, that the saints of God have with so much earnestness prayed that God would give them understanding in his mind and will as revealed in the word, with his reiterated promises that he would so do, is of more weight with me than all the disputes of men to the contrary. And there is no further argument necessary to prove that men do not understand the mind of God in the Scripture in a due manner, than their supposal and confidence that so they can do without the communication of

---

14 2 Cor. 4:6.

a spiritual understanding unto them by the Holy Spirit of God, which is so contrary unto the plain, express testimonies thereof.

3. It is called wisdom. For by this work on the minds of men they are rendered "wise unto salvation." So, the apostle prays for the Colossians, "that God would fill them with the knowledge of his will in all wisdom and spiritual understanding" (Col. 1:9). These things may be the same, and the latter exegetical of the former. If there be a difference, "wisdom" respects things in general, in their whole system and complex; "understanding" respects particulars as they are to be reduced unto practice. Wherefore, the "spiritual understanding" which the apostle prays for respects the mind of God in special or particular places of the Scripture; and "wisdom" is a skill and ability in the comprehension of the whole system of his counsel as revealed therein. He who is thus made wise, and he alone, can understand the things of God as he ought (Dan. 12:10; Hos. 14:9; Ps. 107:43). Although men may bear themselves high on their learning, their natural abilities, their fruitful inventions, tenacious memories, various fancies, plausibility of expression, with long study and endeavors, things good and praiseworthy in their kind and order, yet unless they are thus made wise by the Spirit of God, they will scarce attain a due acquaintance with his mind and will. For this effect of that work is also expressly called "knowledge" (Col. 1:9; 2 Cor. 4:6; Eph. 1:17; Col. 3:10). Wherefore, without it we cannot have that which is properly so called.

This is the second thing designed in this discourse. In the first it was proved in general that there is an effectual operation of the Spirit of God on the minds of men, enabling them to perceive and understand the supernatural revelations of the Scripture when proposed unto them; and in the second is declared what is the nature of that work, and what are the effects of it on our minds. Both of them have I treated merely from Scripture testimony. For in vain shall we seek to any other way or means for what we ought to apprehend and believe herein. Neither is the force of these testimonies to be eluded[15] by any distinctions or evasions whatever. Nor, while the authority of the Scripture is allowed, can any men more effectually evidence the weakness and depravation of their reason than by contending that in the exercise of it they can understand the mind and will of God as revealed therein, without the special aid and illumination of the Spirit of God. Nor can any man on that supposition, with any wisdom or consistency in his own principles, make use in a way of duty of the principal means whereby we may so understand them, as will afterward more fully appear.

---

15 I.e., evaded or escaped.

5

Ignorance

Causes and Remedies

Causes of the Ignorance of the Mind of God Revealed
in the Scripture; and of Errors about It; What
They Are; and How They Are Removed.

THE SUPPOSITION we proceed upon in this discourse is, that *God has revealed his mind and will unto us, as unto all things concerning his worship, with our faith and obedience therein, in the Holy Scripture.* Thereon do we inquire by what means we may attain the saving knowledge of the mind of God so revealed; and my principal design is to show what aid and assistance we receive of the Holy Ghost unto that end. To further us in the knowledge hereof, I shall inquire into the causes and reasons of that ignorance and those misapprehensions of the mind of God as revealed, which are among men, and how our minds are delivered from them.

It may be this part of our discourse might have had a more proper place assigned unto it, after we have given the truth pleaded a more full confirmation. But whereas an objection may arise from the consideration of what we shall now insist on against the truth contended for, I thought it not amiss so to obviate[1] it, as therewith further to illustrate the doctrine itself which we labor in.

HUMAN DEFICIENCY

All men see, and most men complain of, that ignorance of the mind of God, and those abominable errors, attended with false worship, which abound in

1   I.e., anticipate; prevent.

the world. How few are there who understand and believe the truth aright? What divisions, what scandals, what animosities, what violence, mutual rage, and persecutions, do ensue hereon, among them that are called Christians, is likewise known. Hence, some take occasion to countenance themselves in an open declension unto atheism; some, unto a great indifferency in all religion; some, to advance themselves and destroy others by the advantage of their opinions, according as they are prevalent in some times and places. A brief inquiry into the causes of that darkness and ignorance which is in the world among men outwardly owning the doctrine of the gospel, and especially of the errors and heresies which do abound above what they have done in most ages, may be of use to preserve us from those evils. A subject this is that would require much time and diligence unto the handling of it in a due manner. I intend only at present to point at the heads of some few things, the observation whereof may be of use unto the end designed.

Those of the Roman church tell us that the cause hereof is the obscurity, difficulty, and perplexity of the Scripture. If men will trust thereunto as their only guide, they are sure to miscarry. Wherefore, the only relief in this matter is that we give up our souls unto the conduct of their Church, which neither can err nor deceive. So, indeed, said Adam of old, when he was charged with his sin and infidelity: "The woman whom thou gavest to be with me, she gave me of the tree, and I did eat."[2] But whereas it is an evil, yea, the greatest of evils, whose causes we inquire after, it seems in general more rational that we should seek for them in ourselves than in anything that God has done. For he alone is good, and we are evil.

It is granted that God has given us his word, or the Holy Scripture, as a declaration of his mind and will; and, therefore, he has given it unto us for this very end and purpose, that we may know them and do them. But whereas many men do fail herein, and do not understand aright what is revealed, but fall into pernicious errors and mistakes, unto his dishonor and their own ruin, is it meet to say unto God that this comes to pass from hence, because the revelation he has made of these things is dark, obscure, and intricate? Or the Scripture which he has given us does deceive us? Would a due reverence or deferency unto the wisdom, goodness, and love of God unto mankind be preserved therein?

Bold to endure all things
The human race rushes on through every crime.[3]

---

2 Gen. 3:12.

3 In the text: *Audax omnia perpeti Gens humana ruit per vetitum nefas.*—Owen. This quotation is from Horace (65–8 BC), a leading Roman lyric poet. For the Latin text and English translation,

What will not the prejudices and corrupt interests of men carry them out into. God will forever preserve those that are his in an abhorrency of that religion, be it what it will, that by any means leads unto an undervaluation of that revelation of himself which, in infinite wisdom and goodness, he has made unto us.

But is it because there is no reason to be given of this evil from the minds of men themselves that it is thus ascribed unto God? May not as well all the wickednesses that the world is filled with be ascribed unto him and what he has done? Does not each one see a sufficient cause hereof even in himself, if he were not delivered from it by the power of the Spirit and grace of God? Do not other men who fail in the right knowledge of God, especially in any important truth, sufficiently evidence in other things that the root of this matter is in themselves? Alas! How dark are the minds of poor mortals, how full of pride and folly? I shall say with some confidence, he who understands not that there is reason enough to charge all the errors, ignorance, and confusions in religion, that are or ever were in the world, without the least censure of obscurity, insufficiency, or intricacy in the Scripture, on the minds of men, and those depraved affections whose prevalency they are obnoxious unto, are themselves profoundly ignorant of the state of all things above and here below.

We must, therefore, inquire after the causes and reasons of these things among ourselves, for there only they will be found.

And these causes are of two sorts: First, that which is general, and the spring of all others; Second, those which are particular, that arise and branch themselves from thence.

GENERAL CAUSE OF IGNORANCE

The first and general cause of all ignorance, error, and misunderstanding of the mind and will of God, as revealed in the Scripture, among all sorts of men, whatever their particular circumstances are, is the natural vanity and darkness with which the minds of all men are depraved. The nature of this depravation of our minds by the fall, and the effects of it, I have fully elsewhere declared. Wherefore I now take it for granted that the minds of all men are naturally prepossessed with this darkness and vanity, from whence they are not, from whence they cannot be delivered but by the saving illumination of the Spirit and grace of God. But because I have so largely treated of it both in

see Horace, *The Odes: New Translations by Contemporary Poets*, ed. J. D. McClatchy (Princeton, NJ: Princeton University Press, 2002), 22–23.

the *Discourses of the Dispensation of the Spirit*,[4] as also in those concerning the apostasy of these latter times, I shall not again insist upon it.

Two things I shall only observe unto our present purpose, namely, one, that hereby the mind is kept off from discerning the glory and beauty of spiritual, heavenly truth, and from being sensible of its power and efficacy (John 1:5). Two, that it is by the same means inclined unto all things that are vain, curious, superstitious, carnal, suited unto the interest of pride, lust, and all manner of corrupt affections. Hence, whatever other occasions of error and superstition may be given or taken, the ground of their reception and of all adherence unto them is the uncured vanity and darkness of the minds of men by nature. This is the mire wherein this rush does grow.

And the consideration hereof will rectify our thoughts concerning those whom we see daily to wander from the truth, or to live in those misapprehensions of the mind of God which they have imbibed, notwithstanding the clear revelation of it unto the contrary. Some think it strange that it should be so, and marvel at them; some are angry with them; and some would persecute and destroy them. We may make a better use of this consideration; for we may learn from it the sad corruption and depravation of our minds in our estate of apostasy from God. Here lies the seed and spring of all the sin, evil, and disorder, which we behold and suffer under in religious concerns in this world. And if we consider it aright, it will serve,

1. To impress a due sense of our own condition upon our minds, that we may be humbled. And in humility alone there is safety. "His soul which is lifted up is not upright in him" (Hab. 2:4); for he draws back from God, and God has no pleasure in him, as the apostle expounds those words (Heb. 10:38). It was in the principles of our nature to adhere sacredly unto the first truth, to discern and abhor every false way. We were created with that light of truth in our minds as was every way able to guide us in all that we had to believe or do with respect unto God or our own blessedness forever. But in the room thereof, through our wretched apostasy from God, our mind has become the seat and habitation of all vanity, disorder, and confusion. And no way does this more discover itself than in the readiness and proneness of multitudes to embrace whatever is crooked, perverse, and false in religion,

---

4   In the text: book 3, chap. 3.—Owen. The works referenced in this sentence are Πνευματολογια, or, *A Discourse concerning the Holy Spirit* (1674) and *The Nature of Apostasie from the Profession of the Gospel, and the Punishment of Apostates Declared, in an Exposition of Heb. 6, 4, 5, 6: With an Enquiry into the Causes and Reasons of the Decay of the Power of Religion in the World* [. . .] *also, of the Proneness of Churches and Persons of All Sorts unto Apostasie, with Remedies, and Means of Prevention* (1676).

notwithstanding the clear revelation that God has made of the whole truth concerning it in the Scripture. A due reflection hereon may teach us humility and self-abasement. For we are by nature children of wrath, even as others, neither have we any good thing that we have not received. It is better, therefore, to be conversant with such thoughts on this occasion, than to be filled with contempt of, or wrath against those whom we see yet suffering under those woeful effects of the general apostasy from God, wherein we were equally involved with them. Yea,

2. It will teach us pity and compassion toward those whose minds do run out into the spiritual excesses mentioned. The merciful high priest of the whole church has "compassion on the ignorant, and on them that are out of the way" (Heb. 5:2), and it is conformity unto him in all things which ought to be our principal design, if we desire to be like unto him in glory. Want hereof is the ruin of religion, and the true cause of all the troubles that its profession is encumbered with at this day.

It is true, for the most part, there is an interposition of corrupt affections seducing the minds of men from the truth. With these are they tossed up and down, and so driven with the winds of temptations that befall them. But is it humanity to stand on the shore, and seeing men in a storm at sea, wherein they are ready every moment to be cast away and perish, to storm at them ourselves, or to shoot them to death, or to cast fire into their vessel, because they are in danger of being drowned? Yet no otherwise do we deal with them whom we persecute because they miss the knowledge of the truth, and, it may be, raise a worse storm in ourselves as to our own morals than they suffer under in their intellectuals. Concerning such persons, the advice of the apostle is, "Of some have compassion, making a difference, and others save with fear, pulling them out of the fire" (Jude 22–23). Some are so given up in their apostasy as that they "sin unto death"; with such we are not to concern ourselves (1 John 5:16). But it is very rare that we can safely make that judgment concerning any in this world. Sometimes, no doubt, we may, or this rule concerning them had never been given. As unto all others, the worst of them, those that are in the fire, the frame of our minds' acting toward them is here presented unto us; compassion of their present state, and fear of their future ruin, we ought to be possessed with and acted by. But how few are they who are so framed and minded toward them, especially to such as by their enormous errors seem to be fallen into the fire of God's displeasure? Anger, wrath, fury, contempt toward such persons, men think to be their duty; more contrivances there are usually how they may be temporally destroyed than how they may be eternally saved. But such men profess the truth as it were by chance. They never knew what it is to learn it aright, nor whence the knowledge of it is to be received, nor were ever under its power or conduct. Our proper work is to save such persons, what lies in us, "pulling them out of the fire." Duties of difficulty and danger unto ourselves may be required hereunto. It is easier, if we had secular power with us, to thrust men into temporal fire for their errors than to free them from eternal fire by the truth. But if we were governed by compassion for their souls and fear of their ruin, as it is our duty to be, we would not decline any office of love required thereunto.

3. Has God led us into the truth, has he kept us from every false way? It is evident that we have abundant cause of gratitude and fruitfulness. It is a condition more desperate than that of the most pernicious errors, to "hold the truth in unrighteousness";[5] and as good not know the Lord Jesus Christ as to be barren in the knowledge of him. It is not, we see, of ourselves, that we either know the truth, or love it, or abide in the profession of it. We have nothing of this kind but what we have received. Humility in ourselves, usefulness toward others, and thankfulness unto God, ought to be the effects of this consideration.

This is the first general cause of men's misapprehension of the mind and will of God as revealed in the Scripture. The revelation itself is plain, perspicuous, and full of light. But this "light shineth in darkness, and the darkness comprehendeth it not."[6] The natural darkness and blindness which is in the minds of men, with the vanity and instability which they are attended with, causes them to wrest the Scriptures unto their own destruction. And for this sort of men to complain, as they do horribly in the Papacy, of the obscurity of the Scripture, is all one as if a company of blind men should cry out of an eclipse of the sun when he shines in his full strength and glory. How this darkness is removed and taken away by the effectual operation of the Holy Spirit in our illumination, I have elsewhere at large discoursed.[7]

Corrupt affections prevalent in the minds of men do hinder them from a right understanding of the mind of God in the Scripture. For hereby are they effectually inclined to wrest and pervert the truth, or are filled with prejudices against it. This is the next cause of all ignorance and error, where we must seek for the particular causes of them before proposed. The principal reason why the generality of men attain not a right understanding of the mind and will of God in the Scripture, is the corrupt affections that are predominant

---

5 Rom. 1:18.

6 John 1:5.

7 Owen is likely referring to his Πνευματολογια, or, A Discourse concerning the Holy Spirit, bk. 3.

in their own minds, whereby they are exposed unto all sorts of impressions and seductions from Satan and the agents for his kingdom and interest. So one apostle tells us that "unlearned and unstable men do wrest the Scripture, unto their own destruction" (2 Pet. 3:16). And another that these unlearned and unstable persons are "men of corrupt minds" (1 Tim. 6:5; 2 Tim. 3:8), that is, such whose minds are peculiarly under the power of perverse and corrupt affections. For these affections are θελήματα τῶν διανοιῶν, "the wills of the mind" (Eph. 2:3), such as carry it with an impetuous inclination toward their own satisfaction, and such as render it obstinate and perverse in its adherence thereunto. These are the root of that "filthiness and superfluity of naughtiness," which must be cast out before we can "receive the ingrafted Word with meekness" (James 1:21). Some few of them may be named.

1. Pride, or carnal confidence in our own wisdom and ability of mind for all the ends of our duty toward God, and this especially of understanding his mind and will, either keeps the souls of men under the bondage of darkness and ignorance, or precipitates them into foolish apprehensions or pernicious errors. As spiritual pride is the worst sort of pride, so this is the worst degree of spiritual pride, namely, when men do not acknowledge God in these things as they ought, but lean unto their own understandings. This is that which ruined the Pharisees of old, that they could not understand the mind of God in anything unto their advantage. It is the meek, the humble, the lowly in mind, those that are like little children, that God has promised to teach. This is an eternal and unalterable law of God's appointment, that whoever will learn his mind and will as revealed in the Scripture must be humble and lowly, renouncing all trust and confidence in themselves. And whatever men of another frame do come to know, they know it not according to the mind of God, nor according to their own duty, nor unto their advantage. Whatever knowledge they may have, however conspicuous it may be made by their natural and acquired abilities, however it may be garnished with a mixture of secular literature, whatever contempt it may raise them unto of others, such as the Pharisees had of the people, whom they esteemed accursed because they knew not the law, yet they know nothing as they ought, nothing unto the glory of God, nothing to the spiritual advantage of their own souls. And wherein is their knowledge to be accounted of? Indeed, the knowledge of a proud man is the throne of Satan in his mind. To suppose that persons under the predominancy of pride, self-conceit, and self-confidence can understand the mind of God as revealed in a due manner, is to renounce the Scriptures, or innumerable positive testimonies given in them unto the contrary. Such persons cannot make use of any one means of spiritual knowledge that God

requires of them in a way of duty, nor improve any one truth which they may know unto their good. Therefore, our Savior tells the proud Pharisees, notwithstanding all their skill in the letter and tittles of the Scripture, that "they had not heard the voice of God at any time, nor seen his shape, neither had they his Word abiding in them" (John 5:37–38). They had no right knowledge of him, as he had revealed and declared himself.

Men infected with this leaven, having their minds tainted with it, have been the great corrupters of divine truth in all ages. Such have been the ringleaders of all heresies, and such were they who have turned the knowledge of the will of God proposed in the Scripture into a wrangling science, filled with niceties, subtleties, curiosities, futilous[8] terms of art, and other fuel for the minds of fiery contenders in wrangling disputations.

And this kind of self-confidence is apt to befall all sorts of men. Those of the meanest capacity may be infected with it no less than the wisest or most learned. And we frequently see persons whose weakness in all sound knowledge, and insufficiency for the use of proper means unto the attaining of it, might seem to call them unto humility and lowliness of mind in an eminent manner, yet lifted up unto such a degree of spiritual pride and conceit of their own understandings as to render them useless, troublesome, and offensive unto men of sober minds. But principally are they exposed hereunto who either really, or in their own apprehensions, are exalted above others in secular learning, and natural or acquired abilities. For such men are apt to think that they must needs know the meaning of the Holy Ghost in the Scriptures better than others, or, at least, that they can do so, if they will but set themselves about it. But that which principally hinders them from so doing is their conceit that so they do. They mistake that for divine knowledge, which is in them the great obstruction of it.

2. The love of honor and praise among men is another corrupt affection of mind, of the same nature and efficacy with that before named. This is so branded by our Savior as an insuperable obstacle against the admission of sacred light and truth that no more need be added thereunto (see John 5:44; 12:43).

3. A pertinacious[9] adherence unto corrupt traditions and inveterate[10] errors quite shuts up the way unto all wisdom and spiritual understanding. This mined the church of the Jews of old, and makes at present that of the Romanists incurable. What their forefathers have professed, what themselves

8 I.e., futile or trifling.
9 I.e., resolute adherence to an opinion, purpose, or design.
10 I.e., well established.

have imbibed from their infancy, what all their outward circumstances are involved in, what they have advantage by, what is in reputation with those in whom they are principally concerned, that shall be the truth with them, and nothing else. Unto persons whose minds are wholly vitiated with the leaven of this corrupt affection, there is not a line in the Scripture whose sense can be truly and clearly represented. All appears in the color and figure that their prejudices frame in their minds. When the Lord Christ came forth first unto the preaching of the gospel, there came a voice from heaven, saying, "This is my beloved Son, in whom I am well pleased, hear him" (Matt. 17:5). Neither was this command given unto them alone who heard it immediately from the "excellent glory," as Peter speaks (2 Pet. 1:17), but, as recorded in the word, is given equally unto everyone that would learn anything of the mind and will of God in a due manner. No man can learn but by the "hearing of him"; unto him are we sent for the learning of our spiritual knowledge. And no other way does he speak unto us but by his word and Spirit. But where the minds of men are prepossessed with apprehensions of what they have received from the authority of other teachers, they have neither desire, design, readiness, nor willingness to hear him.¶

But if men will not forgo all preimbibed opinions, prejudices, and conceptions of mind, however riveted into them by traditions, custom, veneration of elders, and secular advantages, to hearken unto and receive whatever he shall speak unto them, and that with a humble, lowly frame of heart, they will never learn the truth, nor attain a "full assurance of understanding"[11] in the mysteries of God. These inveterate prejudices are at this day those which principally shut out the truth, and set men together by the ears all the world over about religion and the concerns thereof. Hence is all the strife, rage, tumult, and persecution that the world is filled with. Could men but once agree to lay down all those presumptions which either wit, or learning, or custom, or interest and advantage have influenced them with at the feet of Jesus Christ, and resolve in sincerity to comply with that alone which he does teach them, and to forgo whatever is inconsistent therewith, the ways unto truth and peace would be more laid open than otherwise they are like to be.

4. Spiritual sloth is of the same nature, and produces the same effect. The Scripture frequently gives us in charge to use the utmost of our diligence in the search of and for the finding out of spiritual truth, proposing unto us the example of those that have done so before (Josh. 1:8; Ps. 1:2; Prov. 2:2–6; John 5:39; 1 Pet. 1:10–12). And any rational man would judge that if it had

---

11 Col. 2:2.

not been so expressly given us in charge from God himself, if it had not been a means appointed and sanctified unto this end, yet that the nature of the thing itself, with its importance unto our duty and blessedness, are sufficient to convince us of its necessity. It is truth, it is heavenly truth, we inquire after; that on the knowledge or ignorance whereof our eternal blessedness or misery does depend. And in a due perception thereof alone are the faculties of our minds perfected according to the measure which they are capable of in this life. Therein alone can the mind of man find rest, peace, and satisfaction, and without it must always wander in restless uncertainties and disquieting vanities. It is a notion implanted in the minds of all men that all truth lies deep, and that there is great difficulty in the attainment of it. The minds of most are imposed on by specious appearances of falsehood. Wherefore, all wise men have agreed that without our utmost care and diligence in the investigation of the truth, we must be contented to walk in the shades of ignorance and error. And if it be thus in earthly things, how much more is it so in heavenly?¶

As spiritual, supernatural truth is incomparably to be valued above that which relates unto things natural, so it is more abstruse[12] and of a more difficult investigation. But this folly is befallen the minds of the generality of men, that of all things they suppose there is least need of pains and diligence to be used in an inquiry after those things which the angels themselves desire to bow down and look into, and which the prophets of old inquired and searched after with all diligence. Whatever be their notion hereof, yet practically it is evident that most men, through pride and sloth and love of sin, are wholly negligent herein. At least they will not apply themselves to those spiritual means without the use whereof the knowledge of divine truth will not be attained. It is generally supposed that men may be as wise in these things as they need to be at a very easy rate. The folly of men herein can never be enough bewailed; they regard spiritual truth as if they had no concern in it beyond what custom and tradition put them on, in reading chapters or hearing sermons. They are wholly under the power of sloth as unto any means of spiritual knowledge.

Some, indeed, will labor diligently in the study of those things which the Scripture has in common with other arts and sciences; such are the languages wherein it was writ, the stories contained in it, the ways of arguing which it uses with scholastic accuracy in expressing the truth supposed to be contained in it. These things are great in themselves, but go for nothing when they are alone. Men under the utmost efficacy of spiritual sloth may be

---

12 I.e., difficult to understand.

diligent in them, and make a great progress in their improvement. But they are spiritual objects and duties that this sloth prevails to alienate the minds of men from, and make them negligent of; and what are those duties I shall afterward manifest.

The consideration, I say, of the state of things in the world gives so great an evidence of probability that, what through the pride and self-conceit of the minds of many, refusing a compliance with the means of spiritual knowledge, and excluding all gracious qualifications indispensably required unto the attaining of it. What through the power of corrupt traditions, imprisoning the minds of men in a fatal adherence unto them, preventing all thoughts of a holy, ingenuous inquiry into the mind of God by the only safe, infallible revelation of it; what through the power of spiritual sloth indisposing the minds of the most unto an immediate search of the Scripture, partly with apprehensions of its difficulty, and notions of learning the truth contained in it by other means; and what through a traditional course of studying divinity as an art or science to be learned out of the writings of men—the number is very small of them who diligently, humbly, and conscientiously endeavor to learn the truth from the voice of God in the Scripture, or to grow wise in the mysteries of the gospel by such ways as wherein alone that wisdom is attainable. And is it any wonder, then, if many, the greatest number of men, wander after vain imaginations of their own or others, while the truth is neglected or despised?

5. Again, there is in the minds of men by nature a love of sin, which causes them to hate the truth; and none can understand it but those that love it. In the visible church, most men come to know of the truth of the gospel as it were whether they will or not. And the general design of it they find to be a separation between them and their sins. This sets them at a distance from it in affection, whereon they can never make any near approach unto it in knowledge or understanding. So we are assured, "Light is come into the world, and men love darkness rather than light, because their deeds are evil. For everyone that doeth evil hateth the light, neither cometh to the light, lest his deeds should be reproved" (John 3:19–20). Persons under the power of this frame take up under the shades of ignorance and corrupt imaginations. And if they should attempt to learn the truth, they would never be able so to do.

Satan by his temptations and suggestions does variously affect the minds of men, hindering them from discerning the mind of God as revealed in the Scripture: "The god of this world blindeth the eyes of them that believe not, lest the light of the glorious gospel of Christ, who is the image of God, should shine unto them" (2 Cor. 4:4). The ways and means whereby he does so, the instruments which he uses, the artifices and methods which he applies unto his ends, with his application of himself unto them according to all occasions, circumstances, opportunities, and provocations, in great variety, were worth our inquiring into, but that we should too much digress from our present design.

I have but mentioned these things, and that as instances of the true original causes of the want of understanding and misunderstanding of the revelation of the mind of God in the Scripture. Many more of the same nature might be added unto them, and their effectual operations unto the same end declared; but the mention of them here is only occasional, and such as will not admit of a further discussion. But by these and the like depraved affections it is that the original darkness and enmity of the minds of men against spiritual truth and all the mysteries of it do exert themselves; and from them do all the error, superstition, and false worship that the world is filled with proceed. For,

While the minds of men are thus affected, as they cannot understand and receive divine, spiritual truths in a due manner, so are they ready and prone to embrace whatever is contrary thereunto. If, therefore, it be the work of the Spirit of God alone, in the renovation of our minds, to free them from the power of these vicious, depraved habits, and consequently the advantages that Satan has against them thereby, there is a special work of his necessary to enable us to learn the truth as we ought. And for those who have no regard unto these things, who suppose that in the study of the Scripture all things come alike unto all, to the clean and to the unclean, to the humble and the proud, to them that hate the garment spotted with the flesh and those that both love sin and live in it, they seem to know nothing either of the design, nature, power, use, or end of the gospel.

THE SPIRIT'S REMOVAL OF HINDRANCES

The removal of these hindrances and obstacles is the work of the Spirit of God alone. For,

1. He alone communicates that spiritual light unto our minds which is the foundation of all our relief against these obstacles of and oppositions unto a saving understanding of the mind of God.

2. In particular, he frees, delivers, and purges our minds from all those corrupt affections and prejudices which are partly inbred in them, partly assumed by them or imposed on them. For the artifice of Satan, in turning the minds of men from the truth, is by bringing them under the power of corrupt

and vicious habits, which expel that frame of spirit which is indispensably necessary unto them that would learn it. It is, indeed, our duty so to purify and purge ourselves. We ought to cast out "all filthiness and superfluity of naughtiness," that we may "receive with meekness the ingrafted Word" (James 1:21). To "purge ourselves from these things, that we may be vessels unto honour, sanctified and meet for our Master's use, and prepared unto every good work" (2 Tim. 2:21). If it be not thus with us, let the pride and folly of men pretend what they please, we can neither learn, nor know, nor teach the mind of God as we ought. And what men may do without giving glory unto God, or the bringing of any spiritual advantage unto their own souls, we inquire not, seeing it belongs only equivocally unto Christian religion.¶

But although it is our duty thus to purge ourselves, yet it is by the grace of the Holy Spirit that we do so. Those who, under a pretense of our own duty, would exclude in anything the efficacious operations of the Holy Ghost, or, on the other hand, on the pretense of his grace and its efficacy, would exclude the necessity of diligence in our duties, do admit but of one half of the gospel, rejecting the other. The whole gospel asserts and requires them both unto every good act and work. Wherefore, the purging of ourselves is that which is not absolutely in the power of our natural abilities. For these corrupt affections possess and are predominant in the mind itself, and all its actings are suited unto their nature and influenced by their power. It can never, therefore, by its own native ability free itself from them. But it is the work of this great purifier and sanctifier of the church to free our minds from these corrupt affections and inveterate prejudices, whereby we are alienated from the truth and inclined unto false conceptions of the mind of God. And unless this be done, in vain shall we think to learn the truth as it is in Jesus (see 1 Cor. 6:11; Titus 3:3–5; Rom. 8:13; Eph. 4:20–24).

3. He implants in our minds spiritual habits and principles, contrary and opposite unto those corrupt affections, whereby they are subdued and expelled. By him are our minds made humble, meek, and teachable, through a submission unto the authority of the word, and a conscientious endeavor to conform ourselves thereunto.

It was always agreed that there were ordinarily preparations required unto the receiving of divine illuminations; and in the assignation of them many have been greatly deceived. Hence some, in the expectation of receiving divine revelations, have been imposed on by diabolical delusions, which by the working of their imaginations they had prepared their minds to give an easy admission unto. So was it among the heathen of old, who had invented many ways unto this purpose, some of them horrid and dreadful. And so it is still with all enthusiasts. But God himself has plainly declared what are the qualifications of those souls which are meet to be made partakers of divine teachings, or ever shall be so. And these are, as they are frequently expressed, meekness, humility, godly fear, reverence, submission of soul and conscience unto the authority of God, with a resolution and readiness for and unto all that obedience which he requires of us, especially that which is internal in the hidden man of the heart. It may be some will judge that we wander very far from the matter of our inquiry, namely, how we may come unto the knowledge of the mind of God in the Scripture, or how we may aright understand the Scripture, when we assign these things as means thereof or preparations thereunto. For although these are good things, for that cannot be denied, yet it is ridiculous to urge them as necessary unto this end, or as of any use for the attaining of it. Learning, arts, tongues, sciences, with the rules of their exercise, and the advantage of ecclesiastical dignity, are the things that are of use herein, and they alone. The most of these things, and sundry others of the same kind, we acknowledge to be of great use unto the end designed, in their proper place, and what is the due use of them shall be afterward declared. But we must not forgo what the Scripture plainly instructs us in, and which the nature of the things themselves does evidence to be necessary, to comply with the arrogance and fancy of any, or to free ourselves from their contempt.

It is such an understanding of the Scripture, of the divine revelation of the mind of God therein, as wherein the spiritual illumination of our minds does consist, which we inquire after; such a knowledge as is useful and profitable unto the proper ends of the Scripture toward us, that which we are taught of God, that we may live unto him. These are the ends of all true knowledge (see 2 Tim. 3:14–17). And for this end the furnishing of the mind with the graces before mentioned is the best preparation. He bids defiance unto the gospel by whom it is denied. "God resisteth the proud, but giveth grace unto the humble."[13] Whatever be the parts or abilities of men, whatever diligence they may use in the investigation of the truth, whatever disciplinary knowledge they may attain thereby, the Spirit of God never did nor ever will instruct a proud, unhumbled soul in the right knowledge of the Scripture, as it is a divine revelation. It is these gracious qualifications alone whereby we may be enabled to "cast out all filthiness and superfluity of naughtiness," so as to "receive with meekness the ingrafted Word, which is able to save our souls."[14]

---

13 James 4:6.
14 James 1:21.

Our blessed Savior tells us, that "unless we be converted, and become as little children, we cannot enter into the kingdom of heaven" (Matt. 18:3). We cannot do so unless we become humble, meek, tender, weaned from high thoughts of ourselves, and are purged from prejudices by corrupt affections. And I value not that knowledge which will not conduct us into the kingdom of heaven, or which shall be there excluded. So, God has promised that "the meek he will guide in judgment, the meek he will teach his way; the secret of the Lord is with them that fear him, and he will show them his covenant; And what man is he that feareth the Lord? Him shall he teach in the way" (Ps. 25:9, 12, 14). And so we are told plainly that "evil men understand not judgment, but they that seek the Lord understand all things" (Prov. 28:5).

Now all these graces whereby men are made teachable, capable of divine mysteries, so as to learn the truth as it is in Jesus, to understand the mind of God in the Scriptures, are wrought in them by the Holy Spirit, and belong unto his work upon our minds in our illumination. Without this the hearts of all men are fat, their ears heavy, and their eyes sealed, that they can neither hear, nor perceive, nor understand the mysteries of the kingdom of God.

These things belong unto the work of the Holy Spirit upon our minds, as also sundry other instances might be given unto the same purpose, in our illumination, or his enabling of us rightly to understand the mind of God in the Scripture. But whereas whoever is thus by him graciously prepared and disposed shall be taught in the knowledge of the will of God, so far as he is concerned to know it in point of duty, if he abides in the ordinary use of outward means, so there are sundry other things necessary unto the attaining of further useful degrees of this knowledge and understanding, whereof I shall treat afterward.

Inspiration and Perspicuity

*The Work of the Holy Spirit in the Composing and Disposal
of the Scripture as a Means of Sacred Illumination;
the Perspicuity of the Scripture unto the Understanding
of the Mind of God Declared and Vindicated.*

THERE IS YET ANOTHER part of the work of the Holy Spirit with respect unto the illumination of our minds, which must also be inquired into. And this concerns the Scripture itself. For this he has so given out and so disposed of as that it should be a moral way or means for the communication of divine revelations unto the minds of men. For this also is an effect of his infinite wisdom and care of the church, designing to enlighten our minds with the knowledge of God, he prepared apt instruments for that end. That, therefore, which we shall declare on this head of our discourse is, That *the Holy Spirit of God has prepared and disposed of the Scripture so as it might be a most sufficient and absolutely perfect way and means of communicating unto our minds that saving knowledge of God and his will which is needful that we may live unto him, and come unto the enjoyment of him in his glory.* And here sundry things must be observed.

THE GENRE OF SCRIPTURE

First, the Holy Spirit has not in the Scripture reduced and disposed its doctrines or supernatural truths into any system, order, or method. Into such a method are the principal of them disposed in our catechisms and systems of divinity, creeds, and confessions of faith. For whereas the doctrinal truths of the Scripture have a mutual respect unto and dependence on one another, they may be disposed into such an order, to help the understandings and the memories of men. There is, indeed, in some of the epistles of Paul, especially that unto the Romans, a methodical disposition of the most important doctrines of the gospel, and from there are the best methods of our teaching borrowed. But in the whole Scripture there is no such thing aimed at. It is not distributed into common places,[1] nor are all things concerning the same truth methodically disposed under the same head, but its contexture[2] and frame are quite of another nature. From this consideration, some think they have an advantage to charge the Scripture with obscurity, and do thereon maintain that it was never intended to be such a revelation of doctrines as should be the rule of our faith. Had it been so, the truths to be believed would have been proposed in some order unto us, as a creed or confession of faith, that we might at once have had a view of them and been acquainted with them. But whereas they are now left to be gathered out of a collection of histories, prophecies, prayers, songs, letters or epistles, such as the Bible is composed of, they are difficult to be found, hard to be understood, and never perfectly to be learned. And, doubtless, the way fancied would have been excellent had God designed to effect in us only an artificial or methodical faith and obedience. But if we have a due regard unto the use of the Scripture and the ends of God therein, there is no weights in this objection. For

1. It is evident that the whole of it consists in the advancement of men's own apprehensions and imaginations against the will and wisdom of God. It is a sufficient reason to prove this the absolutely best way for the disposal of divine revelations, because God has made use of this and no other. One, indeed, is reported to have said that had he been "present at the creation of the universe, he would have disposed some things into a better order than what they are in."[3] For vain man would be wise, though he be born like the wild ass's colt. And no wiser or better are the thoughts that the revelations of supernatural truths might have been otherwise disposed of, with respect unto the end of God, than as they are in the Scripture. God puts not such value upon men's accurate methods as they may imagine them to deserve. Nor are they so subservient unto his ends in the revelation of himself as they are apt to fancy; yea, ofttimes when, as they suppose, they have brought truths unto the strictest propriety of expression, they lose both their power and their glory. Hence is

---

1 "Common places" were systematic or topical organizations of doctrine.
2 I.e., the fact or manner of being woven or linked together to form a connected whole.
3 This is likely a reference to a proverbial or stereotypical claim.

the world filled with so many lifeless, sapless, graceless, artificial declarations of divine truth in the schoolmen and others. We may sooner squeeze water out of a pumice stone[4] than one drop of spiritual nourishment out of them.¶

But how many millions of souls have received divine light and consolation, suited unto their condition, in those occasional occurrences of truth which they meet with in the Scripture, which they would never have obtained in those wise, artificial disposals of them which some men would fancy. Truths have their power and efficacy upon our minds, not only from themselves, but from their posture in the Scripture. There are they placed in such aspects toward, in such conjunctions one with another, as that their influences on our minds do greatly depend thereon. He is no wise man, nor exercised in those things, who would part with any one truth out of its proper place where the Holy Spirit has disposed and fixed it. The psalmist says of God's testimonies, they are אנשי עצתי[5], "the men of my counsel" (Ps. 119:24). And no man will make choice of a counsellor, all whose wisdom consists in sayings and rules cast into a certain order and method. He alone is a good counsellor who, out of the largeness and wisdom of his own heart and mind, can give advice according to all present occasions and circumstances. Such counselors are the testimonies of God. Artificial methodizing of spiritual truths may make men ready in notions, cunning and subtle in disputations; but it is the Scripture itself that is able to "make us wise unto salvation."[6]

2. In the writing and composing of the Holy Scripture, the Spirit of God had respect unto the various states and conditions of the church. It was not given for the use of one age or season only, but for all generations, for a guide in faith and obedience from the beginning of the world to the end of it. And the state of the church was not always to be the same, neither in light, knowledge, nor worship. God had so disposed of things in the eternal counsel of his will that it should be carried on by various degrees of divine revelation unto its perfect estate. Hereunto is the revelation of his mind in the Scripture subservient and suited (Heb. 1:1). If all divine truths had from the first been stated and fixed in a system of doctrines, the state of the church must have been always the same, which was contrary unto the whole design of divine wisdom in those things.

3. Such a systematic proposal of doctrines, truths, or articles of faith, as some require, would not have answered the great ends of the Scripture itself.

4   I.e., volcanic glass full of cavities and very low in density that is used especially in powder form for smoothing and polishing; idiomatic for "impossible."

5   *BHS* reads, עֵצָתִי.

6   2 Tim. 3:15.

All that can be supposed of benefit thereby is only that it would lead us more easily into a methodical comprehension of the truths so proposed. But this we may attain and not be rendered one jot more like unto God thereby. The principal end of the Scripture is of another nature. It is to beget in the minds of men faith, fear, obedience, and reverence of God, to make them holy and righteous; and those such as have in themselves various weaknesses, temptations, and inclinations unto the contrary, which must be obviated and subdued. Unto this end every truth is disposed of in the Scripture as it ought to be. If any expect that the Scripture should be written with respect unto opinions, notions, and speculations, to render men skillful and cunning in them, able to talk and dispute about all things and nothing, they are mistaken. It is given us to make us humble, holy, wise in spiritual things, to direct us in our duties, to relieve us against temptations, to comfort us under troubles, to make us to love God and to live unto him, in all that variety of circumstances, occasions, temptations, trials, duties, which in this world we are called unto. Unto this end there is a more glorious power and efficacy in one epistle, one psalm, one chapter, than in all the writings of men, though they have their use also. He that has not experience hereof is a stranger unto the power of God in the Scripture. Sometimes the design and scope of the place, sometimes the circumstances related unto, mostly that spirit of wisdom and holiness which evidences itself in the whole, do effectually influence our minds. Yea, sometimes an occasional passage in a story, a word or expression, shall contribute more to excite faith and love in our souls than a volume of learned disputations. It does not argue, syllogize, or allure the mind; but enlightens, persuades, constrains the soul unto faith and obedience. This it is prepared for and suited unto.

4. The disposition of divine revelations in the Scripture is also subservient unto other ends of the wisdom of God toward the church. Some of them may be named.

(1) To render useful and necessary the great ordinance of the ministry. God has not designed to instruct and save his church by any one outward ordinance only. The ways and means of doing good unto us, so as that all may issue in his own eternal glory, are known unto infinite wisdom only. The institution of the whole series and complex of divine ordinances is not otherwise to be accounted for but by a regard and submission thereunto. Who can deny but that God might both have instructed, sanctified, and saved us, without the use of some or all of those institutions which he has obliged us unto? His infinitely wise will is the only reason of these things. And he will have every one of his appointments, on which he has put his name, to be honored. Such is the ministry. A means

this is not coordinate with the Scripture, but subservient unto it. And the great end of it is, that those who are called thereunto, and are furnished with gifts for the discharge of it, might diligently search the Scripture, and teach others the mind of God revealed therein. It was, I say, the will of God that the church should ordinarily be always under the conduct of such a ministry. And his will it is that those who are called thereunto should be furnished with peculiar spiritual gifts, for the finding out and declaration of the truths that are treasured up in the Scripture, unto all the ends of divine revelation (see Eph. 4:11–16; 2 Tim. 3:14–17). The Scripture, therefore, is such a revelation as does suppose and make necessary this ordinance of the ministry, wherein and whereby God will also be glorified. And it were well if the nature and duties of this office were better understood than they seem to be. God has accommodated the revelation of himself in the Scripture with respect unto them. And those by whom the due discharge of this office is despised or neglected do sin greatly against the authority, wisdom, and love of God. And those do no less by whom it is assumed but not rightly understood or not duly improved.

But it may be said, "Why did not the Holy Ghost dispose of all things so plainly in the Scripture that every individual person might have attained the knowledge of them without the use of this ministry?" I answer, it is a proud and foolish thing to inquire for any reasons of the ways and works of God antecedent unto his own will. "He worketh all things according to the counsel of his will" (Eph. 1:11), and therein are we to acquiesce. Yet we may see the wisdom of what he has done. As herein [1] he would glorify his own power, in working great effects by vile, weak means (1 Cor. 3:7; 2 Cor. 4:7). [2] He did it to magnify his Son Jesus Christ in the communication of spiritual gifts (Acts 2:33; Eph. 4:8, 11–12). [3] To show that in and by the work of his grace he designed not to destroy or contradict the faculties of our nature, which at first he created; he would work on them, and work a change in them, by means suited unto their constitution and nature, which is done in the ministry of the word (2 Cor. 5:18–20).

(2) The disposition of the Scripture respects the duty of all believers in the exercise of their faith and obedience. They know that all their light and direction, all their springs of spiritual strength and consolation, are treasured up in the Scripture. But, in the unspeakable variety of their occasions, they know not where every particular provision for these ends is stored. Hence it is their duty to meditate upon the word night and day, to search for wisdom as silver, and to dig for it as for hidden treasure, that they may "understand the fear of the Lord, and find the knowledge of God" (Prov. 2:3–5). And this being a duty whereunto the exercise of all graces is required, they are all improved

thereby. The soul which is hereby engaged unto constant converse with God will thrive more in that which is the proper end of the Scripture, namely, the fear of the Lord, than it could do under any other kind of teaching.

(3) A continual search into the whole Scripture, without a neglect of any part of it, is hereby rendered necessary. And hereby are our souls prepared on all occasions, and influenced in the whole course of our obedience; for the whole and every part of the word is blessed unto our good, according to the prayer of our Savior, "Sanctify them through thy truth: thy Word is truth" (John 17:17). There is power put forth in and by every part and parcel of it unto our sanctification. And there is such a distribution of useful truths through the whole, that everywhere we may meet with what is prepared for us and suited unto our condition. It is to me no small argument of the divine origin of the Scripture, and of the presence of God in it, that there is no thought of our hearts with respect unto the proper end of the Scripture, that is, our living unto God so as to come unto the enjoyment of him, but that we shall find, at one time or other, a due adjustment of it therein, in one place or other.

There can no frame befall the hearts of believers as unto spiritual things, whether it be as unto their thriving or decay, but there is a disposition of spiritual provision for it; and ofttimes we shall find it then opening itself when we least look for it. Powerful instructions, as unto our practice, do often arise out of circumstances, occasional words and expressions, all arguing an infinite wisdom in their provision, whereunto every future occurrence was in open view from eternity, and a present divine efficacy in the word's application of itself unto our souls. How often in the reading of it do we meet with, and are as it were surprised with, gracious words, that enlighten, quicken, comfort, endear, and engage our souls? How often do we find sin wounded, grace encouraged, faith excited, love inflamed, and this in that endless variety of inward frames and outward occasions which we are liable unto? I shall say with confidence, that he never was acquainted with the excellency of the Scripture, with its power and efficacy, in any holy experience, who is capable of fancying that divine revelations might have been disposed unto more advantage with respect unto our living unto God. And these things are sufficient for the removal of the objection before mentioned.

THE CLARITY OF SCRIPTURE

Secondly, the Holy Spirit has so disposed of the Scripture *that the mind of God in all things concerning our faith and obedience, in the knowledge whereof our illumination does consist, is clearly revealed therein.* There needs no other argument to prove anything not to belong unto our religion than that it is not revealed or appointed in the Scripture; no other to prove any truth not to be indispensably necessary unto our faith or obedience than that it is not clearly revealed in the Scripture. But in this assertion we must take along with us these two suppositions.

1. That we look on the Scripture and receive it not as the word of men, but as it is indeed, the word of the living God. If we look for that perspicuity and clearness in the expression of divine revelation which men endeavor to give unto the declaration of their minds in things natural, by artificial methods and order, by the application of words and terms invented and disposed of on purpose to accommodate what is spoken unto the common notions and reasonings of men, we may be mistaken. Nor would it have become divine wisdom and authority to have made use of such methods, ways, or arts. There is that plainness and perspicuity in it which become the holy, wise God to make use of, whose words are to be received with reverence, with submission of mind and conscience unto his authority, and fervent prayer that we may understand his mind and do his will. Thus, all things are made plain unto the meanest capacity; yet not so, but that if the most wise and learned do not see the characters of infinite divine wisdom on things that seem most obvious and most exposed unto vulgar apprehension, they have no true wisdom in them. In those very fords and appearing shallows of this river of God where the lamb may wade, the elephant may swim. Everything in the Scripture is so plain as that the meanest believer may understand all that belongs unto his duty or is necessary unto his happiness; yet is nothing so plain but that the wisest of them all have reason to adore the depths and stores of divine wisdom in it. All apprehensions of the obscurity of the Scripture arise from one of these two causes.

(1) That the minds of men are prepossessed with opinions, dogmas, principles, and practices in religion, received by tradition from their fathers; or have vehement and corrupt inclinations unto such ways, practices, and opinions, as suit their carnal reason and interest. It is no wonder if such persons conceive the Scripture dark and obscure. For they can neither find that in it which they most desire, nor can understand what is revealed in it, because opposite unto their prejudices, affections, and interests. The design of the Scripture is to destroy that frame of mind in them which they would have established. And no man is to look for light in the Scripture to give countenance unto his own darkness.

(2) It will appear obscure unto all men who come to the reading and study of it in the mere strength of their own natural abilities. And, it may be, it is

on this account that some have esteemed St. Paul one of the obscurest writers that ever they read. Wherefore, as a book written in Greek or Hebrew must be obscure unto them who have no skill in these languages, so will the Scripture be unto all who are unfurnished with those spiritual preparations which are required unto the right understanding of it. For,

2. It is supposed, when we assert the clearness and perspicuity of the Scripture, that there is unto the understanding of it use made of that aid and assistance of the Spirit of God concerning which we do discourse. Without this the clearest revelations of divine supernatural things will appear as wrapped up in darkness and obscurity; not for want of light in them, but for want of light in us. Wherefore, by asserting the necessity of supernatural illumination for the right understanding of divine revelation, we no way impeach the perspicuity of the Scripture. All things wherein our faith and obedience are concerned are clearly declared therein; howbeit when all is done, "the natural man receiveth not the things of the Spirit of God, neither can he know them," until the eyes of his understanding be enlightened.[7]

DIFFICULT PASSAGES

Thirdly, the Holy Spirit has so disposed the Scripture that, notwithstanding that perspicuity which is in the whole with respect unto its proper end, yet are there in sundry parts or passages of it: τινὰ δυσνόητα, some things "hard to be understood"; and τινὰ δυσερμήνευτα, some things "hard to be uttered or interpreted." The former are the things themselves, which are so in their own nature; the latter are so from the manner of their declaration.

1. There are in the Scripture τινὰ δυσνόητα,[8] things deep, wonderful, mysterious, such as in their own nature do absolutely exceed the whole compass of our understanding or reason, as unto a full and perfect comprehension of them. Nor ought it to be strange unto any that sundry divine revelations should be of things in their own nature incomprehensible. For as unto us, many earthly and natural things are so, as David affirms concerning the forming of our natures in the womb (Ps. 139:5–6, 14–16). And our Savior assures us that heavenly things are much more above our comprehension than earthly (John 3:12). Such as these are, the Trinity, or the subsistence of one single divine nature in three persons; the incarnation of Christ, or the assumption of our human nature into personal union and subsistence

---

7   1 Cor. 2:14.
8   This may be an allusion to 2 Pet. 3:16.

with the Son of God; the eternal decrees of God, their nature, order, causes, and effects; the resurrection of the dead; the manner of the operations of the Holy Spirit in forming the new creature in us, and sundry others. Our rational faculties in their utmost improvement in this world, and under the highest advantage they are capable of by spiritual light and grace, are not able, with all their searchings, to find out the Almighty unto perfection in these things. And in all disputes about the light of glory, as whether we shall be able thereby to behold the essence of God, to discern the depths of the mystery of the incarnation, and the like, men do but darken counsel by words without knowledge, and talk of what they neither do nor can understand. But yet the wisdom of the Holy Spirit has in these two ways provided that we shall not suffer from our own weakness.

(1) In that whatever is necessary for us to believe concerning these things is plainly and clearly revealed in the Scripture, and that revelation declared in such propositions and expressions as are obvious unto our understandings. And he who thinks we can believe nothing as unto its truth but what we can comprehend as unto its nature overthrows all faith and reason also. And propositions may be clear unto us in their sense, when their subject matter is incomprehensible. For instance, consider the incarnation of the Son of God, and the hypostatic union therein of the divine and human natures; it is a thing above our reason and comprehension. But in the Scripture it is plainly asserted and declared that "the Word, which is God, and was with God," was "made flesh"; that "God was manifest in the flesh"; that "the Son of God was made of a woman, made under the law"; that "he took on him the seed of Abraham"; that "he came of the Jews according to the flesh," who "is over all, God blessed forever"; and that so "God redeemed his church with his own blood."[9] Thus, plainly and perspicuously is this great matter, as it is the object of our faith, as it is proposed unto us to be believed, declared and expressed unto us. If anyone shall now say that he will not believe that to be the sense of these expressions which the words do plainly and undeniably manifest so to be, and are withal incapable of any other sense or construction, because he cannot understand or comprehend the thing itself which is signified thereby, it is plainly to say that he will believe nothing on the authority and veracity of God revealing it, but what he can comprehend by his own reason that he will believe; which is to overthrow all faith divine.¶

The reason of our believing, if we believe at all, is God's revelation of the truth, and not our understanding of the nature of the things revealed. Thereinto

9 John 1:1; 1:14; 1 Tim. 3:16; Gal. 4:4; Heb. 2:16; Rom. 9:5; Acts 20:28.

is our faith resolved, when our reason reaches not unto the nature and existence of the things themselves. And the work of the Spirit it is to bring into captivity unto the obedience of the faith every thought that might arise from our ignorance, or the impotency of our minds to comprehend the things to be believed. And that new religion of Socinianism, which pretends to reduce all to reason, is wholly built upon the most irrational principle that ever befell the minds of men. It is this alone: "What we cannot comprehend in things divine and infinite, as unto their own nature, that we are not to believe in their revelation." On this ground alone do the men of that persuasion reject the doctrine of the Trinity, of the incarnation of the Son of God, of the resurrection of the dead, and the like mysteries of faith. Whatever testimony the Scripture gives unto them, because their reason cannot comprehend them, they profess they will not believe them.[10] A principle wild and irrational, and which leads unto atheism, seeing the being of God itself is absolutely incomprehensible.

(2) That degree of knowledge which we can attain in and about these things is every way sufficient with respect unto the end of the revelation itself. If they were so proposed unto us, as that if we could not fully comprehend them, we should have no benefit or advantage by them, the revelation itself would be lost, and the end of God frustrated therein. But this could not become divine wisdom and goodness, to make such propositions unto us. For this defect arises not from any blamable depravation of our nature as corrupted, but from the very essence and being of it as created; for being finite and limited, it cannot perfectly comprehend things infinite. But whatever believers are able to attain unto, in that variety of the degrees of knowledge, which in their several circumstances they do attain, is sufficient unto the end whereunto it is designed; that is, sufficient to ingenerate,[11] cherish, increase, and preserve faith and love, and reverence with holy obedience in them, in such a way and manner as will assuredly bring them unto the end of all supernatural revelation in the enjoyment of God.

2. There are in the Scripture τινὰ δυσερμήνευτα, some things that are "hard to be interpreted"; not from the nature of the things revealed, but from the manner of their revelation. Such are many allegories, parables, mystical stories, allusions, unfulfilled prophecies and predictions, references unto the then present customs, persons, and places, computation of times, genealogies, the signification of some single words seldom or but once used in the Scripture, the names of divers birds and beasts unknown to us. Such things

10 See the introduction on Socinianism.
11 I.e., to generate or produce.

have a difficulty in them from the manner of their declaration. And it is hard to find out, and it may be in some instances impossible, unto any determinate certainty, the proper, genuine sense of them in the places where they occur. But herein also we have a relief provided, in the wisdom of the Holy Spirit in giving the whole Scripture for our instruction, against any disadvantage unto our faith or obedience. For,

(1) Whatever is so delivered in any place, if it be of importance for us to know and believe, as unto the ends of divine revelation, it is in some other place or places unveiled and plainly declared, so that we may say of it as the disciples said unto our Savior, "Lo, now he speaketh plainly, and not in parables."[12] There can be no instance given of any obscure place or passage in the Scripture, concerning which a man may rationally suppose or conjecture that there is any doctrinal truth requiring our obedience contained in it, which is not elsewhere explained. And there may be several reasons why the Holy Spirit chose to express his mind at any time in such ways as had so much obscurity attending of them.¶

[1] As for types, allegories, mystical stories, and obscure predictions, he made use of them under the Old Testament on purpose to draw a veil over the things signified in them, or the truths taught by them. For the church was not yet to be acquainted with the clear knowledge of the things concerning Jesus Christ and his mediation. They had not so much as a perfect image of the things themselves, but only an obscure shadow or representation of good things to come (Heb. 10:1). To have given unto them a full and clear revelation of all divine truths would have cast the whole design of God for the various states of the church, and the accomplishment of the great work of his grace and love, into disorder. It was not hard, then, for the church to be taught of old in types and allegories, but it was much grace and mercy that through them the light of the Sun of Righteousness so far beamed on them as enabled them comfortably to wait "until the day did break and the shadows flee away" (as Song 4:6). The fullness and glory of the revelation of grace and truth was reserved for Jesus Christ. God did them no wrong, but reserved "better things for us" (Heb. 11:40).

[2] Whatever seems yet to be continued under any obscurity of revelation, it is so continued for the exercise of our faith, diligence, humility, and dependence on God in our inquiries into them. And suppose we do not always attain precisely unto the proper and peculiar intendment of the Holy Spirit in them, as we can never search out his mind unto perfection, yet are there so many and great advantages to be obtained by the due exercise of those graces

12 John 16:29.

in the study of the word, that we can be no losers by any difficulties we can meet with. The rule in this case is that we *affix no sense unto any obscure or difficult passage of Scripture but what is materially true and consonant unto other express and plain testimonies.* For men to raise peculiar senses from such places, not confirmed elsewhere, is a dangerous curiosity.

[3] As to sundry prophecies of future revolutions in the church and the world, like those in the Revelation, there was an indispensable necessity of giving them out in that obscurity of allegorical expressions and representations wherein we find them. For I could easily manifest that as the clear and determinate declaration of future events in plain historical expressions is contrary to the nature of prophecy, so in this case it would have been a means of bringing confusion on the works of God in the world, and of turning all men out of the way of their obedience. Their present revelation is sufficient to guide the faith and regulate the obedience of the church, so far as they are concerned in them.

[4] Some things are in the Scripture disposed on purpose that evil, perverse, and proud men may stumble and fall at them, or be further hardened in their unbelief and obstinacy. So our Lord Jesus Christ affirms that he spoke unto the stubborn Jews in parables that they might not understand. And whereas there must be heresies, that they which "are approved may be made manifest" (1 Cor. 11:19), and some are "of old ordained to this condemnation" (Jude 4), some things are so declared that from them proud, perverse, and wrangling spirits may take occasion to wrest them unto their own destruction. The truths of Christ as well as his person are appointed to be a stone of stumbling and a rock of offense, yea, a gin and a snare unto many. But this, humble, teachable believers are not concerned in.

(2) The Holy Spirit has given us a relief in this matter, by supplying us with a rule of the interpretation of Scripture, which while we sincerely attend unto we are in no danger of sinfully corrupting the word of God, although we should not arrive unto its proper meaning in every particular place; and this rule is, the analogy or proportion of faith. "Let him that prophesieth," says the apostle, that is, expounds the Scripture in the church, "do it according to the proportion of faith" (Rom. 12:6). And this analogy or proportion of faith is what is taught plainly and uniformly in the whole Scripture as the rule of our faith and obedience. When men will engage their inquiries into parts of the Scripture mystical, allegorical, or prophetical, aiming to find out, it may be, things new and curious, without a constant regard unto this analogy of faith,[13]

---

13 The "analogy of faith" is a general sense of the meaning of Scripture, constructed from the clear or unambiguous passages, used as the basis for interpreting difficult texts. For more on the analogy of faith, see Andrew S. Ballitch, *The Gloss and the Text: William Perkins on Interpreting Scripture*

it is no wonder if they wander out of the way and err concerning the truth, as many have done on that occasion. And I cannot but declare my detestation of those bold and curious conjectures which, without any regard unto the rule of prophecy, many have indulged themselves in on obscure passages in the Scripture. But now suppose a man brings no preconceived sense or opinion of his own unto such places, seeking countenance thereunto from them, which is the bane of all interpretation of the Scripture; suppose him to come in some measure prepared with the spiritual qualifications before mentioned, and in all his inquiries to have a constant due regard unto the analogy of faith, so as not to admit of any sense which interferes with what is elsewhere plainly declared—such a person shall not miss of the mind of the Holy Spirit, or if he does, shall be assuredly preserved from any hurtful danger in his mistakes. For there is that mutual relation one to another, yea, that mutual inbeing[14] of all divine truths, in their proposal and revelation in the Scripture, as that every one of them is after a sort in every place, though not properly and peculiarly, yet by consequence and coherence. Wherefore, although a man should miss of the first proper sense of any obscure place of Scripture, which, with all our diligence, we ought to aim at, yet, while he receives none but what contains a truth agreeable unto what is revealed in other places, the error of his mind neither endangers his own faith or obedience nor those of any others.

(3) For those things which are peculiarly difficult, as genealogies, chronological computations of time, and the like, which are accidental unto the design of the Scripture, those who are able so to do, unto their own edification or that of others, may exercise themselves therein, but by all others the consideration of them in particular may be safely omitted.

And these are the heads of the work of the Holy Spirit on our minds and on the Scriptures, considered distinctly and apart, with reference unto the right understanding of the mind of God in them. By the former sort, our minds are prepared to understand the Scripture; and by the latter, Scripture is prepared and suited unto our understandings. There yet remains the consideration of what he does, or what help he affords unto us, in the actual application of our minds unto the understanding and interpretation of the word. And this respects the means which we are to make use of unto that end and purpose; and these also shall be briefly declared.

---

with *Scripture*, Studies in Historical and Systematic Theology (Bellingham, WA: Lexham, 2020), 66–68; Richard A. Muller, *Dictionary of Latin and Greek Theological Terms: Drawn Principally from Protestant Scholastic Theology* (Grand Rapids, MI: Baker Academic, 1985), 33.

14 I.e., essence; basic nature.

7

Biblical Interpretation

*Means to Be Used for the Right Understanding of the Mind of God
in the Scripture. Those Which Are Prescribed in a Way of Duty.*

THE MEANS TO BE USED for the right understanding and interpretation
of the Scripture are of two sorts. First, that which is general and absolutely
necessary. Second, such as consist in the due improvement thereof.

GENERAL MEANS: READING

The first is *diligent reading of the Scripture, with a sedate,*[1] *rational consideration of what we read.* Nothing is more frequently commended unto us;
and, not to insist on particular testimonies, the whole 119th Psalm is spent
in the declaration of this duty, and the benefits which are attained thereby.
Herein consists the first natural exercise of our minds in order unto the
understanding of it. So, the eunuch read and pondered on the prophecy of
Isaiah, though of himself he could not attain the understanding of what he
read (Acts 8:30–31). Either reading, or that which is equivalent thereunto,
is that whereby we do, and without which it is impossible we should, apply
our minds to know what is contained in the Scriptures. And this is that
which all other means are designed to render useful. Now, by this reading
I understand that which is staid, sedate, considerative, with respect unto
the end aimed at; reading attended with a due consideration of the things
read, inquiry into them, meditation on them, with a regard unto the design

1   I.e., calm.

and scope of the place, with all other advantages for the due investigation of the truth.

Frequent reading of the word more generally and cursorily, whereunto all Christians ought to be trained from their youth (2 Tim. 3:15), and which all closets and families should be acquainted with (Deut. 6:6–9), is of great use and advantage; and I shall, therefore, name some particular benefits which may be received thereby.

1. Hereby the minds of men are brought into a general acquaintance with the nature and design of the book of God, which some, to their present shame and future ruin, are prodigiously ignorant of.

2. They who are exercised herein come to know distinctly what things are treated of in the particular books and passages of it; while others who live in a neglect of this duty scarce know what books are historical, what prophetical, or what doctrinal, in the whole Bible.

3. Hereby they exercise themselves unto thoughts of heavenly things and a holy converse with God; if they bring along with them, as they ought, hearts humble and sensible of his authority in the word.

4. Their minds are insensibly furnished with due conceptions about God, spiritual things, themselves, and their conditions; and their memories with expressions proper and meet to be used about them in prayer or other ways.

5. God oftentimes takes occasion herein to influence their souls with the efficacy of divine truth in particular, in the way of exhortation, reproof, instruction, or consolation, whereof all who attend diligently unto this duty have experience.

6. They come, by reason of use, to have their senses exercised to discern good and evil, so that if any noxious or corrupt sense of any place of the Scripture be suggested unto them, they have in readiness wherewith to oppose it from other places from whence they are instructed in the truth.

And many other advantages there are which men may reap from the constant reading of the Scripture, which I therefore reckon as a general means of coming to the knowledge of the mind of God therein. But this is not that which at present I especially intend. Wherefore

By this reading of the Scripture I mean the studying of it, in the use of means, to come to a due understanding of it in particular places. For it is about the means of the solemn interpretation of the Scripture that we now inquire. Hereunto, I say, the general study of the whole, and in particular the places to be interpreted, is required. It may seem altogether needless and impertinent to give this direction for the understanding of the mind of God in the Scripture, namely, that we should read and study it to that end. For who can imagine how it should be done otherwise? But I wish the practice of many, it may be, of the most, did not render this direction necessary. For in their design to come to the knowledge of spiritual things, the direct immediate study of the Scripture is that which they least of all apply themselves unto. Other writings they will read and study with diligence, but their reading of the Scripture is for the most part superficial, without that intension of mind and spirit, that use and application of means, which are necessary unto the understanding of it, as the event does manifest. It is the immediate study of the Scripture that I intend. And hereunto I do refer, first, a due consideration of the analogy of faith always to be retained. Second, due examination of the design and scope of the place. Three, a diligent observation of antecedents and consequents,[2] with all those general rules which are usually given as directions in the interpretation of the Scripture. This, therefore, in the diligent exercise of our minds and reasons, is the first general outward means of knowing the mind of God in the Scripture and the interpretation thereof.

PARTICULAR MEANS

The means designed for the improvement hereof, or our profitable use of it, are of three sorts: spiritual, disciplinary, and ecclesiastic. Some instances on each head will further clear what I intend.

1. The first thing required as a spiritual means is prayer. I intend fervent and earnest prayer for the assistance of the Spirit of God revealing the mind of God, as in the whole Scripture, so in particular books and passages of it. I have proved before that this is both enjoined and commanded unto us by the practice of the prophets and apostles.[3] And this also, by the way, invincibly proves that the due investigation of the mind of God in the Scripture is a work above the utmost improvement of natural reason, with all outward advantages whatsoever. For were we sufficient of ourselves, without immediate divine aid and assistance, for this work, why do we pray for them? With which argument the ancient church perpetually urged the Pelagians as to the necessity of saving grace. And it may be justly supposed that no man who professes himself a Christian can be so forsaken of all sobriety as once to question whether this be the duty of everyone who has

2 "Antecedents and consequents" are those things that come logically before and those things that logically follow any individual interpretation.

3 Owen seems to be referring either to his Πνευματολογια, or, A Discourse concerning the Holy Spirit or to The Reason of Faith, the first treatise in this volume.

either desire or design to attain any real knowledge of the will of God in the Scripture. But the practical neglect of this duty is the true reason why so many that are skillful enough in the disciplinary means of knowledge are yet such strangers to the true knowledge of the mind of God. And this prayer is of two sorts.

(1) That which respects the teaching of the Spirit in general, whereby we labor in our prayers that he would enlighten our minds and lead us into the knowledge of the truth, according to the work before described. The importance of this grace unto our faith and obedience, the multiplied promises of God concerning it, our necessity of it from our natural weakness, ignorance, and darkness, should render it a principal part of our daily supplications. Especially is this incumbent on them who are called in a special manner to search the Scriptures and to declare the mind of God in them unto others. And great are the advantages which a conscientious discharge of this duty, with a due reverence of God, brings along with it. Prejudices, preconceived opinions, engagements by secular advantages, false confidences, authority of men, influences from parties and societies, will be all laid level before it, at least be gradually exterminated out of the minds of men thereby.¶

And how much the casting out of all this old leaven tends to prepare the mind for, and to give it a due understanding of, divine revelations, has been proved before.[4] I no way doubt but that the rise and continuance of all those enormous errors which so infest Christian religion, and which many seek so sedulously[5] to confirm from the Scripture itself, are in a great measure to be ascribed unto the corrupt affections, with the power of tradition and influences of secular advantages, which cannot firm their station in the minds of them who are constant, sincere suppliants at the throne of grace to be taught of God what is his mind and will in his word, for it includes a prevailing resolution sincerely to receive what we are so instructed in, whatever effects it may have upon the inward or outward man. And this is the only way to preserve our souls under the influences of divine teachings and the irradiation of the Holy Spirit, without which we can neither learn nor know anything as we ought. I suppose, therefore, this may be fixed on as a common principle of Christianity, namely, that constant and fervent prayer for the divine assistance of the Holy Spirit is such an indispensable means for the attaining the knowledge of the mind of God in the Scripture as that without it all others will not be available.

---

4 Owen is probably referring to *The Reason of Faith*.
5 I.e., dedicatedly or diligently.

Nor do I believe that anyone who does and can thus pray as he ought, in a conscientious study of the word, shall ever be left unto the final prevalency of any pernicious error or the ignorance of any fundamental truth. None utterly miscarry in the seeking after the mind of God but those who are perverted by their own corrupt minds. Whatever appearance there be of sincerity and diligence in seeking after truth, if men miscarry therein, it is far more safe to judge that they do so either through the neglect of this duty or indulgence unto some corruption of their hearts and minds, than that God is wanting to reveal himself unto those that diligently seek him. And there are unfailing grounds of this assurance. For [1] faith exercised in this duty will work out all that filthiness and superfluity of naughtiness which would hinder us so to receive with meekness the ingrafted word as that it should save our souls. [2] It will work in the mind those gracious qualifications of humility and meekness, whereunto the teachings of God are promised in a special manner, as we have showed. And [3] our Savior has assured us that his heavenly Father will "give the Holy Spirit unto them that ask him" (Luke 11:13). Neither is any supplication for the Holy Spirit more acceptable unto God than that which designs the knowledge of his mind and will that we may do them. [4] All those graces which render the mind teachable and meet unto the reception of heavenly truths are kept up unto a due exercise therein. If we deceive not ourselves in these things, we cannot be deceived. For in the discharge of this duty those things are learned in their power whereof we have the notion only in other means of instruction. And hereby whatever we learn is so fixed upon our minds, possesses them with such power, transforming them into the likeness of it, as that they are prepared for the communication of further light, and increases in the degrees of knowledge.

Nor can it be granted, on the other hand, that any sacred truth is learned in a due manner, whatever diligence be used in its acquisition, or that we can know the mind of God in the Scripture in anything as we ought, when the management of all other means which we make use of unto that end is not committed unto the hand of this duty. The apostle, desiring earnestly that those unto whom he wrote, and whom he instructed in the mysteries of the gospel, might have a due spiritual understanding of the mind of God as revealed and taught in them, prays with all fervency of mind that they might have "a communication of the Spirit of wisdom and revelation from above" to enable them thereunto (Eph. 1:16–19; 3:14–19). For without this he knew it could not be attained. That which he did for them we are obliged to do for ourselves. And where this is neglected, especially considering that the supplies of the Spirit unto this purpose are confined unto them that ask him, there is no ground of expectation that anyone should ever learn the saving knowledge of the mind of God in a due manner.

I shall, therefore, fix this assertion as a sacred truth: *Whoever, in the diligent and immediate study of the Scripture to know the mind of God therein so as to do it, does abide in fervent supplications, in and by Jesus Christ, for supplies of the Spirit of grace, to lead him into all truth, to reveal and make known unto him the truth as it is in Jesus, to give him an understanding of the Scriptures and the will of God therein, he shall be preserved from pernicious errors, and attain that degree in knowledge as shall be sufficient unto the guidance and preservation of the life of God in the whole of his faith and obedience.* And more security of truth there is herein than in men's giving themselves up unto any other conduct in this world whatever. The goodness of God, his faithfulness in being the rewarder of them that diligently seek him, the command of this duty unto this end, the promises annexed unto it, with the whole nature of religion, do give us the highest security herein. And although these duties cannot but be accompanied with a conscientious care and fear of errors and mistakes, yet the persons that are found in them have no ground of troublesome thoughts or fearful suspicions that they shall be deceived or fail in the end they aim at.

(2) Prayer respects particular occasions, or special places of Scripture, whose exposition or interpretation we inquire after. This is the great duty of a faithful interpreter, that which in, with, and after, the use of all means, he betakes himself unto. An experience of divine guidance and assistance herein is that which unto some is invaluable, however by others it be despised. But shall we think it strange for a Christian, when, it may be after the use of all other means, he finds himself at a loss about the true meaning and intention of the Holy Spirit in any place or text of Scripture, to betake himself in a more than ordinary manner unto God by prayer, that he would by his Spirit enlighten, guide, teach, and so reveal the truth unto him? Or should we think it strange that God should hear such prayers, and instruct such persons in the secrets of his covenant? God forbid there should be such atheistical thoughts in the minds of any who would be esteemed Christians. Yea, I must say, that for a man to undertake the interpretation of any part or portion of Scripture in a solemn manner, without invocation of God to be taught and instructed by his Spirit, is a high provocation of him. Nor shall I expect the discovery of truth from anyone who so proudly and ignorantly engages in a work so much above his ability to manage. I speak this of solemn and stated interpretations; for otherwise a scribe ready furnished for the kingdom of God may, as he has occasion, from the spiritual light and understanding wherewith he is

endued, and the stores he has already received, declare the mind of God unto the edification of others. But this is the first means to render our studying of the Scripture useful and effectual unto the end aimed at.

This, as was said, is the sheet anchor[6] of a faithful expositor of the Scripture, which he takes himself unto in all difficulties. Nor can he without it be led into a comfortable satisfaction that he has attained the mind of the Holy Ghost in any divine revelation. When all other helps fail, as he shall in most places find them to do, if he is really intent on the disquisition of truth, this will yield him his best relief. And so long as this is attended unto, we need not fear further useful interpretations of the Scripture, or the several parts of it, than as yet have been attained unto by the endeavors of others. For the stores of truth laid up in it are inexhaustible, and hereby will they be opened unto those that inquire into them with humility and diligence. The labors of those who have gone before us are of excellent use herein. But they are yet very far from having discovered the depths of this vein of wisdom. Nor will the best of our endeavors prescribe limits and bounds to them that shall come after us. And the reason why the generality of expositors go in the same track one after another, seldom passing beyond the beaten path of former endeavors, unless it be in some excursions of curiosity, is the want of giving up themselves unto the conduct of the Holy Spirit in the diligent performance of this duty.

2. Readiness to receive impressions from divine truths as revealed unto us, conforming our minds and hearts unto the doctrine made known, is another means unto the same end. This is the first end of all divine revelations, of all heavenly truths, namely, to beget the image and likeness of themselves in the minds of men (Rom. 6:17; 2 Cor. 3:18). And we miss our aim if this is not the first thing we intend in the study of the Scripture. It is not to learn the form of the doctrine of godliness, but to get the power of it implanted in our souls. And this is an eminent means of our making a progress in the knowledge of the truth. To seek after mere notions of truth, without an endeavor after an experience of its power in our hearts, is not the way to increase our understanding in spiritual things. He alone is in a posture to learn from God who sincerely gives up his mind, conscience, and affections to the power and rule of what is revealed unto him. Men may have in their study of the Scripture other ends also, as the profit and edification of others. But if this conforming of their own souls unto the power of the word be not fixed in the first place in their minds, they do not strive lawfully nor will be crowned. And if at any time, when we study the word, we have not this design expressly in our minds,

6 I.e., dependability; reliability.

yet if, upon the discovery of any truth, we endeavor not to have the likeness of it in our own hearts, we lose our principal advantage by it.

3. Practical obedience in the course of our walking before God is another means unto the same end. The gospel is the "truth which is according unto godliness" (Titus 1:1). And it will not long abide with any who follow not after godliness according unto its guidance and direction. Hence, we see so many lose that very understanding which they had of the doctrines of it, when once they begin to give up themselves to ungodly lives. The true notion of holy, evangelical truths will not live, at least not flourish, where they are divided from a holy conversation. As we learn all to practice, so we learn much by practice. There is no practical science which we can make any great improvement of without an assiduous practice of its theorems. Much less is wisdom, such as is the understanding of the mysteries of the Scripture, to be increased, unless a man be practically conversant about the things which it directs unto.

And hereby alone we can come unto the assurance that what we know and learn is indeed the truth. So our Savior tells us that "if any man do the will of God, he shall know of the doctrine whether it be of God" (John 7:17). While men learn the truth only in the notion of it, whatever conviction of its being so it is accompanied with, they will never attain stability in their minds concerning it, nor come to the full assurance of understanding, unless they continually exemplify it in their own obedience doing the will of God. This is that which will give them a satisfactory persuasion of it. And hereby will they be led continually into further degrees of knowledge. For the mind of man is capable of receiving continual supplies in the increase of light and knowledge while it is in this world, if so be they are improved unto their proper end in obedience unto God. But without this the mind will be quickly stuffed with notions, so that no streams can descend into it from the fountain of truth.

4. A constant design for growth and a progress in knowledge, out of love to the truth and experience of its excellency, is useful, yea, needful, unto the right understanding of the mind of God in the Scriptures. Some are quickly apt to think that they know enough, as much as is needful for them; some, that they know all that is to be known, or have a sufficient comprehension of all the counsels of God as revealed in the Scripture, or, as they rather judge, of the whole body of divinity, in all the parts of it, which they may have disposed into an exact method with great accuracy and skill. No great or useful discoveries of the mind of God shall I expect from such persons. Another frame of heart and spirit is required in them who design to be instructed in the mind of God, or to learn it in the study of the Scripture. Such persons

look upon it as a treasury of divine truths, absolutely unfathomable by any created understandings. The truths which they do receive from there, and comprehend according to their measure therein, they judge amiable, excellent, and desirable above all earthly things. For they find the fruit, benefit, and advantage of them, in strengthening the life of God in them, conforming their souls unto him, communicating of his light, love, grace, and power unto them.

This makes them with purpose of heart continually to press, in the use of all means, to increase in this wisdom, to grow in the knowledge of God and our Lord and Savior Jesus Christ. They are pressing on continually unto that measure of perfection which in this life is attainable. And every new beam of truth whereby their minds are enlightened guides them into fresh discoveries of it. This frame of mind is under a promise of divine teaching: "Then shall we know, if we follow on to know the Lord" (Hos. 6:3). "If thou criest after knowledge, and liftest up thy voice for understanding; if thou seekest her as silver, and searchest for her as for hid treasure; then shalt thou understand the fear of the Lord, and find the knowledge of God" (Prov. 2:3–5). When men live in a holy admiration of and complacency in God, as the God of truth, as the first infinite essential Truth, in whose enjoyment alone there is fullness of all satisfactory light and knowledge; when they adore the fullness of those revelations of himself which, with infinite wisdom, he has treasured up in the Scriptures; when they find by experience an excellency, power, and efficacy in what they have attained unto; and, out of a deep sense of the smallness of their measures, of the meanness of their attainments, and how little a portion it is they know of God, do live in a constant design to abide with faith and patience in continual study of the word, and inquiries into the mind of God therein—they are in the way of being taught by him, and learning of his mind unto all the proper ends of its revelation.

5. There are sundry ordinances of spiritual worship which God has ordained as a means of our illumination, a religious attendance whereunto is required of them who intend to grow in grace and in the knowledge of our Lord and Savior Jesus Christ.

OBJECTIONS TO SPIRITUAL MEANS

And this is the first head of means for the due improvement of our endeavors in reading and studying of the Scriptures, that we may come thereby unto a right understanding of the mind of God in them, and be able to interpret them unto the use and benefit of others. What is the work of the Holy Spirit herein, what is the aid and assistance which he contributes hereunto, is so manifest from what we have discoursed, especially concerning his operations in us as a Spirit of grace and supplication, not yet made public, that it must not be here insisted on.[7]

It may be these means will be despised by some, and the proposal of them to this end looked on as weak and ridiculous, if not extremely fanciful. For it is supposed that these things are pressed to no other end but to decry learning, study, and the use of reason in the interpretation of the Scriptures, which will quickly reduce all religion into enthusiasm. Whether there be anything of truth in this suggestion shall be immediately discovered. Nor have those by whom these things are pressed the least reason to decline the use of learning, or any rational means in their proper place, as though they were conscious to themselves of a deficiency in them with respect unto those by whom they are so highly, and indeed for the most part vainly, pretended unto.

But in the matter in hand we must deal with some confidence. They by whom these things are decried, by whom they are denied to be necessary means for the right understanding of the mind of God in the Scriptures, do plainly renounce the chief principles of Christian religion. For although the Scripture has many things in common with other writings wherein secular arts and sciences are declared, yet to suppose that we may attain the sense and mind of God in them by the mere use of such ways and means as we apply in the investigation of truths of other natures is to exclude all consideration of God, of Jesus Christ, of the Holy Spirit, of the end of the Scriptures themselves, of the nature and use of the things delivered in them, and, by consequent, to overthrow all religion (see Prov. 28:5).

And this first sort of means which we have hitherto insisted on are duties in themselves, as well as means unto further ends. And all duties under the gospel are the ways and means wherein and whereby the graces of God are exercised. For as no grace can be exerted or exercised but in a way of duty, so no duty is evangelical or accepted with God but what special grace is exercised in. As the word is the rule whereby they are guided, directed, and measured, so the acting of grace in them is that whereby they are quickened, without which the best duties are but dead works. Materially they are duties, but formally they are sins. In their performance, therefore, as gospel duties, and as they are accepted with God, there is a special aid and assistance of the Holy Spirit. And on that account, there is so in the interpretation of the Scriptures. For if without his assistance we cannot make use aright of the

7 Owen seems to be referring to his *The Work of the Holy Spirit in Prayer, as the Spirit of Grace and Supplications; and the Duty of Believers Therein; with a Brief Enquiry into the Nature and Use of Mental Prayer, and Forms* (1682), the first treatise in vol. 8.

means of interpreting of the Scripture, we cannot interpret the Scripture without it. The truth is, they who shall either say that these duties are not necessarily required unto them who would search the Scriptures, and find out the mind of God for their own edification, or so as to expound those oracles of God unto others, or that they may be performed in a manner acceptable unto God and usefully unto this end, without the special assistance of the Holy Spirit, do impiously, what lies in them, evert[8] the whole doctrine of the gospel and the grace thereof.

That which, in the next place, might be insisted on is the consideration of the special rules which have been, or may yet be, given for the right interpretation of the Scriptures. Such are those which concern the style of the Scripture, its special phraseology, the tropes and figures it makes use of, the way of its arguing; the times and seasons wherein it was written, or the several parts of it; the occasions under the guidance of the Spirit of God given thereunto; the design and scope of particular writers, with what is peculiar unto them in their manner of writing; the comparing of several places as to their difference in things and expressions; the reconciliation of seeming contradictions, with other things of an alike nature. But as the most of these may be reduced unto what has been spoken before about the disposal and perspicuity of the Scripture, so they have been already handled by many others at large, and therefore I shall not here insist upon them, but speak only unto the general means that are to be applied unto the same end.[9]

---

8 I.e., overthrow or upset.
9 There was a tradition in England stretching back to the sixteenth century of publications on Scripture and its interpretation. See William Whitaker, *A Disputation on Holy Scripture: Against the Papists, Especially Bellarmine and Stapleton* (1588), and William Perkins, *The Arte of Prophecying* (1592).

Rules for Biblical Interpretation

*The Second Sort of Means for the Interpretation of
the Scripture, Which Are Disciplinarian.*

THE SECOND SORT of means I call disciplinarian, as consisting in the due use and improvement of common arts and sciences, applied unto and made use of in the study of the Scriptures. And these are things which have no moral good in themselves, but being indifferent in their own nature, their end, with the manner of their management thereunto, is the only measure and standard of their worth and value. Hence it is that in the application of them unto the interpretation of the Scripture, they may be used aright and in a due manner, and they may be abused to the great disadvantage of them who use them; and accordingly, it has fallen out. In the first way they receive a blessing from the Spirit of God, who alone prospers every good and honest endeavor in any kind; and in the latter they are efficacious to seduce men unto a trust in their own understandings, which in other things is foolish, and in these things pernicious.

ORIGINAL LANGUAGES

That which of this sort I prefer, in the first place, is the knowledge of and skill in the languages wherein the Scripture was originally written. For the very words of them therein were peculiarly from the Holy Ghost, which gives them to be דברי אמת, "words of truth," and the Scripture itself to be כתובה ישר,[1]

---

1 *BHS* reads, וְכָתוּב.

"a right, or upright, or perfect writing" (Eccles. 12:10). The Scriptures of the Old Testament were given unto the church while it was entirely confined unto one nation (Ps. 147:19–20). Therefore, they were all written in that language, which was common among, and peculiar unto, that nation. And this language, as the people itself, was called Hebrew, from Heber the son of Salah, the son of Arphaxad, the son of Shem, their most eminent progenitor (Gen. 10:21–24). For being the one original tongue of mankind, it remained in some part of his family, who probably joined not in the great apostasy of the world from God, nor was concerned in their dispersion at the building of Babel, which ensued thereon. The derivation of that name from another original is a fruit of curiosity and vain conjecture, as I have elsewhere demonstrated.[2]

In process of time that people were carried into captivity out of their own land, and were thereby forced to learn and use a language somewhat different from their own; another absolutely it was not, yet so far did it differ from it that those who knew and spoke the one commonly could not understand the other (2 Kings 18:26). This was כסדים[3] לשון, "The language of the Chaldeans," which Daniel and others learned (Dan. 1:4). But, by the people's long continuance in that country, it became common to them all. After this some parts of the books of the Scripture, as of Daniel and Ezra,[4] were written in that language, as also one verse in the prophecy of Jeremiah, when they were ready to be carried there, in which he instructs the people how to reproach the idols of the nations in their own language (Jer. 10:11). The design of God was, that his word should be always read and used in that language which was commonly understood by them unto whom he granted the privilege thereof, nor could any of the ends of his wisdom and goodness in that merciful grant be otherwise attained.

The prodigious conceit of keeping the Scripture, which is the foundation-rule and guide of the whole church, the spiritual food and means of life unto all the members of it, by the church, or those who pretend themselves entrusted with the power and rights of it, in a language unknown unto the community of the people, had not then befallen the minds of men, no more than it has yet any countenance given unto it by the authority of God or reason

---

2 Owen is likely referring to *Of the Divine Original, Authority, Self-Evidencing Light, and Power of the Scriptures; with an Answer to That Inquiry, How We Know the Scriptures to Be the Word of God; also, a Vindication of the Purity and Integrity of the Hebrew and Greek Texts of the Old and New Testament; in Some Considerations on the Prolegomena and Appendix to the Late* Biblia Polyglotta. *Whereunto Are Subjoined Some Exercitations about the Nature and Perfection of the Scripture, the Right of Interpretation, Internal Light, Revelation, Etc.* (1659).

3 *BHS* reads, כַּשְׂדִּים.

4 Dan. 2:4–7:28 and Ezra 4:8–6:18; 7:12–26 were written in Aramaic.

of mankind. And, indeed, the advancement and defense of this imagination is one of those things which sets me at liberty from being influenced by the authority of any sort of men in matters of religion. For what will not their confidence undertake to vent, and their sophistical ability give countenance unto or wrangle about, which their interest requires and calls for at their hands, who can openly plead and contend for the truth of such an absurd and irrational assertion, as is contrary to all that we know of God and his will, and to all that we understand of ourselves or our duty with respect thereunto?

When the New Testament was to be written, the church was to be diffused throughout the world among people of all tongues and languages under heaven; yet there was a necessity that it should be written in some one certain language, wherein the sacred truth of it might, as in original records, be safely laid up and deposited. It was left as καλὴ παραθήκη, καλὴ παρακαταθήκη, "a good and sacred *depositum*"[5] unto the ministry of the church, to be kept inviolate by the Holy Ghost (1 Tim. 6:20; 2 Tim. 1:14). And it was disposed into writing in one certain language, wherein the preservation of it in purity was committed to the ministry of all ages, not absolutely, but under his care and inspection. From this one language God had ordained that it should be derived, by the care of the ministry, unto the knowledge and use of all nations and people. And this was represented by the miraculous gift of tongues communicated by the Holy Ghost unto the first-designed publishers of the gospel. In this case it pleased the wisdom of the Holy Ghost to make use of the Greek language, wherein he wrote the whole New Testament originally. For the report that the Gospel of Matthew and the epistle to the Hebrews were first written in Hebrew, is altogether groundless, and I have elsewhere disproved it.[6]

Now, this language at that season, through all sorts of advantages, was diffused throughout the world, especially in those parts of it where God had designed to fix the first and principal station of the church. For the eastern

---

5 Lat. "deposit."

6 *Exercitations on the Epistle to the Hebrews also concerning the Messiah Wherein the Promises concerning Him to Be a Spiritual Redeemer of Mankind Are Explained and Vindicated, His Coming and Accomplishment of His Work according to the Promises Is Proved and Confirmed, the Person, or Who He Is, Is Declared, the Whole Oeconomy of the Mosaical Law, Rites, Worship, and Sacrifice Is Explained: And in All the Doctrine of the Person, Office, and Work of the Messiah Is Opened, the Nature and Demerit of the First Sin Is Unfolded, the Opinions and Traditions of the Antient and Modern Jews Are Examined, Their Objections against the Lord Christ and the Gospel Are Answered, the Time of the Coming of the Messiah Is Stated, and the Great Fundamental Truths of the Gospel Vindicated: With an Exposition and Discourses on the Two First Chapters of the Said Epistle to the Hebrews* (1668), exer. 4.

parts of the world, it was long before carried into them, and its use imposed on them by the Macedonian arms and laws, with the establishment of the Grecian empire for sundry ages among them. And some while before in the western parts of the world, the same language was greatly inquired into, and generally received, on account of the wisdom and learning which was treasured up therein, in the writings of poets, philosophers, and historians, which had newly received a peculiar advancement.

For two things fell out in the providence of God about that season, which greatly conduced unto the furtherance of the gospel. The Jews were wholly possessed of whatever was true in religion, and which lay in a direct subserviency unto the gospel itself. This they gloried in and boasted of, as a privilege which they enjoyed above all the world. The Grecians, on the other hand, were possessed of skill and wisdom in all arts and sciences, with the products of philosophical inquiries, and elegancy of speech in expressing the conceptions of their minds. And this they gloried in and boasted of above all other people in the world. Now, both these nations being dispossessed of their empire, sovereignty, and liberty at home, by the Romans, multitudes of them made it their business to disperse themselves in the world, and to seek, as it were, a new empire; the one to its religion, and the other to its language, arts, and sciences. Of both sorts, with their design, the Roman writers in those days do take notice, and greatly complain. And these privileges being boasted of and rested in, proved equally prejudicial to both nations, as to the reception of the gospel, as our apostle disputes at large (1 Cor. 1–2). But through the wisdom of God, disposing and ordering all things unto his own glory, the design and actings of them both became an effectual means to facilitate the propagation of the gospel. For the Jews having planted synagogues in most nations and principal cities in the Roman empire, they had both leavened multitudes of people with some knowledge of the true God, which prepared the way of the gospel, as also they had gathered fixed assemblies, which the preachers of the gospel constantly took the advantage of to enter upon their work and to begin the declaration of their message. The Grecians, on the other hand, had so universally diffused the knowledge of their language as that the use of that one tongue alone was sufficient to instruct all sorts of people throughout the world in the knowledge of the truth. For the gift of tongues was only to be a "sign unto unbelievers" (1 Cor. 14),[7] and not a means of preaching the gospel constantly in a language which he understood not who spoke.

In this language, therefore, as the most common, diffusive, and generally understood in the world, did God order that the books of the New Testament

---

7   1 Cor. 14:22.

should be written. From there, by translations and expositions, was it to be derived into other tongues and languages. For the design of God was still the same, that his word should be declared unto the church in a language which it understood. Hence is that peculiar distribution of the nations of the world into Jews, Greeks, Barbarians, and Scythians (Col. 3:11), not accommodated unto the use of those terms in Grecian writers, unto whom the Jews were no less barbarians than the Scythians themselves. But as the Scriptures of the Old Testament were peculiarly given unto the Jews, so were those of the New unto the Greeks, that is, those who made use of their language, from whence it was deduced unto all other nations, called Barbarians and Scythians.

It must be acknowledged that the Scripture, as written in these languages, is accompanied with many and great advantages.¶

1. In them peculiarly is it γραφὴ θεόπνευστος, a "writing by divine inspiration" (2 Tim. 3:16). And ספר יהוה, the "book of writing of the Lord" (Isa. 34:16). With a singular privilege above all translations. Hence the very words themselves, as therein used and placed, are sacred, consecrated by God unto that holy use. The sacred sense, indeed, of the words and expressions is the *internum formale sacrum*,[8] or that wherein the holiness of the Scripture does consist; but the writing itself in the original languages, in the words chosen and used by the Holy Ghost, is the *externum formale*[9] of the Holy Scripture, and is materially sacred.

It is the sense, therefore, of the Scripture which principally and for its own sake we inquire after and into; that divine sense which, as Justin Martyr speaks, is ὑπὲρ λόγον, ὑπὲρ νοῦν, καὶ ὑπὲρ πᾶσαν κατάληψεν, absolutely "above our natural reason, understanding, and comprehension."[10] In the words we are concerned with respect thereunto, as by the wisdom of the Holy Ghost they are designed as the written signs thereof.

2. The words of the Scripture being given thus immediately from God, every apex, tittle, or iota in the whole is considerable, as that which is an effect of divine wisdom, and therefore filled with sacred truth, according to their place and measure. Hence, they are all under the special care of God, according to that promise of our Savior, "Verily I say unto you," ἕως ἂν

8 Lat. "internal sacred form."
9 Lat. "external form."
10 This English translation is Owen's. The quotation likely comes from Justin Martyr's (ca. 100–165) *Dialogue with Trypho*, which defends Jesus as the prophesied Messiah. For the Greek text, see W. Trollope, ed., *Justin Martyr's Dialogue with Trypho: Greek Text and Notes*, 2 vols. (Cambridge: G. Bell; J. Hall and Son, 1847). For an English translation, see *Justin Martyr, the Dialogue with Trypho: Translation, Introduction, and Notes*, trans. A. Lukyn Williams (London: Macmillan, 1930).

παρέλθῃ ὁ οὐρανὸς καὶ ἡ γῆ, ἰῶτα ἕν ἢ μία κεραία οὐ μὴ παρέλθῃ ἀπὸ τοῦ νόμου, "Till heaven and earth pass, one jot or one tittle shall in no wise pass from the law" (Matt. 5:18). That our Savior does here intend the writing of the Scriptures then in use in the church, and assure the protection of God unto the least letter, vowel, or point of it, I have proved elsewhere.[11] And himself in due time will reprove the profane boldness of them who, without evidence or sufficient proof, without that respect and reverence which is due unto the interest, care, providence, and faithfulness of God in this matter, do assert manifold changes to have been made in the original writings of the Scripture.

But, as I said, divine senses and singular mysteries may be couched in the use and disposal of a letter. And this God himself has manifested, as in sundry other instances, so in the change of the names of Abram and Sarai, wherein the addition or alteration of one letter carried along with it a mysterious signification for the use of the church in all ages. In translations, nothing of that nature can be observed. And hence a due consideration of the very accents in the original of the Old Testament, as distinctive or conjunctive, is a singular advantage in the investigation of the sense of particular places and sentences.

3. There is in the originals of the Scripture a peculiar emphasis of words and expressions, and in them a special energy, to intimate and insinuate the sense of the Holy Ghost unto the minds of men, which cannot be traduced into other languages by translations, so as to obtain the same power and efficacy. Now, this is not absolutely from the nature of the original languages themselves, especially not of the Greek, whose principal advantages and excellencies, in copiousness and elegancy, are little used in the New Testament, but from a secret impression of divine wisdom and efficacy accompanying the immediate delivery of the mind of God in them. There is, therefore, no small advantage hence to be obtained in the interpretation of the Scripture. For when we have received an impression on our minds of the sense and intention of the Holy Ghost in any particular place, we shall seek for meet words to express it by, wherein consists the whole work of Scripture exposition, so far as I have any acquaintance with it—"The duty of the interpreter is not to say what he wants, but exhibit the sense of what he interprets"[12]—for when the mind is really affected with the discovery of truth itself, it will be guided and directed in the declaration of it unto others.

11 See *Of the Divine Original, Authority, Self-Evidencing Light, and Power of the Scriptures*.
12 In the text: *Interpretis officium est, non quid ipse velit, sed quid sentiat ille quem interpretatur, exponere* (Hieron. Apol. adv. Rufin).—Owen. For the Latin text, see Hieronymus, *Contra Rufinum*, ed. P. Lardet, Corpus Christianorum: Series Latina 79 (Turnhout: Brepols, 1982). For an English translation, see Jerome, "The Apology against the Books of Rufinus," in *Saint Jerome,*

4. The whole course of speech, especially in the New Testament, is accommodated unto the nature, use, and propriety of that language, as expressed in other authors who wrote therein, and had a perfect understanding of it. From them, therefore, is the proper use and sense of the words, phrases, and expressions in the New Testament much to be learned. This no man can make a judgment of in a due manner but he that is skilled in that language, as used and delivered by them. Not that I think a commentary on the New Testament may be collected out of Eustathius, Hesychius, Phavorinus, Julius Pollux,[13] and other glossaries, from whose grammaticisms and vocabularies some do countenance themselves in curious and bold conjectures, nor from the likeness of expression in classic authors. This only I say, that it is of singular advantage, in the interpretation of the Scripture, that a man be well acquainted with the original languages, and be able to examine the use and signification of words, phrases, and expressions as they are applied and declared in other authors. And even to the understanding of the Greek of the New Testament it is necessary that a man have an acquaintance with the Hebrew of the Old. For although I do not judge that there are such a number of Hebraisms in it, in a supposed discovery whereof consists no small part of some men's critical observations, yet I readily grant that there is such a cognation and alliance in and between the senses of the one and the other as that a due comparing of their expressions does mutually contribute light and perspicuity unto them.

By these things great advantage may be obtained unto the right understanding of the sense of the Scripture, or the mind of the Holy Ghost therein. For there is no other sense in it than what is contained in the words whereof materially it does consist, though really that sense itself be such as our minds cannot receive without the special divine assistance before pleaded. And in the interpretation of the mind of anyone, it is necessary that the words he speaks or writes be rightly understood. And this we cannot do immediately unless we understand

---

Dogmatic and Polemical Works, ed. John N. Hritzu (Washington, DC: Catholic University of America Press, 1965), 47–220. Jerome (ca. 347–420) wrote his Apology Against the Books of Rufinus primarily in defense of his translation and utilization of Origen (ca. 185–ca. 253). However, though Jerome said things similar to this, the quotation is not found in that work. A near exact Latin match for the quotation can be found in Hieronymi, "Epistola xlviii (b), seu liber apologeticus, ad Pammachium, pro libris contra Jovinianum," in *Opera omnia*, ed. J. P. Migne, Patrologia Latina 22 (Paris: Migne, 1845), 507. For an English translation, see Jerome, "Letter XLVIII. To Pammachius," in *Jerome: Letters and Select Works*, trans. W. H. Fremantle, vol. 6 of *Nicene and Post-Nicene Fathers*, 2nd ser., ed. Philip Schaff and Henry Wace (Peabody, MA: Hendrickson, 2004), 77.

13 This is a list of ancient and medieval Greek grammarians.

328 CAUSES, WAYS, AND MEANS

the language wherein he speaks, as also the idiotisms[14] of that language, with the common use and intention of its phraseology and expressions.¶

And if we do not hereby come unto a perfect comprehension of the sense intended, because many other things are required thereunto, yet a hindrance is removed, without which we cannot do so, occasions of manifold mistakes are taken away, and the cabinet is, as it were, unlocked wherein the jewel of truth lies hid, which with a lawful diligent search may be found. And what perplexities, mistakes, and errors, the ignorance of these original languages has cast many expositors into, both of old and of late, especially among those who pertinaciously adhere unto one translation, and that none of the best, might be manifested by instances undeniable, and these without number. Such is that of the gloss on Titus 3:10, *Haereticum hominem devita*,[15] which adds, as its exposition, *tolle*.[16] And those among ourselves who are less skilled in this knowledge are to be advised that they would be careful not to adventure on any singular exposition of the Scriptures, or any text in them, upon the credit of any one or all translations they can make use of, seeing persons of greater name and worth than to be mentioned unto their disreputation have miscarried upon the same account. A reverential subjection of mind, and diligent attendance unto the analogy of faith, is their best preservative in this matter.¶

And I fear not to add, that a superficial knowledge in these tongues, which many aim at, is of little use unless it be to make men adventurous in betraying their own ignorance. But the sense and substance of the Scripture being contained entirely in every good translation, among which that in use among ourselves is excellent,[17] though capable of great improvements, men may, by the use of the means before directed unto, and under the conduct of the teaching of the Spirit of God in them, usefully and rightly expound the Scripture in general unto the edification of others; whereof many instances may be given among ancient and modern expositors.

---

14 I.e., idioms.

15 Lat. "avoid the divisive person."

16 Lat. "take up" or "take out." *De vita tolle*, literally "take out a life," was the gloss or interpretation of Titus 3:10 used to justify the execution of heretics. There was an anecdote about John Colet (1467–1519), an English humanist and Catholic reformer, made famous by the later editions of Erasmus's (ca. 1466–1536) *Annotationes*, or annotations on the New Testament, specifically on this verse, which recounts the irony of Colet's holding to the position of executing heretics while at the same time strongly criticizing the institutional church. See J. H. Lupton, *A Life of John Colet* (London: George Bell and Sons, 1887), 202.

17 The Bible translation of widespread use during the second half of the seventeenth century was the Authorized Version (1611), also known as the King James Version. This is true even among English Dissent. The last printing of the Geneva Bible (1560) was in 1644, and the Authorized Version was largely the Geneva Bible without the controversial marginal notes.

This skill and knowledge, therefore, is of great use unto them who are called unto the interpretation of the Scripture. And the church of God has had no small advantage by the endeavors of men learned herein, who have exercised it in the exposition of the words and phraseology of the Scriptures, as compared with their use in other authors. But yet, as was before observed, this skill, and the exercise of it in the way mentioned, is no duty in itself, nor enjoined unto any for its own sake, but only has a goodness in it with respect unto a certain end. Wherefore, it is in its own nature indifferent, and in its utmost improvement capable of abuse, and such in late days it has fallen under unto a great extremity. For the study of the original languages, and the exercise of skill in them in the interpretation of the Scripture, has been of great reputation, and that deservedly. Hence multitudes of learned men have engaged themselves in that work and study, and the number of annotations and comments on the Scripture, consisting principally in critical observations, as they are called, have been greatly increased. And they are utter strangers unto these things who will not allow that many of them are of singular use. But with this skill and faculty, where it has been unaccompanied with that humility, sobriety, reverence of the author of the Scripture, and respect unto the analogy of faith, which ought to bear sway in the minds of all men who undertake to expound the oracles of God, may be, and has been, greatly abused, unto the hurt of its owners and disadvantage of the church.

Abuses of the Languages

1. For by some it has been turned into the fuel of pride, and a noisome elation of mind. Yea, experience shows that this kind of knowledge, where it is supposed signal,[18] is of all others the most apt to puff up and swell the vain minds of men, unless it be where it is alloyed with a singular modesty of nature, or the mind itself be sufficiently corrected and changed by grace. Hence the expressions of pride and self-conceit which some have broken forth into on an imagination of their skill and faculty in criticizing on the Scriptures have been ridiculous and impious. The Holy Ghost usually teaches not such persons, neither should I expect to learn much from them relating unto the truth as it is in Jesus. But yet the stones they dig may be made use of by a skillful builder.

2. In many it has been accompanied with a noxious, profane curiosity. Every tittle and apex shall give them occasion for fruitless conjectures, as

---

18 I.e., considered of great importance; prominent.

vain, for the most part, as those of the Cabalistic[19] Jews. And this humor has filled us with needless and futile observations, which, beyond an ostentation of the learning of their authors, indeed, the utmost end whereunto they are designed, are of no use nor consideration. But this is not all; some men from hence have been prompted unto a boldness in adventuring to corrupt the text itself, or the plain sense of it; for what else is done when men, for an ostentation of their skill, will produce quotations out of learned authors to illustrate or expound sayings in the Scripture, wherein there seems to be some kind of compliance in words and sounds, when their senses are adverse and contrary? Among a thousand instances which might be given to exemplify this folly and confidence, we need take that one alone of him who, to explain or illustrate that saying of Hezekiah, "Good is the word of the Lord which thou hast spoken; he said moreover, for there shall be peace and truth in my days" (Isa. 39:8), subjoins, ἐμοῦ θανόντος γαῖα μιχθήτω πυρὶ, "when I am dead may earth be mingled with fire,"[20] so comparing that holy man's submission and satisfaction in the peace of the church with truth, and the blasphemous imprecation of an impious wretch for confusion on the world, when once he should be got out of it. And such notable sayings are many of our late critics farced[21] with.

And the confidence of some has fallen into greater excesses, and has swelled over these bounds also. To countenance their conjectures and self-pleasing imaginations, from whence they expect no small reputation for skill and learning, they fall in upon the text itself. And, indeed, we are come into an age wherein many seem to judge that they can neither sufficiently value themselves, nor obtain an estimation in the world, without some bold sallies[22] of curiosity or novelty into the vitals of religion, with reflection of

---

19 I.e., the medieval and modern system of Jewish theosophy, mysticism, and thaumaturgy or magic marked by belief in creation through emanation and a cipher method of interpreting Scripture.

20 The Greek line is believed to come from a lost play of Euripides (ca. 480–406 BC) called *Bellerophon*. It was famously quoted in Suetonius's (b. ca. AD 70) life of Nero (37–68), to which the emperor replied, "Nay, rather while I live," subsequently setting Rome on fire. Suetonius, *Lives of the Caesars*, vol. 2, *Claudius. Nero. Galba, Otho, and Vitellius. Vespasian. Titus, Domitian. Lives of Illustrious Men: Grammarians and Rhetoricians. Poets (Terence. Virgil. Horace. Tibullus. Persius. Lucan). Lives of Pliny the Elder and Passienus Crispus*, trans. J. C. Rolfe, Loeb Classical Library 38 (Cambridge, MA: Harvard University Press, 1914). 148–49. While Owen does not make explicit who he is referring to, John Calvin offers a similar criticism of apparently the same commentator(s). See John Calvin, *Commentary on the Book of the Prophet Isaiah*, vol. 3, trans. William Pringle (Grand Rapids, MI: Baker, 2005), 193.

21 I.e., stuffed; filled with.

22 I.e., bursting forth.

contempt and scorn on all that are otherwise minded, as persons incapable of comprehending their attainments. Hence it is that among ourselves we have scarce anything left unattacked in the doctrine of the reformed churches and of that in England, as in former days; neither shall he be with many esteemed a man, either of parts, learning, or judgment, who has not some new curious opinion or speculation, differing from what has been formerly commonly taught and received, although the universality of these renowned notions among us are but corrupt emanations from Socinianism or Arminianism on the one hand, or from popery on the other.[23]

But it is men of another sort, and in truth of another manner of learning, than the present corrupters of the doctrines of the gospel, who, so far as I can perceive, trouble not themselves about the Scripture much one way or another, that we treat about. They are such as, in the exercise of the skill and ability under consideration, do fall in upon the Scripture itself, to make way for the advancement of their own conjectures, whereof ten thousand are not of the least importance compared with the duty and necessity of preserving the sacred text inviolate, and the just and due persuasion that so it has been preserved. For, first, they command the vowels and accents of the Hebrew text out of their way, as things wherein they are not concerned, when the use of them in any one page of the Scripture is incomparably of more worth and use than all that they are or ever will be of in the church of God. And this is done on slight conjectures. And if this suffice not to make way for their designs, then letters and words themselves must be corrected, upon an unprovable supposition that the original text has been changed or corrupted. And the boldness of some herein is grown intolerable, so that it is as likely means for the introduction and promotion of atheism as any engine the devil has set on work in these days, wherein he is so openly engaged in that design.

Limits of the Languages

There are also sundry other ways whereby this great help unto the understanding and interpretation of the Scripture may be and has been abused; those mentioned may suffice as instances confirming our observations. Wherefore, as substantial knowledge and skill in the originals is useful, and indeed necessary, unto him that is called unto the exposition of the Scripture, so in the use and exercise of it sundry things ought to be well considered by them who are furnished therewith: As (1) that the thing itself is no grace, nor any

---

23 See the introduction on Socinianism, its relationship with Arminianism, and the Church of Rome.

peculiar gift of the Holy Ghost, but a mere fruit of diligence upon a common furniture with natural abilities; and nothing of this nature is in sacred things to be rested on or much trusted unto. (2) That the exercise of this skill in and about the Scripture is not in itself, as such, a special or immediate duty. Were it so, there would be special grace promised to fill it up and quicken it. For all gospel duties are animated by grace in their due performance, that is, those who do so perform them have special assistance in their so doing. But it is reduced unto the general head of duty with respect unto the end aimed at. Wherefore (3) the blessing of God on our endeavors, succeeding and prospering of them, as in other natural and civil occasions of life, is all that we expect herein from the Holy Spirit. And (4) sundry other things are required of us, if we hope for this blessing on just grounds. It may be some ignorant persons are so fond as to imagine that if they could understand the original languages, they must of necessity understand the sense of the Scripture. And there is nothing more frequent than for some, who either truly or falsely pretend a skill in them, to bear themselves high against those who perhaps are really more acquainted with the mind of the Holy Ghost in the word than themselves, as though all things were plain and obvious unto them, others knowing nothing but by them or such as they are. But this is but one means of many that is useful to this purpose, and that such as, if it be alone, is of little or no use at all. It is fervent prayer, humility, lowliness of mind, godly fear and reverence of the word, and subjection of conscience unto the authority of every tittle of it, a constant attendance unto the analogy of faith, with due dependence on the Spirit of God for supplies of light and grace, which must make this or any other means of the same nature effectual.

HISTORY, GEOGRAPHY, AND CHRONOLOGY

An acquaintance with the history and geography of the world and with chronology, I reckon also among disciplinarian aids in the interpretation of the Scripture. For as time is divided into what is past and what is to come, so there are sundry things in the Scripture which, in all seasons, relate thereunto.

1. For God has therein given us an account of the course and order of all things, which the Jews call סרר עלם, from the "foundation of the world." And this he did for sundry important reasons, as incident with the general end of the Scripture. For hereby has he secured the testimony that he has given to his being, power, and providence, by the creation and rule of all things. The evidences in them given thereunto are those which are principally attacked by atheists. And although they do sufficiently manifest and evince their own

testimony unto the common reason of mankind, yet sundry things relating unto them are so involved in darkness and inextricable circumstances, if all their concerns had not been plainly declared in the Scripture, the wisest of men had been at a great loss about them; and so were they always who wanted the light and advantage hereof. But here, as he has plainly declared the original emanation of all things from his eternal power, so has he testified unto his constant rule over all in all times, places, ages, and seasons by instances incontrollable. Therein has he treasured up all sorts of examples, with such impressions of his goodness, patience, power, wisdom, holiness, and righteousness upon them, as proclaim his almighty and righteous government of the whole universe. And in the whole he has delivered unto us such a tract and series of the ages of the world from its beginning, as atheism has no tolerable pretense, from tradition, testimony, or the evidence of things themselves, to break in upon. Whatever is objected against the beginning of all things, and the course of their continuance in the world, delivered unto us in the Scripture, which is secured not only by the authority of divine revelation, but also by a universal evidence of all circumstances, is fond and ridiculous. I speak of the account given us in general, sufficient unto its own ends, and not of any men's deductions and applications of it unto minute portions of time, which probably it was not designed unto. It is sufficient unto its end, that its account, in general, which confounds all atheistic presumptions, is not to be impeached. And although the authority of the Scripture is not to be pleaded immediately against atheists, yet the matter and reason of it is, which from its own evidence renders all contrary pretensions contemptible.

2. God has hereby given an account of the beginning, progress, trials, faith, obedience, and whole proceedings of the church, in the pursuit of the first promise, unto the actual exhibition of Jesus Christ in the flesh. Hereunto were all things in a tendency for four thousand years. It is a glorious prospect we have therein, to see the call and foundation of the church in the first promise given unto our common parents; what additions of light and knowledge he granted unto it successively by new revelations and promises; how he gradually adorned it with gifts, privileges, and ordinances; what ways and means he used to preserve it in faith, purity, and obedience; how he chastened, tried, punished, and delivered it; how he dealt with the nations of the world with respect unto it, raising them up for its affliction, and destroying them for their cruelty and oppression of it; what were the ways of wicked and sinful men among them or in it, and what the graces and fruits of his saints; how by his power he retrieved it out of various calamities, and preserved it against

all opposition unto its appointed season—all which, with innumerable other effects of divine wisdom and grace, are blessedly represented unto us therein.

Now, besides that spiritual wisdom and insight into the great design of God in Christ, which is required unto a right understanding in these things as they were types of better things to come and examples of gospel mysteries, there is a skill and understanding in the records and monuments of time, the geographical respect of one nation unto another, the periods and revolutions of seasons and ages, required to apprehend them aright in their first literal instance and intention. And besides what is thus historically related in the Scripture, there are prophecies also of things to come in the church and among the nations of the world, which are great evidences of its own divinity and supporting arguments of our faith. But without some good apprehension of the distinction of times, seasons, and places, no man can rightly judge of their accomplishment.

Secondly,[24] there are, in particular, prophecies in the Old Testament which reach unto the times of the gospel, upon the truth whereof the whole Scripture does depend. Such are those concerning the calling of the Gentiles, the rejection and recovery of the Jews, the erection of the glorious kingdom of Christ in the world, with the oppositions that should be made unto it. And to these many are added in the New Testament itself (as Matt. 24–25; 2 Thess. 2; 1 Tim. 4:1–3; 2 Tim. 3:1–5; 4:3–4). But especially in the whole book of the Revelation, wherein the state of the church and of the world is foretold unto the consummation of all things. And how can any man arrive unto a tolerable acquaintance with the accomplishment of these prophecies as to what is already past, or have a distinct grounded expectation of the fulfilling of what remains foretold, without a prospect into the state of things in the world, the revolutions of times past, with what fell out in them, which are the things spoken of? Those who treat of them without it do but feign chimeras[25] to themselves, as men in the dark are apt to do, or corrupt the word of God, by turning it into senseless and fulsome[26] allegories. And those, on the other side, by whom these things are wholly neglected do despise the wisdom and care of God toward the church, and disregard a blessed means of our faith and consolation.

Some things of this nature, especially such as relate unto chronological computations, I acknowledge are attended with great and apparently inextricable difficulties. But the skill and knowledge mentioned will guide humble and modest inquirers into so sufficient a satisfaction in general, and as unto all

---

24 I.e., with reference to the previous paragraph.

25 I.e., things illusory or impossible to achieve.

26 I.e., abundant; copious.

things which are really useful, that they shall have no temptation to question the verity of what in particular they cannot assoil.[27] And it is an intolerable pride and folly, when we are guided and satisfied infallibly in a thousand things which we know no otherwise, to question the authority of the whole because we cannot comprehend one or two particulars, which, perhaps, were never intended to be reduced unto our measure. Besides, as the investigation of these things is attended with difficulties, so the ignorance of them or mistakes about them, while the minds of men are free from pertinacy[28] and a spirit of contention, are of no great disadvantage. For they have very little influence on our faith and obedience, any otherwise than that we call not into question what is revealed. And it is most probable that the Scripture never intended to give us such minute chronological determinations as some would deduce their computations unto, and that because not necessary. Hence, we see that some who have labored therein unto a prodigy of industry and learning, although they have made some useful discoveries, yet have never been able to give such evidence unto their computations as that others would acquiesce in them; but by all their endeavors have administered occasion of new strife and contention about things, it may be, of no great importance to be known or determined.¶

And, in general, men have run into two extremes in these things; for some pretend to frame an exact computation and consent of times from the Scripture alone, without any regard unto the records, monuments, histories, and signatures of times in the world. Wherever these appear in opposition or contradiction unto the chain and links of time which they have framed to themselves, as they suppose from the Scripture, they reject them as matters of no consideration. And it were well if they could do this unto satisfaction. But how evidently they have failed herein, as, for instance, in the computation of Daniel's weeks, wherein they will allow but four hundred and ninety years from the first of Cyrus unto the death of our Savior, contrary to the common consent of mankind about things that fell out, and their continuance between those seasons, taking up five hundred and sixty-two years, is manifest unto all. The Scripture, indeed, is to be made the only sacred standard and measure of things, in its proper sense and understanding, nor is anything to be esteemed of which rises up in contradiction thereunto. But as a due consideration of foreign testimonies and monuments does ofttimes give great light unto what is more generally or obscurely expressed in the Scripture, so where the Scripture in these things, with such allowances as it everywhere declares itself to

---

27 I.e., absolve or acquit.
28 I.e., pertinacity; stubborn adherence.

admit of, may be interpreted in a fair compliance with uncontrolled foreign testimonies, that interpretation is to be embraced.¶

The question is not, therefore, whether we shall regulate the computation of times by the Scripture, or by the histories and marks of time in the world, but whether, when the sense of the Scripture is obscure in those things, and its determination only general, so as to be equally capable of various senses, that, all things being alike, is not to be preferred which agrees with the undoubted monuments of times in the nations of the world? For instance, the angel Gabriel acquaints Daniel that from the going forth of the commandment to restore and rebuild Jerusalem unto Messiah the prince and his cutting off, should be seventy weeks, to speak only of the whole number in general, that is, four hundred and ninety years. Now, there were sundry commandments given or decrees made by the kings of Persia, who are intended to this purpose. Of these two were the most famous, the one granted by Cyrus in the first year of his empire (Ezra 1:1–4); the other by Artaxerxes in the seventh year of his reign (Ezra 7:11–26). Between the first of these and the death of Christ there must be allowed five hundred and sixty-two years, unless you will offer violence unto all monuments, records, and circumstances of times in the world. It is, therefore, safer to interpret the general words of the angel of the latter decree or commandment, whose circumstances also make it more probable to be intended, wherein the space of time mentioned falls in exactly with other approved histories and records. Neither would I disallow another computation, which, contending for the first decree of Cyrus to be the beginning of the time mentioned, and allowing the whole space from thence to be really five hundred and sixty-two years, affirms that the Scripture excludes the consideration of the years supernumerary[29] to the four hundred and ninety, because of the interruptions which at several seasons were put upon the people in the accomplishment of the things foretold for so many years, which some suppose to be signified by the distribution of the whole number of seventy weeks into seven, sixty-two, and one, each of which fractions has its proper work belonging unto it; for this computation offers no violence either to sacred or unquestionable human authority.[30]

But, on the other extreme, some there are who, observing the difficulties in these accounts, as expressed in the Scripture from the beginning, having

---

29 I.e., additional; surplus.

30 For Puritan eschatology, see Crawford Gribben, *The Puritan Millennium: Literature and Theology, 1550–1682*, rev. ed., Studies in Christian History and Thought (Milton Keynes, UK: Paternoster, 2008).

framed another series of things to themselves openly divers from that ex-
hibited therein, and raked together from other authors, some things giving
countenance unto their conjectures, do profanely make bold to break in
upon the original text, accusing it of imperfection or corruption, which they
will rectify by their fine inventions and by the aid of a translation known to
be mistaken in a thousand places, and in some justly suspected of willful
depravation. But this presumptuous confidence is nothing but an emanation from that flood of atheism which is breaking in on the world in these
declining ages of it.[31]

METHODICAL REASON

The third aid or assistance of this kind is a skill in the ways and methods of
reasoning, which are supposed to be common unto the Scriptures with other
writings. And this, as it is an art, or an artificial faculty, like those other means
before mentioned, is capable of a right improvement or of being abused.
An ability to judge of the sense of propositions, how one thing depends on
another, how it is deduced from it, follows upon it, or is proved by it, what
is the design of him that writes or speaks in any discourse or reasoning,
how it is proposed, confirmed, illustrated, is necessary unto any rational
consideration to be exercised about whatever is so proposed unto us. And
when the minds of men are confirmed in a good habit of judgment by the
rules of the art of reasoning about the ordinary ways and methods of it, it is
of great advantage in the investigation of the sense of any writer, even of the
Scripture itself. And those ordinarily who shall undertake the interpretation
of any series of Scripture discourses without some ability in this science will
find themselves oftentimes entangled and at a loss, when by virtue of it they
might be at liberty and free. And many of the rules which are commonly
given about the interpretation of the Scripture, as, namely, that the scope of
the author in the place is duly to be considered, as also things antecedent
and consequent to the place and words to be interpreted, and the like, are
but directions for the due use of this skill or faculty.

But this also must be admitted with its limitations. For whatever perfection
there seems to be in our art of reasoning, it is to be subject to the wisdom
of the Holy Ghost in the Scripture. His way of reasoning is always his own,
sometimes sublime and heavenly, so as not to be reduced unto the common

---

31 Owen obviously does not state precisely whom he has in mind here, but they are clearly those
who have a low view of Scripture and will do whatever it takes to twist sources into their theological mold.

rules of our arts and sciences, without a derogation from its instructive, convictive, and persuasive efficacy. For us to frame unto ourselves rules of ratiocination,[32] or to have our minds embondaged unto those of other men's invention and observation, if we think thereon absolutely to reduce all the reasonings in the Scripture unto them, we may fall into a presumptuous mistake. In the consideration of all the effects of infinite wisdom, there must be an allowance for the deficiency of our comprehension, when humble subjection of conscience, and the captivating of our understandings to the obedience of faith, is the best means of learning what is proposed unto us. And there is nothing more contemptible than the arrogancy of such persons as think, by the shallow measures and short lines of their own weak, dark, imperfect reasoning, to fathom the depths of Scripture senses.

Again, what sense soever any man supposes or judges this or that particular place of Scripture to yield and give out to the best of his rational intelligence is immediately to give place unto the analogy of faith, that is, the Scripture's own declaration of its sense in other places to another purpose, or contrary thereunto. The want of attending unto men's duty herein, with a mixture of pride and pertinacy, is the occasion of most errors and noxious opinions in the world. For when some have taken up a private interpretation of any place of Scripture, if, before they have thoroughly imbibed and vented it, they do not submit their conception, although they seem to be greatly satisfied in it and full of it, unto the authority of the Scripture in the declaration of its own mind in other places, there is but small hope of their recovery. And this is that pride which is the source and origin of heresy, namely, when men will prefer their seemingly wise and rational conceptions of the sense of particular places before the analogy of faith.

Moreover, there is a pernicious mistake that some are fallen into about these things. They suppose that, taking in the help of skill in the original languages for the understanding of the words and their use, whether proper or figurative, there is nothing more necessary to the understanding and interpretation of the Scripture but only the sedulous and diligent use of our own reason, in the ordinary way, and according to the common rules of the art of ratiocination. For what, say they, can be more required, or what can men more make use of? By these means alone do we come to understand the meaning of any other writer, and therefore also of the Scripture. Neither can we, nor does God require that we should, receive or believe anything but according to our own reason and understanding. But these things, though

32 I.e., precise reasoning.

in themselves they are, some of them, partly true, yet as they are used unto the end mentioned, they are perniciously false.¶

1. For it greatly unbecomes any Christian once to suppose that there is need of no other assistance, nor the use of any other means for the interpretation of the oracles of God, or to come unto the understanding of the hidden wisdom of God in the mystery of the gospel, than is to the understanding or interpretation of the writings of men, which are the product of a finite, limited, and weak ability. Were it not for some secret persuasion that the Scripture indeed is not, what it pretends to be, the word of the living God, or that it does not indeed express the highest effect of his wisdom and deepest counsel of his will, it could not be that men should give way to such foolish imaginations. The principal matter of the Scripture is mysterious, and the mysteries of it are laid up therein by God himself, and that in a way inimitable[33] by the skill or wisdom of men. When we speak of and express the same things according unto our measure of comprehension, wherein, from its agreement with the Scripture, what we say is materially divine, yet our words are not so, nor is there the same respect to the things themselves as the expressions of the Scripture have, which are formally divine. And can we ourselves trace these paths of wisdom without his special guidance and assistance? It is highly atheistic once to fancy it.¶

2. We treat of such an interpretation of the Scripture as is real, and is accompanied with an understanding of the things proposed and expressed, and not merely of the notional sense of propositions and expressions. For we speak of such an interpretation of the Scripture as is a sanctified means of our illumination, nor any other does either the Scripture require or God regard. That to give in this unto us, notwithstanding the use and advantage of all outward helps and means, is the peculiar work of the Spirit of God, has been before demonstrated. It is true, we can receive nothing, reject nothing, as to what is true or false, nor conceive the sense of anything, but by our own reasons and understandings. But the inquiry herein is, what supernatural aid and assistance our minds and natural reasons stand in need of to enable them to receive and understand aright things spiritual and supernatural. And if it be true that no more is required unto the due understanding and interpretation of the Scriptures but the exercise of our own reasons, in and by the helps mentioned, namely, skill in the original languages, the art of ratiocination, and the like, which are exposed unto all in common, according to the measure of their natural abilities and diligence, then is the sense of the

---

33 I.e., incapable of being imitated.

Scripture, that is, the mind of God and Christ therein, equally discernible, or to be attained unto, by all sorts of men, good and bad, holy and profane, believers and unbelievers, those who obey the word and those who despise it; which is contrary to all the promises of God and to innumerable other testimonies of Scripture.

Biblical Interpretation and the Church

Helps Ecclesiastical in the Interpretation of the Scripture.

THIRDLY, THERE ARE MEANS and helps for the interpretation of the Scripture which I call ecclesiastical. Those I intend which we are supplied with by the ministry of the church in all ages. And they may be referred unto three heads, under which their usefulness to this purpose is pleaded: as one, catholic or universal tradition; two, consent of the fathers; three, the endeavors of any persons holy and learned who have gone before us in the investigation of the truth, and expressed their minds in writing, for the edification of others, whether of old or of late. These things belong unto the ministry of the church, and so far as they do so are sanctified ordinances for the communication of the mind of God unto us.

1. It is pleaded by some that the Scripture is to be interpreted according to catholic tradition, and not otherwise. And I do acknowledge that we should be inexpressibly obliged to them who would give us an interpretation of the whole Scripture, or of any book in the Scripture, or of any one passage in the Scripture, relating unto things of mere supernatural revelation, according unto that rule, or by the guidance and direction of it. But I fear no such tradition can be evidenced, unless it be of things manifest in the light of nature, whose universal preservation is an effect of the unavoidable reason of mankind, and not of any ecclesiastical tradition. Moreover, the Scripture itself is testified unto unanimously and uninterruptedly by all Christians to be the word of God; and hereby are all divine truths conveyed down from their origin and delivered unto us. But a collateral tradition of any one truth

or doctrine besides, from Christ and the apostles, cannot be proved. And if it could be so, it would be no means of the interpretation of the Scripture but only objectively, as one place of Scripture interprets another; that is, it would belong unto the analogy of faith, contrary to which, or in opposition whereunto, no place ought to be interpreted. To pretend this, therefore, to be the rule of the interpretation of Scripture actively, as though thereby we could certainly learn the meaning of it, in part or in whole, is fond. Nor, whatever some do boast of, can any man living prove his interpretation of any one place to be dictated by or to be suitable unto universal tradition, any otherwise but as he can prove it to be agreeable to the Scripture itself; unless we shall acknowledge, without proof, that what is the mind and sense of some men who call themselves the church at present was the mind of Christ and his apostles, and of all true believers since, and that infallibly it is so. But this pretense has been abundantly and sufficiently disproved, though nothing seems to be so to the minds of men fortified against all evidences of truth by invincible prejudices.

2. The joint consent of the fathers or ancient doctors of the church is also pretended as a rule of Scripture interpretation. But those who make this plea are apparently influenced by their supposed interest so to do. No man of ingenuity who has ever read or considered them, or any of them, with attention and judgment, can abide by this pretense. For it is utterly impossible they should be an authentic rule unto others who so disagree among themselves, as they will be found to do, not, it may be, so much in articles of faith, as in their exposition of Scripture, which is the matter under consideration. About the former they express themselves diversely, in the latter they really differ, and that frequently. Those who seem most earnestly to press this dogma upon us are those of the Church of Rome; and yet it is hard to find one learned man among them who has undertaken to expound or write commentaries on the Scripture, but on all occasions, he gives us the different senses, expositions, and interpretations of the fathers, of the same places and texts, and that where any difficulty occurs in a manner perpetually. But the pretense of the authoritative determination of the fathers in points of religion has been so disproved, and the vanity of it so fully discovered, as that it is altogether needless further to insist upon it. And those who would seem to have found out a middle way, between their determining authority on the one hand, and the efficacy of their reasons, with a due veneration of their piety and ability, which all sober men allow, on the other, do but trifle, and speak words whose sense neither themselves nor any others do understand.

3. We say, therefore, that the sole use of ecclesiastical means in the interpretation of the Scripture is in the due consideration and improvement of that light, knowledge, and understanding in, and those gifts for the declaration of, the mind of God in the Scripture, which he has granted unto and furnished them with who have gone before us in the ministry and work of the gospel. For as God in a special manner, in all ages, took care that the doctrine of the gospel should be preached *vivâ voce*,[1] to the present edification of the body of the church, so likewise, almost from the beginning of its propagation in the world, presently after the decease of the apostles and that whole divinely inspired society of preachers and writers, he stirred up and enabled sundry persons to declare by writing what their apprehensions were, and what understanding God had given them in and about the sense of the Scripture. Of those who designedly wrote comments and expositions on any part of the Scripture, Origen was the first, whose fooleries and mistakes, occasioned by the prepossession of his mind with platonic philosophy, confidence of his own great abilities, which, indeed, were singular and admirable, with the curiosity of a speculative mind, discouraged not others from endeavoring with more sobriety and better success to write entire expositions on some parts of the Scripture. Such among the Greeks were Chrysostom, Theodoret, Aretine, Oecumenius, Theophylact; and among the Latins, Jerome, Ambrose, Augustine, and others.[2] These have been followed, used, improved, by others innumerable in succeeding ages. Especially since the Reformation has the work been carried on with general success, and to the great advantage of the church. Yet has it not proceeded so far but that the best, most useful, and profitable labor in the Lord's vineyard, which any holy and learned man can engage himself in, is to endeavor the contribution of further light in the opening and exposition of Scripture, or any part thereof.¶

Now, all these are singular helps and advantages unto the right understanding of the Scripture, of the same kind of advantage, as to that single end of light and knowledge, which preaching of the word is, used with sobriety, judgment, and a due examination of all by the text itself. For the exposition of the fathers, as it is a ridiculous imagination, and that which would oblige us to the belief of contradictions and open mistakes, for any man to authenticate them so far as to bind us up unto an assent unto their conceptions and dictates because

---

1 Lat. "by a living voice," orally.
2 Those referenced are Origen of Alexandria (ca. 184–ca. 253), John Chrysostom (ca. 347–407), Theodoret of Cyrus (ca. 393–ca. 458/466), Aretine (unknown), Oecumenius of Trikka (tenth c.), Theophylact of Ohrid (ca. 1055–ca. 1107), Saint Jerome (ca. 347–420), Ambrose of Milon (ca. 340–397), and Augustine of Hippo (354–430).

they are theirs; so they will not be despised by any but such as have not been conversant in them. And it is easy to discern from them all, by the diversity of their gifts, ways, and designs, in the exposition of Scripture, that the Holy Spirit divided unto them as he pleased; which as it should make us reverence his presence with them, and assistance of them, so it calls for the freedom of our own judgments to be exercised about their conceptions. And for those of latter days, though the names of the principal and most eminent of them, as Bucer, Calvin, Martyr, Beza,[3] are now condemned and despised by many, mostly by those who never once seriously attempted the exposition of any one chapter in the whole Scripture, yet those who firmly design to grow in the knowledge of God and of our Lord and Savior Jesus Christ, both do and always will bless God for the assistance he gave them in their great and holy works, and in the benefit which they receive by their labors.¶

These are the outward means and advantages which are requisite, and to be used as anyone's calling, opportunity, ability, and work do require, as helps to attain a right understanding of the mind of God in the Scripture. Now, concerning them all I shall only say, that the Spirit of God makes them useful and prosperous according to the counsel of his own will. Some are prone in the use of them to lean unto their own understandings, and consequently to wander in and after the imaginations of their own minds, corrupting the word of God, and endeavoring to pervert his right ways thereby. Others he leaves in the shell of the text, to exercise their skill about words, phrases, and expressions, without leading them into the spiritual sense of the word, which is its life and power. In some he blesses them to the full and proper end, but not unless they are in a compliance with the spiritual means and duties before insisted on.

CONCLUSIONS

From what has been discoursed concerning the work of the Spirit of God in revealing unto believers the mind of God in the Scriptures, or the sense of that revelation made of it therein, two things will seem to follow. First, that those who have not that assistance granted to them, or that work of his wrought in them, cannot understand or apprehend the truth or doctrine of faith and obedience therein revealed. For if that work of the Spirit be necessary thereunto, which they are not made partakers of, how can they come

3 Those referenced are Martin Bucer (1491–1551), John Calvin (1509–1564), Peter Martyr Vermigli (1499–1562), and Theodore Beza (1519–1605), representatives of the early Reformed tradition.

to any knowledge or understanding therein? Secondly, that those who are so influenced and guided must understand the whole Scripture aright, and be freed from all mistakes in their conceptions about the mind of God, both which are contrary to the experience of all men in all ages, seeing many persons visibly destitute of any saving work of the Holy Ghost upon their minds, as is evident in that no renovation of them or reformation of life does ensue thereon, have yet attained a great acquaintance with the truth as it is revealed in the word, and many who are truly enlightened and sanctified by him do yet fall into sundry errors and mistakes, which the differences and divisions among themselves do openly proclaim. And the Scripture itself supposes that there may be diversity of judgments about spiritual things among those who are really sanctified and believers.

A brief answer unto both these exceptions will lead this discourse unto its close. I say, therefore, to the first:¶

1. That there are in the declaration of the mind of God in the Scriptures sundry things that are common unto other writings, both as to the matter of them and the manner of their delivery. Such are the stories of times past therein recorded, the computation of times, the use of words, phrases of speech, figurative and proper, artificial connections of discourse, various sorts of arguments, and the like; all [of] which persons may come to the understanding of, and be able to make a right judgment concerning, without any special assistance of the Holy Spirit, the things about which they are conversant being the proper object of the reasonable faculties of the mind, provided there be a common blessing on their endeavors and exercise.¶

2. The main doctrines of truth declared in the Scripture are proposed in such distinct, plain enunciations, in propositions accommodated unto the understandings of rational men, that persons who, in the use of disciplinary and ecclesiastical helps, attend unto the study of them without prejudice, or prepossession with false notions and opinions, with freedom from the bias of carnal and secular interests and advantages, and from the leaven of tradition, may learn, know, and understand the sense, meaning, and truth of the doctrines so proposed and declared unto them, without any special work of saving illumination on their minds. The propositions of truth in the Scripture, I mean those which are necessary unto the great ends of the Scripture, are so plain and evident in themselves, that it is the fault and sin of all men endued with rational abilities if they perceive them not, and assent not unto them upon the evidence of their truth, or of the mind of God in those places of Scripture wherein they are declared; which is the substance of what we plead concerning the perspicuity of the Scripture against the Papists.¶

3. Considering the natural vanity of the mind of man, its proneness to error and false imaginations, the weakness of judgment wherewith it is in all things accompanied, whatever it attains in the knowledge of truth is to be ascribed unto the guidance of the Spirit of God, although not working in it or upon it by a communication of saving light and grace. For,¶

4. The knowledge of truth thus to be attained is not that illumination which we are inquiring after, nor does it produce those effects of renewing the mind, and transforming it into the image of the things known, with the fruits of holy obedience, which are inseparable from saving illumination.

In answer unto the second pretended consequence of what we have discoursed, I say,¶

1. That the promise of the Spirit, and the communication of him accordingly, to teach, instruct, guide, and lead us into truth, is suited unto that great end for which God has made the revelation of himself in his word, namely, that we might live unto him here according to his will, and be brought unto the enjoyment of him hereafter unto his glory.

2. That unto this end it is not necessary that we should understand the direct sense and meaning of any single text, place, or passage in the Scripture, nor yet that we should obtain the knowledge of everything revealed therein. It suffices, in answer to the promise and design of the work of the Holy Ghost, that the knowledge of all truth necessary to be known unto that end be communicated unto us, and that we have so far a right understanding of the sense of the Scripture as to learn that truth by the use of the means appointed unto that end.

3. We are not hereby absolutely secured from particular errors and mistakes, no more than we are from all actual sins by the work of the Spirit on our wills; that of both kinds, while we live in this world, being only in a tendency toward perfection. There is no faculty of our souls that is absolutely and perfectly renewed in this life. But as the wills of believers are so far renewed and changed by grace as to preserve them from such sins as are inconsistent with a holy life according to the tenor of the covenant, which yet leaves a possibility of many infirmities and actual sins, so their minds are so far renewed as to know and assent to all truths necessary to our life of obedience and a right understanding of the Scripture wherein they are revealed, which yet may be consistent with many mistakes, errors, and false apprehensions, unto our great damage and disadvantage. But with this must be added, that such are the teachings of the Spirit of God as to all divine truths whatever, both in the objective revelation of them in the word, and in the assistance he gives us by his light and grace to perceive and understand the mind and

whole counsel of God in that revelation, that it is not without our own guilt, as well as from our own weakness, that we fall into errors and misapprehensions about any Scripture proposals that concern our duty to God. And if all that believe would freely forgo all prejudices or preconceived opinions, and cast off all impressions from worldly considerations and secular advantages, giving themselves up humbly and entirely to the teaching of God in the ways of his own appointment, some whereof have been before insisted on, we might "all come in the unity of the faith, and of the knowledge of the Son of God, unto a perfect man, unto the measure of the stature of the fullness of Christ" (Eph. 4:13). And these things may suffice to illustrate the work of the Holy Ghost in our illumination, with respect unto the external objective causes thereof, or the Holy Scripture itself.

There is yet another work of the Holy Ghost with respect unto the Scripture, which although it fall not directly under the present consideration of the ways and means of saving illumination, yet the whole of what we have discoursed is so resolved into it, in the order of an external cause, as that it may justly claim a remembrance in this place; and this is, his watchful care over the written word, in preserving it from destruction and corruption, from the first writing of it unto this very day. That it has been under the special care of God, not only the event of its entire preservation, considering the opposition it has been exposed unto, but also the testimony of our Savior as to the books of the Old Testament, than which those of the New are certainly of no less esteem or use, do sufficiently evince: "Till heaven and earth pass, one jot or one tittle shall in no wise pass from the law" (Matt. 5:18). That by the law the whole writings of the Old Testament are intended, the context does declare. And what he affirms, that it shall not by any means pass away, that is, be abolished or corrupted, that he takes on himself to preserve and secure. Two things the Scripture in itself is subject unto: First, destruction or abolition, as unto the whole or any necessary part thereof. Second, corruption of the writing, by changes, alterations, and falsifications of the copies of it. And by both of these it has been attempted, and that both before and since the time of the promulgation of the gospel, the stories whereof are known. And yet is it come safe off from all, not only without ruin, but without wound or blemish. For anyone to suppose that this has been done by chance, or by the care of men alone, without the special watchful providence and powerful actings of the Spirit of God, in the pursuit of the promise of Christ that it should not fail, which expressed a care that God had taken on himself to make good from the beginning, is not only to neglect the consideration of the nature of all human affairs, with the revolutions that they are subject unto, and the deceit and violence wherewith the Scriptures have been attacked, with the insufficiency of the powers and diligence employed for their preservation, but also to countenance the atheistical notion that God has no special regard to his word and worship in the world. Indeed, for a man to think and profess that the Scripture is the word of God, given unto men for the ends which itself declares, and of that use which it must be of in being so, and not believe that God has always taken and does take special care of its preservation, and that in its purity and integrity, beyond the ordinary ways of his providence in the rule of all other things, is to be sottish[4] and foolish, and to entertain thoughts of God, his goodness, wisdom, and power, infinitely unworthy of him and them.¶

There have of late been some opinions concerning the integrity and purity of the Scriptures invented and maintained, that, I conceive, take off from the reverence of that relation which the Scripture has, in its integrity and purity, unto the care and glory of God. Hence it is by some maintained that some books written by divine inspiration, and given out unto the church as part of its canon, or rule of faith and obedience, are utterly lost and perished. That the law and Scripture of the Old Testament before the captivity were written, though in the Hebrew tongue, which, they say, was not originally the language of Abraham, derived from Heber, but of the posterity of Ham in Canaan, yet not in the letters or characters which are now in use, but in those which a few wicked idolaters called Samaritans did use and possess, being left unto them by Ezra, and new characters invented by him, or borrowed from the Chaldeans for the use of the church. That the vowels and accents, whereby alone the true reading and sense of it is preserved, are a late invention of some Masoretic rabbis; and that the original text is in many places corrupted, so as that it may and ought to be corrected by translations, especially that of the LXX,[5] with sundry other such imaginations, which they countenance with uncertain conjectures and fabulous stories.[6] And I cannot but wonder how some seem to take shelter unto their opinions, especially that of preferring the translation of the LXX unto the original Hebrew text, or, as they fondly speak, "the present copy of it," in the Church of England, whose publicly authorized and excellent translation[7] takes no more notice of, nor has any

---

4   I.e., drunken; dumb.

5   I.e., "The Seventy," the number of translators in the third- and second-centuries BC who translated the Old Testament into Greek. This is often a reference to the Septuagint.

6   Owen obviously does not explicitly identify whom he has in mind, but clearly they are those who elevate translations of the Bible over the original Hebrew and Greek in an effort to support their theological ends.

7   This is a reference to the Authorized Version (1611), also known as the King James Version.

more regard unto that translation, when it differs from the Hebrew, as it does in a thousand places, than if it had never been in the world.¶

And as no translations are in common use in the whole world but what were immediately traduced out of the Hebrew original, excepting only some part of the vulgar Latin, so I verily believe that those very Christians who contend for a preference to be given unto that of the LXX, now they have got their ends, or at least attempted them, in procuring a reputation of learning, skill, and cunning, by their writings about it, would not dare to advise a translation out of that to be made and composed for the use of that church which they adhere unto, be it what it will, to the rejection and exclusion of that taken out of the original. And to have two recommended unto common use, so discrepant as they would be found to be, would certainly be of more disadvantage to the church than by all their endeavors otherwise they can compensate. Yea, I am apt to think that they will not be very urgent for an alteration to be made in the church's translation in those particular instances wherein they hope they have won themselves much reputation in proving the mistakes of the Hebrew, and manifesting how it may be rectified by the translation of the LXX. For whatever thoughts may be in their minds concerning their learned disputes, I doubt not but they have more reverence of God and his word than to break in upon it with such a kind of violence, on any pretense whatsoever. As, therefore, the integrity and purity of the Scripture in the original languages may be proved and defended against all opposition, with whatever belongs thereunto, so we must ascribe their preservation to the watchful care and powerful operation of the Spirit of God absolutely securing them throughout all generations.

General Index

Abel, sacrifices in faith, 84
abiding in Christ, 248
Abraham
    anxious inquiring of, 146
    command to sacrifice his son, 83
    immediate revelation granted to, 82
    taught family in the fear of God, 84
acknowledgement, 44, 258
Act of Toleration (1689), 8, 26
Act of Uniformity (1662), 6
advocate, 58
allegories, 47, 305, 306
allusions, 47, 304
ambition, 120
Ambrose, 343
analogy of faith, 47, 50, 139, 306–7, 311,
    328, 329
anointing of the Spirit, 60, 149, 246
antecedents and consequents, 311
antichrists, preservation and deliver-
    ances from, 248–49
antinomianism, 20, 22
Apocrypha, 112, 194n4
apostasy, 283
apostles, 164
    extraordinary office of, 63
    as eyewitnesses of Christ's glory, 161
    inspiration of, 163, 224, 250
    as poor, low, and despised, 116–17
    preaching of, 40, 190
Aretine, 343
Aristotelianism, 274n10

Arminians, 17, 29–30
Artaxerxes, 336
assent of faith
    with assurance, 39, 57, 188–89
    from external arguments, 135
    of the nature of that on which it is
        built, 33, 35, 130–31
    to Scripture, 173–74
assurance, 57, 125, 126, 215, 225
assurance of adherence, 39, 188
assurance of evidence, 39, 188
atheism, 83, 106, 111, 155, 169, 280
Augustine, 119, 155, 203, 343
authorial intent, divine and human, 48
Authorized Version (1611), 328n15
awe and wonder, as evidence of divine
    authority of Scripture, 185

Babylonian captivity, and preservation of
    Scripture, 102
Baptista of Mantua, 204–5
Barbarians, 325
Barebones Parliament (1553), 5
Basil, 202
Bauthumley, Jacob, 20
Baxter, Richard, criticism of Owen, 14
believers
    given the Spirit, 59
    preservation of, 61
believing the Scriptures to be revelation,
    33, 88, 89, 92, 135–37, 198
Bellarmine, Robert, 206

Beza, Theodore, 344
Bible. *See* Scripture
biblical interpretation, 47–49, 309–19
  and the church, 50, 341–44
  diversity of judgments among believ-
    ers, 345
  errors and mistakes in, 280
  rules for, 49–50, 319, 321–40
  two means, 42, 225
Biblical languages, 321–32
  abuses of, 329–31
  and interpretation, 49
  limits of, 331–32
Biddle, John, 31
Bishops' War (1629–1640), 3
blasphemy, 169
blessedness, 106–7
Bonaventure, 188
Book of Common Prayer, 3, 5, 6, 15, 50
books of Moses, 85, 228
British Empire, anti-Catholicism of, 12
Browne, Robert, 17
Brudenell, Lord, 11
Bucer, Martin, 344
Burroughs, Edward, 24

Cabalistic Jews, 330
Calvin, John, 68, 150, 207, 344
Cano, Melchor, 137, 206
carnal weapons, 117
Cartesianism, 31
catechisms, 295
Catholic Church. *See* Roman Catholic
  Church
catholic tradition, and biblical interpre-
  tation, 341–42
Caton, William, 24
Causes, Ways, and Means of Understand-
* ing the Mind of God* (Owen), 13, 22,
  27, 32, 40–50
celebrity pastors, 70
Chaldeans, 322, 348
Charles I, King, 2, 9, 20
Charles II, King, 5–6, 11, 12
Chauncy, Isaac, 14

children of God, 53
chronological computations of time, 49,
  307, 334–37
Chrysostom, John, 343
church
  authority of, 108
  and biblical interpretation, 50, 341–44
  edification of, 62
  not infallible, 226
  outward call as essential but insuf-
    ficient, 65
  testimony and declaration of Scrip-
    ture, 34, 108–16, 156, 164
  visible and invisible, 63
church fathers, 50, 342, 343
Church of England, 2, 4–6
  appeal to reason, 32–33, 242n18,
    261n18
  movement toward Roman Catholic
    liturgical practices, 10, 30
  Owen's opposition to, 13–14
  Puritan opposition to, 12, 13
Cicero, 175
Clarendon Code, 6
clearer passages, inform reading of difficult passages, 47, 306
Clement of Alexander, 201–2
"cloud of witnesses," 115
Colet, John, 328n14
collation, 47
Comforter, office of, 58–59
communication of the Spirit, 60–62
communion with God, through liturgical forms, 15
compassion, toward the ignorant,
  283–85
confessions of faith, 296
conjectural knowledge, 104, 254
conscience, 182–83
consolation, from word of God, 185–86
contemplation, 56
Conventicle Act (1664), 6
Conventicle Act (1670), 7
conversion, as divine effect of the word
  of God, 181–82

conviction, as divine effect of the word
of God, 182–85
Coppe, Abiezer, 20
Corporation Act (1661), 6
corrupt affections, 46, 283–85, 312
corrupt traditions, 45, 286–87, 289
Cotton, John, 68
Council of Trent (1545–1563), 220n3
counsel of God, 244
covetousness, 120
creeds, 296
Crell, Johann, 29
Cressy, Hugh, 16, 50
Cromwell, Oliver, 1, 4, 5, 10–11, 18, 21,
25, 31
Cromwell, Richard, 1, 5, 8
"cunningly-devised fables," 111, 128,
160–61, 199
curiosity, in interpretation, 329–30
Cyrus, 335–36

Daniel, seventy weeks of, 335–36
darkness of understandings, 238, 239,
281
of the world, 184
David, faith of, 146
Declaration of Indulgence (1672), 7
decrees of God, 47, 303
Defense of the Gospel (Owen), 31
delight in God. See enjoyment of God
design for growth and progress in
knowledge, 49, 316–17
devil, as "god of this world," 104, 105,
138, 179, 274, 289
Dewsbury, William, 24
Didymus the Blind, 247
Digby, Kenelm, 11
Diggers, 19, 22
Dionysius of Halicarnassus, 119
Directory for Public Worship
(Westminster Assembly), 5
discerning of spirits, as extraordinary
gift, 64
disciplinarian means of biblical interpretation, 42, 49, 225, 321–40, 345

Discourse of Spiritual Gifts (Owen), 13,
22, 62–67
Dissertation on Divine Justice (Owen), 31
divine author, intended meaning of, 48
divine efficacy, revealed in Scripture,
179–80
divine excellency, revealed in Scripture,
177–78
divine faith, 35, 132, 136
divine revelation. See revelation
divisions and scandals among
Christians, 280
doctrine, spiritual gifts concerning, 66
doctrines, 295–96, 297
double veiling, 43, 231–32
duty of right understanding of Scripture,
43, 44
duty of prayer, 54, 56
for oneself, 51
pray for others, 51
as well as possible, 51

early church, extraordinary gifts and
offices in, 64
ecclesiastical means of interpretation, 50,
341–44
education in arts and sciences, as means
of right biblical interpretation, 42
Edward, King, 9
Egyptians, wisdom of, 100
Elisha, servant of, 235
Elizabeth, Queen, 9
empiricism, 253–54
English Baptists, 17–18
English Catholics, 9–10
English Civil War, 4, 10, 30
English Dissent, 1, 2
enjoyment of God, 54, 103, 106–8, 189,
304
enlightening of understanding, 45,
267–68
Enlightenment, 31
Enoch
immediate revelation granted to, 82
walked with God, 84

enthusiasms, 223, 226, 265, 318

Episcopius, Simon, 29, 31, 247n4

"etcetera oath," 3

Euripides, 330n18

Eustathius, 327

evangelist, as extraordinary office, 63

external arguments, 34–35, 99–126

    rebukes unbelievers, 199–200

    insufficiency of, 35–36, 127–51

external senses, 253–54

extraordinary gifts of the Spirit, 63–65, 272

extraordinary offices in the church, 63

faculties and powers of the soul, abuse of, 169

faith

    as assent upon testimony, 38

    built and resolved into Scripture itself, 166

    as divine and supernatural, 126

    established by the word of God, 186

    as extraordinary gift, 64

    as gift of God, 129

    infallibility of, 34, 93–94

    knowledge from, 168

    part of obedience, 128

    rests on truth and authority of God alone, 166

    and unbelief, 53

faith and obedience, 128

    all things concerning revealed in Scripture, 302

    as great ends of Scripture, 297–98, 299

false knowledge, 44–45, 258–60

false worship, 183, 279

Farnworth, Richard, 24

Feake, Christopher, 21

Fell, Margaret, 24

Fifth Monarchists, 6, 20–21, 22, 25

Five Mile Act (1665), 7

Fletcher, Elizabeth, 26

formal object of faith, 34, 92–96, 125, 153

Fox, George, 23, 24

free prayer, 50

"full assurance of understanding," 41, 44, 145, 221–22, 225, 254, 255, 258, 260

genealogies, 307

General Baptists, 17–18

Geneva Bible (1560), 328n15

geography, and biblical interpretation, 49, 334

Glorious Revolution (1688–1689), 7, 12

glory of God

    revealed in Jesus Christ, 274–75

    as proper purpose of prayer, 54, 56

God

    authority and veracity of, 34, 37, 94–95, 127–29, 153–54, 156–57, 200, 303

    as Father of glory, 240

    as God of truth, 243

    as only true God, 268

    perpetual care over Scripture, 101

    righteous vengeance of, 122–23

    self-subsistence of, 197

    sovereign will and pleasure of, 122

    works of creation and providence, 38, 169–70, 172, 174–75

Godhead, eternal power of, 173

godliness, 129, 315, 316

godly fear, 46, 292

Goodwin, Thomas, 68

gospel

    prejudices against, 274

    same from the beginning, 121

    times of prevalency, at the sovereign disposal of God, 122

graces bestowed for benefit of others, 63

graces bestowed for individual's good, 63

grammatical sense, 48

"greatness of God's power," 235

Grecian monarchy, and preservation of Scripture, 102

Greek language, 323–25

Greeks, wisdom of, 100, 118, 120, 324

Gregory of Valencia, 206–7

Gribben, Crawford, 1
Grotius, Hugo, 29, 31

Hammond, Henry, 30
hard to interpret, 47, 302, 304–7
hard to understand, 47, 302
healing gifts, as extraordinary gifts, 64
Hebrew language, 322, 326, 331
Helwys, Thomas, 17
Henry VIII, King, 9
Hesychius, 327
history, and biblical interpretation, 49,
    332–34
holiness, as proper purpose of prayer, 54
Holy Spirit
    abides in us, 246
    aid and assistance in interpretation,
        318–19
    assists, helps, and relieves against
        temptation, 146
    authored the whole of Scripture, 37
    care in the preservation of Scripture,
        347–49
    as comforter, 58–60
    in composing and disposal of Scrip-
        ture, 46, 295
    as an earnest, 60, 61–62, 149
    as efficient cause of faith, 193, 205,
        223
    enables us to believe the Scripture to
        be the word of God, 89
    external work of evidencing Scrip-
        ture's divinity, 39, 190
    gift of, 59, 240, 313, 240
    and illumination of minds, 42, 43, 67,
        81, 224–26, 230, 252
    immediate inspiration of Scripture,
        94, 96
    implants spiritual habits and prin-
        ciples, 46
    infallibility of, 44
    infallibly secures faith, 186
    infinite condescension of, 59
    as infinitely wise, 256
    inhabitation of, 60

internal testimony of, 36–37, 39,
    133, 156, 189, 200, 205, 245,
    272–73
leads us into the truth, 243–46
love of, 59, 256
mission of, 58, 244
objective work of, 140, 200
outpouring of, 52
power of, 59
as principal efficient cause of Scrip-
    tural understanding, 43–44
produces faith in us, 34, 94
produces infallible certainty, 35–36
removal of hindrances, 290–93
as a seal, 60, 61, 149
as Spirit of revelation, 234
as Spirit of truth, 156, 243, 256
as Spirit of wisdom and revelation,
    239, 240–42
subjective work of, 140
teaches us to understand aright the
    mind and will of God, 254
as an unction, 60
work in prayer, 52–54
Holy Spirit as Comforter (Owen), 13, 22,
    47–62
Hooker, Thomas, 68
Hooton, Elizabeth, 23
"hope of God's calling," 235
Horace, 280n3
Hubberthorne, Richard, 24
human authorial intent, 48
human faith, 35, 131, 135
human responsibility, to use means for
    biblical interpretation, 266–67
human wisdom, 99–100
humility, 46, 282, 291–93
    in instruction, 257
    in interpretation, 305, 306, 313, 329
    as means of attaining growth in spiri-
        tual gifts, 67
hypostatic union, 303

idolatry, 52, 104, 184
ignorance, 45–46, 104–5, 279–93

illumination, 27–28, 33–34, 36, 41–42,
    48, 67, 89–90, 137–42, 184, 199
  as grasping of content, 45
  as internal subjective revelation, 234
  nature and effects of, 45, 265–78
  necessity of, 42–43, 234–38
  from supernatural revelation, 82
  and use of reason, 266
immediate inspiration, 96, 140, 149, 163,
    165, 224, 225
inbred principles of natural light, 38,
    167–68, 172, 174, 252, 272
incarnation, 7, 134, 302, 304
Independency, at the Westminster As-
    sembly, 5
Indians, 105, 124
indifference to religion, 280
individualism, 70
indwelling of the Spirit, 60
infallible certainty, 35, 36, 68
"inner light" (Quakerism), 23, 26–28, 40
inspiration, 163
instinct. See inbred principle of natural law
institutionalism, 70
intellect, use in prayer, 57
internal testimony of the Holy Spirit,
    36–37, 142–51, 205
  as efficacious persuasion, 143–46
  not new immediate revelation, 142–43
  not the reason of faith, 36, 142–43
invisible church, 63
Irish Rebellion, 12
irrationalism, of Quakers, 40
Islam, 85

Jacob, Henry, 17
James I, King, 9
James II, King, 7, 12
James Stuart, 11
Jerome, 326–27n10, 343
Jessey, Henry, 21
Jesuits, 10
Jesus Christ
  as image of the invisible God, 273–74
  intercession of, 146

sealing of, 61
signs of, 160
Jews
  boasting of, 118, 120, 324
  despised by nations and ignorant and
    barbarous, 99
  interpretation of the Old Testament,
    48
  knowledge of Scripture, 44, 259
John, testimony on Scripture, 110
joy, 186
Julius Pollux, 327
justification, and necessity of obedience,
    266
Justin Martyr, 325

kingdom of heaven, 139, 240, 241, 244,
    293
knowing all things, 248
knowing the only true God, 268–69
knowledge
  degree of, 249, 304
  distinct from acknowledgement, 44,
    258
  through the exercise of the mind,
    271–72
  as spiritual gift, 66
  three ways of, 38, 167–68, 214
Koran, 103

Laud, William, 3
Laudianism, 3, 8
Leavens, Elizabeth, 26
Levellers, 18, 19
light
  illumination as, 45
  Spirit's work as, 276–77
  word of God as, 230
light and darkness, 276–77
light of nature, 167–68, 169, 170–72, 197
light shining in a dark place, 36, 38, 103,
    106, 138, 141, 179, 184
light shining into our hearts, 45, 273,
    274–75
Lilburne, John, 18

Lockean epistemology, 31
Long Parliament, 4
Louis XIV, King, 11
love of honor and praise, 45, 286
love of sin, 45, 289–90
lusts, 147–48, 155

Mahometism (Islam), 85
manna, 87
martyrs, testimony of, 112–13, 114–16
Mary Stuart, 8
Mary Tudor, 9, 12
Mass, 52
material object of faith, 34, 92, 125, 154
Mather, Nathaniel, 69–70
meditating on Scripture as means of ap-
    prehending Scripture, 42, 87, 225,
    228, 257
meekness, 46, 257, 291–93
    in interpretation, 313
    as means of attaining growth in spiri-
    tual gifts, 67
mental prayer, 16, 52, 56–57
minds darkness of, 238, 281
mind and will of God, 213
    revealed in Scripture, 34, 88–89, 219,
    280
    understandable by all men, 222
minister, spiritual gifts of, 65–66
ministry of the church, 249, 255
    declares the Scripture to be the word
    of God, 108
    extraordinary and ordinary, 164–66
ministry of the word, 33, 88, 156, 192
miracles, 159–60, 195
    as extraordinary gift, 64
    as God's attestation of apostles and
    their ministry, 114, 128
Missal, 51–52
moderate Calvinism, 3
Mohammed, 117
Mohammedans, 106, 124, 183
Moors, 147
moral certainty, 36, 154
    as effect of reason, 129–30

insufficient from external arguments,
    34–36, 127–51
Mortimer, Sarah, 28n77
Moses, veil of, 43, 231
Moses and the prophets, 159–60
Muggleton, Lodowicke, 21
Muggletonians, 21–22
mutual instruction of one another,
    87–88
mysteries of the gospel, 172, 235, 244
    contempt of, 262
mystical stories in Scripture, 47, 305, 306

nations, walk in their own ways, 85
natural blindness and darkness, 138
natural law, 18, 29, 30, 31
natural light. See light of nature
Naylor, James, 24, 25
Nemesius, 202
new birth, 47, 303
new immediate revelations, 42, 224, 226,
    234, 250
New Model Army, 4
New Testament
    canon of, 194
    completion of books of, 86, 234
    on the writings of the Old Testament,
    163
Noah, immediate revelation granted to,
    82

Oates, Titus, 11
obedience, 128, 316. See also faith and
    obedience
objective revelations, 250
obligation to believe, 164–66
Old Testament, 86
    canon, 194
    darkness and obscurity in, 230–31
    prophets, 163
    types and shadows of, 231–32, 334
"opening of the eyes of our understand-
    ing," 45, 137, 139–40, 229, 233, 239,
    241, 267–68
oracles of God, 102, 114, 164, 194

ordinary believers, understanding of
Scripture, 221
ordinary gifts of the Spirit, 62, 65–67, 272
Origen, 343
outward means appointed by God, 236,
238, 255, 265, 266–67, 270, 273,
275, 277, 293, 344
Overton, Richard, 18
Owen, John
on assurance, 13
as a brilliant synthesizer, 67
contribution to pneumatology, 1–2
as Cromwell's personal chaplain, 8
energized publishing career, 1
on prayer book worship, 14
preached at Rump Parliament, 8
as a Puritan, 69
on Roman Catholicism, 12–13
as student at Oxford University, 8
subjectivist piety of, 69
as vice-chancellor at Oxford University, 26
Oxford University, 8, 26

parable, of rich man and Lazarus,
159–60
parables, as hard to interpret, 47
Paraclete, 58
parents, ministry to instruct their children, 84
Particular Baptists, 17–18
Paul
concept of double veiling, 43, 231–32
on faith resting on the Word of God,
162
Pelagians, 227, 255
Pentecost, and descent of the Spirit, 245
Perkins, William, 68
Persian monarchy, and preservation of
Scripture, 102
persuasion of mind, 198–99
Peter
on faith resting on authority and truth
of God, 160–62
testimony about Scripture, 110

winnowed by Satan, 146
Pharisees, pride of, 242, 285–86
Phavorinus, 327
Philip, and Ethiopian eunuch, 88, 245,
273, 309
Philistines, put out eyes of Samson, 223,
255
Pittis, Thomas, 15–16
pity, on the ignorant, 283–85
"Popish Plot" (1768), 11
prayer
according to one's abilities, 55
according to the will of God, 51
boldness and confidence in, 54
for enabling of God, 43
as external performance, 55
for help in understanding the Scriptures, 48–49
human deficiency in practice of, 53
and improvement of holiness, 54
includes intense, sincere acting of
minds, 51
and interpretation, 48
as means of right biblical interpretation, 42, 225, 311–15
proper purposes of, 54
for the Spirit of wisdom and revelation, 239, 263
as spiritual gift, 55–56, 67
for understanding Scripture, 227, 230,
234, 257
preaching, 40, 190
efficacy of, 58, 117–21
instrumental cause of teaching of the
Spirit, 247
as ordinary ministry of the church,
165
Presbyterianism, at the Westminster
Assembly, 5
pride, 45, 120, 121, 258, 263, 281, 282,
285–86, 289, 291, 329
private interpretation, 40
privatism, 70
probability, 35, 39, 254
profaneness, 169

prophecies, interpretation of, 305, 306, 334

prophecy, as extraordinary gift, 64

prophets

extraordinary office of, 63

immediate inspiration of, 163, 165, 224, 250

preaching by immediate inspiration of the Holy Spirit, 165

Prophets (books of the Old Testament), 228

Pro Sacris Scripturis Exceritationes adversus Fanaticos (Owen), 27

Protestants, on Scripture, 205

providence, 169–70

and preservation of Scripture, 101

Psalms, 228

Puritans

on biblical chronology and prophecy, 49n95

at the Westminster Assembly, 4–5

Quakers, 23–28, 32, 40, 70, 261n18

quenching the Spirit, 55

Racovian Catechism, 31

radical sectarians, 261n18

Ramism, 49n96

Ranters, 20, 22

rational considerations, 38, 76, 168, 170, 171, 309, 337

rationalism, 253–54

of Socinians, 40, 44

readiness to conform mind and heart, 49, 315–16

reading Scripture, 87, 309–11

reason, 31–32, 42, 169, 253–54, 255

and biblical interpretation, 49, 337–40

depraved and corrupt, 135

finite, limited, and weak, 135, 339

insufficient for understanding the mind and will of God, 224, 236–39

and moral certainty, 35

required for instruction, 271–72

and revelation of works of creation and providence, 172–73

in the use of external means, 266

Reason of Faith (Owen), 13, 27, 32–40

Reeve, John, 21

Reformation, 343

regeneration, 59, 181

regulative principle of worship, 14

Religious Society of Friends, 25

Remonstrant crisis, 29

Restoration of English monarchy, 1, 2, 5, 30

resurrection of the dead, 134, 303, 304

revelation, 33

certainty of, 34

as communication of light, 139

contained in Scripture, 198

consonance of, 170–71

external arguments for, 35–36, 97–126

infallibility of, 172–73

nature of, 37–39, 167–86

only foundation and reason of faith, 37, 89, 153–66

only objective cause of illumination, 33, 82

originally given immediately, 33, 82–83

as proper object of faith, 35, 127–29

requires exercise of faith, conscience, and obedience, 83

self-authenticating, 169–76

sufficient guide unto all duties of faith and obedience, 83–84

veracity of, 34, 94–95

Revelation (book), 334

reverence, 46, 292, 329

revolutionary sectarians, 17–23

"riches of glory," 235

righteous judgment of God, 122–23

Roman Catholic Church, 70

on assurance, 13, 36, 142, 251

on authority of the church, 109, 136, 219–20, 252–53, 256

on authority of Scripture, 148–49

in England, 9–17

false worship of, 50
neglect of ordinary gifts, 62
on obscurity, difficulty, and perplexity
of Scripture, 280
on tradition, 40, 44, 94
on transubstantiation, 171
worship of, 13
Roman Empire, 118, 120
and preservation of Scripture, 102
rule of the church, spiritual gifts for, 67
Rump Parliament (1648-1653), 4, 8
Rushworth, John, 11

Salmon, Joseph, 20
Samaritan woman, 180, 192
sanctification, by the word of God, 181
Satan
blinding by, 105, 138, 179, 274, 289
malicious craft of, 83, 138, 101
prejudices produced by, 36
temptations by, 274, 285, 289–90
saving grace, 62–63, 311
saving knowledge of the mind and will
of God, 89, 277, 279, 295
scholasticism, 274n10
Scripture
antiquity of, 34, 98–100
authority of, 27–28, 32–33, 38
to be read in language commonly
understood, 322
clarity of, 47, 300–302
composing and disposal of, 46, 293,
296
designed to reveal God to us, 103–6
difficult passages of, 302–7
diligent use of, 256
direct sense of, 346
divine content of, 34, 103–8
divine origin of, 38, 91, 103
divine power and efficacy of, 187
effects of, 34, 116–26
errors and misapprehensions about,
346–47
external form of, 325
genre of, 46, 295–300

great ends of faith and obedience,
297–300
on illumination, 267–78
infallibility of, 34
internal sacred form of, 325
literal sense of, 233
makes preaching necessary, 298–99
neglect of, 272
only external means of supernatural
illumination, 33, 43, 86
opposition to authority of, 147–49
perceived as obscure, 296, 301
perspicuity of, 41, 214–15, 345
phraseology of, 319, 328, 329
preservation of, 34, 100–103, 347–49
as rule of faith and obedience, 40, 234,
306
as self-authenticating, 33, 37–38, 157,
158–63, 169–76, 177–86
spirit of wisdom and holiness of, 298
sufficiency of, 33, 85–86, 161, 250
things common with other writings,
345
truth and divinity proved by rational
arguments, 190–91
in unknown language, 322
as word of God, 81, 88, 127, 147,
197–98, 219
Scythians, 325
sealing of the Spirit, 61, 149
Second Council of Orange (529), 129,
204
seducers, preservation and deliverances
from, 248–49
Seekers, 20n57
self-conceit, in interpretation, 329
self-confidence, 286
self-denial, 257
sensuality, 120
Septuagint, 348–49
set forms of prayer, 50–51, 54–55, 57
Shepard, Thomas, 68
Short Parliament, 3
Simmons, Martha, 25
simplicitate credendi, 155

sin unto death, 283
sloth, 45, 287–89
Smyth, John, 17
sobriety, in interpretation, 329
Socinianism, 16, 28–32, 40, 44, 236,
    242n18, 304
Socinus, Faustus, 28–29, 247n4
Solemn League and Covenant, 4, 6
Son of God, gives understanding,
    268–69, 270–71
Spanish Armada, 12
special revelation, priority of, 38, 171–76
speculation, 44
spiritual blindness, 36, 38, 179, 184
spiritual excess, 70
spiritual gifts, extraordinary and
    ordinary, 58, 62
spiritual means of interpretation, 48–49,
    311–17
    objections to, 317–19
spiritual wisdom, 241–42
"Spirit of wisdom and revelation," 140,
    141, 239, 250, 262, 313
Spurr, John, 4n5, 5n7
Stapleton, Thomas, 205–6
study of the word, 33, 87, 257
subjective revelations, 250
submission of soul and conscience, 46,
    292
subordinate means of making Scripture
    effectual, 87–88
subtilitate disputandi, 155
Sun of Righteousness, 84
superstition, 52, 104, 184
suppressing the truth in unrighteous-
    ness, 38, 122, 284
synagogues, 324
Synod of Dort (1618–1619), 29

"taught of God," 138, 245, 252, 255
teachability, 67, 291, 306
teachers, not lords over the faith, 250
telescope, 43, 235
Ten Commandments, 127
testimony of the Holy Spirit, 39

Theodoret, 343
Theophylact, 343
thoughts of heavenly things, 310
"Thus saith the Lord," 37, 127, 153, 157,
    163, 170
times of ignorance, 123
tongues, as extraordinary gift, 64
Torah, 228
Tory royalists, 7
tradition, 42
    and biblical authority, 220n3
    and biblical interpretation, 50
    Roman Catholic Church on, 40, 44, 94
translation out of darkness into light, 268
transubstantiation, 52
Trinitarian relations, 59
Trinity, 28–29, 30, 47, 134, 302, 304
"True Levellers." See Diggers
trust in God, 45, 260
truth, in things natural and civil, 244
trying the spirits, 261

unbelief, 169, 173, 306
unbeliever, knowledge of, 44–45
unction of the Spirit, 246–54, 263
understanding, 45, 269–71, 277–78
    as spiritual gift, 66
unfulfilled prophecies, as hard to
    interpret, 47
unregenerate
    can pray unto the edification of others,
    56
    use of set forms of prayer, 55
unvocal prayer, 56
utterance, as spiritual gift, 66–67

vanity, 281, 346
veil of Moses, 43, 231
veil of sin, darkness, and blindness, 43,
    231–32
Venner, Thomas, 6
Vermigli, Peter Martyr, 344
Vindication of the Late Reverend and
    Learned John Owen (anonymous),
    14

visible church, 63
Vulgate, 220n3

weapons of warfare, 62
Westminster Assembly, 4–5
Whigs, 7
Whitaker, William, 68
Whitehead, George, 24
wicked, lack wisdom, 241
will of God. See mind and will of God
William of Orange, 7
Winstanley, Gerrard, 19
wisdom
  as gift, 241
  Spirit's work as, 45, 278

as spiritual gift, 66
wisdom and revelation, 239–40
wisdom of the world, 99–100, 105, 241
"wonderful things" of the Scriptures,
  42–43, 227–30, 235, 255, 260, 268
word of knowledge, as extraordinary
  gift, 63–64
word of wisdom, as extraordinary gift, 63
Work of the Holy Spirit in Prayer (Owen),
  13, 15, 16, 50–57
worldly wisdom, 241
worship, 14
  ordinances of, 49, 317
  spiritual gifts for, 67
written prayers, 51

Scripture Index

Genesis

3:12 .... 280n2
4:26 82
5:29 82
10:21–24 322
15:2 146
18:19 82
22:2 83

Exodus

9:1 .... 127n1
20:2 .... 127n1, 128n2
31:2–6 82
34:29 231

Deuteronomy

4:2 86
4:6–8 100
6:6–7 .... 86, 87
6:6–9 310
6:7 87
11:18–19 87
12:32 86
17:8 228
29:4 137
29:29 158
31:11–13 158
32:4 94

Joshua

1:8 .... 87, 228, 287

2 Samuel

7:28 95

1 Kings

4:31–34 82

2 Kings

6:17 235
18:26 322

2 Chronicles

20:20 .... 94, 95, 127n1, 176

Ezra

1:1–4 336
4:8–6:18 .... 322n2
7:11–26 336
7:12–26 .... 322n2

Nehemiah

8:8 88

Job

32:8 277
36:22 .... 243, 252

Psalms

1:2 .... 87, 228, 287
8:3 170
9:10 260
19:1 .... 174n4, 175n5
19:1–2 83

19:1–3................ 170, 177
19:7–8................ 86
19:7–9................ 163, 177
24:7–8................ 240
25:9 293
25:12 293
25:14 293
36:9 230
43:3 230
45:5 185
77:11 228
78:11 228
81:12 85
94:9 .... 240n16
104 177
107:43 278
115 .... 202, 202n7
116:11 .... 146n28
119 .... 42, 87, 163
119:18 .... 42, 82, 139, 209,
                227–32, 239n13,
                255n14, 265, 267,
                268n4
119:24 297
119:27 139
119:33–34 227
119:34 .... 88, 139, 277
119:105 230
119:130 88
119:144 .... 209, 277
138:2 .... 138n18, 173
139:5–6 302
139:14–16 302
147:8–9 177
147:19–20 .... 177, 322

Proverbs
1:6 88
2:2–6 287
2:3–5 .... 299, 317
26:12 241
28:5 .... 293, 318

Ecclesiastes
12:10 321

Song of Songs
4:6 305

Isaiah
1:3 168
5:4 270
7:9 176
8:19–20 .... 105, 158
8:20 .... 86, 88, 127n1, 163,
                228, 250
9:6 229
11:2 240
11:2–3 235
11:3 240
25:7 .... 227, 232
28:9 88
29:11–12 88
30:15 95
34:16 325
39:8 330
43:10–12 98
44:18–20 170
44:19–20 173
46:5–8 170
46:8 173
54:13 .... 135n12
57:15 .... 95, 127n1
60:2 184
61:1 273
65:16 .... 243n1

Jeremiah
5:12 113
10:11 322
23:28 83
23:28–29 .... 112, 159
23:29 184

Daniel
1:4 322
2 20
2:4–7:28 .... 322n2
12:3 88
12:10 .... 241, 278

Hosea
2:8 168
6:3 317
8:12 229
14:9 .... 88, 227, 241, 278

Habakkuk
1:11 118
2:4 282

Zechariah
1:6 184
12:10 52

Malachi
4:4 163
4:4–6 86

Matthew
5:14–15 88
5:18 .... 101, 326, 347
6:23 276
8:29 .... 148n32
11:25 .... 129, 139
11:27 139
13:11 .... 129, 135n11, 139,
                    240
15:16 88
16:17 .... 135n10
17:5 287
18:3 293
21:42 164
22:37 269
24–25 334
28:20 245

Mark
12:30 269
15:18 .... 148n35
16:16 .... 165, 176

Luke
1:4 .... 86, 225, 258
1:17 241
2:32 .... 81, 235

9:35 .... 127n1
10:27 269
11:13 .... 240, 313
11:35 276
13:3 .... 85n6
16:27–31 159
16:29 164
16:31 .... 71, 164
24:25–27 162
24:26–27 87
24:27 88
24:32 87
24:44 .... 228, 233
24:44–45 .... 227, 232–33
24:45 .... 88, 139, 232, 265,
                       267

John
1:1 .... 303n8
1:5 .... 276, 282, 284n6
1:9 27
1:14 .... 161, 303n8
1:45 164
2:22 92
3:12 302
3:19–20 289
4:29 180
4:40–42 93
4:42 .... 192, 195
5:37–38 286
5:39 287
5:44 286
6:45 .... 129, 138, 243,
                      245n3, 252, 255,
                      271, 272
7:17 316
8:12 .... 195n5
9:25 .... 184n20
9:39–40 242
12:43 286
14–16 244
14:16 .... 58, 245, 246
15:4 .... 248n7
16:13 .... 43, 243–46, 271
16:13–15 261

16:29 .... 305n11
17:3 269
17:17 .... 94, 300
17:20 .... 112, 245
20:30–31 160
20:31 86
21:24 110

Acts
1:1 86
1:4 245
2:1–4 245
2:13 .... 195, 195n6
2:33 299
2:41 .... 195n6
3:7–8 195
3:14 246
4:13 116
5:32 114
7:2 240
8:13 195
8:21 195
8:28–30 92
8:30–31 309
8:31 .... 88, 246
8:35–36 88
13:47 81
14:15–17 170
14:16 .... 85, 104n8
16:14 .... 81, 273
16:21 118
17:18 116
17:23 104
17:24–28 170
17:30 .... 104n8, 123n33
18:13 118
18:24–25 164
18:28 164
19 120
19:19 236
20:20 237
20:21 244
20:27 .... 237, 244
20:28 .... 303n8
20:32 181

22:20 114
24:14 164
26:17–18 267
26:18 81
26:22 164
26:22–23 92
26:24 161
26:25 .... 161n9
26:27 92
27:31 .... 148n33
28:23 164

Romans
1 104
1:16 .... 181, 192
1:17 170
1:18 .... 85, 284n5
1:18ff 104
1:19 .... 82, 169, 197n1
1:19–21 83
1:20 .... 173, 174n3, 175n6
1:20–21 170
1:21–25 171
1:28 173
2:5 .... 123n34
2:14–15 .... 82, 169
3:2 164
3:31 266
6:17 315
8:13 291
8:26 53
9:5 .... 303n8
10:2 258
10:14–15 .... 164, 192
10:17 .... 156n7, 162
11:33 235
11:34 .... 122n31
12:2 .... 137, 259
12:6 306
16:25 235
16:25–26 .... 162, 164

1 Corinthians
1 117
1–2 324

1:18................... 241
1:21................... 105
1:23................... 179, 241
1:23–24.............. 269
1:26................... 179
2...................... 256
2:4–5................. 117, 128, 190
2:9.................... 154
2:9–10............... 82
2:13................... 128
2:14................... 138, 236, 269, 276,
                      302n6
3:7.................... 299
3:18................... 241
4:7.................... 240, 242
6:11................... 291
6:18–19.............. 169
8:1.................... 258
10:20 104
11:19 306
12:3 129
12:4–11 63
14 324
14:22 .... 324n5
14:23–24............ 179
14:24–25............ 179, 183, 190
14:36–37............ 128
15:3–4............... 92, 117

2 Corinthians
1:21–22.............. 246
1:24................... 95n5
3...................... 259
3:13–14............. 231
3:13–18............. 43, 227
3:16–18............. 231
3:17–18............. 246
3:18................... 82, 185, 232n5, 274,
                      315
4:3–7 117
4:4.................... 81, 104, 138, 184,
                      185, 274, 275, 290
4:6.................... 82, 138, 184, 185,
                      252n10, 273, 276,
                      277n14, 278

4:7.................... 116, 128, 299
5:18–20.............. 88, 299
10:4–5............... 121, 184
12:1................... 235
12:7................... 235

Galatians
1:1.................... 164
1:8.................... 164
1:12................... 235
2:2.................... 235
4:4.................... 303n8
4:6.................... 53

Ephesians
1:11................... 299
1:13................... 68
1:13–14.............. 68n103
1:16–19.............. 313
1:17................... 140n22, 240, 250n8,
                      258, 262n21, 278
1:17–18.............. 81, 235
1:17–19.............. 43, 82, 139, 227,
                      233–42
1:18................... 137, 265, 267, 269
1:18–19.............. 137
2:3.................... 269, 285
2:8.................... 129
2:20................... 108, 161, 162
3:5.................... 140
3:8.................... 235
3:9–10............... 140
3:14–19............. 238, 313
3:16................... 246
3:16–19............. 137
4:7.................... 244
4:8.................... 299
4:11–12.............. 299
4:11–15.............. 88
4:11–16.............. 299
4:12–15.............. 255
4:13................... 249, 258, 347
4:14................... 243, 251
4:18................... 269
4:20–24.............. 291

4:30 68
5:8 .... 268, 276, 276n12
6:18 54

Philippians
1:9 .... 254, 258
1:19 246
1:29 129

Colossians
1:6 258
1:9 278
1:9–10 258
1:13 .... 265, 268
1:15 .... 273n9
1:21 269
2:2 .... 139, 145, 251,
                        252n9, 258, 260,
                        287n11
3:10 .... 258, 278
3:11 325
3:16 87

1 Thessalonians
1:5 145
2:13 .... 88, 131, 154, 163,
                        180
4:9 255

2 Thessalonians
2 334
2:11 .... 123n32
2:11–12 85
3:2 .... 176n9

1 Timothy
1:15 161
2:4 258
3:15 .... 88, 108
3:16 .... 303n8
4:1–3 334
6:5 285
6:20 .... 260, 323

2 Timothy
1:14 323
2:7 .... 88, 277
2:21 291
2:25 258
3:1–5 334
3:7 258
3:8 285
3:14–17 .... 191, 292, 299
3:15 .... 87, 297n5, 310
3:15–17 .... 86, 162
3:16 .... 88, 127n1, 325
4:3–4 334

Titus
1:1 .... 258, 316
1:2 94
3:3–5 291
3:10 .... 328, 328n14

Hebrews
1:1 .... 88, 297
1:1–2 .... 82, 86, 95
1:3 .... 273n9
1:9 .... 246, 273
2:4 .... 114, 163
2:16 .... 303n8
3:5 231
4:12 .... 180, 180n14
5:2 283
5:11 273
5:14 .... 146n27, 254
6:1 249
6:4 81
8:10 269
10:1 305
10:38 282
11:1 .... 115, 170
11:6 154
11:40 305
12:1 115

James
1:5 .... 241, 241n17
1:17 240

1:18 181
1:21 .... 181, 285, 291,
292n14
3:17 .... 241n17
4:6 .... 292n13

1 Peter
1:10–11 .... 224, 272
1:10–12 287
1:11–12 250
1:13 269
1:18 .... 186n21
1:23 181
2:2 181
2:9 .... 81, 265, 268

2 Peter
1:2–3 258
1:8 258
1:16 .... 128n4
1:16–21 .... 110, 160–61
1:17 287
1:17–18 161
1:19 .... 105, 179n12, 184,
250
1:19–21 88
1:20 161
1:20–21 113
1:21 .... 163, 164, 250
2:5 82
2:20 258
3:1 269
3:2 162
3:16 .... 285, 302n7

1 John
1:1 161
1:2 269
2:20 .... 44, 60, 243, 246, 271,
273
2:24 248
2:27 .... 44, 60, 243, 246,
256n15, 261, 271,
273
3:3 260
4:1 .... 250, 261n17
5:6 .... 94, 251
5:10 .... 113, 181, 252
5:16 283
5:20 .... 88, 137, 265, 268

Jude
3 .... 262n20
4 306
10 168
14–15 82
22–23 283

Revelation
1:6 .... 247n6
2:13 114
3:7 246
6:9–11 112
17:6 114
19:9 110
20 20
20:4 112
22:6 110
22:18 86